PROFITS
OF WAR

PROFITS OF WAR

INSIDE THE SECRET
U.S.-ISRAELI ARMS
NETWORK

Ari Ben-Menashe

SHERIDAN SQUARE PRESS
NEW YORK

ISBN 1-879823-01-2

Published in the United States by
Sheridan Square Press, Inc.
145 West 4th Street
New York, NY 10012

Distributed to the trade by
National Book Network
4720-A Boston Way
Lanham, MD 20706

10 9 8 7 6 5 4 3 2 1

This book is dedicated to Ellen Ray,
who changed my life.

Acknowledgments

WRITING INTELLIGENCE REPORTS does not make one an author. This book would not have been possible without the heroic efforts of Richard Shears and Isobelle Gidley, who listened to me recount my experiences for months on end, painstakingly turning my recollections into a book. Nor could it have been possible without the meticulous craftsmanship, writing, and editing of Zachary Sklar, who, almost singlehandedly, turned that first version into the book you are about to read.

Twelve years as an intelligence officer also does not prepare one for the Byzantine world of publishing. I am most indebted to John Young, my agent, and Patrick Gallagher and Paul Donovan of Allen & Unwin Australia, who together had faith in this project at its inception. Then, I especially needed the counsel, friendship, and courage of Ellen Ray, Bill Schaap, and Danny Mintz of Sheridan Square Press in New York, who brought this book to fruition.

Of course, had I not been acquitted of the charges leveled against me by the U.S. government, my memoirs would be a futile dream. For this I will always be grateful to Thomas F.X. Dunn, who not only successfully defended me but also continued to encourage my efforts to tell my story.

I must also thank the journalists, researchers, friends, and family who had enough respect for me to listen to what I had to say and maintain my faith that it would, ultimately, be made public. My mother, Khatoun, my brother-in-law Michael, and Marian Gail were extremely supportive. Robert Parry, Gary Sick, and Phil Linsalata heard me out—and assisted me—when I needed it most. In Australia, Grant Vandenberg, Jan Roberts, and Mark Corcoran were also very helpful.

vii

Finally, I want to thank those of my former colleagues in Israeli intelligence—who must remain unnamed—who have renewed contact with me over these last few years, despite personal dangers to themselves and their careers.

Ari Ben-Menashe
Sundown, New York
July 1992

Contents

Introduction

EARLY ONE MORNING in the spring of 1990, I lay on my bunk in the Metropolitan Correctional Center in New York, unable to sleep, my mind restless. I stared at the ceiling of my tiny cell, and the fluorescent lights stared back, unblinking. I glanced over at the depressing furnishings—a sink, a toilet, two metal cabinets.

This was federal prison—my home for the time being. It wasn't terribly violent—no murders, no gang rapes. My neighbors on the high-status white tier, as opposed to the black and Hispanic tiers, were mostly white-collar criminals. John Gotti, the Mafia don, had been here for a short time, but had been released on bail. (He won that case, but he was to return later.) Adnan Kashoggi spent a few nights in residence. And Joe Doherty, the Irish revolutionary, was present all the time I was.

The conditions weren't that awful either—nothing like what I had been subjected to at El Reno in Oklahoma while being transported across the country. No overcrowding, no debilitating noise, no guard brutality as in many state and city jails. MCC was more like a third-class, flea-bag hotel—with one important exception. You weren't free to leave.

Below me, on the lower bunk, my cellmate, Nick Lante, later convicted of conspiracy to sell heroin in the "pizza connection" case, snored. How in the world had I ended up here? Living with this guy? In this place? What had gone wrong?

The events of the last few months flashed through my mind. In the fall of 1989 I had been on top of the world—a healthy 37-year-old Israeli citizen, married with a delightful young daughter, a prestigious job in the Prime Minister's Office, a considerable amount of money in the bank, and a two-week vacation in Australia awaiting me. Then one day I was arrested and tossed into jail in Los Angeles on phony charges of illegally trying to sell three C-130 transport planes to Iran.

I'd been expecting something to happen for a while—in Australia, Israel, the U.S., anywhere, anytime. I didn't know exactly what, but ever since my friend Amiram Nir had died in a mysterious "plane crash" in late November 1988, two years after his involvement in the Iran-contra affair had been revealed, I'd been worried.

So this was it—an arms-dealing rap. Actually I felt a measure of relief. At least it wasn't death. Nobody was likely to kill me in jail in the custody of the U.S. government.

But then the reality began to sink in, and I felt deeply hurt. I'd been set up, betrayed, by the American and Israeli governments. The Americans I could understand. I knew a lot about the CIA's arms deals with Iran and Iraq; in fact part of my job had been to threaten to go public with that information if the CIA didn't halt chemical weapons sales to Saddam Hussein. Naturally, the Americans were not pleased.

But the Israelis, my own people, my own government that I'd served for all my adult working life—that was hard to swallow.

I'd started working for the government as a codebreaker on the Iranian desk in Signals Intelligence during my three years of compulsory military service, 1974 to 1977. Then, as a civilian, I'd put in ten years with Israel's military intelligence, in the prestigious External Relations Department; from 1980 I also served on the Joint Committee for Iran-Israel Relations. Finally, I had spent two years as a roving troubleshooter for Prime Minister Yitzhak Shamir, working directly out of his office, with the title of special intelligence consultant.

It was secret missions for Israel that had resulted in my being jailed. When word of Shamir's communications with the PLO leaked out and embarrassed the government, someone had to be sacrificed. I was the one.

That's how I had ended up at Metropolitan Correctional Center, in this metal bunkbed, staring at the fluorescent lights, unable to sleep. I had believed that my work was part of the effort to ensure the survival of the State of Israel and the Jewish people. But here I was in prison, my future in peril, and nobody was coming forward to help me. When I was needed by my employers,

I was always there. When I needed them, they turned their backs on me. Shamir, for whom I had felt great respect, and who had known my father since the 1940s, had had a hand in setting me up. And then two lawyers representing the Israeli government had visited me in prison and asked me to make a deal—plead guilty, keep silent, go live in obscurity somewhere. I'd refused, and now that government was publicly denying that I'd ever worked for it.

I had expected this official government response. But from those I'd worked with and considered my friends I had also expected some support. There were ways it could have been done without their risking their own lives or careers. But no one did anything. No one would even acknowledge they knew me.

My own wife told me on the telephone from Israel that there was nothing she could do for me. She refused to come to New York. My sisters wouldn't talk to me, out of fear. Everyone except my mother had abandoned me—and she was being hassled and threatened by the Israeli government. I never had felt so alone.

My choices seemed pretty clear:

I could do what the Israeli government lawyers had offered to arrange—keep silent, plead guilty, get a deal from the judge, be totally discredited, accept a lot of money from the Israeli government, and go off to live in the boonies somewhere.

I could plead not guilty, but not say much about what had really gone on, and see what might develop as my trial approached.

I could go public with my story, talk to journalists, plead not guilty, go to trial and tell the truth as my defense—that I had sold billions of dollars' worth of weapons to Iran, but that I had been acting on behalf of my government in everything I had done, usually with the full knowledge and cooperation of the U.S. government as well.

I mulled the options. The first seemed the easiest. I could conceivably return to my country, try to save my marriage, at least see my daughter, perhaps get a decent job, and have enough money to live comfortably. But I would be pleading guilty to something I hadn't done, and my reputation would be destroyed forever. Worse still, the memory of what had happened to Amiram Nir stuck in my mind. I, too, would probably be killed a couple of years down the road, just to make sure I'd remain silent.

The second option offered no answers and not much hope. Besides, I was sick of living with uncertainty.

As for the third choice, I had, of course, signed the Official Secrets Act in Israel, which forbade me from revealing anything publicly about my work. But since I'd been set up and left out in the cold, I no longer felt constrained to play by the rules of my former masters. All bets were off. If I did talk, however, it meant that I would never be able to return to Israel. I would lose my wife and daughter forever. My passport might be revoked, and I would have a hard time getting a job. Still, this seemed the most pragmatic choice because it was least likely to lead to my death. It's always more difficult to kill someone who has a high profile. When you're making allegations the government doesn't want anyone to believe, killing you only makes people believe them more.

Equally important, I was furious. I'm not the kind of person who can take betrayal lying down. I prefer to fight back.

Finally, I felt the story I had to tell could be of service, that people needed to know what had actually happened, unbeknownst to them or the press, over the last decade—how Israel and the U.S. had prevented peace in the Middle East, how the American government was still supplying chemical weapons to Saddam Hussein, how Ronald Reagan and George Bush had swapped arms with the Iranians for a delay in the release of the hostages to win the 1980 election, and much more.

I asked myself, "Is anyone going to believe me? Will the American and Israeli governments deny everything and brand me a nut, totally discrediting me?" That was a distinct possibility. But I remembered Watergate and how there had been denial after denial—until the truth came pouring out.

On that quiet spring morning, I chose the third option. I did not plead guilty, and I eventually won my case in court. I talked to journalists. And now I have written this book about my career in Israeli intelligence.

It is not a pretty story, and I am no longer proud of my part in it. It is a tale of the 1980s—of big money, insatiable greed, and unfathomable corruption. It is a tale of government by cabal—how a handful of people in a few intelligence agencies determined the policies of their governments, secretly ran enormous operations without public accountability, abused power and public trust, lied, manipulated the media, and deceived the public. Last but not least, it is a tale of war—armies, weapons, hundreds of thousands of deaths—war run not by generals on the battlefield but by comfortable men in air-conditioned offices who are indifferent to human suffering.

This book is both a memoir and an exposé. It is also, in part, an act of atonement. I only hope that my story will in some small way contribute to the difficult process of righting the terrible wrongs of the 1980s and help remove from power those who were responsible.

BOOK ONE

DOLLAR MACHINE

1

Youth

PERHAPS IT WAS written that political chaos would follow me through life. I was born into it in Tehran, Iran, in 1951. My parents, affluent Iraqi Jews, had been married in Baghdad in 1945, but settled in Tehran the same year. Briefly, in late 1950 and early 1951, they visited Israel to explore the possibility of moving there. On that trip, in Jerusalem, I was conceived. But my parents, for the time being, decided to return to Iran, a country deeply divided against itself.

Shortly after their return, the Majlis—the Parliament—passed an act nationalizing oil. The British Anglo-Iranian Oil Company withdrew, and Prime Minister Mohammed Mossadegh found himself in charge of a nation that was in an uproar, with fierce rows among the country's leaders and rioting in the streets.

Even within the Jewish community in Iran there were divisions. The Iraqi Jews, who had a highly developed sense of Western and European culture and Jewish awareness, would not mix with the Iranian Jews, who regarded themselves as Iranians who happened to have another religion.

Those Iranian Jews who emigrated to Israel were generally financial refugees without emotional connection to their new home. They certainly didn't leave Iran because of oppression. There was little anti-Semitism in Iran, and still isn't, even under the new regime. Historically, it was Cyrus the Great, the Persian king, who granted the Jews freedom, and, later, Islam recognized Judaism and the Prophets of Judaism. Even though Reza Shah Pahlavi, the father of the last Shah, sided with the Nazis during the Second World War, he never adopted Hitler's anti-Semitic ways, and most Iranians harbored none of the hatred of Jews that existed in Europe.

The Iraqi-Jewish community living in Tehran was closely knit, with its own social club, synagogue, and school. Nevertheless, most of the city's Iraqi-Jewish children attended the American Community School, where the first language taught was English, followed by French and Farsi, or Persian. At home, Arabic was spoken because of the parents' background, so I, in keeping with many other sons and daughters of Iraqi Jews, was brought up with four languages. (Later I also learned Hebrew and Spanish.) As for my sense of identity, I never felt Iranian even though I was born in Iran. I was Jewish.

Like all the boys in the Iraqi-Jewish community, I was taught to pray in Hebrew toward the bar mitzvah at the age of 13. After finishing high school, most Iraqi-Jewish children would be sent to university in the United States. Although proud to be Jewish, their parents saw no future in sending their sons and daughters to Israel, which they regarded as a nation of poor refugees and Hasidic Jews from Eastern Europe. The U.S. Embassy was well aware of the status of Iraqi Jews and readily granted visas for the teenagers, who often stayed on in America, married, and settled down.

My father Gourdji, though, was something of an oddball in all this. He had received a French education in the Alliance School in Baghdad, and before entrenching himself in Iran, he had traveled the world extensively, spending time in India, France, Palestine, and the Soviet Union.

In Palestine, during 1940, he hooked up with a group of Jewish terrorists who called themselves LEHI—a Hebrew acronym for Fighters for the Liberation of Israel. Although the organization had a reputation as rightwing, many of its members were formerly part of the communist movement. They were better known as the Stern Gang, after their leader David Stern, who was virulently anti-British.

Stern's successor, Yitzhak Shamir, who later became prime

minister of Israel, was equally anti-British and was even willing to negotiate with the Nazis for Jewish lives. He offered to fight alongside German troops against the British if the Germans would allow the Jews who were interned in European concentration camps to emigrate to Palestine. As expected, the British and U.S. governments and the Jewish labor movement, whose leader, David Ben-Gurion, was comfortably ensconced in New York, did everything in their power to thwart such a plan, and the Stern people were persecuted and hunted down, even by other Jews in Palestine.

Shamir and his colleagues from the Stern Gang are anti-American to this day, because they believe that the slaughter of six million Jews in Europe could have been prevented with a bit of American cooperation. Most of the people affiliated with the Stern Gang were not welcome to stay in the State of Israel after it was established because the Labor coalition government that took over looked askance at them. Shamir himself was an exception, becoming a prominent figure in the Mossad, the Israeli intelligence agency. Prime Minister Ben-Gurion said of him, "If a terrorist, let him be my terrorist."

My father, finding Israel less than welcoming, set up shop in Iran. He joined his brother in the import-export business. From the Soviet Union, for example, he imported furs and leather. Later, during the 1950s, he acquired the Mercedes Benz/Bosch car and spare-parts franchise for Iran. But my father always yearned to pull up roots and go to live in Israel whenever the political climate changed.

For my part, I loved to listen to my father talk about his travels and his philosophies. Sometimes we'd go up to the walk-on roof of our three-story house in the northern suburbs of Tehran for long discussions. At other times, we'd find a shady spot in the yard. And while I was taught languages, math, geography, and history at the American School, it was from my father that I really learned about life.

He enjoyed talking about his experiences in the Soviet Union. While my three sisters and I grew up surrounded by the American propaganda that was flooding Iran in the 1950s and 1960s, which portrayed the Soviet Union as an evil place, my father would say, "It's really just another way of life. In the Soviet Union you don't see indigent people in the streets. Everybody has a bare minimum to live, and they get their basic needs from the state. If they don't have any business initiative, they won't find themselves living in dire poverty or close to starvation. Growing up with a bare minimum is better than starving."

This was his way of explaining the differences between East and West to growing children. His was an unusual philosophy then in an affluent, capitalist, American-oriented society. My father expressed his views openly, and there was no doubt why he was never fully accepted by others in the Iraqi-Jewish community.

Despite my father's socialist sympathies, the Labor coalition in power in Israel was not acceptable to him. This was not because of ideology, but because he saw these so-called socialists as "peasants" whose main aim was to enrich themselves—bringing economic chaos while making it clear that Middle Eastern Jews, regardless of their education, would always be second-class citizens in Israel. Furthermore, the Labor coalition "socialists" were, ironically, intertwined with the capitalist United States.

My father supported the Gahal (today known as the Likud Party), a merger of Menachem Begin's Herut Party and the Israel Liberal Party. Although they saw themselves as a conservative party because of their strong emphasis on Jewish identity, they also supported progressive social programs. Their leaders, Begin and Yitzhak Shamir, became folk heroes to the party loyalists. I would compare the Gahal—and today's Likud Party—to the Peronists in Argentina: rightwing populists. The Labor coalition, which later became the Labor Party, was in favor of close relations with South Africa and of cutting relations with the Soviet Union altogether; on the other hand, the Likud tried to open up relations with the Soviet Union and tone down the ties with South Africa.

Because of what I learned from my father, I was fascinated during my school years in Tehran with the concept of world revolution—not as a violent uprising but as a redistribution of wealth. From my youthful philosophical perspective, centrally controlled economies and ways of life were a necessary first step in educating the masses and preparing them for a more open society.

*   *   *

By July of 1966, when I was 14, I was feeling increasingly foreign in Iran, with my Iraqi-Jewish background and my American schooling. Like most adolescents, I was searching for my identity, a place I could feel at home. Under the influence of my father and sharing the vision of an Israeli state, I decided I wanted to live in Israel. So my mother—a pragmatic and street-smart woman—took me and my sisters Claris, Evon, and Stella, to Israel, where Stella and I were enrolled at the American International School in Kfar Smaryahu, north of Tel Aviv. My two oldest sisters went to college. Five years later, my parents moved from Tehran to Israel, lock, stock, and barrel.

I had the best of both worlds. Most of the pupils at the school were white Americans or the children of foreign diplomats stationed in Israel. There weren't too many Jewish resident children attending the school, and while sometimes I felt something of a misfit, we all got along well. When I left at the end of each day, I would mix with Israeli kids in Ramat Gan, the Tel Aviv suburb where we were living. Once in a while I'd go to a party, take a girlfriend to the cinema, or just go for a long walk, some three or four kilometers, to the sea.

After their graduation from high school at the age of 18, my Israeli friends were drafted into the army. My American pals left for the U.S. to attend university. I, meanwhile, found myself in a peculiar situation once again. Because I still had an Iranian passport, I could not be drafted. So I joined a kibbutz. I was a religious Jew at the time, hardly orthodox but at least keeping kosher and observing the sabbath. I was the only one on this socialist kibbutz who wore a yarmulke. Even though I did not identify with their way of life, I wanted to experience the East European ethos, and rub shoulders with the avant garde. Curiously, it was a move that set me on the road to a life enmeshed in political intrigue.

Half of each day at Kibbutz Mishmar Hasharon was spent studying Hebrew, the rest doing volunteer work in the fish ponds, engaged in the extremely difficult task of sorting out male and female trout. Sometimes I would work through the night in the bakery, preparing for the early morning sale of bread.

My roommates that year, 1969, were two non-Jewish volun-

teers in their 30s. One was an Australian member of the Church
of God, Michael Dennis Rohan, the other an American Baptist
named Arthur. They were in the kibbutz because they had had
visions of Christ ordering them to come to the Holy Land. The
kibbutz was an economical way of doing the Lord's work. As long
as they went about certain daily tasks, they didn't have to pay
anything for their keep.

Rohan, a tall slim man with thinning brown hair, had a vision
that he was to be the king of Israel who would prepare the way for
the return of Christ. Arthur's vision was slightly different; he saw
Christ's return as imminent and knew that the Jews had to be
saved from themselves. God had sent them His only son 2,000
years earlier, and they had not accepted Him.

It was a crazy situation. There I was keeping an eye out for any
girls I might be able to lure into my bed—life in a kibbutz is not
all work and prayer—while sharing a room with two Westerners
who were following a different kind of heavenly calling. Not that
Rohan was not human. He fell for a very attractive Hebrew
teacher who came into the kibbutz daily. He sent her his photo-
graph with a note that he would be king of Israel one day and he'd
like her to be his queen. She ignored him.

At night Rohan, dressed in his khaki work clothes, talked to
me about the Temple Mount in Jerusalem. For Moslems this was
the holiest place after Mecca and Medina. On the mount is El
Aqsa Mosque which has been built over a rock imprinted with a
footstep said to be that of the Prophet Mohammed, who ascended
to heaven from that spot.

"To rebuild the temple, this mosque has to be destroyed,"
Rohan told me. "In order for Jesus to come back, the Third Temple
has to be built, but this can only be done by getting rid of the
mosque." The Second Temple had been destroyed by the Romans.

Rohan started receiving visits from two men wearing
yarmulkes—who, he explained, were from the Jewish Defense
League, a New York-based extreme rightwing organization associated with Rabbi Meir Kahane. Rohan never said how he got
involved with them. A month after I met him, Rohan packed his
bags to leave for Jerusalem. "I'm going to prepare the way for the
second coming of Christ," he said. Then he astonished me by

donning a suit and tie. With a wave of his bony hand, he set out on the Lord's work.

Two weeks later I learned that Rohan had meant all he had said. The news was dominated by a report that the El Aqsa Mosque had been burned in an arson attack. Moslems around the world were outraged and were calling for a *jihad*, a holy war, against Israel. Some Arab newspapers claimed that Israeli military helicopters had firebombed the mosque, but I guessed something far different—which was soon to be confirmed.

Rohan was waiting for me in my room, again dressed in his smart suit. "I've just got back from Jerusalem," he said. "If you'd permit me, I'd like to stay here for the weekend." His bed was still free.

I made no mention of the news at that stage. "Dennis, I have no problem," I said, "but you realize that if you stay longer than a few days, you'll have to register."

That evening, joined by Arthur, we started talking again, and this time I mentioned the burning of the mosque. "Is this a sign that the Third Temple is going to be built?" I asked.

"Yes," he said.

"Did you have anything to do with it?"

"It was God's work, but through my hands."

"Dennis, you realize the whole world is looking for who did it. What are you going to do about it?"

"I'm going to turn myself in."

I didn't know whether to trust him to do that or not. But I knew that action had to be taken. Israel was being blamed for what he had done.

He asked to be left to have a good sleep that night, promising he wouldn't leave.

Arthur said, "Dennis, I'll be praying all night for your soul."

At breakfast the next morning, I asked Rohan if he had any matches.

"Sure I do," he said. "I used them for a good cause."

After breakfast, with Rohan's permission, I went to a pay phone and called the police emergency 100 number, identified myself to an officer, and told her that the most wanted man in Israel was in my room at the kibbutz. When I said he was an Australian, she told me she had had a lot of crank phone calls and her patience was running out, but she listened to me carefully.

Forty-five minutes after the call, the kibbutz was invaded by heavily armed Israel Police Border Guards, the police paramilitary unit, in their green uniforms. They surrounded the block in which our room was located. Then three officers in civilian clothes knocked on the door. Dennis was treated kindly, handcuffed, and led away to be charged with grand arson of a holy site.

I traveled later to Jerusalem with Arthur, the two of us just scruffy young guys from the kibbutz, and the Israeli police put us up at the King David Hotel, the best in town. We were interrogated about Rohan for hours, and when I mentioned the Jewish Defense League, my interrogators jumped. They said it was vital I not say anything about Rohan, particularly his connections with the JDL.

"There should be no traces of Jewish hands in this," said one of the senior officers.

Rohan never had a trial. He pleaded guilty at a public hearing and was sent for psychiatric observation, and was later declared by the court to be mentally ill. He was committed to a psychiatric hospital south of Haifa.

Three months later Rohan turned up at my flat in Ramat Gan, where I was then living.

"I escaped," he said. "But don't worry. I only came to say hello. I'm going back later."

This time he gave me more details, explaining he had carried out the deed in coordination with the JDL. But he believed his lawyer, Yitzhak Tunic, who was later to be appointed as the state comptroller—the ombudsman—had "sold him down the river" because he was afraid Rohan might mention the JDL if he took the witness stand. My own subpoena had been canceled because there were worries that I might also mention the JDL.

"Is it Russia," he asked, "where a man of God is put away and accused of being crazy?"

All this made me think: Is there any justice in the world? In some respects, the Israeli court system was one of the fairest in the world, yet "for reasons of State interests" this case had been suppressed. Rohan had been prepared to admit the crime and was willing to go to jail for ten years or more for what he believed in, but he wanted a platform to talk about his motives. The Israeli legal system was not going to allow that to happen.

Rohan gave himself up to the authorities after chatting with me. Three months later he was deported to Australia.

In 1972 while studying political science and modern history at Bar Ilan University, along with working toward a teacher's license, I became pals with another student, Adel Mohammad Atamna. An Israeli citizen, he was a Palestinian from an Arab village, Kfar Kara'a, located inside the pre-1967 Israeli border. At the time, I was renting a small apartment in Qiryat Ono, not far from the university, and Adel had been renting a flat close by because his village was two hours' drive from Tel Aviv. One day, he invited me to his home, set in a traditional Arab village, which itself lay within a Westernized society. It amazed me how he was able to live in both worlds.

Our friendship developed further when his Jewish landlady got cold feet about having an Arab on her property and threw him out. When I found out why he was looking so miserable, I decided to give my apartment to him while I stayed at my parents' house. He started calling me his brother. One day in late 1972 he said, "I've found you a job. How would you like to teach English in our village high school?"

I loved the idea. There was an abundance of Jewish English teachers, but none wanted to teach in an Arab village. Although I had not yet obtained my degree or my teaching license, I was able to get a temporary permit. So I started teaching teenage boys and girls three times a week, traveling the two hours each way by bus.

One day, out of the blue, I received a letter from the Prime Minister's Office. In essence, it said: Dear Sir, We have a very interesting position to offer you with a lot of future prospects. We would like you to come for an interview in Tel Aviv.

An address and a date were specified. If I couldn't make it, I was told to phone and ask for Kohava.

At the time I was dating a woman three years my senior who had just finished serving in the army and was working for the SHABAK—the secret police-style internal security service. When I showed her the letter, she smiled.

"This is from the Mossad or the SHABAK," she said. "This is a SHABAK interview address. They're going to offer you a great job, I'd say."

The address turned out to be a regular apartment building. I walked up to the third floor and knocked on the door. A young man answered. He led me into a room and asked me to sit and wait for ten minutes. I found out later that I was under observation throughout that period.

A man in his early 50s called me into a larger room and, when I was seated, said right away:

"Whatever I'm going to tell you right now is governed by the Official Secrets Act. You are not permitted to divulge this conversation or even that it took place or where we met. Please sign this statement which holds you to secrecy."

He handed me a piece of paper, which I signed.

"We have been looking at your background, your file," he said.

"Who are you? What file?"

"The El Aqsa Mosque affair. We've read about the way you helped."

It was never stated, but I assumed he meant that they were pleased I had cooperated when asked to keep my mouth shut about the possible Jewish Defense League involvement.

"Who are you?" I asked again.

"We're from the Prime Minister's Office, and the internal security of the Jewish state is on our shoulders. You have the privilege of being invited to join our family."

He explained that I was not being invited just yet. I had to go through security clearance, my background would be checked further, and I would have to pass tests. But he said my file left him convinced they would be in a position to make me an offer.

"Even though you are not an Israeli citizen yet, you are going to become one, which will make you subject to the draft." What he said was quite true. At this point I intended to become an Israeli citizen. In 1973 I actually got the final papers.

"We can make you a better offer than going into the army," said my host. "You will sign a contract to work for us for at least five years and you will stay teaching in the Arab village where you are working right now. All you have to do is just answer some questions once in a while to the person in charge of security in that area. You will be getting a salary from the school and a salary from us. And who knows, if you're good, you could be promoted to chief of security in that region and you could eventually be stationed abroad—the future is open to you."

I looked at him without saying a thing.

"If you are agreeable, we will schedule you for tests right away."

"You want me to be a *manyak* [Hebrew slang for a snitch]?" I asked.

He was taken aback. This was something he had not expected.

"No, no—we want you to be an undercover agent for the most prestigious and noble organization in the State of Israel. We want to put some of the burden of the security of the Jewish state, which I personally believe is a great honor, on your shoulders."

He was asking me to spy on my friends, to spy on Adel.

"No, thank you," I said. "I'm not prepared to betray friendships."

"But these are Arabs, our enemies."

"Stop the nonsense. Sure they're Arabs, but they're also Israeli citizens."

He suddenly became very angry. "You know what will happen if you turn this down. They'll take you into the army."

"I don't mind serving my country. I just don't want to be a *manyak*."

I left with his final words ringing in my ears: "We'll give you a week to change your mind. After that, we're gone."

When I got home, my girlfriend was waiting. I told her what had happened.

"Are you crazy?" she asked. She spent the following week trying to persuade me to accept the offer. But I never called them back.

A year later, in 1973, after I had become an Israeli citizen but while I was still studying and teaching, I received another letter. This time, it was from the Ministry of Defense, inviting me to an interview in Tel Aviv. They had a "very special" position to offer me in connection with my upcoming military service.

It was a different apartment. A young woman who opened the door took me in to meet a chubby, balding man who introduced himself as Lt. Col. Sasson. He brought out a file and said he understood I was about to be drafted by the military. He had an offer, but before it was made, he asked me to sign a secrecy statement. I had a feeling of *déjà vu*.

"You have to serve three years in the military. But if you pass all the tests and if you get a security clearance, we will ask you to sign on for an extra two years for career service, meaning you will serve five years in the military. We will give you a very special position and we'll also send you to officers' school."

"Great," I said. "What am I supposed to do?"

"When will you be ready to join the military?"

"My studies finish some time at the end of this year."

Because of my background, my education, and my fluency in Farsi, Hebrew, and English, I had been selected to work for Military Intelligence. As long as I didn't have to spy on my friends, I had no problem with this. I was committed to Israel and wanted to serve the country—all the better if it was a good, prestigious job as well. I agreed to undergo security clearance procedures.

They began the following morning. At the offices of Field Security I was asked to fill in tens of pages of questions that covered my background, the names of my family and friends, and others who could provide references. This was followed by three days of psychological and aptitude tests.

I was to be assigned to work at the Iranian desk at the code-cracking SigInt—Signals Intelligence—unit. But there were more tests to come, including a physical, in order to be able to join the military in a special unit.

My draft date was set for May 6, 1974. When I asked why this was so far away, I was told I had been scheduled for a pre-military course in codebreaking starting in Jerusalem in mid-November 1973. It turned out that my basic training would be in a special infantry unit known as Golani, in which I would undertake a special high-explosives sabotage course. This would be followed by an officers' course, and then I was to be put into the code-breaking unit.

"Why," I asked, "is all this necessary for a man who's to be working as a codebreaker?" I was told I asked too many questions. Lt. Col. Sasson asked if I was going to sign for the extra two years or not. If I refused, I would be assigned to a regular army unit for three years. I signed.

During my codebreaking course, I was introduced to the Iranian method of cryptography. It was pointed out that all the Iranian embassies around the world used a model of the Swiss Haglin coding machine, and they transmitted in Farsi, but using the Roman alphabet.

We were taught the method of breaking the code sent by the Haglin machine. Using a computer, even without knowing the starting point of the machine, the Israelis had found a method of breaking the code. But a new problem came up. The Iranians started double-coding—making a code out of a code—and nobody was able to break it. The only way the Israelis could read communications was by "acquiring" the black book that was sent weekly by diplomatic pouch to the communications officer in the unofficial Iranian embassy in Ramat Gan in Israel.

For "security reasons," Iranian diplomatic pouches had to lay over for 24 hours at Ben-Gurion Airport before the embassy received them. This allowed the SHABAK to get into the pouches. These pouches are sealed, but the SHABAK people were experts at breaking the seals and then repairing them after the black book had been "borrowed" and photocopied. On one occasion a sloppy job was done on the resealing, but that was quickly overcome— the Iranian communications officer was also the man in charge of picking up the pouch. When he discovered the broken seal, he was paid handsomely, which made life a lot easier thereafter. He simply photocopied the weekly code and passed it to us.

After my course was finished, I was stationed in Unit 8200, in the code-breaking department in the non-Arab branch of SigInt. Unit 8200 was housed in a base consisting of a number of white and grey concrete buildings located near a country club some ten kilometers north of Tel Aviv. Close by, on an elevation, was a grey-white building known as the villa, belonging to Mossad, where top-secret security meetings were held. About a kilometer away were several intelligence corps service bases and the intelligence school.

Each department in Unit 8200 was run on a need-to-know basis. A person from one department could not enter another without special permission. The unit commander was Col. Yoel Ben-Porat, known as Buffy, the Hebrew acronym of his name. The number-two person in the code-breaking department, Lt. Col. Sasson Yishaek, was the man who had recruited me, as "Lt. Col. Sasson."

The department's commander, Col. Reuben Yirador, had been involved in a discovery a few years earlier. In 1972 he had decoded a Soviet intercept which had not been encrypted in the regular way. It was one of the same VENONA intercepts that British MI-5 agent Peter Wright mentions in his book *Spycatcher*, although he doesn't say it was the Israelis who cracked this code in Rome. Col. Yirador found out that the Soviets were bugging the office of the prime minister of Israel, Golda Meir. The bugs had been planted by two technicians, Soviet immigrants to Israel, who were working in the Prime Minister's Office. Someone leaked the fact that the Israelis were on to the bugging by the Soviets. The two technicians disappeared from Israel before they could be arrested.

The discovery of the bugs meant, of course, that the Soviets were privy to many of the goings-on in Golda Meir's office in 1972—a very significant year. The Soviets had a special interest in Israel that year because it was then that Golda Meir had met Leonid Brezhnev in Finland, and had rejected his proposal for a comprehensive peace settlement in the Middle East. As a result of that meeting and the bugging, Egyptian President Anwar Sadat was well informed by the Soviets about Israel's attitude. The intelligence he had been fed may well have prompted Sadat to launch a war against Israel to force it to sit down at the peace table.

The branch of Unit 8200 I was assigned to was headed by an older civilian woman, Shulamit Ingerman, one of Israel's best cryptographers, who had twice won the highest award for contributions to Israel's security. A likable woman who cared more about her career than her sloppy appearance, she introduced me to the Iranian team of six.

While it was accepted wisdom that—like Israel's encrypting system—NATO and Soviet codes could rarely be broken because the coding method was always being randomly changed, my task of reading the Farsi material was not difficult. This was because the "starting point" was being stolen from the Iranian pouch. It was only a matter of translation. However, it was still necessary to try to crack the code because at some point the black book might not be available.

One night, when I was duty officer and working with a young woman in the unit, I decided to try looking for the secret of the code around the word *noghteh*, which in Farsi means "full stop" or "period." This, of course, appears frequently in telegrams, and the messages to and from Tehran were no exception. The Iranians used the letter W to represent the spaces between words, but our computer had been designed to delete the Ws. I instructed the computer to put the Ws back in and to look for the word *noghteh* with Ws on each side. I believed that if we could find a certain frequency of these stops and spaces we would crack the code. Sometime in the dead of night we broke through. No longer would we need the little black book.

The young woman on duty and I shrieked with joy. I immediately called Shulamit, Col. Yirador, Col. Buffy, and Lt. Col. Yishaek. They said they'd be around right away.

The only problem I had that night was that, against regulations, I did not have a uniform on. I was wearing shorts, having traveled in for my night shift by bicycle from Ramat Gan—it was a pleasant ride. On their arrival shortly after 3:00 A.M., the heavy brass of the unit expressed their delight and extended their congratulations. Suddenly Buffy turned to me with a stern face and demanded: "When is your shift over?"

I told him at eight in the morning.

"At 8:05 you will come to my office to stand court martial for being insubordinate and out of order."

Everyone in the room was taken aback.

"Sir?" I asked.

"The next time you break a code," he said, "make sure you are in uniform."

At eight in the morning I made my way in a borrowed uniform to Buffy's office. He told me right away that he was sentencing me to 14 days in jail for disorderly conduct. He ordered me to sit. I sat. Then he broke into a smile and said, "But I'm suspending the sentence. I have a driver outside with a car. Go home, take a shower, have a shave, and be back in an hour."

I did as I was told. Then other members of the Iranian desk and I were taken to see the director of Military Intelligence, Maj. Gen. Shlomo Gazit, where we were all commended.

Life with the military held promise. Or so I thought.

2

Codebreaker

BETWEEN 1975 AND 1977, the Iranian desk in Unit 8200 was reading coded messages faster than the Iranians. They came in, we threw them into the computer, translated them, and sent them on to various interested intelligence quarters. Breaking the code had opened doors to a wealth of material from around the world.

The monitoring of the Iranians, along with other signals, was carried out through the satellite station in Bet Ella in the foothills of the Judea mountains, half an hour's drive from Jerusalem. There were also various Unit 8200 listening stations in northern Israel, the Sinai, and overseas. Located in innocuous-looking buildings in Japan, Italy, and Ethiopia, these powerful listening posts could intercept, among other signals, all the traffic in and out of the Iranian Foreign Ministry, the Royal Court, the SAVAK, and Iranian military intelligence. The listeners zeroed in on Tehran, the hub, and other Iranian embassies.

Under the Shah, Iran had good relations with what we referred to as the "moderate pro-American Arab countries"—Egypt, Jordan, and the Emirates, including Kuwait. We were getting no intelligence on these nations from the Americans. With the code broken, however, we were able to find out what various Iranian emissaries were reporting back to Tehran. In addition, the

18

Iranians had good contacts with the Soviet Bloc, and what the Soviets told Tehran they also unwittingly told us.

There was one other vital source of information—Ardeshir Zahedi, the Iranian ambassador to the U.S. Zahedi reported directly back to the Shah's office in the Royal Court what was being said in the U.S. capital about Middle East policy and the Americans' initiatives with Anwar Sadat's Egypt.

While we "read" a great deal of important material, we also noticed how much junk came through the code system. We found out just how lazy some ambassadors were—they merely translated newspaper editorials into Farsi and sent them as their well-informed analyses of what was going on in their respective countries. Among the "newspaper clippers" was the Iranian ambassador to Israel, who was obviously an avid reader of the *Jerusalem Post*, at the time the only English-language daily in Israel. He would translate the editorials and, passing them off as his own assessments, direct them to his foreign minister. This was done with such regularity that finally we saved ourselves a great deal of translation time—we would cut out the editorial from the paper and clip it to the printout of the coded message, then send it on to our analysts. Often, they had already read the editorials anyway.

It wasn't all office work in Unit 8200.

Friday morning, July 2, 1976, I was ordered to report to Lt. Col. Yishaek's office. I found a number of other officers there, all experts in various languages. We were then asked to accompany him to the office of Col. Yosef Zeira, a very stern department commander in Unit 8200.

The colonel locked his door. Then he turned to us all and said, "From now until Sunday morning you are all going to 'disappear.' No going home, no telephone calls. You have simply vanished."

No one protested. Whatever this was about, it was all part of our work. Our families and friends would simply have to understand.

"You're all going on a trip to Kenya," the colonel said. Then he told us that Israel had decided to mount a commando raid to rescue the Israeli and other passengers on board an Air France jet that had been hijacked June 27 while flying to Paris from Tel Aviv. Members of the Baader-Meinhof Group had boarded the plane on a stopover in Rome, diverted it to Athens, and then finally landed it at Entebbe Airport in Uganda. The non-Israeli passengers had, by Friday, been released.

At that time relations between Israel and Idi Amin were at their lowest. The self-proclaimed president of Uganda had been a close friend of Israel and had been installed in a military coup, planned and led by the former Israeli military attaché in Uganda, Col. Baruch Bar Lev. But now, after Col. Muammar Qaddafi of Libya had promised money to black African nations if they cut ties with Israel, relations between Israel and Uganda had deteriorated. Amin, however, still wore the paratrooper's wings bestowed on him by the Israeli military when he had undergone training in Israel.

The details of the Israeli rescue are, of course, well known. What isn't known is the misery that at least one of the backup teams endured. We were told we would be flying to Nairobi in an Air Force Boeing 707, which would be used as a listening post. The plan was to fly there, park on the airfield, and tap into radio frequencies to establish if any messages were being passed, in any language, that the Israelis were on their way. I was told to scan for Farsi.

In addition to being used for our various language skills, we were also ordered to sign for combat gear—if extra manpower were needed, we would be the first to be airlifted to Entebbe as backup. Now I could see that my training with explosives might come in handy after all.

The Boeing 707 that took off from Israel carried no markings. I had been assigned a seat at the rear with my equipment: earphones and a scanner. This, I was told, would be where I would stay for however long the rescue operation took. During the flight the toilets broke down. My seat was right by the toilet door. By the time we touched down shortly before dawn that morning, the air conditioning had also failed. Sweat poured from all our bodies as the plane taxied to its position in a dark corner of the Nairobi airfield. By the following night the heat and stench were unbearable.

In stark contrast to the commando raid at Entebbe, I had absolutely nothing to do but listen to the crackling earphones and try to overcome waves of nausea. We were self-sufficient for food and water, although I couldn't face eating anything. After who knows how many hours, the technicians on board were able to repair the toilets and the air conditioning, and I then continued listening for Farsi in *relative* comfort.

Many hours later a shout went up. The raid had been a success. Our job was over—if it could be called a job.

When we arrived back at the airfield in north-central Israel, the nation was in a jubilant mood. Everyone involved in the operation, no matter what their role, was lauded as a hero. A young woman I was going out with at the time forgave me for disappearing on her and hugged and kissed me. I tried to tell her that all I had done was sit in a sardine can beside a smelly toilet listening to stereophonic crackling, but she didn't care. I was her hero, she said.

One night in 1976 while I was duty officer in Unit 8200, I read a telegram sent from the Iranian Embassy in Ramat Gan to Tehran. I couldn't believe my eyes. The ambassador talked in detail about a meeting he had had with the Lockheed Aircraft Company representative in Israel who had passed on details of Lockheed bribes paid to Defense Minister Shimon Peres. The sum involved was the equivalent of $3.5 million. I remembered the Lockheed bribe scandal that had hit Japan, but no one had heard of Israeli involvement in such things.

The intercepted telegram dealt with the sale of C-130 aircraft to Israel and the possibility of Israel purchasing more C-130s as opposed to other transport. I double-checked the translation. There was no way I could have been mistaken. By now, Lt. Col. Yishaek had become commander of the department, replacing Col. Yirador, who had remained in Military Intelligence. It was the middle of the night, but I knew how explosive this material was. A sleepy voice answered Yishaek's number.

"Sir," I said, "you need to come here right away."

"I hope this is important."

"Sir, I wouldn't have called you for anything less. It's more than important—it's extremely sensitive."

"Unless this is as big as the Egyptians declaring war on Israel, I'll have your balls cut off for getting me out of bed at this time."

"It's worse," I said.

He arrived 20 minutes later, in uniform, unshaven.

"OK," he said, "what's so important?"

I told him to sit and read the computer. He said he couldn't read Farsi. I told him I deliberately hadn't translated it. I went through it for him word by word, whispering, so a woman soldier working in another part of the office couldn't hear. He asked me to translate it again.

"Are you sure?" he asked.

"Sir, I am absolutely sure."

The telegram also detailed in which of Shimon Peres's brother's business accounts in Europe the bribe money had been deposited. Other than his "analyses" plagiarized from the newspaper, the ambassador was very credible.

Yishaek got on the phone and told Buffy to come right away. By the time he arrived, I had the translation on paper. Buffy read it, his brow furrowed under the fluorescent lighting. Known for his good relations with Peres, Buffy looked up finally and sighed heavily.

"I want the original telegram, the translation, your log, and anything else connected to this erased," he said slowly and deliberately.

I told him it couldn't be done. The monitoring of embassies inside Israel was not carried out by Military Intelligence, but by the SHABAK, and the telegrams in and out of the Iranian building were accounted for by the SHABAK. They sent the telegrams to us every day, we would decode the letters, and early the following morning they would demand every telegram back with its translation. It wasn't a matter of just fixing the local log. The SHABAK had a log, too.

However, the following morning, the SHABAK, for the first time, did not ask for the telegram. Before I went home, I was called into Buffy's office. He told me, "We all know that you are a good officer. You are a patriot. You love your country. And I know that nothing of this matter will leak out."

The young woman who had been working with me immediately received transfer orders to another unit of 8200 in northern Israel, and within a short time Col. Ben-Porat was promoted to the rank of brigadier general and later appointed official spokesman of the Israel Defense Forces. I don't know if Peres actually received the bribe. I do know that after I stumbled on the accusation and passed it on to my superiors, it was covered up. No public disclosure or inquiry was ever made.

In April 1977, Lt. Col. Yishaek told me that I was required to travel to Italy, to work in our Rome listening station. Alarm bells rang in my head. Only recently two members of Military Intelligence working in that station had been killed, and although nobody claimed responsibility, suspicion had fallen on the Palestine Liberation Organization.

In the aftermath of the massacre of Israeli athletes at the 1972 Olympic Games in Munich, a battle was raging in Europe between Mossad agents and a Palestinian group called Black September. They were killing each other at every opportunity. We knew there was a leak somewhere at the embassy in Rome; someone was passing on to the Palestinians the names and activities of Israeli military and security personnel. The chances were that I would be a marked man as soon as I arrived. Obviously one's life is put at risk at times in the service of one's country, but I simply didn't want to be one of those who could die in this senseless situation.

"I'm not going," I said. "You can say or do what you like, but I won't go."

Yishaek was furious. "You'll be court-martialed for insubordination," he said.

"So be it," I replied. "At least I'll still be alive."

The next morning, I was called to the Administrative Officers' Bureau, where two military policemen were waiting. I was taken before a military tribunal on a charge of serious insubordination. I refused an attorney and was found guilty. The sentence was 14 days in jail and reduction in rank from lieutenant to corporal. I was also told I would no longer have the honor of serving the extra two years in the military. I would be released after I completed my regular military service.

I was taken to a military prison near Haifa to serve my 14 days. Two days later, to my surprise, I was released and sent straight back to my unit. Shulamit Ingerman was waiting to tell me that Lt. Col. Yishaek had overreacted and she had gone over his head to obtain a pardon from the director of Military Intelligence—

only someone with a rank of major general or above can overrule a military tribunal.

"Your rank can be restored right away if you agree to sign again for the extra two years' service," said Shulamit.

My regular military service was due to end in less than a month, and if I were to keep to the contract, I would be doing an extra two years as a career officer. This was my opportunity to scrap the contract and I took it. I told Lt. Col. Yishaek, "Thanks for the pardon. But I'm not going to stay here any longer."

If truth be told, I was bored. We had broken the code. I didn't want to spend another two years there. I was looking in another direction—I wanted to work in the deepest sanctum of Israeli intelligence: the External Relations Department of the Israel Defense Forces/Military Intelligence. I wanted to serve Israel where I would have the most impact. I was ambitious, and with my unique background and skills, I felt the ERD offered the most challenging future for me.

I obtained an interview with the office of the chief personnel officer of the intelligence corps. I expressed my hopes of joining Military Intelligence as a civilian in the External Relations Department, where almost everyone else was a civilian anyway.

On May 3, 1977, I was released from the military. I was then scheduled for a number of interviews, including one with the chief of External Relations, Col. Meir Meir.

"I think," he said, "we could draw on your Iranian expertise."

At the same time I was offered a job in Mossad operations, to be stationed in Europe. I declined, pinning my hopes on getting assigned to External Relations. The SHABAK also offered me work in their Iranian Unit, and there was a possibility of joining the Foreign Ministry. I still wasn't interested. I knew what I wanted.

Finally the message came back. I had been accepted in External Relations.

Had I known what was in store, I might have considered it safer to go to Rome.

3

Love in the
Time of Revolution

AUGUST 15, 1977. How could I ever forget my first day in the External Relations Department of the Israel Defense Forces/ Military Intelligence? My right cheek was badly swollen with an abscessed tooth and I could hardly speak because of polyps on my vocal cords. It was three weeks before I felt normal again. Spooks, too, are human.

IDF/MI/ERD was the most prestigious department in the intelligence community. Its status went back to the 1974 Agranat Commission which the prime minister had appointed to investigate the intelligence failures of the 1973 war, when Israel had been surprised on Yom Kippur by the Syrian-Egyptian attack.

Several of the important recommendations in the commission's secret report were implemented immediately by the government. One that I was well aware of converted Military Intelligence into the senior intelligence agency, giving it more powers than Mossad. As a result, the National Assessment, the intelligence term for the immediate security situation in the country and what the security arrangements were to be, would be solely the responsibility of the director of Military Intelligence. It was not to be a pooled responsibility of the various intelligence agencies—this one was his alone.

A further effect of the recommendations was the creation of the External Relations Department of Military Intelligence. This was built around an existing unit called Foreign Liaison. When I joined External Relations in 1977, it had four branches:

There was the Special Assistance Branch (SIM), through which special military assistance was to be given to other countries and various "liberation movements." The Mossad department that had been in charge of external military assistance now became a liaison department between foreign countries and SIM.

Then there was the branch in which I was initially employed, known as RESH—the pronunciation in Hebrew of the letter R. R branch was in charge of intelligence exchange with foreign intelligence communities and general relations with foreign intelligence networks. The Mossad, in fact, had a large parallel branch called Tevel, but once R branch gained prominence, Tevel had a problem. It arose because in order to receive intelligence information from foreign countries, it was necessary to give them something in return. And what countries in the West wanted most was technical information about Soviet weapons systems; in other words, military information. The Mossad no longer had access to the analytical departments of the military to gain this information—they had to go through the R branch. The result was that the once-powerful Tevel now found itself also playing the part of a liaison department with the R branch.

A third branch, known as Foreign Liaison, was charged with taking care of Israeli military attachés outside Israel as well as Israeli military personnel serving in foreign countries. It was also in charge of liaison with foreign military personnel and foreign military attachés in Israel.

The fourth branch, Intelligence 12, was a general liaison branch with the Mossad.

Other than these four branches, the External Relations Department also had an operations officer who was directly subordinate to the chief of ERD and who took care of various logistical matters such as passports, intelligence exchange conferences, diplomatic pouches coming in and out, security, and so on. He also had under his control the ERD conference halls, where secret intelligence meetings were held.

While working in the R branch, I was assigned by the office of the director of Military Intelligence to work with the Iranians. The director's office wanted someone who was knowledgeable about Iran to be a direct liaison with the Iranian intelligence community. The Mossad representative in Tehran at the time was very ineffective, and finally the director and the chief of Tevel agreed to his recall. The deputy military attaché in Tehran, Col. Yitzhak Cahani, who acted as the External Relations Department's representative, was also rather unsuccessful with intelligence work, as he didn't speak Farsi and didn't understand the situation on the ground.

Starting in late September 1977, I became a Middle East commuter, traveling back and forth between Tel Aviv and Tehran. Because I was born in Tehran, I was still regarded in Iran as an Iranian citizen and therefore subject to Iranian laws, even though I had by now taken out Israeli citizenship. I wasn't supposed to have a foreign diplomatic passport—which Israel had issued to me—because the Iranians deemed dual citizenship illegal. The difficulty was overcome when the Israeli government issued me a diplomatic passport in which the place of birth was conveniently not mentioned. I used it only when I went to Tehran.

As a result of the establishment of diplomatic relations in the late 1960s between Iran and Israel, the Iranians had a full embassy in Ramat Gan with a SAVAK representative, a military attaché, a commercial attaché, a consul, and an ambassador. But it wasn't officially designated as an embassy and it did not have a sign on the door or a flagpole. Officially, the Iranians had an interests section in the Swiss Embassy in Tel Aviv, but it didn't really exist, and callers to the Swiss Embassy who asked for it would be referred to the unofficial Iranian Embassy in Ramat Gan.

Israel had the same unofficial status in Tehran. The building on Kakh Avenue had no sign on the door, but everyone knew what it was. The reason for this elaborate charade was the Shah's concern that his relationship with Arab nations would be disrupted. They were fully aware of the unofficial arrangement, but this ruse allowed the Arabs to turn a blind eye.

My trips to Tehran were a source of ill will toward me from Col. Cahani and the Mossad, because I had taken over some of their territory. However, they could say nothing: I had been commissioned by the big boss, the director of Military Intelligence.

In Tehran I would often meet the SAVAK representative, as well as officials from Iranian Military Intelligence. Mostly the meetings were held in my room at the Carlton Hotel, not far from the unofficial Israeli Embassy.

Besides sharing information about Iraq and other Arab countries, the Iranian intelligence people and I also exchanged technical information. For example, Israel at the time was developing a tank called Merkava at the Israel Military Industries. The tank developers were interested in knowing the composition of metal sheets, developed by the British and used on their advanced battle tanks, some of which had been supplied to the Iranians. This metal, known as Chobham armor, was thought to be impenetrable by indirect rocket or missile hits. On instructions from my superiors, I asked the Iranian military, through their foreign liaison department, if we could have a sample of the metal.

"The only way you can get a sheet of this metal would mean us cutting up a tank," said my Iranian counterpart.

"Fine," I said. "Why don't you do it?"

And they did. They cut a sheet of Chobham armor off one of their tanks and dispatched it to Israel in a diplomatic crate. It didn't destroy the tank—but it made it less secure because the hole had to be patched with inferior metal. Later, in the early 1980s, the British realized that the Merkava tanks had features of the British armor.

We were exchanging a great deal of intelligence with the Iranians on Iraq, which we saw as a mutual enemy, even though the Shah had officially settled his disputes with the Iraqi leadership. We were also passing to them information on the activities of anti-Shah Shi'ite Iranians living in Lebanon. It was from there that information about the impending Iranian revolution first started to leak out.

"You must be careful," I told my Iranian colleagues. "We think you're in for big trouble here."

Apart from these intelligence-swap meetings, I had another task in Tehran—putting together an analysis of the underground

Tudeh Party of Iran, a pro-Soviet group. My research visits to Tehran University resulted in my meeting two special friends who were to play major roles in my life and in the complex political scene in the Middle East.

One was a man calling himself Mahmoud Amirian, an alias, who was writing a doctoral dissertation on Marxism. He used an alias because he had been jailed in the late 1960s by the SAVAK for subversive activity. When he was released, he left Iran and lived in Baku, in the Soviet Union, just over the Iranian border, until 1976, when he came back to Tehran using an alias and a French passport. He came in as an Iranian expatriate who was born and lived in Paris. He had effectively "laundered" himself.

After we became friendly and I had found out who he really was, he revealed that he was one of the leading members of the Tudeh Party in charge of foreign liaison. An extremely well-educated man, he believed in "the cause." Even though he knew I was in Israeli intelligence, he told me he trusted me.

The other man I met at Tehran University in 1977 was Sayeed Mehdi Kashani, who was doing a Master's thesis on the Shi'ite community of southern Iraq. A few years older than I, he was the son of Ayatollah Abol Qassem Kashani, who at the time was an opposition Shi'ite leader living in the holy city of Qom. Like Amirian, Kashani had been jailed for subversive activities against the Shah.

My meeting these two men was not entirely accidental. I had been directed to them by the research department of IDF/MI. Israel had an intelligence network within Tehran, using the local Jewish community, and possessed a lot of information about the opposition in the capital. Kashani and Amirian both introduced me to their friends in the Iranian opposition. I heard enough to convince me to write reports for Israel early in 1978 declaring without reservation that the Shah was about to be overthrown. I also pointed out that it was the first time that opposition circles were no longer wishfully thinking; they were talking realistically.

The intellectuals and the middle class in Tehran, I reported, were fed up. There was extreme corruption in higher circles, prices were skyrocketing, and food production in Iran, which had been the bread basket of the Middle East, had come to a halt as a result of the Shah's White Revolution, breaking up the feudal system. He had distributed land to the peasants to keep them happy, but he had destroyed their life-support systems. In times past, the feudal lords had provided villagers with seeds, a marketing system, transportation, water, and so on, but after these lords had been dispossessed and the land divided up, the peasants' infrastructure was destroyed. Who was to take care of their marketing?

The Shah wasn't interested—his attention was on the military, not food production. As a result, food production in Iran came almost to a standstill, and by 1978 most supplies were being imported. The peasants managed because they found ways of providing for themselves. The rich were all right, too, because they could afford to buy the high-priced imported foodstuffs. The people who suffered were those caught in the middle, the intellectuals and the middle class.

They were battling extremely high food prices, and on top of that the infrastructure of the city of Tehran was not capable of handling the traffic, which came to a standstill. Even my superiors laughed at me when I wrote that the traffic might be one of the reasons the Shah would be overthrown. But it was true. It was quite clear that people were fed up with taking hours to get to work and back.

The middle classes spearheaded the revolution, but the Shi'ite fundamentalists quickly jumped on the bandwagon. My talks with Kashani's Shi'ite friends left me no doubt that they were extremely well-organized through the mosques, the one perfect infrastructure remaining. Discontent spread through the university, intellectual circles, and the mosques. A report I sent back in February 1978 pointing out the "mosque network" was dismissed by Military Intelligence and Mossad analysts, who thought it too theoretical.

I believed that my sources were impeccable and my assessments on the mark. I had gone deeper than any other Israeli intelligence official. I spoke the same language as my contacts, both in tongue and, to a large degree, thought. I was convinced that it would not be long before I was proved correct.

*   *   *

Despite the volatile situation in Iran, my controllers in the External Relations Department decided they could use me in an entirely different part of the world—Central and South America. Apart from Iran, Israel's main military exports were going to those two regions. There were direct government sales as well as sales through a private network coordinated by Ariel Sharon, at that time minister of agriculture. With the swing toward leftwing governments, there was a danger that these markets might be closed down. If the Sandinista National Liberation Front (FSLN) took over from President Anastasio Somoza Debayle in Nicaragua, for example, it was likely they would obtain their military equipment from the Soviet Union.

Upon learning of close contacts between the Tudeh Party and the commanders of the Sandinistas, my controllers asked me if I could get my Iranian friends to help arrange a meeting between an Israeli intelligence official and the Sandinistas. Although I wanted to concentrate all my talks with my contacts on the coming changes in Iran, I did what I was asked.

I wasn't sure of the roots of contact between the Tudeh Party and the Sandinistas, but I assumed they arose through connections in Moscow and Havana.

"Can you arrange a meeting?" I asked Amirian.

"I will try," he said, and I knew as soon as he said it that there would be no problems.

It took Amirian just a short time to get back to me. The path had been cleared for a meeting with the Sandinistas. My superiors were delighted and had no hesitation in deciding who should travel to Central America: me. I realized there was a very good reason for my selection. My superiors wanted me out of Iran for a while for my own safety. Although my warnings of an impending uprising against the Shah had not been treated seriously, everything that I had reported had been passed on to the Americans as a matter of policy. In turn, the Americans had referred my reports back to Iranian intelligence. I was being placed in an extremely delicate position, and it was felt I should be pulled out of Tehran for a few weeks at least.

Not that the mission to Nicaragua was going to be a piece of cake. No one knew how I would be received by the Sandinistas and what they might decide to do with me once I was in their territory. And there would be no backup. I had to go in complete secrecy. Even the Israeli intelligence network stationed in Central America could not be informed of the mission, out of concern about a possible leak to the right wing.

I did not like the idea of leaving my post in Iran unattended even briefly when the country was at such a critical juncture. I felt I should return to Tehran as soon as possible, but I was excited about my new mission.

Late in March 1978, I flew to the United States and from there traveled to Managua. The city, leveled by an earthquake in 1931, badly damaged by fire four years later and then hit again by a major earthquake in 1972, was now in a state of great uncertainty, with recent fighting in the streets between Somoza's troops and the Sandinistas.

The leftwing movement had not forgotten Somoza's father's act of treachery in 1934 when, as head of the National Guard, he had invited Augusto Sandino, the revolutionary patriot after whom the movement is named, to a banquet and then murdered him. But now, with 500,000 homeless, a death toll of more than 30,000 from the political fighting between the Somoza government and the Sandinistas, and an economy that was in ruins, everyone knew it would not be long before Somoza was overthrown.

On arrival at the Intercontinental Hotel, a vast concrete structure rising up from old Managua, I phoned a number that had been given to me by an FSLN representative I had met in Washington while en route to Central America. The woman who answered said she would call for me at eight the following morning.

She arrived as arranged, dressed in jeans, a light-blue blouse and sneakers. I'll always remember that first image of her . . . tall, slim, with green eyes, light-olive skin, and jet-black hair. She flashed a bright smile as she held out her hand.

"I'm Marie Fernanda," she said. "We're in for a bit of a trip."

Then she led me outside and with a soft chuckle introduced me to her old, mud-splattered yellow Fiat. That car was to be the catalyst for some of the happiest and most tragic moments of my life.

Less than ten kilometers out of Managua we reached the first military roadblock. Marie pulled out a press card that identified

her as a Colombian journalist. She was going north, she told the
inquisitive government soldiers, to write a story. I was merely
introduced as her companion. We were waved through.

Skirting Lake Managua, we smashed over potholes as the road
narrowed, but at least the traffic was thinning out. An hour later
we hit a small town. The National Guard was everywhere with
roadblocks at each end of the town. We were told that if we kept
going we would be risking our lives because we would be entering
areas held by the revolutionary forces.

"That's why I'm here," Marie told the officers. "To cover the
war."

Twenty minutes on, we came to another roadblock. Russian
submachine guns were trained on us.

"These are friends," said Marie. "They know the car." I was
happy to hear her reassurance. A group of unkempt young men in
"odds and ends" paramilitary dress approached, Kalashnikovs
slung over their shoulders. After a few words of greeting, they
moved back the barbed-wire barriers and we continued.

Now that she was in territory held by the FSLN, Marie lost her
nervousness. Her voice now full of confidence, she let me have it.

"I don't understand you people," she said angrily. "You Israelis
and the Jews who have suffered so much are now helping this
Nazi Somoza. You don't care about what he has done to the
Nicaraguan people."

There wasn't much I could say. It was true we were supplying
Somoza.

She had not finished: "It's very bad that your country that was
created on a socialist-egalitarian basis has turned into a fascist
state which helps the Nazi dictators of South America."

I let her run with it. The fertile countryside, with rocky outcrops pushing through dense vegetation, flashed by.

"Where did you learn your English?" I asked. I'd taken her point.
I wanted to talk about other things.

"In the United States. I lived there for a few years. Don't think
we are all peasants," she said, her voice brimming with dignity
and indignation. "While the revolution is for the peasants, it is
being run by enlightened professionals."

She told me she was taking me to the Sandinista military
headquarters in the area. There I could present my case—"and it

had better be good." I wasn't there to present a case, of course. My assignment was to find out what the Sandinista policies might be when they came to power and try to establish lines of communications.

Civilian traffic had been replaced by jeeps filled with youths, all clutching Kalashnikovs. It was obvious who controlled this part of the country. It was a long, hot drive, during which we stopped at small towns for cold drinks or to fill up with gas from old-fashioned, hand-cranked pumps. I asked where they got their gas.

"We have a supply system," she said. "We Sandinistas have everything under control. All civilian needs are being met."

Finally we reached a heavily guarded military base. The guards moved aside as Marie turned into the gates.

"Welcome to the regional headquarters of the Sandinista military forces," she said. An officer in full uniform, who explained he was "foreign liaison," led me to a prefabricated building that had been comfortably fitted out with a bed and shower. This was my room. It was obvious I'd be spending the night here. Marie was given a similar "villa" next to mine.

She came in and sat on the bed. She told me she was 21, and that her role with the Sandinistas was also foreign liaison. "And maybe one day," she added, "I'll be foreign minister of a liberated Nicaragua."

She was so earnest and serious. I wanted to see that bright smile I'd seen earlier.

"Marie Fernanda, can I call you Freddie?" I asked, which made her laugh.

"Sure," she said.

There was a shy awkwardness between us. I was deeply attracted to her, and she knew it. I asked her why there had been no sound of gunfire. "Is this war? It's so quiet."

"There's a lull. The biggest fighting is a long way away, near Costa Rica. But soon there will be no more war. It's been a long struggle, but Somoza is finished." Having said that, she left.

Later that afternoon I was taken to the commander's office. A bespectacled man in his mid-30s greeted me with a warm handshake, then introduced me with great modesty to a number of his companions.

"I hope you had a nice trip to Managua, and I hope soon we will be able to meet there, too," he said in good English, with a trace of a Spanish accent. We sat around in the office, and he made it clear that the Sandinistas would like to have a relationship with Israel.

"We respect the Israeli people very much," he said. "We identify with the Jewish plight because we are facing the same type of Hitler in our country. We have faced him for many years. It's too bad that your government is aiding him and selling him arms." So I got it again, this time from the top man. But I had expected it.

I outlined our thoughts about our links with Central America. I repeated to him, as I had to Freddie, that I had no excuses to offer—Israel was selling arms to Somoza in a big way: artillery, machine guns, mortars, and soon it would be helicopters. I could have given him the usual spiel that Israel wasn't to blame, that independent arms brokers were the real culprits. That was the accepted Israeli line, but I suspected that my hosts knew better.

However, I did have a point to make. A number of Sandinistas were being trained by our enemies, the PLO, in Lebanon. The commander shrugged.

"We have a war to win, Mr. Ben-Menashe. Your country is arming Somoza, we receive some training from the PLO. Who is to judge who is right? But I can only ask you to tell your government to stop arming Somoza and start siding with the people of Nicaragua. You could begin by providing us with any medical aid or field hospitals which you can spare. There is still a lot of blood that is going to be shed."

I made a note of his requests, and we established a means of contact through a Sandinista liaison office in South America. Of course, I had no authority to make any promises. I was there to sound them out—and tell them that Israel would like to keep its embassy running in Managua when the Sandinistas were in control and that we could act as a go-between for them with the U.S.

My hosts said that they would support any peace moves in the Middle East—but also emphasized that Israel should recognize the PLO.

"Although we recognize Israel's right to exist, we recognize the PLO as the legitimate representative of the Palestinian people," the commander said. It was clear that my hosts didn't want to commit themselves one way or the other.

"The Sandinistas are a very democratic movement, from the social democrats down to supporters of Soviet communism," the commander continued as we sipped sweet tea. "When we take over, there will be democratic elections. We are spearheading the revolution for the people of Nicaragua. We are not against a free market, but we don't believe the peasants should be starved out."

The commander was drawing a picture of a socialist country with freedom of the press, freedom of speech, free education, and a good health and welfare system.

I explained that I had been working in Iran. "Another revolution," he said with a laugh. "You must enjoy them."

He was interested to know if the Tudeh Party was going to have any part in the government after the Shah was toppled. I told him the Shah was going, but I certainly didn't think the left would take over. The new leaders would be religious.

"Are they going back to the Dark Ages?"

"Dark Ages or not, I think you'll find that religion, rather than accepted government principles, will soon be Iran's driving force."

We were served dinner in the office area. The air was thick with the smoke from the Marlboro cigarettes my hosts were smoking. "Not everything American is bad," the commander laughed.

Back in my room, Freddie showed up. "How was your discussion?" she wanted to know. I told her that it had gone well. She made coffee. My pulse pounded, and it wasn't the drink.

In the morning, we headed south, the Sandinistas again showing respect for my lovely companion. Back in government-held territory, the Fiat started to act up. Then, with a loud bang and gushing of steam, the radiator blew. Fortunately, we were close to a small village where we found a cantina and called a mechanic. The car would take several hours to repair, and we knew we'd never get back to the capital in time to beat the curfew. If you drove around the city after curfew, you were likely to be shot.

There was only one room available above the cantina with two beds. Freddie kissed me warmly, then told me she was going to sleep. I climbed into my own bed, my mind racing over the events of the previous day. Freddie, breathing softly in the darkened room, was foremost in my mind. She was no ordinary peasant woman, that was for sure. Apart from her beauty, she had a fast mind. I watched her sleep, so peaceful, and then dozed off myself.

We were back at the Intercontinental Hotel shortly after noon the following day. Freddie said she'd show me around the city. We sipped the strong, locally produced coffee, and wandered through the streets. She showed me the monument to the poet Rubén Darío and took me around areas that had been rebuilt following the devastating 1972 earthquake. And that night she stayed with me. The smell of her skin, her sparkling green eyes, overwhelmed me. I was her first lover.

She left at ten the following morning. I phoned Israel and reported that all was well. At noon there was a call from the lobby. Three men had come to see me. It was important, said the porter, that I meet them.

I guessed who they were as soon as they entered the room. Dressed in dark suits with bulges under their jackets, it was obvious they were from state security. They wasted no time.

"Where were you in the last few days?" the most senior, a well-built man with neatly trimmed hair, wanted to know. "Who are you working for?"

"None of your business."

He banged on the coffee table. "It is our business. If you don't already know it, we make everything our business in Nicaragua."

I told them I would not speak to them further until I had talked with my ambassador and that if they didn't let me call him there would be an "incident." They found the number and dialed it themselves. They wanted to be sure whom I was talking to. I asked for the ambassador. I didn't even know his name, because I hadn't told the embassy I was there. When I was finally put through, I spoke to the ambassador in Hebrew, explaining I was an Israeli citizen and that I worked for the government.

"We weren't informed," was the terse reply.

"I know you weren't informed. But please call the Tel Aviv office of Col. Meir Meir, chief of External Relations. And do it quickly, or you're going to be involved in something far bigger."

"Such as?"

"Such as trying to get an Israeli intelligence officer out of a Nicaraguan jail."

It was about 12:30 P.M. in Nicaragua, evening in Israel. There was still a chance Col. Meir would be in the office.

I hung up and waited. There was an awkward ten minutes as the security men and I sat staring at one another. I could see their patience was running out. Then the ambassador called back. He said he was coming around right away. Minutes later he hurried into the room. He gave me a cold glare, then told my visitors:

"I'm taking responsibility for this man. You have nothing to be concerned about. He'll be leaving the country tomorrow. He's just an Israeli adventurer traveling around Latin America."

They didn't believe him, but they had no authority to interfere with an Israeli citizen who had come under the official charge of his ambassador.

As soon as they left, he turned on me angrily. They had confirmed my identity in Israel, but he was not happy that he had not been informed. He wanted to know whom I had met, so he could prepare a report. I told him that Israel would tell him. And I sat and smiled at him until he left.

I spent that night with Freddie. I gave her my home and office numbers in Tel Aviv and the Carlton Hotel number in Tehran. As I traveled to the airport the next morning, there was a lump in my throat. I had already started to miss her.

A few weeks later, in April of 1978, she called me at my office in Tel Aviv. She was in Lisbon, Portugal, and she had a proposition to put to me. A short holiday in Athens, if I could manage to get the time off. I was owed a lot of days, so I made the arrangements and flew to Athens.

The first two days were magical, as we strode hand in hand around the ancient city. On the third day she told me she was pregnant.

"What should we do?" she asked.

I had no idea. I was totally unprepared for this.

"We're kind of an unlikely pair," she said.

That was putting it mildly. She was a socialist Catholic, a Sandinista, subject to party discipline. I was Jewish, working for Israeli intelligence, and my country was supplying her most hated enemy with weapons. There could be serious personal, political, and professional consequences for both of us.

"It would be awfully hard for us to be together to raise a baby," I said. "We live on opposite sides of the world."

"Opposites attract."

Yes, it was true. She was beautiful, passionate, sweet, fascinating, different from anyone I'd known. I wanted her. I wanted the baby. But I knew if we were ever together, my job would be in jeopardy. I'd be considered a security risk. My brain was saying one thing, my heart another.

Later that day we took a bus to Soúnion, where the Adriatic and the Mediterranean meet. As we looked at the two seas merging, she turned to me and said, "I don't think I could ever have an abortion."

"Yes, but we barely know each other. Who are you? I don't know. Who am I? You don't know."

She looked up at me with that radiant smile, gleaming white teeth against olive skin. Then she kissed me. "I want the baby, Ari."

"Okay," I said, still confused. "It's your choice. Maybe it's destiny."

Which it was.

By April 1978, my warnings about an imminent revolution in Iran had been accepted by my superiors. Later that month, I sat in as my report was handed around at an intelligence exchange conference in Tel Aviv involving Israeli Military Intelligence and Mossad analysts on one side, and American CIA and Defense Intelligence Agency analysts on the other. This time my heart sank.

One American analyst dismissed my conclusions as baloney, saying that what was happening in Tehran was nothing more than a lot of shouting by a bunch of noisy kids in the street and that the demonstrations and unrest had been going on generally in Iran since the 1950s. It was not a friendly meeting—in fact, there was an outright confrontation on the subject between the two sides. We were trying to tell the U.S. representatives that there would be a change in status quo in the Middle East and Israel could not depend on Iran for any military backup against the Arabs. It had always been accepted that if ever Israel was stormed by the Arabs, the Americans would come to the rescue, using Iran as a staging ground. Now the Shah was going to go, and Israel's security would be weakened. It was as simple as that.

The American analysts wouldn't listen.

That was a slap in the face for the Israeli intelligence network and for me personally. A further shock came later.

President Jimmy Carter, in a public speech, declared that the Shah of Iran was an ally and a friend and stood like a rock in the Middle East. We just couldn't believe it. The Americans had not only dismissed our warnings but had not even bothered to do any serious checking themselves. They had completely misread the threat to the Shah's rule.

It wasn't until the end of that year that the Carter administration finally admitted that the Iranian ruler was about to go. In December 1978, the CIA enlisted the aid of the Israeli intelligence community and the SAVAK in a plan to kill Ayatollah Ruhollah Khomeini, the Islamic cleric who was coordinating the upsurge of opposition from Paris. Put together by the prime minister's counterterrorism adviser, Rafi Eitan, the plan was for an Israeli hit team to fly to France without the permission of the French authorities and "eliminate" Khomeini. On the same day, the Iranian generals would declare martial law in Iran and, after order had been restored a month or so later, the SAVAK would move in and arrest or remove the generals and restore total power to the Shah.

On paper the plan could have worked, but the human element was too weak. There was no way on earth that the Shah, the generals, and the SAVAK had the ability to pull off their end of the bargain. The military and the SAVAK had been too well infiltrated; and they were all too busy shipping their booty out of the country to escape the inevitable doomsday.

Nevertheless, preparations continued. The Israeli selected to lead the raid on Khomeini's residence in the outskirts of Paris was Col. Assaf Heftez, chief of the Israeli Police Border Guard special antiterrorist unit—a highly trained commando team set up to deal with hijackings and other terrorist incidents. There is no doubt the team would have successfully carried out its part and returned home without being caught, but the Shah did not have the backbone or the loyalty of his people necessary to retain his grip on the Peacock Throne.

The plan, however, was still put to the Shah by the recently retired Israeli ambassador to Iran, Uri Lubrani. It was instantly rejected.

"I will not allow any more Iranians to be massacred," said the Shah. "For the generals to carry out martial law will mean bloodshed in the streets of Tehran. We will handle the situation ourselves."

This was new. The Shah of Iran was showing concern for the people of Iran!

Lubrani told the Israeli intelligence community that the Shah could not stay in power and that no general in Iran could stage a military coup. The country was lost to the Shi'ite leadership, he said. It was just a matter of time.

In December 1978, I decided to let my CIA colleagues know what I thought of them. I was furious and personally offended that all my earlier reports had been dismissed. Nothing had been done about our warnings and then at the end of 1978, when it was too late, they had come up with an impossible plan that would have created more bloodshed.

"You guys better start listening a bit more instead of thinking you are always right," I told an official by phone. I don't recall who hung up first.

In that same month, with the assassination plan abandoned, a serious attempt was made to get Ayatollah Khomeini to agree to talks. Israel wanted to know where it stood when he came to power. Prime Minister Menachem Begin agreed with the intelligence departments that nothing would be lost by trying to talk to Khomeini. But who was going to do the talking on Israel's behalf?

The task fell on the shoulders of an unlikely person—Ruth Ben-David.

In the early 1950s this charming, gracious French Catholic woman lived in Paris and entertained ultra-orthodox Jews who used to visit from Jerusalem. Rabbi Amram Blau, then head of an orthodox Jewish sect in Jerusalem known as Neturei Karte, meaning Guardians of the Citadel, was among those who visited Paris. Being a widower, he craved female attention. He was introduced to the stunningly attractive woman with whom he whiled away the hours. Eventually they fell in love. They decided to marry, and she converted to orthodox Judaism.

Before her husband died, she frequently accompanied him when he traveled to Turkey to attend seminars at which Jewish rabbis and Shi'ite mullahs entered into religious debates and tried to establish how theology could be brought back to earthly government. In those meetings Ruth met the exiled cleric, Ayatollah Khomeini. When Rabbi Blau died, his son from his first marriage took over the leadership of the Neturei Karte. But it was Ruth who was recognized as the matriarch of the sect.

Prime Minister Begin entrusted Ruth Ben-David with visiting Ayatollah Khomeini in Paris on his behalf in December 1978. She was to sound him out about how he would see relations with Israel if he were to take over—and what his attitude to the Jews in Iran would be.

Khomeini gladly received the emissary, his old friend. It was said she was the only woman he would sit alone with in a closed room. She had a long conversation with him at his residence outside Paris, and she reported back personally to Begin.

According to accounts directed to intelligence analysts from the Prime Minister's Office, the meeting with the Ayatollah was very friendly. Khomeini made it clear that the Iranian Jews were Iranian citizens and Islam respected Judaism and all other religions that were not seen as heresy. He would not allow Baha'is to practice their religion in Iran, because in Islamic law it is stated that prophets who came before the Prophet Mohammed, including Moses and Jesus Christ, were true prophets, but anyone who came after him claiming to carry the word of God was a heretic, and heretics should be put to death. The Prophet Mohammed was the seal. Khomeini added that the Israeli state in Palestine was also a heresy and should not exist. However, the first interest of the Islamic state was to bring Islam and Islamic government to the Moslem populations in the Arab countries and rid the Moslem world of heretic governments. He also said that Mecca and Medina had to be liberated from the Saudis.

His message to Begin was clear: Don't worry, Israel. First on my agenda is to deal with my Arab enemies. Then I will deal with Israel.

This news was well received in Israel. Some Arab countries—Jordan, Iraq, Saudi Arabia, Kuwait, Egypt, and the Emirates—were going to have an active, formidable enemy. They were not only going to have to deal with Israel now, but also Iran. The Shah, in his last years, had started lining himself up with moderate pro-American Arabs, which could have become a deadly coalition against Israel. As the situation looked at this new stage, it seemed fortunate that the plan to assassinate Khomeini had not gone forward.

Shortly before Christmas 1978, I asked for a vacation. My superiors were happy to remove me from the scene for a while because I had upset the Americans by speaking my mind to them. I had already called Managua and made arrangements. I flew to Lisbon and took a cab to the Penta Hotel. Freddie had arrived ahead of me. She threw open the door. I'd seen her a few times since April, but not like this. She was huge. Our baby was due in two months.

"You're beautiful, Freddie," I said.

It was a blissful two weeks that we spent together in Portugal. As we strolled along the Atlantic at Estoril, she told me of the arrangements she'd made for the birth of our child.

I took her hand. "I'm glad we decided to have it," I said.

She smiled, that smile that had won my heart in war-ravaged Nicaragua. The Sandinistas had almost won control, even occupying the national palace for a few days in August that year.

"It looks like you might be foreign minister soon, after all," I said. But it was only half a joke. I didn't want her to be swallowed up by a far-away bureaucracy.

All too soon, it was time for me to go back to Tel Aviv. She patted her tummy.

"Don't worry about us," she said. "And you'll see us again when you can, huh?"

I took her in my arms. One day, I thought, I'd stop saying goodbye to this woman. It was not easy living without her.

4

Groundwork

AT 12:30 P.M. on January 16, 1979, four helicopters had lifted off from the grounds of Tehran's Niavaran Palace, their rotors sweeping aside the snow. There was nothing to indicate to a would-be assassin which aircraft carried His Imperial Majesty Mohammad Reza Pahlavi Aryamehr, Shahanshah of Iran, King of Kings, Shadow of the Almighty, Center of the Universe.

The Shah's departure from Iran would bring about a tumultuous upheaval in the Middle East. It would also lead to a new threat to the existence of Israel, and ultimately bring my country into fierce conflict with the United States. As I studied the intelligence reports of the Shah's last minutes in the country he had ruled for nearly 40 years, I could be sure of one thing: When the Shah and his Empress stepped from their helicopter at Mehrabad Airport and two officers of his Royal Guard fell to their knees and tried to kiss his feet, it was the end. He would never return.

"How long will you be away, sir?" a guard had asked.

"It depends on the state of my health," he had replied wistfully as the Empress, her chestnut hair pushed up under a fur hat, linked her arm through his. His body was riddled with cancer. He was a broken man.

"I am sure," said the Empress, "that the independence of this country and the unity of the nation will remain. We have faith in

44

the Iranian nation and in the culture of Iran. I hope and I know God will always be behind the Iranian nation."

But God had been showing His displeasure. Shops, banks, and offices were closed as mobs roamed, chanting, "Death . . . death to the Shah." Many of his close friends had simply deserted him. The rich families he knew so well had already traded in millions of rials for dollars, francs, and Deutschmarks, and fled to relatives in the West, leaving behind the crackle of gunfire and the sound of people wailing over freshly dug graves.

Oil production had come to a standstill. Scores of freighters lay idle in the Persian Gulf, waiting for customs officials to return to work. Moscow had sent an aircraft to pick up 70 Soviet oil researchers and their families. Americans and other foreign nationals crammed onto U.S. Air Force planes. Iran was out of control; for each fanatical white-shrouded protester the troops had shot down, another had sprung up to fill the gap.

As their Imperial Majesties walked toward their silver and blue Boeing 707, two officers spontaneously turned to face each other, holding up a copy of the Koran for them to pass under. Then, as the street mobs shouted with joy and smashed the statues erected in his honor, the King of Kings, a small parcel of Iranian soil tucked in his pocket, took the controls of the aircraft and flew off into the sunless sky. The Shah's rule was over.

Israel decided to act fast to protect its interests. On board one of the last flights that El Al made into Tehran before the airport was closed were 48 Israeli aircrews, all wearing civilian clothes.

A few days later, with the full cooperation of the commander of the Iranian Air Force—who was later executed—48 F-14 jets were flown out of Iran to an air force base in northern Sinai. (They were later sold by Israel to the Taiwanese.) As proof of the Carter administration's blindness, the U.S. had delivered these planes to the Shah in September 1978, even before the U.S. Air Force was supplied with its own. The Shah, whose regime was crumbling around him, had paid through the nose for them. The U.S. was relieved that the F-14s had not fallen into the "wrong hands." The Israelis had corrected the situation.

The Regency and the Supreme Military Councils set up for the Shah's absence were unable to function, and Prime Minister Shahpour Bakhtiar, who, as a Mossadegh supporter and a member of the National Front, was the last prime minister appointed by the Shah as a compromise with the opposition, proved equally helpless. On February 1, 1979, Ayatollah Ruhollah Khomeini arrived in Iran from Paris. Amidst wild scenes of rejoicing, ten days later Bakhtiar went into hiding before eventually finding exile in Paris himself.*

The Israeli Embassy in Tehran was handed over to the Palestine Liberation Organization by the new Iranian regime, and it became the PLO Embassy. There was a complete breakdown in relations between Israel and Iran, although the American Embassy in Tehran continued operating.

Meanwhile, the last 17 Israelis who had been left behind in Iran—officials at the embassy and others, who were in hiding—were flown out by the U.S. Air Force to Frankfurt and then by El Al to Tel Aviv.

Khomeini won a landslide victory in a national referendum, and on April 1, he declared Iran an Islamic republic, just as my contacts had predicted months before.

The first prime minister appointed by the revolutionary government of Ayatollah Khomeini was Mehdi Bazargan. A member of the National Front and a supporter of Mossadegh, Bazargan represented Khomeini's compromise between the fundamentalists and the middle class. Bazargan believed that the Soviets and the U.S. were both evil, but preferred the U.S. to the godless communists. He did not accept the Ayatollah's thesis that Iran could exist without the backing of any superpower. He made it clear that he would like to see relations with Washington normalized. He allowed the U.S. Embassy in Tehran to operate, and he continued to deal with the Americans.

Bazargan's faction found itself in a tense power struggle with the extremist fundamentalist group that wanted neither Americans in Iran nor any relationship with the U.S., which was seen as "the Great Satan." There seemed to be no hope of an immediate repair of relations between Israel and Iran. Israel was still licking its wounds after the pullout from Iran, but at the same time, Israeli intelligence was keeping a close eye on the fluid situation there.

* Bakhtiar was assassinated in Paris in 1991.

Contrary to U.S. intelligence reports, our information suggested that things within Iran were breaking down fast, that a showdown was looming among Iran's various religious and political factions, and that, above all else, the clergy was there to stay. We were also convinced that a confrontation between the Arab states and the Iranians was not far off, centering on a clash between Iran and its neighbor Iraq. Israel had many friends in the Iranian military who hated Iraq. Even though Iraq had a big Shi'ite community in the south, there was a long-standing enmity between the Shi'ite Iranians and the Sunni leadership of Iraq. A border conflict had been settled by the Shah in 1975, but the new Iranian regime announced it would not recognize the settlement. It claimed that Shatt al-Arab, Iraq's main outlet to the Persian Gulf, was actually an Iranian waterway and that Bahrain was also its territory.

One of the first signs of a clash between the Iranians and the Arabs came during the visit to Iran of Col. Qaddafi's right-hand man, Maj. Abdul Salam Jalloud, to present the Libyan leader's congratulations to the new regime. While Jalloud was there, his Iranian hosts asked him about the fate of Sheikh Mussa Sadr, a Shi'ite leader from southern Lebanon who had disappeared on a visit to Libya in 1978. The Libyans were believed to have killed him for preaching Shi'ite Islam rather than their brand of the religion. Jalloud was not allowed to leave Iran for three weeks while the Iranians demanded an explanation. He was finally allowed to fly out only after Qaddafi personally intervened and spoke to Khomeini.

Another sign of discord between Iran and the Arabs was the expulsion of Palestine Liberation Organization personnel from Iran. After PLO members were found to be speaking about pan-Arab nationalism and socialism in gatherings of Iranian citizens of Arab descent in the southern part of the country, the Islamic government authorities ordered that all PLO members other than a skeleton staff at the Tehran embassy be expelled from Iran.

Big trouble was looming. As early as September 1979, Israeli intelligence reports from Baghdad had warned that Iraq was preparing for a full-scale invasion of southern Iran. Baghdad's aim was to annex the oil-rich Iranian province of Khuzistan, which runs along the Persian Gulf to Iraq. And Baghdad had reason to be

confident—it saw the Iranian military in a state of complete dis-
integration. Most of the generals and admirals had either escaped
Iran or been executed. For the time being, all the American-
trained pilots of the Iranian Air Force were in jail—every single
one of them. The charge: They had not been diligent and had
allowed the F-14 jets, commandeered by Israeli pilots, to fly away
from the Iranian base.

The only officer of note still alive in the country was the
commander of the navy, Adm. Ahmad Madani. In the 1960s, he
had been the youngest admiral in the Shah's navy, but in 1970 he
had been forced to resign, because of charges of alleged corruption.

In fact, he was becoming too outspoken in his criticism of the
Shah's regime, something the Shah did not tolerate, even in
muted terms.

Adm. Madani denied the accusations but was nevertheless
forced out of the navy. For the next nine years, he taught at
various Iranian universities, constantly harassed by agents of the
Shah. His popularity with opponents of the Shah grew, and, immediately after the revolution, in February 1979, Khomeini restored him to commander of the navy and appointed him defense
minister. In April of that year, he left the post of defense minister
to become the governor of the strategic Khuzistan province on
the Iraqi border. He remained a close adviser to Khomeini on all
defense-related matters.

When reports of Iraqi preparations to invade Iran started arriving in Tel Aviv, we became extremely concerned. We believed the
Iranian military could not withstand an Iraqi attack, and the idea
of a Greater Iraq with the largest known oil reserves in the
world—bigger than those of the Soviet Union and of Saudi
Arabia—sent shivers through both the Israeli intelligence community and the political leadership.

Prime Minister Begin personally relayed our intelligence reports to President Carter, though he had little faith it would do
much good. Begin still loathed Carter for the peace agreement
forced upon him at Camp David. As Begin saw it, the agreement
took Sinai away from Israel, did not create a comprehensive
peace, and left the Palestinian issue hanging on Israel's back. He

had signed it only because of Carter's pressure and because Defense Minister Ezer Weizman and Foreign Minister Moshe Dayan, both of whom wanted to ingratiate themselves with the Americans, had urged him to. In addition, while Begin accepted that the downfall of the Shah had been inevitable, he considered the disorderly fall of Iran into the hands of Shi'ite extremists to be a direct result of Carter's ineptitude. Begin had always been convinced that a regime friendly to the West could have been established instead.

As Israeli fears of an imminent Iraqi attack on Iran grew, Begin made it clear to Carter that the U.S. urgently needed to throw its support behind the government of Mehdi Bazargan, who was up against Iran's extremist Shi'ite groups. Bazargan was willing to negotiate with the Americans and was prepared to accept help in reorganizing his military. But Carter and his administration, in particular National Security Adviser Zbigniew Brzezinski, dismissed outright Begin's suggestions that the U.S. support Bazargan. While we were stressing the urgency of the situation, the wrong-headed U.S. view, from the administration down to the CIA and DIA analysts, was that Iran should be allowed to slowly disintegrate from within until a real leader emerged, supported by the Americans.

Israel pushed its concerns further at an Israel-U.S. intelligence exchange conference in late September 1979, which I attended. Present at the meeting in one of Israel's intelligence conference halls were analysts from the CIA and the DIA and, on the Israeli side, from Mossad and Military Intelligence. It was overseen by my department, External Relations.

First there was an opening statement read by the deputy director of Military Intelligence for production (research). Prepared by other analysts and myself, the report emphasized the Iraqi threat to Iran and what it could mean to Israeli and U.S. interests.

The U.S. attitude—indifference, lack of understanding, call it what you will—was made perfectly clear. Dr. Jack Vorona, the head of the U.S. delegation, was not a Middle East expert, but the assistant deputy director of DIA for technical affairs. He just didn't want to listen to what we had to say. He was more concerned about getting details, as he and his colleagues had in the past, about Soviet-made military equipment. As I sat at that meeting, I couldn't help thinking that the Americans were just putting their heads in the sand.

The Director of Central Intelligence, Stansfield Turner, wasn't expected to understand the situation, but what about his deputies? What about Robert Gates, who had attended various meetings with senior Israeli intelligence officers about events in the Middle East in the late 1970s, while assigned to the National Security Council? He was quiet, young, officially described as a Soviet expert, and known as a "Bush boy." Surely he had some influence. Surely he realized how explosive the situation had become.

Whatever Gates might have been aware of, it was clear that the U.S. administration either did not understand the dangers or did not want to. According to Israeli intelligence estimates, Saddam Hussein had a master plan to make Iraq a nuclear power, to develop his own atom bomb. After taking over southwestern Iran with conventional weapons, we believed his next plan would be to threaten the oil-rich Arabs of the Gulf and Saudi Arabia and become the regional power, backed up by an arsenal of nuclear weapons.

Hussein's overall plan was not feasible, but it was feasible that he could take over Khuzistan. That he could get hold of an atomic bomb was quite possible too.

The U.S. was simply not heeding Bazargan's precarious situation. The Iranians were frustrated—and they were scared. They wanted to draw attention to themselves because, if the Iraqis prevailed, Iran would be reduced to nothing. The Islamic revolution would be remembered as nothing more than Iran's vehicle to destruction.

Prime Minister Bazargan desperately needed American arms and help against the Iraqi threat. It was up to President Carter to prop up him and his government. It was up to Carter to maintain the balance in the Middle East and keep Bazargan in power against the enormous opposition inside his country. There was great pressure on Bazargan to move against the Americans. To withstand it, he needed an American military airlift. It never came. Instead, the Americans decided on a hands-off policy toward Iran.

For the Israelis, the Carter administration's shortsighted attitude was a source of great frustration. All Israel could do was continue to press home its concerns, not only to America but also to its European friends, although at this point we could hardly include France among these. Thanks to the French government, the Iraqis had already been provided with technicians, know-how, equipment, and a nuclear reactor, and were working on developing a nuclear bomb.

On November 4, 1979, the axe fell. The U.S. had not come to Bazargan's aid, and the extremist faction in Iran prevailed. In a desperate attempt to draw attention to themselves, the extremists unleashed a number of radical "students" who took over the U.S. Embassy and held the staff hostage. In exchange for the release of the hostages, they demanded the immediate return of the Shah to Iran to face trial. The following day, Bazargan resigned.

Instead of trying to play down the issue, Carter personally took responsibility for the negotiations over the captives, leaving the radicals with no question as to the hostages' high value as bargaining chips. It was his greatest mistake. By making the hostages the biggest national and international subject on his agenda, Carter had himself become a captive.

He immediately announced a full embargo on trade with Iran. He froze all money belonging to the Iranian government in U.S. banks, and he made a very public issue of the crisis. His desperate actions humiliated his own country, fueled the contempt the Iranians already felt for the U.S., and gave them more ammunition against the Carter administration.

Quietly, the Carter administration was trying to deal with the Iranians on other astonishing levels. Three Iranian brothers living in the West had come forward to offer their services, and Carter played right into their hands. The Hashemi trio—Cyrus, Jamshid, and Reza—claimed they had connections in Iran with Ahmed Khomeini, the son of the Ayatollah, and could use their friendship with him to help secure the release of the hostages. The brothers also said they were cousins of the influential Hojjat El-Islam Ali Akbar Hashemi Rafsanjani.

To this day, it is difficult to understand how the Carter administration relied on them. The Hashemis never negotiated successfully with anybody of rank in Iran. But they did make a great
deal of money in arms sales. Using their suddenly gained influence with the White House, the brothers started selling small
quantities of military equipment to the Iranians, supposedly to
get their goodwill to release the hostages.

The Hashemi brothers' Tehran contact, Iran Najd Rankuni,
was head of the Dervish movement and a son-in-law of Rafsanjani, who was to become president of Iran. At the time, Rankuni,
as opposed to his father-in-law, was connected with the Iranian
Revolutionary Guards. He did not have direct access to the Supreme Council, which actually called the shots in Iran, and there
was no way that he could set up a serious dialogue between the
Americans and the Iranians for the release of the hostages.

Carter's inept handling of the situation enraged some intelligence
experts outside the administration. In December 1979, a well-
known retired CIA officer, Miles Copeland, gathered a group of
CIA-connected officers and their associates who had been purged
from the agency by Adm. Turner and were very unhappy with the
Carter administration and the CIA leadership. Copeland had
helped Kermit Roosevelt and the Iranian military restore the
Shah of Iran to power in 1953, after the Shah had been overthrown by Mohammed Mossadegh during the turmoil that followed the nationalization of Iranian oil. After mobilizing the
Iranian military against Mossadegh, CIA officers had flown to
Iran with bags full of $100 bills. They walked through the bazaar
handing out money to whoever shouted: "Long live the Shah."

A good friend of the late Egyptian President Gamal Abdel
Nasser, Copeland was known for his anti-Israel stand. Israeli
intelligence believed him to be the man responsible for the U.S.
pressure put on Israel, Britain, and France in 1956 to pull out of
the Suez Canal area. He was also thought to have been the man
behind the push for the Israelis to withdraw from the Sinai. While
the United States was pressuring the Israelis over the Sinai, the
Soviet Union invaded Hungary without U.S. reaction. Copeland

was criticized for this. Nevertheless, he was still highly regarded for his analytical abilities.

Besides the purged group gathered around Copeland, William Casey, a former intelligence officer and close associate of Republican presidential candidate Ronald Reagan, came into the fold. The group also included Robert McFarlane, a former Marine colonel who had served in Vietnam, and a number of others with CIA connections. They decided that the U.S. administration under Carter was incapable of dealing with the Iran issue. They also saw eye to eye with Israel on the strategic situation in Iran. The Copeland group and the Israeli government both wanted to make sure the Iranians were not defeated in the Khuzistan if and when Iraq attacked, and to make sure that President Carter's blunders were not repeated.

A meeting between Miles Copeland and Israeli intelligence officers was held at a Georgetown house in Washington, D.C. The Israelis were happy to deal with any initiative but Carter's. David Kimche, chief of Tevel, the foreign relations unit of Mossad, was the senior Israeli at the meeting. He had a secret operation, which had begun in September 1979, to supply Iran with small arms and some spare parts. These arms were routed through South Africa, and their transport was handled by South African intelligence logistics teams. This operation was unknown at the time to the Mossad chief, to the director of Military Intelligence, or to the prime minister. Kimche, who needed a well-informed Iranian affairs briefer, asked Col. Meir, head of ERD, to send me to Washington with him on the Mossad budget. Meir agreed, so I went.

The Israelis and the Copeland group came up with a two-pronged plan to use quiet diplomacy with the Iranians and to draw up a scheme for military action against Iran that would not jeopardize the lives of the hostages, who, following the release of 14, now numbered 52.

As part of that plan, Earl Brian, an acquaintance of former Iranian Prime Minister Bazargan, arranged an urgent meeting in late January 1980 in Tehran to discuss the hostage situation. Those present would be Brian, McFarlane, and Bazargan. Bazargan arranged for *laissez-passer* through the Iranian Embassy in Ottawa. Even though his faction had lost control in November

1979, Bazargan was still thought to be very close to Ayatollah Khomeini, as well as to Hojjat El-Islam Mehdi Karrubi, the powerful member of the ruling Supreme Council of Iran who was in charge of foreign relations.*

Brian spoke some Farsi. While California state secretary of health and welfare during Ronald Reagan's governorship, he dealt with the Iranian government in trying to put together an Iranian medicare plan, which never came to fruition. During frequent visits to Tehran in the mid-1970s, he became acquainted with Bazargan. McFarlane was chosen to go with Brian because he was an aide to the powerful Republican Sen. John Tower, chairman of the Armed Services Committee, who was also connected to CIA circles through Gates and close to one of the Republican candidates for the presidency, George Bush. The Israelis also pushed for these two to travel to Iran because they both had special relationships with the Israeli intelligence community.

Those relationships went back to 1978, when Rafi Eitan, newly appointed counterterrorism adviser to Prime Minister Begin, visited the United States. Eitan believed that the U.S. had amassed a great deal of information about Palestinian terrorists around the world that it was not sharing with Israel. The purpose of his 1978 trip to Washington was to build a network within the United States that would provide Israel with this information. Eitan's operation was being funded from the budget of the small Ministry of Defense intelligence agency, LAKAM, the scientific liaison bureau set up to gather and exchange technology and intelligence with foreign military industries.

During the Washington visit, Eitan was introduced to Sen. John Tower and his senior aide, Robert McFarlane. Eitan went out of his way to befriend McFarlane, whom he viewed as potentially a very useful contact. He invited McFarlane to Israel. After one or two meetings, the two developed a close relationship. McFarlane proceeded to introduce Eitan to a number of his friends, among them Earl Brian, who had significant intelligence connections.

All these people had access to some of the information Eitan was after. They also had Republican connections, and the Repub-

---

* Bazargan still lives in Tehran, is very influential with members of the clergy, and is an accepted negotiator between the West and the Iranian clergy.

licans were prepared to do almost anything to get back into the White House. They got on very well with the diminutive Israeli, and by the end of 1978, much that reached the Senate Armed Services Committee also found its way to Eitan's desk.

So it was no surprise that the Israelis were in favor of McFarlane and Brian taking a commercial flight from Europe to Tehran to meet Bazargan. That initial meeting in January 1980 set in motion a series of top-secret conferences that remained hidden from the American people but were to have a dramatic effect on events in the Middle East in the coming months. Having agreed that there was room to discuss the hostage situation, Brian, McFarlane, and Bazargan arranged a meeting for early March 1980 in Madrid. Those attending would be Mehdi Karrubi and a close associate of Ronald Reagan's, yet to be decided on.

After leaving Iran, Brian and McFarlane visited Rafi Eitan in Israel and told him all about their meeting in Tehran. Little was going to happen in Iran that the Israelis would not know about.

Several weeks after that first meeting in Tehran in January 1980, I got a phone call at my home in Israel from my old friend from Tehran university days, Sayeed Mehdi Kashani, one of the contacts who had warned me of the threat to the Shah. Kashani's father, Ayatollah Abol Qassem Kashani, was now a member of the ruling Supreme Council. He pulled no punches. Iran, he said, wanted equipment for its military forces.

"I don't know if I can help," I said. "You know it's not up to me."

"But you have connections, Ari. And whether you like it or not, I'm coming to see you. I'm already in Europe. I've booked an Air France flight."

"Hold it. What kind of passport do you have? You know you can't get in with . . ."

"Don't worry about it. I'm on my way."

He gave me a flight number. I reported to my superiors, and they told me to meet him at the airport.

In late February, Kashani sailed through immigration at Tel Aviv's Ben-Gurion International Airport with—a Philippine passport. His father had been a close friend of Ferdinand Marcos, and the younger Kashani had managed to become an honorary

Filipino. It had been a couple of years since I'd seen him, but he was much as I remembered, a jovial, handsome man in his 30s, impeccably dressed in a double-breasted blue suit, carrying only a suithanger, a small bag, and a briefcase. I welcomed him, we kissed three times in the Iranian tradition, and I drove him to the Hilton Hotel in Tel Aviv.

He came for breakfast the next morning at my parents' apartment in Ramat Gan. Our conversation was in Farsi.

"I came here as a friend," he said, "but I'm also on a mission for my father. We need spare parts for our aircraft. And we will pay."

I repeated what I had already told him, that I had no authority. But of course I promised to see what I could do.

I was well aware of the importance of helping the Iranians because of our mutual antipathy toward Iraq, and, not wanting to waste any time, I bypassed my immediate superiors and telephoned the office of the director of Military Intelligence, Maj. Gen. Yehoshua Sagi.* I spoke to his chief of staff, Maj. Moshe Hebroni. When I explained Kashani's request and the circumstances under which he was in Israel, Hebroni told me to bring him straight to the general headquarters of IDF/MI.

In his meeting with Gen. Sagi, Kashani began by repeating the already known facts about McFarlane's and Brian's visit to Tehran. But he revealed something new—that the senior American who was to meet Hojjat El-Islam Karrubi in Madrid concerning the hostages was the director-designate of Reagan's presidential campaign, William J. Casey.

Kashani said that the secret ex-CIA-Miles Copeland group was aware that any deal cut with the Iranians would have to include the Israelis, because they would have to be used as a third party to sell military equipment to Iran. He also said something that McFarlane and Brian had not mentioned to their Israeli contact, Rafi Eitan: that Casey was going to invite the Israeli Labor Party leader Shimon Peres, who was looking like the man who would succeed Likud's Begin, to participate in the ongoing meetings and coordinate the sales of weapons to Iran from Israel.

This news alarmed Sagi, who immediately called in Rafi Eitan.

---

* Maj. Gen. Sagi's name is spelled Saguy in most English books. Sagi, however, is how he himself spells it when signing his name in English.

Kashani repeated what he had already told us, and Eitan was disturbed. Clearly it would be a problem to have the opposition leader sitting in on these secret meetings.

Sagi told Kashani that his request for military aid from Israel would be put to the prime minister himself. Kashani was asked to remain in Israel for a few days to await an answer.

The following morning I was summoned to the director's office and told that Prime Minister Begin had given the green light for the sale to Iran of non-American military equipment, preferably non-lethal. The Iranians wanted spare parts for their F-4s, but it was decided instead to sell them tires, a gesture toward our Iranian friend which, if discovered by the Carter administration, would cause less of a rupture than had we sold technical parts. As it was, we realized the Americans would be upset should the deal be uncovered. There was a strict embargo on trade to Iran, particularly military equipment.

Later I worked out a deal with Kashani in the hotel. We would sell Iran 300 tires for the planes for $900 each, an exorbitant price—we were making $400 on each tire. We wanted the money in advance, in cash. Kashani asked, "You don't trust us?"

I told him I would be held responsible for the money by the producer of the tires. I held out my hands. "Where am I going to get the money to pay in advance?"

He laughed.

Kashani left a few days later. He hadn't succeeded in getting any weapons, but he had tires—and that was better than nothing. Within three days he had opened a numbered account at Banque Worms in Geneva, where he deposited $270,000. He phoned me. "The money is there. I'd like a date from you when the tires are going to be delivered." He left me a phone number in Paris where I could call him.

After making our arrangements with the Alliance Tire Factory in Israel, including a guarantee for payment, we went to SIBAT, the Ministry of Defense's office for foreign defense exports, to get an export license. Obtaining such export licenses is a complicated bureaucratic matter. The process was expedited through the intervention of Maj. Hebroni.

I was given a blank export license for 300 tires without markings. I took it and went to the factory. I was told there would be a problem if we wanted the tires right away, because markings couldn't be removed that quickly. I told them to blot them out. It could be done with heat.

Three days later two crates of tires marked "Diplomatic Cargo" were flown out of Israel to Vienna via El Al. After the Israeli diplomatic marks were removed, Israeli Embassy personnel transferred the tires from El Al's cargo area to the appropriate people at Iran Air. Meanwhile, I flew to Geneva and drew a bank check for $150,000 in favor of Alliance, Israel. I drew another for $14,000, payable to El Al, for the freight and insurance. A third bank check was made out to cash for $106,000.

I took the check back to Israel and dropped it on the director's desk.

"Our profit from the tires," I said.

"Hey," Sagi laughed, "this is good business."

Thus was born the new extra-budgetary Likud/intelligence community slush fund. It was the seed which grew into hundreds of millions of dollars, kept secret by one of the biggest cover-ups the world has known.

Somehow the Carter administration found out about the sale right away. On April 27, President Carter called Menachem Begin and chewed his ear off.

"You're selling military equipment to Iran while American citizens and diplomats are being held hostage by the Iranians," was the gist of Carter's complaint.

Begin didn't say anything to upset the president. Carter would have thrown a fit had he known that there were negotiations between Iranians, Israelis, and Americans about the hostages. President Carter at this point must have been rather sensitive to anything that had to do with the hostages and Iran. It was only three days after the American military rescue mission, code-named Operation Eagle Claw, had disastrously failed.

On the night of April 24, 1980, four air force C-130s had flown a team of more than 100 men under the command of Col. Charles Beckwith to a desert spot in Iran they dubbed Desert One, where they were to transfer to eight navy helicopters coming in on a different route. The helicopters were to refuel and take commandos to another spot, 50 miles from Tehran, called Desert

Two. From there, they were to travel by truck into downtown Tehran to rescue the hostages.

The plan fell apart at Desert One. One of the helicopters never made it, two others clogged with desert sand. One crashed into a C-130. The mission was doomed to fail before it began. The question remains who inside the Carter administration wanted to sabotage the president. Interestingly, Oliver North and John Singlaub, who later were to be involved in the Iran-contra scandal under the Reagan administration, were part of this failed operation.

There were two other attempts in April 1980 to negotiate with the Iranians to get the hostages out. The PLO's Yasser Arafat, who was aligned with Syria at that moment, went to Iran to meet with Ayatollah Khomeini on the hostage subject. Arafat was trying to score points with Carter but was rebuffed by the Iranians. Around the same time, Algerian Foreign Minister Abdelaziz Bouteflika, a well-respected diplomat, met with various Iranian leaders, including Khomeini, on the subject of the hostages. The Algerian failed to broker an accord because he was not able to guarantee arms sales to Iran.

Meanwhile, in March, the first meeting between the Iranian Supreme Council's Mehdi Karrubi and Reagan associate William Casey had taken place in Madrid's Ritz Hotel. Also attending on the Iranian side were my friend Kashani and an aide from the Iranian Ministry of Defense, Dr. Ahmed Omshei. No Israelis were present. On the U.S. side, Casey was accompanied by McFarlane and a surprising character, Donald Gregg, a member of Carter's National Security Council under Brzezinski. I was fascinated and puzzled to hear that Casey was there with a Carter man, but the account Kashani gave me cross-checked with McFarlane's information passed to Rafi Eitan.

McFarlane also reported that Casey had met separately with opposition leader Shimon Peres to discuss his willingness to provide military equipment to Iran. Kashani said that Peres also met separately with Karrubi. The reason the Americans insisted that Peres meet with Karrubi was what we'd already heard—they thought the Likud coalition was going to crumble, and expected elections in Israel at any time. Peres had tried to explain his visit to Spain as a call on Prime Minister Adolfo Suárez.

That first Madrid meeting, as reported by Robert McFarlane to Rafi Eitan, was arranged to explore future relations between the United States and Iran and to discuss supplying arms to Iran against the imminent Iraqi threat. Also discussed was the release of all Iranian monies frozen in U.S. banks and the influence the Iranian government would exert over the radical students to release the hostages. Iran, it was made clear, would make moves to normalize its relations with the United States. Karrubi emphasized how impossible it was to deal with the Carter administration and indicated that he and the Supreme Council were more than happy to deal quietly with the Republicans.

Another rendezvous in Madrid was arranged for May. As the meeting wound up, the Iranians repeated that they did not have much time. The military needed an instant boost because of the threat from Iraq. They were willing to reach an agreement with any officials who could assure them that the Carter administration would carry out any deals struck.

When word reached Begin that Peres had met secretly with a senior Iranian in Madrid, the infuriated prime minister called Peres into his office and gave him a warning: If he ever did such a thing again without the knowledge of the government, it would be seen as treason and he would have to pay the price—whatever that meant.

So the scene was set. All concerned knew their parts. Secret meetings were to be held between the CIA "renegades" and the Republicans on one side and the Iranians on the other. Although the Israelis would not be present, they would be kept informed. The president of the United States—and, of course, the American people—would be kept in the dark.

5

The Agreement

KHOSRO FAKHRIEH TOOK a gulp of his beer and stared me straight in the eyes. He was a stocky man, and his double-breasted suit made him look even broader.

"I'm deadly serious, Mr. Ben-Menashe," he said. "We want to deal with the Americans, but not the Americans who are in power. And we're relying on Israel to make the arrangements."

It was early May 1980. The first of the secret meetings between Casey and Karrubi had already been held in Madrid two months earlier. But Tehran wanted to involve Israel in the deal, if only to ensure, initially, that nothing went wrong.

I had flown to Vienna to meet Fakhrieh, a close aide to Supreme Council member Ayatollah Hashemi (who was assassinated a few years later), on the instructions of the director of Military Intelligence, who had asked me to keep in touch with my Iranian friends. I was not to commit myself on anything. Accompanied by my long-time contact Sayeed Mehdi Kashani, I had checked into the Hilton Hotel; Fakhrieh was also staying there. We met in his room. A cloud of cigarette smoke billowed around his face as he talked.

"I'll be frank with you, Mr. Ben-Menashe," he said. "We want to rid ourselves of this heretic menace from the west"—he was, of course, talking about Saddam Hussein of Iraq—"but we will have nothing to do with Carter."

It wasn't difficult to read the desperation in his words. I watched him stub out yet another cigarette.

"There is a problem," I said. "Carter is the president, and he is the only one with the legal—and I repeat, legal—power to talk to you people."

Fakhrieh chuckled. "You need not be so cautious. It's quite clear to us, as it must be to you, that the embarrassment Iran has caused him will cost Carter the election later this year. With that in mind, we're willing to make a secret deal with the Republicans—and the CIA."

I asked him what he had in mind, knowing that what he told me would be the official Iranian line.

"America gets back their people, our money is freed from U.S. banks, and we also get our arms from Israel, with the blessing of your U.S. masters. We are willing to trust the Americans—who are usually not trustworthy—in reaching such a deal."

Fakhrieh revealed that at the next meeting in Madrid, to be held later in May, Karrubi would meet Casey again. But there would be another man present, representing a second Republican presidential candidate, George Bush. His name: Robert Gates.

Gates had visited Tel Aviv numerous times for intelligence exchange meetings. A career CIA official who at times served on various National Security Councils, he became a close associate of George Bush's when Bush was Director of Central Intelligence. Shortly before the Iranian revolution, Gates made several trips to Israel to meet intelligence community officials to discuss Iran's uncertain future. I briefed him and his aides on Iran several times, and I quickly reached the conclusion that he was not the Soviet analyst he was always represented to be—he just didn't seem to know very much about the Soviet Union, nor did he seem very interested in it. Israeli intelligence had also learned of his connections with Ariel Sharon, Mike Harari, and arms sales to Central American governments.

Robert Gates was the new player at the second Madrid meeting. It took place at the end of May. As before, they met at the Ritz Hotel. Those present on the U.S. side, in addition to Gates, were William Casey, Robert McFarlane, and Earl Brian. Representing the Iranians were Mehdi Karrubi, Sayeed Mehdi Kashani, Ahmed Omshei, and this time an addition—the man I had met in Vienna,

Khosro Fakhrieh. By now the power structure of the Republican ticket had been defined. Casey was representing Ronald Reagan, while Gates—although he was officially executive assistant to CIA Director Stansfield Turner, a Carter appointee—was there representing George Bush.

No Israelis were present. Although Israel was determined to keep its finger on the pulse, it did not want to be seen to be intervening, especially after the outraged Carter phone call to Prime Minister Begin following the sale of the aircraft tires to Iran. Begin was worried that if Congress heard that Israel was meeting the Iranians along with a group of Americans that were not part of the official government, this would be perceived as subversion of legal government in the United States.

As before, Israeli intelligence received reports on the second Madrid meeting from Kashani, McFarlane, and Brian. At this meeting, as reported to me by Kashani, it was made clear to the Americans that in return for a promise that they would release frozen Iranian monies after the Republicans took office in January 1981, and that Israel would not be castigated by the Republicans or Congress for selling arms to Iran, the hostages would be released right away.

"You want to know something, Ari?" said Kashani. "These Americans don't want their people released yet. They've now come up with another proposal that a very high official of the future U.S. administration should meet with Hojjat El-Islam Karubi and work out the details of the deal with Iran. It's obvious these guys are procrastinating."

The reason was obvious, too. Even though steps could be taken immediately to free the hostages, Carter, as president, would get all the credit. Indeed, we also learned that the Hashemi brothers, on behalf of the Carter administration, had made contact with some Iranian officials at about the same time. Since they could not promise major arms sales through the Israelis, though, they got nowhere.

"Why don't they just come straight out and say they don't want their people released before January?" Kashani wondered.

So we knew as early as May 1980 that the Iranians were prepared to talk seriously about freeing the hostages. If they could receive U.S.-made equipment through Israel, the captives would be freed. Although they didn't want to deal directly with Carter, they would be happy to use the CIA as an intermediary. And yet Kashani and I had no doubt that the Republicans and their unofficial CIA friends were going to keep Carter in the dark and continue their negotiations at a pace that suited them.

Intelligence reports continued to flow in about the Iraqi build-up on the eastern border with Iran. The Soviets were arming the Iraqis, but Moscow was so uncertain what to do that it sent queries to Israel asking for an assessment of the Iranian situation, acting through the quasi-official representative of the KGB in Israel, the Russian Orthodox Church's Papal Nuncio in Jerusalem.* The KGB's contacts with Israeli intelligence had gone through him ever since Israel and the Soviet Union cut diplomatic ties in 1967. Moscow was officially represented at the time by an Interests Section in the Finnish Embassy in Tel Aviv. The queries were left unanswered because Israel did not want to pass intelligence to the Soviets who could, in turn, hand it on to Iraq.

War drums were beginning to be heard around Europe, and the United States, egged on by the Iranian opposition, asked for help from Israel to launch a coup d'état against the Iranian government. The Israeli government, having decided by then that it was in Israel's interests to keep Khomeini in power, didn't respond to the American request.

About two weeks after Reagan and Bush officially won the Republican nominations for president and vice president in mid-July 1980, the third Madrid meeting took place. Parallel meetings between the Iranians and the Hashemis, representing the Carter administration, also occurred. The same issues were discussed, along with future U.S.-Iranian relations under a Reagan-Bush administration. If it was not clear beforehand, the cards were now on the table: The Americans would not commit themselves to any deal regarding the hostages before January 20, 1981, when the new president would be sworn in. They said they could not let Israel sell arms to the Iranians, despite the pleas from Tehran, until the Republicans were in power.

* The Russian Orthodox Church has its own Pope, and his representative in Jerusalem is officially known as the Russian Orthodox Papal Nuncio.

"Fine. These guys want to be popular with the American people," Kashani told me in a phone call from Europe. "Why not get the prisoners released after the November elections?"

"How do I know?" I said. "Ask your American friends." But the answer was obvious. The Republicans were going to wait until they could take all the credit.

At the beginning of August, a bizarre directive to the Israeli intelligence community on a "need-to-know" basis came out of the Prime Minister's Office. The document, which was read to me and others at a meeting called by the director of Military Intelligence, Maj. Gen. Sagi, revealed that the Israeli Cabinet had decided it would be "appropriate" for the Israeli security and defense forces to cooperate with elements in the United States that were not necessarily members of the present administration or blessed by the administration. In essence, the prime minister was telling his intelligence network that we were to cooperate with the Republican camp.

Now that the go-ahead had been given by the prime minister, who was also defense minister, the instruction that went out to me and other intelligence officials was to see what we could do for the Iranians—but to be careful. The Carter administration should not know what was going on. As Sagi pointed out, the prime minister was still very sensitive about Israel being seen as subverting the legal government of the United States.

The second half of August 1980 was a very interesting period. I called Kashani, now back at his Paris number. He had been flying back and forth from Tehran by private plane, keeping in touch constantly.

"I have good news for you," I said. "We're ready to help. Prepare your wish lists."

I heard his sigh of relief on the other end. "I'm very happy, Ari. And please send my regards to your mother. I still remember her cooking."

At Kashani's suggestion, we arranged a meeting in Amsterdam.

"You think it's secure? We won't be spied on there?" I asked.

"Oh no, nothing to do with that," he laughed. "The women in Holland are very pretty."

I expected Kashani to be alone when we met at the Marriott Hotel in the middle of August. But he brought with him a battery of six Iranian officials from the Defense Ministry. I was surprised. I had come alone.

We spent a few minutes warming up. All seven men were expensively and elegantly dressed, and one was enjoying beer—forbidden in Iran. Another of Kashani's companions, Cyrus Husseinzadeh, spoke Hebrew and was in SAVAMA, the revolution's version of the Shah's secret police, SAVAK. He told how he had originally been a member of the SAVAK and had been trained in Israel by SHABAK, the Israeli secret police and internal security service. He'd taken a course in counterintelligence, but "after I saw the atrocities committed by my superiors in the SAVAK, I refused to take part and joined the revolution."

After a while the Iranians handed me a 50-page file—their shopping list—that included everything a nation preparing for war required: aircraft, tanks, anti-aircraft missiles, anti-tank missiles, artillery shells, aircraft wheelbases, mortars, grenades, and many other spare parts.

They stressed the immediate need for supplies. There was no problem about the payment. As one of them told me, "As a sign of good faith, when you guys move, we will initially deposit $1 billion U.S. in a bank of your choice in Europe."

We talked about the hostages. "It's not up to us when they're released," I was told. "It's up to the Americans. They have the final say. The ball is in their court."

Kashani insisted on paying my hotel bill. As I checked out, he mentioned he would like to put a proposition to me—to come and stay at his holiday house in Marbella, Spain, for two or three days. After that he would like to fly back with me to Israel. I didn't want to offend him, but I said I had to call my office first. I phoned Tel Aviv and mentioned the "shopping list."

"Go with him to Spain," said Sagi's chief of staff, Hebroni. "Enjoy yourself. And if he wants to come to Israel to spell out his requests, let him come."

At Amsterdam's Schiphol Airport, Kashani insisted on paying for the round-trip ticket to Marbella. The courtship with the Israelis had begun in earnest: It was now "unofficially official." And during the three days we spent at his modest red-roofed house overlooking the Mediterranean, waited upon by a North African maid, he expressed his relief that Iran would finally be getting Israeli military equipment with American blessing.

"Let's not get ahead of ourselves," I cautioned as we drank tea during one of those hot Spanish evenings. "We haven't got real American blessing. We've only got a nod from the shadows. And Sagi hasn't seen the details of your list yet. I don't even know if we've got all that stuff."

Kashani used his Philippine passport to get into Israel. And the following day, after breakfast at my parents' home—a treat he insisted on, as he fondly remembered his earlier visit—he watched as Gen. Sagi went through the Iranian weapons list.

"Of course, we're happy to cooperate," Sagi told him. "But I honestly don't know how much we can do until the new administration takes over in the U.S. A lot of these weapons and parts are American-made. But we'll certainly look into your request as far as it concerns Israeli-made materials."

It was my turn to do the entertaining, driving the Iranian around Jerusalem and taking him to Hebron to the place where the patriarch Abraham is believed to be buried. The Moslems, who believe that Abraham was their forefather, as do the Jews, call the site Haram El-Ibrahimi. The Moslems wanted a mosque on the site, the Jews a synagogue. The building is now alternately used both as a mosque and a synagogue, an arrangement imposed by the Israeli military.

"What do you think, Ari?" he asked as we strolled. "Do you think we can get enough from your people to arm us sufficiently?"

"As the boss said, we'll do what we can for you. Your enemy is also ours, don't forget."

On September 2, 1980, all Israel's fears came true when the Iraqis attacked southern Iran in the first big border clash, the precursor to the offensive that began on September 22. Saddam Hussein had decided that he should establish his control over Shatt Al-Arab and then go on to take over the oilfields in Khuzistan, Iran's southwestern province on the Persian Gulf. Iraqi troops poured into Iran, but the Iraqi Army was not as good as we had feared.

Their air force was also ineffective in its attempts to destroy Iranian Air Force bases. The Iraqis quickly became bogged down by a surprisingly good defensive campaign launched by the Iranian military. Although the Iranians basically had only equipment left over from the Shah's time, much of it unusable because it had not been serviced and maintained, there was still enough to keep the invaders at bay.

Earlier that year, Iran had established an elected government, in which Abol Hassan Bani-Sadr had defeated Adm. Madani. However, even by the time of the invasion, the real shots were still being called by the Supreme Council. Bani-Sadr, as commander-in-chief, personally intervened to free from jail all the Iranian Air Force pilots who had been imprisoned for allowing the Israelis to steal their F-14 jets at the start of the revolution. But he insisted they each swear on the Koran to serve their country—this wasn't a war for the Mullahs, he told them, but for the very existence of Iran.

Despite the strong defensive position taken by the Iranians, the Israeli government and intelligence community were extremely worried about Iraq's incursion. It would be in Israel's interest to flood Iran with military equipment, but we had to be cautious. Much of the material we had was American, and if that went to Tehran without the release of the hostages and Carter's okay, there could be serious repercussions in the U.S. Congress with its Democratic majority.

Within a few days of the September 2 incursion, Kashani called to tell me that a fourth meeting had recently taken place between the Iranians and the Americans, this time in Barcelona. An important decision had been reached: that a top-secret meeting between George Bush and Hojjat El-Islam Karrubi would be held in Paris. The Iranians wanted assurances from a Republican leader at the highest level that if they held off the release of the 52 Americans until the Reagan administration took office, they would be supplied with military equipment to defend themselves against the Iraqis, and their monies frozen in the U.S. would also be released.

"It's also been decided that Israeli representatives should come to Paris," said Kashani. "Although Bush and Karrubi will be making the ultimate decision, we'll be setting up numerous discussions between other officials and aides."

So this time it was the vice president of the anticipated Republican administration who would be in attendance. Carter would be furious if he knew what George Bush's intentions were, but then, of course, Bush's presence in Paris was not expected to leak out to the Carter people. Kashani had made no mistakes with his information concerning the Iranian decision to meet Bush—the same details were fed to Rafi Eitan from his U.S. contacts, McFarlane and Brian.

"By the way," said Kashani, "we're still after anything you can give us for our war effort. The Americans have told us to hold out. They'll help, but only after the Republicans have taken over and the hostages have been released."

Some time around September 10 I was called into Sagi's office for an official briefing on a letter that had been sent by Stansfield Turner, curiously directed to the head of IDF/MI and not to the American's counterpart in Israel, the Mossad chief. In it, Turner outlined his thoughts about the Middle East situation; the most interesting part of the letter was his forecast that no matter who was elected as president of the United States, he expected to continue leading the CIA in 1981.

According to Sagi, there had also been phone calls from Casey to Begin and Sagi and to Nachum Admoni, the acting director of Mossad, in which Casey outlined his contacts with the Iranians. He confirmed he had met various Iranians in Spain and was about to reach an agreement with them. There would be a meeting, to which the Israelis were invited, in mid-October 1980. The Israelis were to be the channel used to sell arms to Iran. None of this was news to us, of course.

The Israeli intelligence community remained extremely concerned about the Iraqi threat to Iran. If Iraq won that struggle, Israel would have a major problem on its hands with that land mass and those oil reserves in the hands of Saddam Hussein. We started looking for a way to solve the problem of supplying arms to Iran and getting the hostages freed before January. Perhaps, it was suggested, we, the Israelis, could reach an independent deal with the Iranians, get them to release the hostages, and then present it to the Americans as a *fait accompli*. This way the Iranians would have their way, without having to deal with the Carter people, and on the other hand the Reagan people would have to accept it because it would have all been happily completed.

It was an interesting proposition, particularly since Begin was unhappy about the idea of an Israeli delegation participating with Carter's opposition at the Paris meeting. The prime minister was a very legalistic man who believed in law and order around the world.

So the *fait accompli* plan went ahead. First, Begin sent Khomeini's old friend, Ruth Ben-David, as his direct emissary to see the Ayatollah in Tehran in mid-September. Her mission was to get Khomeini's agreement to release the hostages immediately in exchange for Israeli guarantees of arms to Iran. Khomeini agreed in principle, and the details were left to be worked out by others at another meeting. Sagi briefed me on all this and then instructed me to ask Kashani to arrange a meeting between a senior Israeli delegation and an Iranian who could actually carry out the release of the hostages.

We met in Amsterdam in the second half of September. The Israelis included David Kimche, head of Tevel; Uri Simchoni and another man from IDF; Shmuel Morieh from SHABAK; and myself. From the Iranian side, there were Kashani; Ahmed Khomeini, the son of the Ayatollah; Khosro Fakhrieh; and Ahmed Omshei. The Iranian team was regarded as extremely high-level because of the presence of Ahmed Khomeini.

The meeting in the Marriott Hotel lasted nearly two days. At the end of it, we had a working agreement. The Iranians would arrange for the release of the hostages in the first week of October. They would be flown to Karachi, Pakistan, where a U.S. Air Force plane would be waiting. The cash side of the arrangement was that Israel would pay $52 million, through Kashani, so he could pay off the radical leaders. After the release, Israel would start supplying military equipment to Iran, for which Iran would pay. In addition, Israel would exact a commitment from the Republicans that, when they came to power in the U.S., they would release all frozen Iranian funds in American banks.

Just what the Americans would think of the deal was anybody's guess. But my superiors, at least, were happy. The scheme was then put to Casey by my boss, Maj. Gen. Sagi. The response was cool. Casey said that he didn't believe the Iranians would go ahead with the deal, and he proposed that an Iranian representative secretly travel to the U.S. to present the case. So the Americans were still employing their delaying tactics.

It was agreed that the Israelis would escort an Iranian official to the U.S. if Tehran agreed. The Iranians were desperate to try anything as long as they could receive arms from somewhere, so they agreed to send a representative. The American contingent said they would arrange a U.S. visa for the Iranian official in Germany, even though the State Department was not under their control.

We were told that the Americans would be represented at the Washington meeting by Robert McFarlane; Richard Allen; James Baker III, former campaign manager for George Bush; and Lawrence Silberman, a close friend of Bush's. The choices of McFarlane, Baker, and Silberman were all understandable, considering their connections. But Allen was a mystery; he was a man with connections to the Carter administration. We did not know, until McFarlane told Eitan, that Allen had a deal with the Reagan camp that assured him the position of national security adviser for Reagan.

These four people were to meet an Iranian emissary and an Israeli intelligence officer—I was designated—on October 2. In Frankfurt I was waiting to meet their man—Dr. Ahmed Omshei, who was by now a familiar face. He collected his visa, and we flew to Washington via New York. The details of this meeting were coordinated by Hushang Lavi, an Iranian Jew living in the U.S. and working for Israeli intelligence. Lavi was a known arms dealer who left Iran under the Shah to live in the United States. From the U.S. he frequently visited Israel and was recruited by Mossad in the late 1970s as an intelligence asset to further Israel's arms-sales policies. His work for the Israeli government ended in 1983 because he refused to heed warnings about his unauthorized moonlighting in arms with the Hashemi brothers, among others.

As it turned out, James Baker did not attend the October 2 meeting, held in the lobby of Washington's L'Enfant Plaza Hotel. But the other three were there; I said nothing while they listened politely as Dr. Omshei once again outlined the Israeli plan accepted by the Iranians. The meeting lasted just half an hour, during which Omshei suggested that the planned Paris conference between Bush and Karrubi would now not be necessary because the Israelis were negotiating on America's behalf for the release of the hostages.

McFarlane smiled and slowly nodded. "I'll report to my superiors," he said. I didn't understand what that meant. Just who were his superiors?

Two days later I was back in Tel Aviv. I was whisked off instantly to see Sagi in his office.

"I hope you enjoyed your sightseeing trip to Washington, Ari," he said.

I immediately sensed a problem. "You're going to tell me it's all fallen apart."

"Was it ever together in the first place?"

No, I conceded. It had been too much to hope that the Americans would accept our plan.

The Paris meeting was still on. So we continued to make our arrangements to send a team of six who would discuss the minor details of the hostage release while Bush and Karrubi set the official seal on the arrangement. My assignment was to confirm my friendship with the Iranians, to get a list of all their addresses, phone numbers, and telex numbers, and to establish contact points throughout Europe as a prelude for what would certainly be a deal in which Israel would sell arms to Tehran.

When I called Kashani and told him that the Americans had quashed the Israeli plan and there would be no immediate supplies of equipment to Iran, he was devastated.

Iran had been ready to release the hostages months earlier. Israel had been prepared to negotiate a new arms deal. And, all along, the proposals had been delayed or downright ignored. It was clear to everyone involved that the Republicans and their CIA representatives were going to work this thing out all by themselves and take all the glory on inauguration day.

"It's a blow, Ari," he said. "We're desperate. If nothing else, can you supply us right away with wheelbases for the F-4s?"

"I'll do what I can," I said, and hung up.

My superiors made an instant decision. The wheelbases, 60 of them, could come out of air force stock. It was arranged with Kashani that a French aircraft chartered by the Iranians would fly into Ben-Gurion Airport in late October, pick up the cargo, fly back to Paris, and then go on to Tehran. I asked the Iranians to make payment to Banque Worms.

The six of us, five men and a woman, who were chosen to go to Paris were briefed thoroughly about what was to take place there and what our roles would be. As it turned out, the Paris meeting went precisely according to plan. Simon Gabbay, my father's cousin, who was the head of a Jewish organization in Paris, and was for many years an Israeli intelligence asset, coordinated the meetings between the Israeli and Iranian delegations. The purpose of his participation was to eliminate contact between Israeli and Iranian embassy personnel. Gabbay continued to serve this function in years to come.

We six Israelis flew by El Al from Tel Aviv to Orly Airport in mid-October and were as inconspicuous as possible. Arrangements for security had been made. Upon arrival we were met by two Mossad representatives stationed in the Israeli Embassy in Paris. The two senior Israelis—David Kimche and Shmuel Morieh—were driven to their quarters at the Ritz Hotel; I rented a car and drove the remaining four of us—Uri Simchoni, Rafi Eitan, a woman from Mossad, and myself—to the Eiffel Tower Hilton, where we were to stay. That day my only business was to remain in contact with Israel by a secure phone in a safehouse on the rue du Faubourg Montmartre.

Over the next few days, between calls to Israel, I had the opportunity to meet both the Iranians and some of the American contingent, including Robert Gates and George Cave, a long-time CIA official. Cave was officially purged from the CIA in 1977 but was active until 1989. My career and his were somewhat parallel—he is an Iranian expert and speaks, reads, and writes Farsi well. At times he was "downplayed" as a low-level translator, but in reality he was an active CIA operative, a member of what we in Israel called the "Iran Group," headed by Robert Gates, which was created as a result of this Paris meeting. Because of his expertise on Iran, he took part with the Israelis in the arms sales. Cave became well-known in Washington circles and was very close to Gates.

Gates and Cave came to the room of one of the Israeli contingent, and we talked about the Iran-Iraq war in general. My colleagues and I tried to keep our contact with the Americans as brief as possible, as we'd been ordered. I kept in close association with the Iranians—including Kashani, Omshei, and Fakhrieh—obtaining from them the names of contacts in their embassies and in their Melli Bank branches in London and Paris. These would be needed for future negotiations in the planned arms trade. By the third day, I had nearly completed my role in the mission.

The evening before the big meeting, the two Israeli seniors were to be received by Hojjat El-Islam Karrubi, who had just arrived in Paris. I was asked to go with them to Karrubi's suite at the Hotel Montaigne, a small establishment within walking distance of the Hilton. As Karrubi's two bodyguards watched carefully, I came face to face for the first time with this influential member of Iran's Supreme Council. He impressed his guests as an immensely shrewd and religious man. He spoke English and French and made it quite clear that he believed in the Islamic revolution in his country. He took the familiar position that any cooperation between Iran and Israel on Iraq should not be taken as a sign that the Islamic government would recognize Israel, but should be seen only as a matter of expediency.

The next morning, French security officers were scattered through the lobby of the Ritz Hotel hours before the top-secret meeting was due to take place in an upper-level conference room. I had one more task, which necessitated my going to the Ritz to meet the Iranians. Accompanied by my colleagues, and fully aware that we should keep our distance from the Americans at this important gathering, we walked past the vigilant eyes of the French security men to be confronted by two U.S. Secret Service types. After checking off our names on their list, they directed us to a guarded elevator at the side of the lobby.

Stepping out of the elevator, we found ourselves in a small foyer where soft drinks and fruits had been laid out—the hotel had tactfully chosen refreshments that were not forbidden by anyone's religious beliefs. The Americans—Gates, McFarlane, Cave, and Donald Gregg, who worked in President Carter's National Security Council as CIA liaison—were among those already present, chatting with the Iranians. There was no sign of Bush or Karrubi.

I approached the Iranians to complete my final assignment. This was to arrange the route and clearance designator of the plane that would be picking up the wheelbases from Israel. Ten minutes later, Karrubi, in a Western suit and collarless white shirt with no tie, walked with an aide through the assembled group, bade everyone a good day, and went straight into the conference room.

A few minutes later George Bush, with the wispy-haired William Casey in front of him, stepped out of the elevator. He smiled, said hello to everyone, and, like Karrubi, hurried into the conference room. It was a very well-staged entrance. My last view of George Bush was of his back as he walked deeper into the room—and then the doors were closed.

Bush, Casey, Karrubi, and his aide would have no interruptions as the fate of the hostages was sealed. Iran's future arms purchases from Israel met, for the time being, with unofficial U.S. approval. I learned the details of the deal days later in Sagi's office in Israel. It was exactly as had been arranged in Amsterdam in September by the Israelis: The hostages would be released in exchange for $52 million, guarantees of arms sales for Iran, and unfreezing of Iranian monies in U.S. banks. The only difference was the timing of the hostages' release. Instead of immediately, the Republicans insisted that it take place on January 20, 1981, upon Ronald Reagan's inauguration.

It was such a secret arrangement that all hotel records of the Americans' and the Israelis' visits to Paris—I cannot speak for the Iranians—were swept away two days after we left town.

Shortly after the Iranians received their wheelbases, Carter called Prime Minister Begin and raged at him. No one knew how Carter had found out, but this time Begin gave back as good as he got, pointing out that the Iraqis were about to control the biggest known oil reserves in the world and were a danger to the very existence of Israel.

Kashani was happy to have received the wheelbases, but was upset that the arms sales were not going to start until the Reagan

Bush administration took office. "The Americans have screwed up from the very beginning," he fumed. "Their people could have left Iran in mid-1980, and now our land is being abused by the Iraqis."

On November 4, 1980, America held its elections. No one who had been involved in the secret meetings in Paris had any doubts about the outcome—or about how much longer the hostages would continue to eat rice in their Tehran "prison."

There are few rules in the murky depths of espionage, arms deals, and political trade-offs, but there are some rules, nevertheless. In 1980 we all saw that the Americans had gone beyond the pale.

6

The Man
with the Suitcase

THE DELAY UNTIL after January 20, 1981, in getting U.S.-approved military aid to Iran worried a great many people at the highest levels of the Israeli government. If Iran was going to defend itself against Iraq's invasion, it needed weapons immediately. Saddam Hussein loomed as an expansionist presence in the Arab world— the single most dangerous threat to Israel's existence. From Israel's point of view, he had to be stopped.

In the fall of 1980, Prime Minister Begin ordered Director of Israel Defense Forces/Military Intelligence Yehoshua Sagi and acting Director of Mossad Nachum Admoni to appoint an IDF/MI-Mossad Joint Committee for Iran-Israel Relations. Coordinating the efforts of both intelligence services, the Joint Committee was assigned the task of supplying Iran with arms in its war with Saddam Hussein.

The rationale for helping the Khomeini government was straightforward. If the Iranians fought the Iraqis, their soldiers would be killed instead of ours. Moreover, the war not only diverted Arab attention away from Israel, but also drained the Arab countries of money. From Likud's point of view, since Camp David, Israel had lost its edge as a strategic asset to the U.S. in the

Middle East. The "moderate" Arab countries—Egypt, Saudi Arabia, Jordan—were still anti-Israel, but they were accepted by the United States. Israel was becoming increasingly isolated. So as we now saw it, the rise of Khomeini was one of the best things that had happened to us in years. He was radical, anti-American, and anti-Arab. He was doing our job, and we believed it was in our national security interest to support him.

The five initial members of the Joint Committee, who with one exception were present at the historic Paris meeting of October 1980, were hardly gun-toting James Bond types. Rather, they were unimposing, weathered men who collectively possessed a wide range of experience in and understanding of international politics, history, business, banking, law, and weaponry:

—David Kimche, the senior member, head of Tevel at the time, was an intellectual who had a doctorate in social sciences and had spent most of his career in intelligence.
—Shmuel Morieh had been the legal adviser to SHABAK, Israel's internal security apparatus. An Iraqi Jew, he handled legal questions and contracts for the committee.
—Uri Simchoni, a brigadier general, was at various times assistant deputy chief of staff for operations for the Israel Defense Forces and military attaché in Washington. He had also been the chief of the élite Golani infantry brigade.
—Moshe Hebroni, a young major, was chief of staff for the director of Military Intelligence.
—Rafi Eitan was the counterterrorism adviser to the prime minister. A small man who walked like a rabbit and wore cheap sports jackets, he was the only veteran covert-action mastermind on the committee.

All of these men shared two attributes: They had brilliant minds, and they had no qualms about using deadly force to achieve their goals. In addition, they had access to all information in Israeli intelligence, and they were authorized to spend a great deal of money. That combination spelled enormous power.

I was appointed on November 28, 1980, to join this select group. At 29, I was by far the youngest member, but I was fluent in

Farsi and had the most personal experience and contacts in Iran. Clearly, I was to be the legs to carry out the Joint Committee's initiatives; the others were to be the brains.

The job excited me. I had no problem with the political goal of containing Iraq, and I took the pragmatic view that arming Iran was as good a way as we could hope for. Of course, over the entire eight years of the Iran-Iraq war that were to follow, during which hundreds of thousands of people died and as many were wounded, I was never once to set foot on a battlefield to witness the grim results of our work.

In December 1980, I received an important assignment. Sagi called me into his office. I guessed that the urgent summons would have something to do with Israel's covert dealings with Iran. But his first words surprised me: "Ari, I'm giving you the enviable task of picking up $52 million."

Before I could say anything, he added: "What I'm going to ask of you is not part of the committee work—it's part of a deal we've arranged with the Americans over the release of the hostages. In simple terms, $52 million has to be delivered to the Iranians before the new president's inauguration on January 20."

"That's fine," I said. "And which bank do I collect it from?"

Sagi paused and paced up and down the office for a while. "It's actually not that simple. You're going to have to take a trip to Guatemala. There, the Saudi ambassador will hand over to you $56 million . . ."

"$52 million."

"No, $56 million. An extra payment has to be made."

The extra $4 million, I was instructed, was to be deposited in the Valley National Bank of Arizona at its main branch in Phoenix on Camelback Road. I was given a bank account number. The name of the account holder was Earl Brian. The remainder of the money, $52 million, was to be handed over to Kashani in Europe.

I couldn't help wondering: Why Guatemala? . . . Why the Saudis? . . . Why Earl Brian?

The director looked hard at me. "I don't have to spell out for you how most of the payment has been worked out," he answered. "You were present when the Iranians made it clear that their radical leadership had to be paid $52 million. Ayatollah Khomeini is not totally in control, and they don't want a political confrontation in Iran. The Americans cannot arrange the money from the U.S. budget because the Americans we're dealing with are not in the government—yet. So they've asked their Saudi friends to help them."

"Is this Saudi money?"

"No, it's CIA-connected. But the Saudis helped arrange for the banking of it."

Pieces of the jigsaw began to fall into place. I, like many others, was aware of a band of former Israeli intelligence officers who were running a drug- and arms-smuggling operation in Central America, backed by the CIA.

"Is this drug profit money from Central America?"

"Don't ask too many questions, my friend."

Sagi was being very cautious, even with me. Although he refused to confirm my suspicion, I had been working with Israeli intelligence long enough to conclude that the money had come from narcotics deals arranged in Central America by some Israelis for the CIA, and that it had been laundered by the Saudis. My assessment was to prove correct.

"Shit, they're asking me to carry their dirty drug money," I thought with a false indignation. If my sense of morality was so offended, I could have resigned right then. But I didn't. I hate to admit, it was too hot a job, too exciting to turn down.

I told Sagi I would not go into the U.S. with so much money without a customs declaration, and I insisted that someone in authority receive the money from me. I also insisted on getting a customs receipt because I was going to deposit part of the money in an American bank.

"Someone in authority will be at Miami airport waiting for you," said Sagi. "We are going to ask Robert Gates himself to meet you." That was fine with me. If Gates was going to be my safe ticket into the U.S. with millions upon millions of illicit dollars, I'd be more than happy to meet up with him once again.

Then Sagi gave me a second task: to deposit in Europe two checks, our profits from the Iranians for the secret sale of tires and wheelbases for F-4 jets. The profit from the tires had been $105,000 and from the wheelbases another $850,000. So before the Joint Committee had even started its work of selling equipment to the Iranians, we had a profit of $956,000 to initiate the slush fund. This would be "operations money" for the committee. Sagi also instructed that there should be three signatories—myself and two others—for this special account. And the comptroller of Mossad, he said, was to be kept informed of deposits and withdrawals. Both payments—to the Iranians and to our slush fund—were to be deposited initially at Banque Worms in Geneva.

Late in December I phoned my Iranian contact, Sayeed Mehdi Kashani. I told him payment of the $52 million was imminent. Kashani promised to make arrangements for me at Banque Worms, which the Iranians would also be using. He would leave the key to his safe deposit box with the bank manager along with instructions that I be allowed to open the box and deposit the money on presentation of my passport. I gave Kashani my passport number.

At the beginning of January I flew through Miami to Guatemala City. I checked into the Fiesta Hotel and the following morning called the number given me for the Saudi ambassador for Central America, who was usually resident in Costa Rica, but was in town for our meeting.

"I believe we have to meet," I said.

"Yes," he said. "I think that is necessary before any transactions take place."

That evening I drove a rental car to Antigua, the old Spanish capital of Guatemala, at present a playground of the wealthy. Bright lights pinpointed restaurants and night spots that had sprung up against a backdrop of old monasteries and convents, many of them severely damaged by earthquakes over the centuries.

I found the Italian restaurant I had been told to go to and made myself comfortable at a table—I was some 15 minutes early for the 7:00 P.M. rendezvous. At exactly seven there was a commotion. Diners peered out through the windows as a waiter hurried to the door. A black Mercedes stretch limousine had pulled up in the cobblestone street. I didn't have any trouble recognizing my contact, an immaculately dressed man in his early 40s with a little goatee. He spotted me, too, as soon as he entered the restaurant. We dined on pasta, he drank wine, and we chatted about the Iraqi-Iranian situation for a while. Then he turned to business.

An assistant to the chief of Saudi Security and Intelligence would come to my hotel in the morning and deliver $56 million to me. Of this, $40 million would be in the form of 40 $1 million bank checks, drawn to cash on Banque Worms.

"The remainder, Mr. Ben-Menashe, will be in cash."

"But that's $16 million."

"Don't worry," he said. "Although $4 million will be in $100 bills, the rest will be in $1,000 bills."

"It sounds like an awful lot of paper," I said. "I'm going to need a huge suitcase!"

He exploded in a roar of laughter and assured me they would supply the suitcase. I laughed with him, but I knew that $16 million in cash spelled trouble. I asked that he give me bank receipts on the amount I'd be carrying in cash to show I'd collected it legally.

The phone in my room rang on the dot of nine the following morning. The caller from the lobby identified himself as Faissal Ghows from Saudi Arabia.

"Why don't you come up?" I said. I walked to the window and stared out over the largest city in Central America with its curious mix of crumbling old red-roofed houses and modern multistory office and apartment blocks. Faissal Ghows was a name I knew . . . from somewhere.

He was well built, a man about my age, and he came into the room lugging a huge black Samsonite suitcase with a fat brown leather attaché case under his arm. I had a glimpse of a muscular security guard in the hall before the door closed. I stared at the newcomer. I definitely knew him.

He was inspecting me closely, too. "Did you grow up in Tehran?" he asked.

"Yes!"

He slapped me on the shoulder. "But yes, yes, we have met! I should have recognized you. We were classmates. I was the son of the Saudi ambassador in Tehran. We were in the same class in the American Community School."

It all came flooding back. I still had an old school yearbook photo of him at home in Israel.

Ghows dumped the suitcase on the bed and handed me a key. "Why don't you open it?" he said.

I turned the key and lifted the lid. I'd never seen so much money. The suitcase was jammed with $1,000 and $100 bills.

"Sixteen million dollars," he said. Then from the attaché case he brought out a large white envelope. "And here's $40 million in $1 million checks." I stared at them. The checks were drawn on the very bank that I would be paying the money back into. But of course money always has to travel in order to be well laundered.

"Why don't you count them?" he asked.

I counted out the checks. Exactly 40. Not one less, not one more. People didn't make mistakes with that kind of money.

My eyes went back to the cash in the suitcase.

"Want to count it?" asked Ghows. And before I could say anything, he took a money-counting machine from his attaché case. We spent the next hour or so checking the money. It was all there, all right. I set aside $4 million, Earl Brian's money, and stuffed it into plastic laundry bags I'd found in one of the cupboards. Then I put the plastic bags on top of the other money and closed the lid. Ghows handed me the withdrawal papers from Banque Worms.

"This will prove you didn't knock someone on the head and steal their money," he said.

"How did you get the money here?"

"That's our business," he said, deadly serious.

I called Israel later that morning—it was evening there—and explained I would be leaving for the United States early the following morning. I gave the number of the Eastern flight I would be taking to Miami, and reminded my office that I expected to be received in the customs area, as promised, by Robert Gates.

"Don't worry," I was told. "It will all be arranged."

I also asked that the banker in Phoenix be told I would be paying in $4 million and to expect me at his branch.

That night I slept fitfully. Occasionally I sat up in bed and checked the suitcase and the briefcase containing the checks Ghows had left me.

The Eastern flight was to leave for Miami at 8:00 A.M. At 5:00 A.M. I put the suitcase, the briefcase, and a garment bag, which also held the money-counting machine, in the back seat of the rented car and drove to the airport. I returned the car, paid the airport tax, and then went to check in at the Eastern Airlines counter.

"Do you have any luggage?" I was asked.

"No, I'm carrying all my luggage on the plane."

The check-in clerk, a Japanese woman, stared at the suitcase. "You can't take that on board," she said.

"I'm flying first class, and I have the right to take the luggage with me. There'll be enough room in first class."

"No, it's not possible. It must go into the hold. You will get your luggage back at the other end."

I was not to be moved. She called the supervisor, who saw the determined look on my face, checked that first class was virtually empty, and told the woman: "Passenger privilege—let him take it on board."

Guatemala City Airport had no x-ray machine at the time, but as I approached the customs area, everyone stared at me. I was weighed down with baggage. Security guards were waiting to go to town on me. But I showed them my diplomatic passport, and they had to stand aside. My passport was stamped, and I went through.

Shortly before the flight, I and another person flying first class were called on board. The flight crew questioned my right to bring the suitcase with me, but I explained that permission had been granted, and after a little commotion I was allowed to take my seat.

Thirty-two thousand feet over the Caribbean, I felt a tinge of apprehension as the enormity of my mission swept over me. For months, the world had watched and waited as efforts were made at the diplomatic level to secure the freedom of the 52 Americans being held hostage in the U.S. Embassy in Tehran. No one knew anything of the deceit that had been played out in Madrid, Barcelona, Amsterdam, and Paris. The hostages themselves certainly knew nothing about the way they had been used for political gain. Now the stalemate between the Iranians and the United States was about to be broken. All I had to do was make sure the contents of the suitcase and the leather briefcase that rested on my lap were safely delivered.

As the plane began its descent over Florida, I wondered what lay ahead. Would Robert Gates really be there to meet me? Or was

I going to be pounced upon by a team of customs officials and FBI agents who'd been tipped off about a big-time money launderer? Who knew what convoluted plot had been hatched? In this game too many heads roll, there is much double-dealing. Even the position I held in Israeli intelligence would not protect me from being used if it were expedient.

A sense of relief overwhelmed me as I saw Gates's familiar figure standing right by the exit to the tunnel running from the aircraft. He was accompanied by another man, and both were chuckling as they watched me approach with my load. Gates shook my hand warmly, said how good it was to see me again, and introduced his companion as a special customs agent.

The customs man said, "I'll carry this for you," and picked up the suitcase. He seemed surprised at how heavy it was. It weighed, according to the scale in the Fiesta Hotel in Guatemala City, about 110 pounds.

Gates took my garment bag. I carried the briefcase.

I had already filled in my customs card, but had not declared the money on it. I gave the card to the agent, who said he would take care of it and asked me to follow him through passport control into a small private office. There, with Gates looking on, he asked how much money I had.

"I would like a customs slip for $56 million," I said. The two men smiled at each other.

At my request, I was given two receipts, one for $52 million, the other for $4 million. Theoretically, I could have gone through without a declaration because of diplomatic immunity. But I wasn't taking any chances. I wanted this money to go through legal channels to cover me in case any awkward questions were asked later.

I picked up the garment bag and the briefcase. Gates immediately offered to carry the suitcase. He, too, seemed surprised by its weight. Dropping it onto its wheels, he followed me out into the main terminal. It was an extraordinary scene, this high official of the Central Intelligence Agency* shoving a suitcase

---

* At the time, Gates was officially the national intelligence officer for U.S.S.R./Eastern Europe, a post he held from October 1980 till March 1981, when he became director of the DCI's executive staff.

jammed with $16 million through the bustling crowds of businesspeople, tourists, and locals. No one recognized him. No one had a clue about the fortune that was passing by under their noses. In retrospect, I wonder how he would have reacted had the suitcase suddenly burst open and the money spilled out across the floor.

We flew to Phoenix on Eastern, first class, with a changeover in Atlanta. I had the same difficulty convincing the airline staff to let me on the plane with the suitcase. Gates certainly wasn't going to expose his identity by trying to pull rank. I finally managed to get the go-ahead to take it on board.

On the flight to Phoenix, Gates made no reference to the money, or even to the fact that it had gotten through safely. It was almost as if he expected nothing to go wrong. Instead, he briefed me on how Israel should handle American arms sales to Iran. This was clearly the reason he accompanied me to Phoenix.

"When the Iranians give you their requirements," he said, "a decision will have to be made whether the equipment is going to come from your stocks, from the U.S., or from other quarters. You and your people are to contact my office and talk only to me or my assistant, Clair George."

Reagan was about to take office, but the embargo on sales to Iran was obviously going to stand for a long time to come. The official embargo, that is. Gates, of course, was talking about something different.

"If the U.S. government agrees that the requested equipment can be supplied, we'll go to the companies that make it, buy it, and put it together at an air base," said Gates. "It will then be Israel's responsibility to pick it up from there. You're also going to need Israeli end-user certificates."

These were documents in which Israel would promise that arms obtained from the United States would not be sold to any other country. Gates's request was, of course, just a formality. The end-user certificates in this case were pointless—except to cover the U.S. end in case the arms deals became public. Then it could simply blame Israel for illegally reselling U.S. arms.

Payments from the Iranians for the weapons they were to receive were discussed. The Iranians would pay the Israelis, and the

Israelis would in turn pay the Americans through numbered accounts in Europe, according to issued instructions.

"I don't have to impress on you the necessity to keep this quiet," said my traveling companion. "And, of course, if any of this is made public, in either the near or distant future, we will deny all knowledge." Because I was a representative of the Israeli government, he trusted that every word he'd spoken would be reported back to my superiors.

On arrival in Phoenix, Gates helped me lift the suitcase into a rental car. His job, to instruct me on the procedures of the arms sales, was over for the time being. As I bade him goodbye and prepared to drive to the hotel, he said, "Good luck. I won't say goodbye—I guess we'll be seeing each other."

"By the way," I said, "what's the extra $4 million for?"

"Oh . . . just operating funds." He smiled and walked away.

At the hotel I called an Israeli friend living in Phoenix and asked if I could leave a suitcase in a safe place for the night. He offered me his house and came to pick me up. Back at his home we shoved the suitcase under his bed. "What the hell have you got in here, Ari—bricks?" he asked.

"Just a few prized possessions," I replied.

We went out for the evening, after I'd made sure that his family was remaining in the house. However, I carried with me the briefcase containing the $40 million in checks.

In the morning, my friend brought the suitcase back to the hotel. While he waited, I quickly opened it in the bathroom and took out the $4 million I had placed in the plastic laundry bags in Guatemala. Then, with the money covered with sweaters, I persuaded my friend to take me and the suitcase back to his house. He was puzzled by my movements, but we were good enough friends that I knew he wouldn't ask questions.

Later that morning I made my way to the Valley National Bank. I gave the banker who had been told to expect me the $4 million and asked him to put it in Earl Brian's account, as arranged. The customs slip to show that I'd declared this money and that it was "legitimate" was essential for the deposit.

"That's a lot of money to be walking around with," the banker said.

I shrugged, thanked him for his assistance, and left.

The following morning I picked up the suitcase from my friend's house, threw it in the back of my rented car—it was now $4 million lighter, of course—and checked in for a TWA flight to New York with an ongoing connection to London, and on to Geneva by British Airways. I had to go through the same taxing routines as before, persuading airline staff to let me take the suitcase on board the aircraft. It was only because I was traveling first class and had a diplomatic passport that I was able to pull it off.

I arrived in Geneva late in the morning on a cold January day and took a taxi directly to Banque Worms. At the safe deposit area, I asked for the manager and told him that Kashani had left a key for me. I produced my passport; he checked the number, then asked me to follow him downstairs, through a steel-barred door, to a large safe deposit box. He turned one of the box's locks with his own key, and then I used the key that Kashani had left for me. When the manager had gone, I opened the box, picked up bundles of money, and just threw them in, along with the envelope containing the $40 million in checks. I closed the box and left the bank, carrying the empty suitcase, my briefcase, and the garment bag. I felt considerably lighter.

I took a taxi to the Geneva Hilton and made a call to Israel. Everything, I reported to Sagi's chief of staff, had been delivered. But I still had to open the special account with the profits from the sales of the tires and the wheelbases to Iran. A "friend"—a Mossad agent—would be calling on me, I was told.

The agent said little when he arrived at the hotel. He gave me an envelope containing two checks totaling $955,000. It seemed such small change. He also gave me the documentation for the company in whose name I later opened an account at Banque Worms. Business was booming at Worms.

I phoned Kashani, who was in Geneva and had left his number with Sagi's office. "The money for the students is in the bank," I told him. "And I think that soon we'll all be ready to start business. You get your money and release the Americans, and the weapons can start flowing."

Later Kashani visited me at the hotel and gave me a new list of equipment the Iranians wanted. I promised to do what I could. I checked out of the hotel and made my way to the airport. Behind in the hotel room I'd left an empty suitcase. The hotel might send it back to me; they might not. As far as I was concerned, I didn't want to see it again.

On January 20, 1981, the world turned on its TV sets to watch the inauguration of Ronald Reagan and George Bush as president and vice president of the United States. Just as Reagan was being sworn in, there was a flash announcement from Associated Press. I was one of the few who felt no emotion or surprise at the news that the hostages in Tehran had been released.

7

The First Billion

THE REPUBLICANS RENEGED on the deal to release all Iranian monies frozen in the U.S., and I was among the first to hear of Tehran's anger through my long-time friend Sayeed Mehdi Kashani.

He rang me from Vienna in late January 1981. "We were swindled out of the prisoners," he complained. "The Americans have let a lot of our money go, but they're sitting on $11 billion of Iranian government funds in the Chase Manhattan Bank."

"Hold on," I said. "How can you be swindled out of something you had no right to?"

We both laughed. But then he said, "I hope you Israelis will keep your word. We need that equipment."

"We promised to help, and we will. Don't put us in the same bed as the Americans. A decision about the subject was made at the highest levels of the Israeli government."

At the beginning of February 1981, I flew to Vienna for an arms-supply conference with Kashani and Omshei. In the wake of the hostages being freed and the money being paid to the "students," the Iranians were eager to get down to the serious business of arms supply.

Acting on instructions from the Joint Committee for Iran-Israel Relations, I put a proposal to the two Iranians on what we could sell them from our stockpiles. They could receive existing

F-4 electronics and spare parts; 300,000 122mm artillery shells; 51mm mortars and rockets to be carried by infantry soldiers; 100,000 Kalashnikov AK-47s with ammunition; and air-to-surface missiles. They also wanted engines for their British-made Chieftain tanks. In stock, Israel had 1,000 German-made engines that would fit the tanks. This is where we were to make our greatest profit. The engines were worth between $30,000 and $40,000 each. We offered them to the Iranians at the outrageous take-it-or-leave-it price of $450,000 each.

They were also interested in buying fighter aircraft which we could not sell to them at the time, but we offered them ten old C-130 Hercules aircraft for $12 million each. Their national airline, Iran Air, which was flying 747s and 707s, was also in desperate straits, I was told. The 747s were already grounded for lack of spare parts because the U.S. embargo against Iran covered even commercial engines. The embargo had not been lifted, but now, to boost the airline, the Iranians were not only looking for spare parts for the old fleet but hoping to buy British Tristars.

I added up the bill. The grand total was one billion dollars, give or take a million. Israel's profit—50 percent. The slush fund looked like it was going to do very well.

The Iranians screwed up their faces at the price. They knew Israel was ripping them off. But they had little choice. They said they would take the offer back to Tehran. "But you must come to Tehran, too," said Kashani. "The Defense Ministry will certainly want to talk to you about the details."

My first trip to post-revolutionary Tehran took place in late February 1981. Some colleagues were worried because there were extremist factions in the country who despised the Israelis. I felt there wouldn't be any problem because I had been told that Ayatollah Ali Reza Hashemi of the Supreme Council had assured my safe passage. Besides, Ari Ben-Menashe was to change his identity.

Wearing an English-made suit, with a borrowed Rolex watch on my wrist, I arrived at Vienna airport under the guise of Canadian businessman William Grace. Immigrants to Canada had their origins in numerous countries, and there was nothing to connect me with my true identity or to suggest that I was an Israeli . . . no nametags on my clothes, no Israeli-made socks or shoes, and definitely no Ari Ben-Menashe passport or credit cards. "William Grace's" Canadian passport had been prepared for me by Mossad. I carried no luggage.

As arranged with the Iranians, I booked an Austrian Airlines flight that was due to leave Vienna for London at the same time that an Iran Air flight was due to depart for Tehran. Accompanied by a Mossad agent who was playing the part of my traveling companion, I collected my boarding pass and went through to the transit area. Vienna had been specially chosen—it was an airport where incoming and outgoing transit passengers mingled.

Omshei was waiting for me. I gave my companion my used ticket and the boarding pass, along with my passport. From Omshei I collected a boarding card for the Iran Air flight. He also gave me Iranian travel papers identifying me as William Grace, which would see me safely through immigration in Tehran. We couldn't risk any officials tipping off the radicals that an Israeli— even under Canadian guise—had arrived in Tehran. On the other hand, it had been easy enough for Omshei to obtain a boarding pass for me—after all, Iran Air was the government airline. We had put a complete smokescreen over the movements of Ari Ben-Menashe, alias William Grace.

Omshei was delighted that I was on the way to Tehran. He and the Supreme Council felt that it would not be long now before they had their weapons, as long, he said, as a minor obstacle could be overcome. He didn't tell me what it was.

As we approached Tehran, all the women passengers, who were on the left side of the 707, started wiping off their lipstick and bringing out their body-shrouding chadors. Some headed toward the toilet clutching dark stockings. Goodbye Western decadence for the time being.

My travel documents weren't necessary. Waiting on the tarmac when the plane landed was a Ministry of Defense car. It took us straight out, bypassing customs and immigration. I was driven to the former Hilton Hotel where a suite had been reserved for me. I had an early night. I didn't want to risk walking around the streets of Tehran.

Accompanied by Kashani and Omshei, I was driven the follow-ing morning to the Office for Purchase of Military Equipment in the Ministry of Defense building. Eight men sat around a conference table. The air was thick with smoke.

I made my presentation, outlining the equipment on offer.

"It's far too much money," snapped one of the officials. This was obviously the "minor problem" Omshei had warned me about.

"But we're taking an enormous risk," I protested. "The problems for Israel are immense, as I'm sure you all understand."

"The charges are outrageous."

However, the officials agreed to present the Israeli bill to the Supreme Council. They also asked about the logistics of getting the equipment to Tehran. I suggested that they get over their first hurdle and obtain the Supreme Council's ratification of the deal. I was asked to wait another couple of days.

On the way back to the hotel, Omshei said he would pick me up at 5:00 P.M. for dinner, but at about 3:30 he called and said a very important issue had arisen. The commander of the air force wanted to see me right away. We met in the hotel restaurant.

"Iran has a particular problem with the Iraqis," said the commander. "On the outskirts of Baghdad they have installed a nuclear reactor. It's worrying us."

I knew all about the reactor, referred to as Tammuz 17. For some months in 1979, when relations with Iran were on hold, I'd worked on the Signals Intelligence exchange desk of the External Relations Department. Part of my job had been to review and disseminate KH-11 satellite intelligence about Tammuz 17 that came from the U.S. as a result of the Camp David agreement. The reactor had been given to Iraq by the French to start bomb-grade metal enrichment, and, according to Israeli intelligence, the Iraqis were well on the way to setting it up for military purposes.

"We've tried to hit it twice—once in September and then again a week ago—and we've failed," the commander told me.

"What do you want from Israel?"

"Intelligence—technical information about that reactor. We know you've been collecting data about it. We're well aware of Mossad's activities in France to try to stop the building of this reactor because you're obviously as worried about it as we are. We need all you can give us."

I started taking notes. The commander bit into his food. "We believe that sometime by the end of this year, around November or December, it's going to be activated, and any bombing of the site after that will be a nuclear disaster. It must be taken out before the end of this year."

He gave me the name of an official at the Iranian Embassy in Paris to whom information could be passed. "Remember," said the commander, "that by helping us, you will also be helping Israel, the Middle East, and the rest of the world. If Iraq gets the nuclear bomb, God help us all."

He didn't have to emphasize his concerns to me. We knew that Saddam Hussein was desperate for Middle East supremacy, and he was already stockpiling deadly chemicals and working furiously on his own nuclear bomb.

Early the next morning, Omshei and Kashani came for breakfast and told me that in the afternoon we would be meeting the chief of the air force again. Omshei suggested that in the meantime we take a ride around Tehran. He had an old grey Citroën. We drove through the teeming streets, where shrouded women hurried by with shopping baskets, to the northern suburb of Shemran, where we stopped for the delicious ice cream I remembered fondly from my childhood. I've tasted ice cream all around the world, and the Iranian product seemed to me second to none.

As we drove further north, the car's radiator boiled over. Omshei was petrified. Here he was with a broken-down car at the side of the road with an undercover Israeli intelligence official whose presence, if discovered, would have outraged the masses— and he was responsible for my safety. He loved his car, and he was worried about me. He didn't want to leave it, or me, alone. Trucks rumbled by as Omshei paced up and down, considering what for him was apparently a maddening situation.

"All we need is a carload of radicals to pull up and start asking questions and we're both in trouble," he repeated again and again during the next 15 minutes.

Finally I persuaded him to accompany me on foot to a shop that had a telephone. He called the Defense Ministry. Two hours later, with Omshei now in a state of absolute panic, a tow truck arrived. We then took a taxi to the hotel. I was left in no doubt that the Iranians in power were extremely concerned about my safety—and that of their cars.

During the afternoon meeting with the air force commander,

he asked for air and satellite photos of the Iraqi reactor building and neighboring structures. The next morning, I was told, I would be seeing Ayatollah Hashemi, as well as the new defense minister and Hojjat El-Islam Karrubi—the man who had attended the top-secret meeting with George Bush in Paris four months earlier.

The three men were all smiles when I bade them good morning in a small room in the Parliament building. It was all systems go, they announced. The Supreme Council had given their assent to pay Israel the fortune being asked for the military equipment.

"How would you like the payments made?" asked Karrubi.

"Please put your one billion dollars in a numbered account in Austria."

"Just like that?" asked the defense minister. "Can we trust you?"

"You can trust us. But it must be cash. Letters of credit are troublesome."

"We'd prefer to pay you cash on delivery."

I smiled and shook my head. "We can't deliver until we get the money," I explained. "We have to buy the matériel from the industries."

The defense minister laughed and clapped his hands together in mock applause. "You Israelis have an answer for everything," he said. But he promised that in four days Omshei would call me in Israel and give me the account numbers and the withdrawal codes for the money.

"You understand that we have no other choice but to pay this high price," said Karrubi. "But I hope you will look into the air force request concerning the reactor."

It was agreed that included in their $1 billion would be insurance, war risk coverage, and transportation costs. Now came the question of logistics. I proposed that Israel should charter cargo aircraft from an Argentinean company that would fly to Tel Aviv. These would then be loaded with the weaponry and equipment and flown to Tehran, but only after the pilots had given a flight plan to the Tel Aviv tower that would indicate they were flying to Portugal. Over Cyprus they would change the flight plan and give the Cyprus tower a new routing—to Tehran. The secrecy of the missions would be so high that even Israel's own flight controllers could not know the destination of the cargo planes.

I returned to Israel, using the same trick at the Vienna airport as before, only this time in reverse. In the transit lounge, I was met by a Mossad man who gave me back my passport. I handed it in to immigration and walked out into the main terminal, where I checked in for a flight to Tel Aviv.

The money from the Iranians was paid almost immediately. It was placed in five different numbered accounts, each holding $200 million, in the Girozentrale Bank in Vienna.

Military Intelligence Director Sagi was delighted that the deal had been completed. He instructed the deputy director general of the Ministry of Defense to start getting the equipment together. It was decided that all the matériel would be put in a warehouse in a military hangar at Ben-Gurion International Airport. The logistics people at IDF/MI arranged for the charter flights and for insurance with Lloyd's of London. They would pay high insurance rates for agricultural and "other" equipment flying from Portugal to Tehran. The coverage was 110 percent and applied only from the time the aircraft were over Cyprus to when they landed in Tehran. This hid the contents and the takeoff point.

While the mechanics of the airlifts were being sorted out, Sagi, deciding to act on the Iranian request for information on the Iraqi reactor, ordered a photo reconnaissance flight. It was a dangerous proposition. If anything went wrong, Israel risked detection and could be accused of taking sides with the Iranians.

Four days later we were studying the aerial photos. They were excellent, clearly identifying the location and the buildings. Copies were made for the Iranians and sent to the Israeli military attaché in Paris. He, in turn, handed them over to STEN—our code name for Iranian Military Intelligence—through Simon Gabbay, the Israeli contact with the Iranians in Paris. But a question arose. Did we really want to risk leaving the attack on the reactor to the Iranians? They'd already tried to destroy it and failed. Yet it would be in Israel's interests for the complex to be destroyed. There was one simple answer, and it came straight from Prime Minister Begin's office: We would do the job ourselves.

Israel Aircraft Industries set to work building a number of

piercing bombs, with a sharp nose that could tear through a building's exterior a fraction of a second before exploding. It would also be a "smart" bomb, designed to lock onto a homing device inside the reactor. Mossad was in charge of planting this device, at first a seemingly impossible task; but money opened many doors. For the right kind of fee, some people, including French technicians working in the nuclear reactor in Iraq, would be more than happy to plant a homing device on Israel's behalf. And when you are a trusted employee, it's not so difficult to bypass security.

There was one loose end to tie up. Israeli jets would need landing rights in Iran should they be crippled in a dogfight or start to run low on fuel. To obtain this kind of permission meant further delicate negotiations with the Iranians.

With the help of Omshei, Kashani, and the commander of the Iranian Air Force, a meeting was arranged in mid-March 1981 between President Abol Hassan Bani-Sadr of Iran, who was also commander-in-chief of the Iranian forces, and Professor Moshe Arens, Israel's ambassador to the United States and a close confidant of Prime Minister Begin.

The meeting took place in southern France. Arens flew in on Pan Am direct from Kennedy Airport to Nice. Bani-Sadr flew by private plane from Tehran to Paris and down to the south. The two men met for six hours in their hotel, and the date for the attack on the reactor was fixed: June 7. The air force base designated for landing rights was just south of Tabriz in northern Iran.

The pilot chosen by the Israeli Air Force to lead the strike team was Col. Yoram Eitan, son of Lt. Gen. Rafael Eitan, chief of the general staff of the Israeli Defense Forces (no relation to Rafi Eitan in intelligence). Israel built a dummy reactor in the Negev Desert to practice the strike. On the morning of May 4, a Sunday, one of the rehearsing planes came down, killing the pilot instantly. The news was broken to Gen. Eitan. He'd lost his son.

The lead pilot chosen in his place was Yair Shamir, also a colonel in the air force and the son of the man who was to become prime minister, Yitzhak Shamir. Three days before the planned raid, the Mossad network in Baghdad informed headquarters that the homing device had been put in place.

At 5:30 P.M. on June 7, 1981, six F-15 jets carrying the bombs and eight F-16 escorts took off from Ramat David Airfield and headed east. Six bombs were dropped. Two failed to explode, but that didn't matter—only one direct hit was necessary. The reactor was destroyed. There were no signs of enemy aircraft; no dogfights. It was not necessary to land in Iran. On the return flight the jubilant pilots were met over Jordan by refueling aircraft, but refueling was also not necessary. The operation had been perfect in every respect.

Israeli intelligence had recommended to the prime minister and the government not to admit publicly that Israel was responsible for the attack, in order to give Saddam Hussein an out. Without such a public admission, he would not have been forced to commit himself publicly to retaliation. But Menachem Begin, who had scheduled early elections for June 30, made the announcement because he believed it would stand him in good stead with the Israeli public. The Iranians were, of course, ecstatic. The commander of the Iranian Air Force was connected to Begin through a Paris operator and personally thanked him. For diplomatic purposes, President Bani-Sadr issued a loosely worded condemnation saying Israel had violated the sovereignty of another nation. He kept the lid on his private jubilation.

Meanwhile, the weapons flights from Ben-Gurion Airport to Tehran, which had started in early March 1981, were going well, even though at the start we had come up against an enormous logistical problem—how to transport the bulky shells. Finally it was decided to ship them by freighter directly from the Port of Ashdod in Israel to Bandar Abbas in southern Iran. The rest of the equipment went by air. Between March and August some 40 Argentinean-registered cargo flights left Tel Aviv.

At the end of June we heard from the KGB. The Soviet Union's security and intelligence service, through its representative in Israel, presented a formal letter of inquiry to the chief of staff of the director of Military Intelligence, originating from the Directorate of Foreign Relations of the KGB. The letter demanded explanations from Israel about flights originating in Tel Aviv and flying close to the Turkish-Soviet border and down to Tehran. Sagi's chief of staff handed the letter to me, and I presented it to the Joint IDF/MI-Mossad Committee for Israel-Iran Relations. I believed that an explanation should be given to the Soviets. However, Israeli arrogance came into play. The prevailing opinion, without consulting the Prime Minister's Office, was to answer the letter by stating that the government of Israel does not discuss its foreign and security policies. The Soviets were basically told to get lost.

It was an abrupt, stupid answer. Signed by the chief of External Relations of IDF/MI, it was handed to the Soviet representative in Israel in the first week of July. On July 18 the Soviet reply came back. One of the cargo planes was downed, killing the three Argentinean crew members. F-4 parts were scattered all along the Armenian-Turkish border. So the Soviets found out what was on the planes.

The Soviets took great pride in announcing to the world that the plane had been carrying American weapons systems to Iran. Israel denied all knowledge of this. The flights continued, but this time further below the border, after Robert Gates had made sure there would be no Turkish objections. By mid-August 1981, this stage of the shiploads and flights was completed.

8

The Ora Group

MY RELATIONSHIP WITH Freddie, although intermittent, remained warm and loving. Despite the rapidly changing events in Iran which kept me busy, she was always in my thoughts. She had given birth to a little girl we'd decided to call Herut. The first time I saw my daughter at the Lisbon hotel Freddie had checked into, I wept with happiness. But I didn't know where our future lay.

With Herut in the care of a nanny in Managua, we had continued to meet throughout 1980 in Portugal whenever we could arrange a date. My schedule was hectic, and Freddie didn't like traveling with the baby, so by mid-1981 she announced that she'd had enough.

"I love you, Ari. I want to be nearer to you," she said during one of our strolls through Lisbon. "I've decided to give up my job and come and live here in Portugal."

I was thrilled. It would certainly make life easier for both of us. My shuttling between Israel, Europe, the U.S., and Iran didn't take me very near Nicaragua. Lisbon, on the other hand, was centrally located in all my travels—I would meet the Iranians there because Portugal still had diplomatic relations with Iran—and Freddie felt comfortable there because she had many friends. "Great," I said. "Now we'll be able to see each other more often."

"That's a laugh," she said. Her brow furrowed. Something more was wrong.

"Ari," she said, "I want you to leave your job. It's dangerous work, and we just don't get to see you enough."

I knew I couldn't do that. I was excited about the work my colleagues and I were doing for Israel and was feeling very self-important. Besides, what was there for me to do in Portugal?

Despite her disappointment at my reaction, Freddie gave up her job in Managua and moved to Lisbon, where, with the baby in the care of a nanny she brought with her, she started working for the Portuguese national airline, TAP, as a public relations officer. Freddie didn't really approve of my work and continued to press me to leave it, but she agreed to put me in touch with the president of TAP. That meeting eventually resulted in the Israeli government chartering planes out of Portugal to carry weapons to Iran. Suffice it to say, this was not exactly what Freddie had envisioned as the fruits of our relationship when she moved to Portugal.

By March 1981, the Joint Committee had set up the necessary mechanisms for handling the secret sales of weapons to Iran that had been promised in the October Paris agreements. A number of trading companies with various names made the contacts with the Iranians and with weapons manufacturers and arms brokers, found out what weapons were needed, arranged the logistics of the shipments, and set up the discreet transfer of millions upon millions of dollars.

Israel was operating under a general agreement of cooperation that Prime Minister Begin had secretly reached in principle with William Casey in August 1980. The details of the weapons sales to Iran had been worked out in December 1980, and David Kimche, the senior member of the Joint Committee, was dealing directly with the CIA's Robert Gates on their implementation. In early 1981, Gates gave the go-ahead for unsophisticated weapons to go to Iran. The arrangements for these sales were handled by the Joint Committee in meetings north of Tel Aviv, with the cooperation of the CIA.

But Gates refused at this early time to allow the sale of sophisticated U.S. electronic equipment to Iran. Our friends in Tehran were desperate to have this matériel for their air force and air and ground defenses, and Israel, of course, wanted to help them as much as possible in their war against Iraq. The Iraqis were still bogged down in southern Iran, neither advancing nor retreating. The Joint Committee felt that Iran could do with more sophisticated weapons—for a price, of course. So the Joint Committee sent two of its members—Rafi Eitan and me, both using aliases— to New York to start an undercover operation that would acquire the technology the Americans balked at and sell it to Iran.

The New York office was on John Street, in the Wall Street area. Out of it we built a team of about 50 people, many of them small arms brokers who shopped for electronic equipment from U.S. companies and arranged for delivery to Iran. All sales had to be accompanied by end-user certificates, which stipulated that the equipment was going to Israel, that Israel had licensed the broker to buy it, and that it would not be resold to any other country. These certificates were necessary under U.S. law. We had empty pads of such certificates that we would fill out and then send duplicates to the Israeli Ministry of Defense to keep on file in case anyone ever bothered to check.

The electronic equipment, which was not particularly bulky, was usually flown by the IDF's weekly Boeing 707 flight from New York to Tel Aviv, or by El Al cargo. From Tel Aviv, Argentinean charters would carry it to Tehran. If the volume was too great, then we would charter other planes, usually from TAP in Portugal or Guinness Peat in Ireland, to make the Tel Aviv- Tehran run.

Eitan oversaw the whole operation, and I personally spent a lot of my time shuttling back and forth between Tel Aviv and New York, stopping often in Portugal and meeting the Iranians there to receive their latest requests for equipment.

Initially, our overhead was paid for through the Joint Committee's operating budget, which was separate from Mossad's and the IDF/MI's. The Joint Committee became self-sufficient as the slush-fund profits, both from our undercover New York operation and from other sales that were tacitly approved by the Americans, rapidly grew. Since the transactions went through a number of trading companies, we needed a flagship to hold the slush fund. When the Joint Committee was trying to decide what to call this mother company, the name "Ora" came to my mind. Ora means "light" in Hebrew, but I actually was thinking of a young woman who worked in my office in Tel Aviv, with whom I had a bond that wasn't quite love but was more than friendship. Thus was born the Ora Group, which was to handle billions of dollars in the next few years.

The John Street operation was running very smoothly, with electronics ostensibly heading off to Israel, but finding their way to Iran, until one of the employees in the office, a Swiss woman, caught on to what was happening. She spilled the beans to Leslie M. Gelb, who was working out of the Washington bureau of the *New York Times*. She told him how the office she worked for, which on the face of it was involved in the vague business of imports and exports, kept changing its name and appeared to be sending lots of electronic material to Israel, although there were people in the office speaking Farsi all the time. That was quite true—Hushang Lavi, who was working with us, and I frequently spoke Farsi.

On March 9, 1982, a *New York Times* "news analysis" by Gelb blithely noted that, "Israel has been secretly supplying American-made arms to Iran." We quickly learned that Gelb had a source in our own office. Rafi Eitan, with his reputation for ruthlessness, set the dogs loose.

The dogs in this case were a group of South African intelligence heavies, whose job was to ensure the safe transfer of arms from anywhere in the world to South Africa. They were a wild bunch, and because of Israel's friendship with South Africa, it was an accepted arrangement to ask for favors. As Eitan and I made our hurried exit from the United States, the dogs bit.

To this day, I don't know how they did it, but the Swiss woman who blew the operation suddenly found herself being bundled on a cargo plane loaded with arms, bound for Pretoria. Although Eitan was all for killing her, the rest of the committee, including me, said no. Instead, the terror-stricken woman was given a very severe lecture on the realities of life and dispatched to Europe from South Africa. With the journalist's major source silenced, the office closed down, and not a word from either the U.S. or Israeli government, there was nothing left for any other newspaper to follow up on.

The blowing of the John Street operation was exactly the kind of thing the Israelis had been worried about from the start of the arms sales in 1981. We were well aware that if there were a mistake and the whole trade were exposed, the U.S. could turn around and point the finger at Israel, bringing world condemnation. Whenever U.S. officials were caught red-handed doing something illegal, they usually lied like crazy and accused everyone else. None of us could forget Watergate. And this was bigger than Watergate.

We took two precautions. The first involved Defense Minister Ariel Sharon, who had been appointed to that position earlier in 1981. He was a great supporter of the weapons sales to Iran, and he decided to try to lobby the U.S. government into reaching strategic agreements with Israel. As it turned out, the two American officials used in lobbying for these agreements were CIA Director William Casey's deputy, Robert Gates, and Robert McFarlane, who at that point was on the National Security Council.

Sharon had been a prominent general but was thrown out of the military in 1970 as the result of an interview he gave to *Playboy* magazine criticizing then-Prime Minister Golda Meir. He came back on the scene in the 1973 war when, as a reserves general, he saved the day on the Egyptian front. He stayed on in the military for a few more years, until the Labor Party decided not to appoint him chief of the general staff. Disgruntled, Sharon then left the military altogether. However, he still had political ambitions. In the 1977 election he ran for the Knesset as head of a political party called Shlom Zion (Peace to Zion). As soon as his party won two seats in the Knesset, he joined the Likud Party coalition, and became minister for agriculture. In 1981 he had been elevated to the position of defense minister.

But in the interim, between 1975 and 1977, Sharon was a private citizen who was trying to build a fortune dealing in arms in Central America. He had a network of people working with him there, one being the disgraced Mossad agent Mike Harari, who had just left Israel because of his failure in the "Moroccan Waiter Affair," where the wrong man was shot dead in Lillehammer, Norway, during an attempted hit on Ahmed Salame, a Palestinian who had been involved in the massacre of Israeli athletes at the 1972 Olympic Games in Munich. Harari was a close associate of Panama's military intelligence chief, Manuel Noriega.

Sharon's network had been able to provide military equipment from Israel to various Central American countries, including El Salvador, Guatemala, Panama, Costa Rica, and even Mexico. This was never official Israeli government policy, and it was frowned upon by the cabinet itself, but Sharon was too wild a goose for anybody to handle. So Sharon's private network bought their weapons from Israeli government factories and got their export licenses from the Israeli government. Gates had developed a professional interest in the arms network that Sharon and his former intelligence cowboys were operating in Central America. By 1981, Sharon and Harari were running what Harari described as more of a CIA network than an Israeli operation—and were filling their private bank accounts at the same time.

It was in 1981 that they started supplying a secret army in Central America, the contras, who were trying to destabilize and eventually bring about the downfall of the Sandinista government of Nicaragua, which had come to power in 1979. The contras did not have any money—Congress was not then willing to fund them—and desperately needed cash to buy their arms.

Sharon, with all his power, could not force the prime minister or the leaders of the Israeli intelligence community to pay for weapons from the slush fund that had grown out of the Iran arms sales. So, with the backing of Gates and the CIA, some members of the group created their own fund. They did this, according to Harari, by transporting cocaine from South America to the United States via Central America. A major player was Manuel Noriega, who had known George Bush since he had been the CIA chief in the mid-1970s. Hundreds of tons of cocaine poured into the United States, and another handy slush fund was created.

Because of the close relationship between Gates and Sharon and the special relationship between Robert McFarlane and Rafi Eitan, the strategic U.S./Israeli agreement sought by Sharon was reached. The signing of the strategic agreement by Sharon and the

U.S. was made public, but the contents were kept secret and are still not available through any Freedom of Information Act requests.

However, one part of it was that any U.S. arms sold to Israel involving technology that was 20 years old or more could be resold at the discretion of the Israeli government. The agreement was very loosely worded—it could be interpreted to mean that Israel was allowed to resell brand-new American weapons as long as the technology behind them was at least 20 years old.

This was our first ploy to overcome American denials, if any. If Israel were discovered to be selling arms to the Iranians, we would simply brandish the agreement the Americans had signed . . . with its gaping loophole.

Our second protection involved the money from the arms sales—when letters of credit or cash were paid to us to purchase U.S. arms, we simply and quite blatantly ran the sums through U.S. banks.

A letter of credit from the Iranian government would be issued to an Israeli "front" company by a European-based Iranian company through the London or Paris branch of Iran's Bank Melli. It would be endorsed by the National Westminster Bank in England, and we would then ask for it to be transferred to an American bank. Favorites were the Chicago-Tokyo Bank in Chicago, the Chemical Bank in New York, Bank One in Ohio, and the Valley National Bank of Arizona. Then the banks would have to explain these letters of credit, in U.S. dollars, to the U.S. Treasury if they were to accept them. According to U.S. Treasury regulations, letters of credit for sums in excess of $10,000 had to be approved by Treasury.

Since the sales were a U.S.-sanctioned operation, the CIA would have to ensure that Treasury issued an acceptance. Once the letter of credit was approved, it was moved back again to Europe. Except for the John Street operations in 1981-82, this was to be the way almost all the American-supplied arms sales to Iran were handled from late 1981 until late 1987.

The Soviet shootdown in July 1981 of the Argentinean cargo aircraft carrying weapons to Tehran convinced us that we needed a smokescreen to conceal the movement of the massive amounts of weapons we were shipping.

The smokescreen involved the Israelis making deals with a number of private arms brokers and businesspeople throughout Europe. Their companies would be used as a cover for our own operations. The dealers would purchase equipment from around the world and sell it on our behalf to the Iranians. The money would come to us from Iran, and we would open letters of credit to the dealers—after we had raked off our profit.

One of the arms brokers we dealt with was John Hortrich, an American businessman living in southern France. Like many others we were to employ, he had a murky background but was perfect for the job. He had grown up in Connecticut and gone to medical school, but dropped out. He joined the Marine Special Forces, making it only to the rank of sergeant, and served in Korea as a medic. On his release from the military, he started working as a salesman for Revlon in New York. There he met another, younger, cosmetics salesman, Richard J. Brenneke, with whom he was to keep in contact for many years and who was to figure in the arms-to-Iran story.

Hortrich, according to his own account, was very unhappy working for Revlon. He wanted out. After he married a Cornell graduate, he and his bride decided to settle in the Virgin Islands, where he opened a liquor business, selling to Europe, the United States, and South America. He eventually became the biggest alcohol wholesaler in the Caribbean.

One day in the mid-1970s while on a visit to southern France, he fell madly in love with the young half-French, half-Portuguese proprietor of the small hotel, the Mas Bellevue, where he stayed. Hortrich returned to the Virgin Islands and put a proposition to his wife: that they liquidate the business and go and live in the south of France. With a total of $11 million, they arrived in Nice, and Hortrich decided to go back into business—with an office in St. Tropez at the hotel Mas Bellevue.

While setting up the office, Hortrich met a prominent French businessman, Bernard Velliot, who was connected to French intelligence. They decided to go into the oil and arms business together, even though Hortrich had no experience in such matters. Velliot introduced Hortrich to various crude-oil and arms brokers and a number of stockbrokers and bankers in Europe. In 1979 Hortrich made a terrible mistake and invested $7 million in cocoa futures. He lost the lot. And since he had set up home in St. Tropez, he had made no money in spite of a lot of bragging. In 1980, he mortgaged his home to Banque Worms in Geneva, and banker Jacques Mathenet, a long-time friend, lent him $300,000.

Meanwhile, the Iranians were holding out their hands to everyone for weapons because the main arms sales to Iran had not begun yet. Some of these requests reached Hortrich's ears through Bernard Velliot. Hortrich managed to contact an Israeli arms dealer, Yitzhak Frank, who was working out of London and was well connected to the Israeli intelligence community. Hortrich asked Frank if he could get hold of F-4s to sell to Iran. As a result of these inquiries, I called Hortrich and decided he was worth trying to recruit into our service. He had a couple of good qualifications—he was dabbling in arms, and he was desperate for money.

After meeting Hortrich in Nice, I decided we were going to "pick him up"—our phrase for taking someone on. He was to be used in smokescreen operations as an information and disinformation person, but not in any direct sales negotiations. Whenever we needed someone to enter a deal and screw it up, or someone to leak information in the United States, or make various contacts around the world, he would do it. With the new name we had given him—John de Laroque—he was one of the few outsiders we recruited who would not be duped.

With de Laroque in place, we were ready to put up our smokescreen. The idea was to use sleight-of-hand all around Europe to obscure our operations. Arms traders were duped into setting up deals with the Iranians, not realizing that before negotiations ended, everything would fall apart. What we did was create a bogus international arms market in which it seemed that just about every broker and every country was trading with Iran. In hotel lobbies, on park benches, in private homes there were fantastic proposals between hopeful arms dealers and "desperate" Iranians. Telexed lists circled the globe with orders for aircraft, missiles, tanks, bombs, and artillery, accompanied by figures with more digits than telephone numbers. Of course, the deals couldn't be allowed to go too far. As soon as it looked as though

an arrangement was drawing embarrassingly close to completion, John de Laroque—the former John Hortrich—would step in
and put a wrench in the works, and it would be back to square
one. To keep the dealers keen, Israel would pay their traveling
expenses, though it was well worth the payout to hide the real
deals that were going on between Israel and Iran.

After the John Street operation had been compromised and we
had hastily left the U.S., the Joint Committee decided we should
move to Montreal. But after several months there, we found it too
out-of-the-way to do our work efficiently, so we moved again—
this time to London.

There the operations resumed smoothly. Matters were helped
considerably by the fact that by this time the U.S. had decided it
would cooperate in selling American electronic equipment to
Iran. Thus, our separate undercover operation was no longer
needed, and the Joint Committee was reunited.

My life was divided between Israel, Europe, and the U.S.. with
side trips to various other parts of the world. I didn't have much
time for Freddie and our daughter, Herut, who were living in
Portugal.

My job for the time being mostly consisted of shopping for
weapons and equipment, handling money, and handling our
agents. The others in the Joint Committee in Tel Aviv were in
charge of setting up the business structures—a complex job indeed.

The way the Joint Committee was set up, profits from our arms
sales were not funneled back to the budget or the Finance Ministry, where they would have to come under parliamentary supervision. Instead, the idea was that the operating budget of the Joint
Committee would be taken from the profits of the arms sales—
under the supervision of the Mossad comptroller. The profits
ballooned almost immediately into a huge extra-budgetary slush
fund.

Disbursements were requested from the Mossad comptroller
through either of two channels. One was on behalf of the heads of
the intelligence community—the chief of Mossad or the boss of
IDF/MI; the other was directly from the Prime Minister's Office,

through the first cabinet secretary, Aryeh Naor, or the counterterrorism adviser, Rafi Eitan. The comptroller would then issue the disbursement orders.

In order to have deniability, the people appointed as fronts for these extra-budgetary funds were the signatories for the cut-out companies that were set up in Europe and other parts of the world. These accounts were owned, theoretically, by these companies.

I had been selected as one of three signatories, and the arrangement was that if money had to be released, two out of the three had to sign. Too many signatories would have confused the process; only one would have created difficulties should he or she unexpectedly become incapacitated or die. According to the rules set by the committee, aside from full committee meetings, these three people were not to be in the same place at the same time. Powers of attorney were given by myself and the two others to remaining members of the committee to be used in case of death or other eventualities. Two of us physically had to be at the bank unless two had given full powers of attorney to the bank officer, or to a single member of the selected three.

To avoid placing all the golden eggs in one basket, 200 bank accounts were opened in 27 reputable banks around the world, but at any given time only about a quarter of these accounts were active. Accountants in Vienna, London, Sydney, New York, and Tel Aviv had the power to shift these monies from account to account once every few months, but they had no power to draw money. This was a safeguard to ensure that funds did not go astray and end up in an account that nobody else knew about—it was insurance against the individual accountants, who were changed within their firm from time to time. Anyone on the track of the money would have trouble keeping up.

By 1983 the slush fund was running like a well-oiled machine. Once a year the 200 numbered accounts in Europe would be changed, and the names of the paper companies would be altered. The only name that was never changed was that of the holding group, Ora.

The unwritten rule we operated under was that Israel would not go directly to the arms manufacturers or the weapons industries. Whenever we deemed it necessary to buy American equipment from the United States, either from the manufacturers or from stocks held by the U.S. military, we would approach the designated CIA people. They in turn would purchase the arms and place them at the ready for our collection in warehouses. These were usually at Marana, a CIA airbase near Tucson, Arizona. The first batch of weapons was flown out of there in October 1981. If, on the other hand, we were buying U.S. matériel from NATO stocks in Europe, the hand-over would be at Liège, Belgium. Israel would fly in chartered cargo planes to pick up the matériel, and then the aircraft would return to Tel Aviv. From there they would either fly directly to Tehran or to a second country before carrying the weapons on to Iran. Sometimes a third country would be used. In 1983, for example, to cover our tracks—and as a lesson learned from the downing of one of our planes—aircraft loaded with arms landed in Western Australia, en route to Tehran, with the permission of the Australian Security Intelligence Organization, which knew what was on board.

Other favorite countries used in the smokescreen were Guatemala, Peru, Kenya, Paraguay, and South Africa. If Paraguay was used, the planes flew on to South Africa—the same route normally taken by the CIA when shipping arms to South Africa. So Paraguayan officials who were aware of the South African trade assumed that an aircraft landing in Asunción and filled with weapons was on its way to South Africa, when in fact its final destination was Iran.

The division of the spoils depended on the origins of the weapons and the costs involved in shifting them. Everyone did well out of the trade. The Americans made their profits by selling to us, we made our profits by selling to the Iranians, and the Iranians got their weapons—although the price they had to pay was astronomical.

In the beginning, Israeli end-user certificates were given to the CIA for the weapons, but after mid-1982 the practice stopped. When we bought equipment from European countries, however, they would not release it without Israeli end-user certificates to cover themselves from their own parliaments—even though they knew that the matériel was going to Iran. The countries involved were Austria, Belgium, and Sweden—until that country's prime minister, Olof Palme, said no.

Britain was also involved, but Margaret Thatcher's government had a slightly different way of carrying these things out. Unknown to the British people, their government had been supplying military equipment to the South Africans for years. Mossad files are full of incidents of Liberian-registered ships leaving Southampton loaded with artillery shells and electronics for South African fighter aircraft. Prime Minister Thatcher allowed the use of the same channels to supply matériel for Iran. The equipment at first included spare parts for Chieftain tanks and later Marconi radar equipment and electronics for the American F-4 planes that the Iranians had.

With these arrangements in place and working well, and a huge disinformation campaign going on in Europe with arms dealers and would-be dealers, we also needed a network of trusted agents around the world to help keep the operation running. I had already found a good operator in the man we were now calling John de Laroque. There was one other major player in the network— Nicholas Davies, the London *Daily Mirror*'s foreign editor.

Davies had been recruited by Mossad in the 1970s. The connection had come through a former British Special Airborne Service (SAS) officer, Anthony Pearson, who ran a company called Strategic Intelligence Services. The firm, located in the mid-1970s at 55 Sutherland Street, London SW1, provided espionage services to Israel, among others.

Pearson was known for recruiting mercenaries out of Lafayette, Louisiana, and sending them to remote parts of the world. In southern Sudan in the early 1970s his men helped the Moslem government's troops in fighting against the Christian-Animist revolutionaries. In the Seychelles in November 1981, some of his men participated in an unsuccessful coup, getting only as far as the airport, where they were arrested for bringing in AK-47s in golf bags. According to Mossad files, Pearson also could arrange an assassination for $50,000—splitting the fee with the hit man, who would be recruited in Louisiana.

When I met him, Nick Davies was involved with the Pearson group, but not in its more exotic adventures. He simply took photographs and made reports on Arab nations while he was on overseas journalistic assignments and passed them on to Mossad. At the time, Davies was married to an Australian-born actress, Janet Fielding, who had starred in the *Dr. Who* television series. He was paying child support and alimony to his first wife, and he was also making substantial payments on old debts from an unsuccessful printing business he'd tried to set up in the 1970s. Israeli intelligence knew he was hungry for money, and suggested I meet him to sound him out for assignments in our arms-dealing operations.

We met for the first time in the lobby of London's Churchill Hotel in the first half of 1983. Pearson and an associate, a former colonel in the Jordanian Army named Mohammed Radi Abdullah, were also present. Davies struck me as just what we had in mind—intelligent, well-traveled, and a charmer. In addition, he had a taste for the good life, which meant he'd always need money, and he was close to Robert Maxwell, who at that time did not yet own the *Daily Mirror*, but did have a relationship with Israeli intelligence.

At an opportune moment, I told Davies, "We're looking into you working for us on a full-time basis."

"Do you want me to leave my job at the *Mirror*?" he asked. The tone of his voice suggested that was the last thing he wanted to do.

"No," I said, "of course not." I didn't need to tell him that his job was a perfect cover.

"By the way," he said, "you know Mr. Maxwell is trying to buy the *Mirror*."

"Yes," I said, "I know." The whole of the Israeli intelligence community knew. And we were all hoping he would succeed.

Davies was interested but couldn't decide for sure whether he wanted to become involved in the arms game. Taking photographs for Mossad was one thing. Getting caught up in brokering massive amounts of weapons was something else. But his interest was such that he asked me to his house for lunch, where I met his slim and very attractive wife. He seemed anxious to please Janet, and I got the impression he was afraid of losing her. From a purely mercenary point of view this was good; it made him vulnerable.

I arranged a trip to Israel for him—the Israeli military spokesman's office had a practice of inviting journalists from around the world on free trips to Tel Aviv. I went to his beach-side hotel in Tel Aviv, and we reached an agreement. He would cut off all other unofficial "business" relationships, including those with Pearson and Radi, and he would be used as a London office conduit for arms, our contact man for various Iranian and other deals. His home address would be used on stationery, and during the day his direct office phone number—822-3530—to which only he had access as the *Daily Mirror's* foreign editor, would be used by Israel's Iranian contacts. The Foreign Desk never had a truer definition.

After we officially signed him up, and it was agreed he would work in liaison with me, his financial worries ended. Over the years he was to receive more than $1.5 million on an official basis from Israel—all of it coming from the slush fund—but he was also able to rake off other amounts by making sure, for example, that contracts were drawn up with certain dealers. His earnings were paid to him, and he deposited them into bank accounts in the Grand Cayman, Belgium, and Luxembourg.

What he did with the money was none of our business, but we did know that his second wife, Janet Fielding, divorced him and sued for £50,000 and that he said he paid her off. The money he received enabled him to pay his debts to the banks, but he didn't spend his money in an obvious way. Following our advice, he kept his office car, a silver Ford Escort, provided by the *Mirror*. But he did buy a four-story house at 1 Trafalgar Avenue, in the Elephant and Castle area of London. The phone number—231-0115—was important, because the premises were used by us as an office.

It wasn't long before Davies was traveling the world for us—to America, Europe, and Iran. And he was very good at what he did. We would phone him, sometimes two or three times a day, on the foreign editor's phone, mostly collect calls from pay phones, hundreds of calls that bypassed the *Daily Mirror* switchboard. When he answered, he would just say, "Nick Davies."

Davies was called in only if we needed to use our "London office." When a request came in from the Iranians, we would judge which country was best suited to provide the requested weapons and who was in the best position to talk in that country on our behalf. In Davies's case, he would call dealers or the supplier and introduce himself as a representative of the Ora

Group, an Israeli company based in London. He would set up a meeting, usually for a weekend, and he would fly to the capital city concerned and set up the deal, arranging for the number of weapons to be supplied and how payment was to be made. The dealers or manufacturers he contacted would often call Israel, if they had any contacts, to verify that he was genuine. There was a memo in SIBAT, the Ministry of Defense's foreign sales office, that any questions about Davies and other key members of our arms network should be referred to me.

The sales and the smokescreens worked brilliantly. We became very good at setting up the deals, disguising them, and delivering the goods. There were deals going on all the time in the years from 1981 to 1987, far too many to enumerate. But the 1983 deal for TOW missiles serves as an excellent example of the kind of operation we were running.

The Iranians wanted to get hold of this weapon, an electronically guided anti-tank missile. The Iranians knew that the only way to stop the waves of Iraqi-operated Soviet tanks crossing the border was to get their hands on TOWs. Israel had 4,000 TOWs in stock, and they were getting old. Their power supplies were due to run out in two years, in 1985.

In late 1983 I traveled to Iran, using the same "boarding-card swap" as before, and met the speaker of the Iranian Parliament, Hojjat El-Islam Ali Akbar Hashemi Rafsanjani. We spent some time discussing the politics of the region. Then Rafsanjani got down to business, telling me quite frankly, "We are growing desperate. The Iraqi forces look like they're overrunning us. We must have weapons that can stop their tanks. You know what I'm talking about. We want your TOW missiles."

A deal was later struck with my old friend Sayeed Mehdi Kashani. Iran would get the 4,000 TOWs for $13,000 each, and they would be shipped from Israel direct to Bandar Abbas on a Liberian-registry ship. Kashani, however, asked for $800 extra to be charged on each TOW, bringing the total that Iran had to pay to $13,800 each. The added $800 per missile was to be paid into a separate account in Europe. Kashani insisted it was a special fund for the revolution, whatever that meant.

The Joint Committee decided on two moves before the sale went ahead: putting into action a big deception or disinformation campaign and obtaining explicit permission from the Americans for the sale, even though theoretically we had general permission to make such sales.

The explicit permission was given to a committee member over the phone by Gates, and it was taped in our office. The deception campaign we came up with worked like this:

We arranged for a French-registry, twin-engined Cessna to fly to Tel Aviv's Ben-Gurion Airport and cause a stir by trying to land without identifying itself or requesting permission from the control tower. Predictably the control tower took the necessary steps, and within minutes the unidentified aircraft found an Israeli fighter jet on each wingtip. This time the occupants had no hesitation in revealing who they were—one was Kashani; the other a Frenchman, Jean-Paul Yves. They were permitted to land, but were instantly detained until the purpose of their flight could be determined. It was a weekend, and I was summoned from home to go to the airport to establish what they were doing in Israel. I held back a grin as I saw Kashani sitting in an office, his Philippine passport on the desk in front of him.

The prearranged plan for the two men to draw attention to themselves had worked. The two were eventually allowed into the country, but security men followed them to their hotel. The word quickly went around that two arms dealers, with $70 million to spend, had arrived in Tel Aviv in the hope of purchasing weapons from Israel for sale to Iran. It had been left to me to make sure that the right people heard about it.

I approached an Israeli arms dealer, a former lieutenant colonel in the Israeli military, Arieh Jacobson, who had been introduced to me by a former major, Israel Goldsmith. I told Jacobson that Israel had to do a secret deal with Kashani for the sale of 4,000 TOW missiles to Iran and that there could be a nice financial spinoff for whoever could arrange it.

Jacobson was very impressed by the proposition and was keen to get involved in the deal. He told me he would work on it with another arms dealer, former Brig. Gen. Abraham Bar David. With dreams of making a fat profit, they went to SIBAT, and supposedly secret discussions began. But word leaked out, and it wasn't long before half the world heard that two arms dealers were in Israel trying to negotiate the purchase of TOW missiles.

Kashani and Yves eventually left empty-handed. The world learned that Israel would have no part in selling TOWs to Iran, but it was also leaked that Bar David and Jacobson would be continuing their negotiations with the Iranians. Officially there had been no deal. In the eyes of the world the Israeli government had put its foot down.

No one, especially not Bar David or Jacobson, knew that the whole scenario had been one big smokescreen, because, while Kashani and the former Israeli officers were negotiating madly, and telexes were flying back and forth around the world, the TOW missiles were quietly shipped to Iran. It was a brilliant piece of deception that meant duping a number of our own people, and I know that when those involved learn for the first time how the wool was pulled over their eyes, they are not going to be at all happy. But everyone who deals with arms, officially or unofficially, can expect to be tripped up once in a while.

The payout arrangement for that first shipment, totaling $55,200,000, was designed to hide that massive sum. It was agreed that the money would be spread out through various branches of the Allied Irish Bank.

Under the agreement drawn up by Kashani and Omshei, we were not to touch the money until the TOWs reached Iran. In fact, our committee paid the Israeli Ministry of Defense only $3,000 for each missile—a total payment of $12 million. Kashani's account received a total of $3,200,000. A further $800,000 was used for transport and insurance. The rest, $39,200,000, was profit for the slush fund.

As far as the world was concerned, Israel—and the Americans—had clean hands, but on the war front, the reality was that the Iranians were blasting the Iraqis with U.S.-made TOWs. Once they got through the first 4,000, another 4,000 were to come from NATO stocks in Europe, followed by a further 4,000 from the U.S., coming through Guatemala and Australia—12,000 TOWs in all up to 1987. These, we believed, eventually changed the face of the war.

*　*　*

Iran was so grateful for Israel's assistance that the committee was told, "Anything you want from us, you have only to ask." And there was something we, and the Americans, were very interested in getting our hands on. The battle tank most used by the Iraqis was a Soviet T-72. However, a number of the more advanced T-80s had already been sold to Iraq. The Soviets were, in fact, using the conflict to battle-test them, and these were what we wanted.

In 1985, the Iranians captured three T-80s, two riddled with holes, the third with damaged chains only. We told the Iranians we'd like to have that one. They happily obliged, and the tank was shipped to us from Bandar Abbas. We shared knowledge about the T-80 tank with the Americans at technical DIA and IDF/MI conferences, but we never revealed that we had actually got hold of a T-80. The Americans were told that the information came from two Jewish immigrants from the Soviet Union who had worked as engineers at the T-80 plant.

While our slush funds grew steadily, unusual overhead costs diminished the profits. True, we were selling weapons to the Iranians with a 50 percent to 400 percent mark-up on the ex-factory price, but the actual cost of procuring and delivering them was high, too. There was a huge network of arms brokers to be paid, money to be handed over to those involved in "smoke-screen" deals, bribes to be paid to politicians and civil servants, campaign "donations" to be made around the world, and other expenses. The "donations" sometimes cost more than the weapons themselves.

Contributions were even made from the slush fund, albeit indirectly, to U.S. politicians, including Democrats on the Iran-contra panel. This may be one reason that the full story behind the Iran-contra scandal never materialized. Even though Israel leaked details about some of Oliver North's activities, the Democrats, many of whom were well aware of what was going on, kept quiet about the huge flood of arms that had been running to Iran through Israel. Tel Aviv, not wanting its own arms deals with Tehran to be exposed, had paid them off through various, often convoluted, contributions to the American Israel Public Affairs

Committee (AIPAC). I don't know who at AIPAC knew the ultimate source of these contributions, but it was clear someone did.

In Britain our committee passed money in the same fashion to the Jewish Reform Movement, confident that this money would be channeled to the Conservative Party. Because of the friendship with Britain, the Mossad European operations headquarters was moved in 1982 from Paris to London and set up in a building on Bayswater Road.

A further example of the very special friendship that Israel established with Britain came when the Falklands war erupted. Israel froze the sale of weapons to Argentina, despite existing contracts for Kfir aircraft. As a result, the British government, covertly but officially, reimbursed Israel for its losses on the contracts. Of course it was known throughout the intelligence community that Israel was also keeping British politicians happy through the Jewish Reform Movement's Torah Fund. The friendship soured, however, in 1988, when Margaret Thatcher supported the sale of military equipment for unconventional warfare to Iraq. It was particularly abhorrent for Israel that her son was involved in it.

Aside from the contributions being made in the United States and Britain, payments were being made all around the world, and those who received them kept their mouths shut—even in faraway Australia. Australia was often used by the Joint Committee for "parking purposes," aircraft refurbishment, and stationing of slush-fund monies. In 1982 I first visited Australia to hire an accounting firm and open accounts in four major banks. Eventually monies deposited in Australian banks reached the amount of approximately $82 million U.S.

Starting in early 1986, 12 C-130 aircraft we had purchased from Vietnam were shipped to Western Australia for repairs and refurbishment. In 1987, while the Iran-contra hearings were going on in the U.S. Congress, some of the arms going to Iran were temporarily parked in Western Australia. Approximately 60 containers of artillery shells from North Korea were parked in Fremantle Port. Four thousand TOW missiles that went from the U.S. to Guatemala were shipped to Western Australia and held for approximately two months at a naval base on Stirling Island.

Silkworm missiles purchased from China for Iran were also parked at Stirling Island for approximately two months.

In February 1987 a "contribution" was made to the West Australian Labor Party by our U.S. counterparts in the CIA. In gratitude for the use of Australian soil for the transfer of arms to Iran, Richard Babayan, a contract operative for the CIA, received a check for $6 million U.S. from Earl Brian, who was acting on behalf of Hadron, a CIA "cut-out." Babayan traveled to Perth and stayed at the home of Yosef Goldberg, an Australian businessman of Israeli origin who was well connected to Israeli intelligence and to the local Labor Party headed by Brian Burke, then premier of Western Australia. Babayan handed the check to Goldberg, who in turn gave it to Alan Bond in his role as the guardian of the John Curtin Foundation funds. This money was passed on by one of Robert Maxwell's companies in Australia to be held by the Pergamon Press Trust Fund in Moscow. Babayan later corroborated the details of this operation in a sworn affidavit.

Despite the high costs involved, profits were still made on the sales to Iran. At various times the fund reached peaks of more than $1 billion. At its height it stood at $1.8 billion, with money constantly coming in and going out—a huge turnover that would have made a successful conventional enterprise very envious. The Likud leaders running the government intended to use the money for three main purposes.

The first was to finance activities of Yitzhak Shamir's faction of the Likud Party. Between 1984 and 1989 no less than $160 million was funneled to Shamir's faction, handled by the deputy minister in the Prime Minister's Office, Ehud Ulmart, who was very close to the prime minister. Other funds were contributed to the whole Likud Party, especially to its 1984 and 1988 election campaigns. That amount totaled about $90 million.

Second, the slush fund helped finance the intelligence community's "black" operations around the world. These included funding Israeli-controlled "Palestinian terrorists" who would commit crimes in the name of the Palestinian revolution but were actually pulling them off, usually unwittingly, as part of the Israeli propaganda machine.

A key player in some of these operations was the former Jordanian Army Col. Mohammed Radi Abdullah, the man who was with Pearson and Davies when I made our approach to Davies. Today in his early 50s, Radi was decorated by King Hussein of Jordan for his bravery in the 1967 Middle East war. However, his family fell out with the king because they were not willing to participate in the mass slaughter of Palestinians by the Jordanian Army in 1970. The family emigrated to London. The colonel married a woman related to Saddam Hussein and went about setting up a number of companies, including shipping offices in Cyprus and Sicily.

Radi became known as a businessman who championed Arab and Palestinian causes in Europe. But he missed his homeland and the days when he was lauded as a hero. He fell to the ways of the West, started drinking heavily and spent a fortune on gambling and women.

In the mid-1970s, to recoup his losses, Radi went to work for Pearson, who was supplying intelligence information to Israel. With Radi's unwitting help, Pearson began to acquire intelligence about Palestinian organizations in Europe. The way he did it was by selling arms to those organizations. An arms dealer named John Knight, who ran a company called Dynavest Limited, located at 8 Waterloo Place, London SW1, and another dealer who operated out of Sidem International Limited, Appleby House, 40 St. James' Place, St. James' Street, London SW1, acquired arms from Yugoslavia. They would sell them to Radi, who would in turn sell them to the Palestinian terrorist, Abu Nidal, and other Palestinian groups. Radi was unaware of Pearson's Israeli connection, as were the others involved.

While it may seem curious that Pearson, a man working with Mossad, was encouraging a Jordanian to sell weapons to Israel's enemies, it was actually all part of a very cunning plot. In doing business with these groups, Radi learned what they were going to use their weapons for and unsuspectingly passed the information on to Pearson. Pearson, in turn, passed on to Mossad the intelligence about the movements of the groups and the number of weapons they had.

Based on Radi's unwitting tips, over a two-month period 14 or 15 Palestinians were wiped out. Word went out among the

Palestinian groups that Radi was working for Israeli intelligence and, fearing for his life, he took a trip to Baghdad and presented his case to Abu Nidal himself. Abu Nidal believed his story that he had been used—which he had—and put the word out that Radi was "clean." The blame was placed on Yasser Arafat's group—Palestinian factions at that time were warring among themselves.

Radi went back to his drinking and womanizing, and the money he made selling arms for Pearson all drained away. At that very vulnerable point, in 1978, Pearson stepped in again and offered Radi a £200,000 loan. This time, Pearson made it quite clear to him that the money was coming from an Israeli source. The desperate Radi accepted the loan and was recruited to work for an antiterrorist group in Israel run by Rafi Eitan.

The group's methods were rather unconventional, one could say heinous, but it had operated successfully for years. An example is the case of the "Palestinian" attack on the cruise ship *Achille Lauro* in 1985. That was, in fact, an Israeli "black" propaganda operation to show what a deadly, cutthroat bunch the Palestinians were.

The operation worked like this: Eitan passed instructions to Radi that it was time for the Palestinians to make an attack and do something cruel, though no specifics were laid out. Radi passed orders on to Abu'l Abbas, who, to follow such orders, was receiving millions from Israeli intelligence officers posing as Sicilian dons. Abbas then gathered a team to attack the cruise ship. The team was told to make it bad, to show the world what lay in store for other unsuspecting citizens if Palestinian demands were not met. As the world knows, the group picked on an elderly American Jewish man in a wheelchair, killed him, and threw his body overboard. They made their point. But for Israel it was the best kind of anti-Palestinian propaganda.

In 1986, Radi was involved in another slush-fund black operation—the well-documented attempt to blow up an El Al plane. Or at least what was publicly perceived to be an attempt. In fact, it was a cold, calculated plan conceived by Rafi Eitan to discredit the Syrians. At a secret meeting in Paris, Eitan told Radi that he wanted to implicate the Syrian Embassy in London in terrorism and have all the Syrian diplomats thrown out of England. Radi had a 35-year-old cousin, Nezar Hindawi, living in London, who had two things going for him—he was friendly with the Syrian Air Force intelligence attaché in London; and he had a problem with an Irish girlfriend who told him she was pregnant.

Radi went to his cousin and offered him $50,000. At the same time he told Hindawi that he wanted him to do some work on behalf of Palestine that would also rid him of his troublesome girlfriend.

"This money I'm offering you," Radi told Hindawi, "is from our Syrian brothers on behalf of the Palestinians. We want to blow up a Zionist plane. All you have to do is make sure the girl gets onto an El Al plane with explosives in her bag."

Radi arranged for his cousin to meet the Syrian intelligence officer, and Hindawi later came away with the clear impression that what he was doing was for the Arab cause. In accordance with his briefing, Hindawi told his 32-year-old girlfriend, Ann-Marie Murphy, a chambermaid at the Hilton Hotel on Park Lane, that he loved her and wanted to marry her. He was eager to introduce her, his future bride, to his old Palestinian parents who lived in an Arab village in Israel. He told her to go and visit them and receive their blessing. Then, when she arrived back in England, they would get married. Overjoyed, she agreed to go, not realizing that the address he gave her in Israel was bogus.

As far as Hindawi knew, the woman was going to be sacrificed. All he had to do was tell her that he wanted her to take a bag of gifts to his parents. But because he didn't want to risk her being stopped for having too much carry-on luggage, he would arrange for a "friend" who worked at the airport to pass her the bag when she entered the El Al departure lounge. She would pass through the regular Heathrow security checks and then be given the package containing the bomb.

Hindawi had been told that a Palestinian cleaner would pass the deadly package to Ann-Marie. In mid-April 1986, he kissed her goodbye and watched her walk through passport control to what he expected would be her death, along with that of all the other 400-plus passengers on board the El Al jumbo jet.

In the El Al departure lounge, an Israeli security man dressed in casual clothes—the "Palestinian cleaner"—passed the girl the parcel. She took it. But within seconds she was asked to submit to a search. The security people, who were in on Rafi Eitan's plan, could not afford any accidents. When the bag was opened, plastic explosives were found in a false bottom.

Ann-Marie was rushed off to be interrogated by British security. Sobbing, she told the story of the rat of a boyfriend. Police arrested Hindawi at the London Visitors Hotel, between Notting Hill and Earl's Court, after his brother convinced him to give himself up. He spilled the beans and told them that a Syrian intelligence officer had asked him to carry out the task. But Radi was not implicated. He was under MI-5 protection. As a result, Margaret Thatcher closed down the Syrian Embassy in London. Rafi Eitan had had his way, Hindawi was jailed for 45 years, and Ann-Marie went home to Ireland where she gave birth to a daughter.

These were the kinds of black operations our slush fund was financing.

The third and last main purpose for the slush-fund money was to finance the housing projects in the West Bank and Gaza Strip for Jewish settlers who had been taking over Palestinian land there. Since many members of the U.S. Congress saw these housing projects as a provocation that would impede peace in the Middle East, a lot of U.S. aid to Israel prohibited the use of the money for building in the West Bank. As part of the coalition, the Labor Party, keen to participate in a peace conference, was also against a government project for West Bank housing.

The answer, as far as Likud was concerned, was to draw on the slush fund. Tens of millions of dollars were used in the West Bank and the Gaza Strip to help build the foundations for new Jewish settlements and to buy the land from the Arabs. Although much land was simply confiscated and more taken through condemnation for government purposes, many Arabs, forbidden by the PLO to sell land to the Jews in the West Bank, nevertheless did so at inflated prices, even though they were putting their lives at risk should they be caught.

What they did was sell to various foreign Jewish front companies that were actually financed by the Joint Committee. Many West Bank Arabs became wealthy selling their land, taking the money and emigrating to other countries. As far as Likud was concerned, it was money well spent, because it was encouraging the Arabs to emigrate, while leaving land for the Jews to move onto. Their houses would also be subsidized by the slush fund.

Whenever money was to be disbursed in a big way for the West Bank, the aid of Rabbi Menachem Schneerson, the Lubavicher Rebbe, whose court is in Brooklyn, New York, was enlisted. He gave his blessing, and through his financial institutions, large amounts of money were funneled to Drexel Burnham, the now bankrupt brokerage house where crooked stockbroker Michael Milken built his junk-bond fortune. At times, billions of dollars paid out by the Iranians for arms they were going to receive— along with profits from earlier deals waiting to be disbursed— were held at various interest rates by Drexel on behalf of our front companies after they were funneled through American banks. These large deposits added to Drexel's stature, and Drexel's share of the profits from these deposits helped it underwrite huge quantities of junk bonds.

As long as there were always large amounts on deposit, there was no problem. But in 1987, the committee and Schneerson parted ways. This happened partly because Schneerson's allegiance to the Likud Party was brought into question and partly because of the formation of the orthodox Shas Party, which was at odds with the Rebbe. Shas was controlled by an Iraqi-Jewish rabbi, Ovadia Yousef, who had been the Sephardic chief rabbi of Israel. The Likud Party always considered Yousef's support essential because he had a great following in Israel's Middle Eastern Jewish communities. Up to 1987, some of the profits made for the slush fund by Drexel were used to finance the Lubavicher *yeshevot* (colleges), but this was stopped, and that money went instead to the Shas *yeshevot*.

At the same time, the Joint Committee was afraid that because the funds were being held in the U.S. at Drexel, they might be frozen, if and when the Israelis and the Americans found themselves at odds. For all these reasons, the committee decided to withdraw the funds from Drexel and from the Lubavicher court's control. This only added to Milken's growing troubles, and ultimately contributed to the fall of Drexel.

*   *   *

From March 1981 to the end of 1987 Iran spent the incredible sum of more than $82 billion on equipment sent from the United States, Israel, Europe, South America (especially Brazil and Argentina), and South Africa. The Iranians gratefully received it all—old tanks, aircraft (including old French Mirages from Argentina), TOWs, electronics, radar systems, small arms, artillery, Hawk air-to-ground missiles, Chinese Silkworm missiles, North Korean Scud missiles, Katusha shells captured in Lebanon by Israel, cannons—hundreds of thousands of tons of weaponry, whether it came straight from the factory or was the remnant of some long-dead war. Vast profits were made by the middlemen.

Iran, maintaining an army of approximately 800,000 men, faced a formidable Iraqi military force which was adding to its already well-equipped arsenal from the Soviet Union and France. Iraq was soaking up sophisticated weapons—MiG fighters, SU fighters, and French Mirage 2000s. Like the Iranians, they too were spending a fortune. As arms suppliers, the Western world and the Soviet Union could rub their hands together in glee.

As someone has pointed out, if a question had been put to a computer about what needed to be done to: 1) get the Arabs off Israel's back; 2) part the Arabs from their money; 3) keep the Iranians contained—and part them from their money; 4) keep the oil flowing; 5) make sure the world recycled its old military equipment; 6) keep the Soviets happy; and 7) make a lot of arms dealers and defense contractors rich, it could not have come up with a better solution than the Iraq-Iran war.

9

Promis

DURING 1983 ISRAEL experienced a political upheaval that would ultimately change the lives of many around the world. It began with Prime Minister Menachem Begin's refusal to shake hands with German Chancellor Helmut Kohl. Three days before Kohl was due to arrive in Israel, Begin resigned. He wanted nothing to do with a nation that was associated with the deaths of so many Jews in the war.

But it wasn't only Kohl's visit that brought about Begin's resignation. Begin believed that he personally had let down the nation over the Lebanese war. Former Defense Minister Ariel Sharon, he said, had disappointed him. Sharon's step-by-step invasion had dragged the cabinet deeper and deeper into the war and had brought about a national crisis in Israel and a public relations disaster abroad.

Then on September 16 and 17, 1982, came the massacres at Sabra and Shatila refugee camps in Beirut. Despite his well-known libel suit in New York, Sharon, it now seems clear, was aware in advance that something was going to happen. And he knew what would be the result if the Lebanese Christian militias—the Phalangists—were let into the camps. Pierre Gemayel, the father of murdered Bashir Gemayel, leader of the Christian forces and president-elect of Lebanon who had been killed in a huge bomb blast a number of days earlier, had sent a letter to

Sharon, a close friend. Gemayel, who modeled his Phalangist movement on that of Generalissimo Francisco Franco's, wrote to tell him that he would take revenge for his son's death. Many Palestinians would die. The letter came to Ben-Gurion Airport one evening in a Phalangist diplomatic pouch, which was brought to their Jerusalem office. A courier rushed the letter to the ERD duty officer, who opened it and made a number of copies. He called Sagi's office and reached Hebroni, who was duty officer that night. The original was sent by pneumatic tube to Hebroni, who read it and called Sagi at home. Hebroni made copies for the office and had the original delivered by hand to Sharon's office, where it was placed on his desk.

The evening after the letter arrived, I was walking down the street in Tel Aviv with a colleague who, like me, was aware of the letter's contents. At the time, I was about to leave for England and Ireland to oversee the movement of more weapons to Iran.

"This guy's talking about a massacre," said my friend. "It won't happen. Don't you think we would prevent something like that?"

Sharon's face flashed through my mind. I knew what a wild card he was. "No," I said, "I don't."

Three days later Israeli troops let the Phalangist forces into Sabra and Shatila. I had already arrived in London, and it was the Jewish New Year when the shocking news of the massacre flashed around the world. The next day I saw the pictures on TV in my Belfast hotel room. I wanted to vomit. The massacre could have been prevented.

A commission of inquiry headed by Supreme Court Justice Yitzhak Kahan found that while the Israeli government was not involved, it was warned in advance that a tragedy like that could happen and took no action to prevent it. Worse, it had sealed off the area as a military operations zone, preventing the Palestinians from escaping. Although the full report of the commission remains highly classified, many of us in ERD saw it; the members clearly believed that Sharon had seen the warning letter.

As a result of the inquiry, three months after the massacre, my boss, Maj. Gen. Sagi, was thrown out of office. Sharon was forced to resign as defense minister, to be replaced by Moshe Arens, the Israeli ambassador to the United States. But interestingly, Sagi's chief of staff, Moshe Hebroni, was allowed to spend three months as head of branch in the External Relations Department—time enough to wipe out any stray documentation that might implicate him and his boss in the massacres.

When the new prime minister, Likud's Yitzhak Shamir, took office in 1983, he immediately cleaned house, especially in the intelligence community, of which he had been a member for many years. Several members of the Joint Committee were forced out, including senior member David Kimche. This shakeup left Rafi Eitan essentially running the Joint Committee.

Eitan and Shamir had been close for years. Both were tough Mossad veterans who had resigned from the intelligence service in the early 1970s when they realized they were not going to get any top jobs under Labor Party rule. When Likud finally came to power, Begin decided to use Eitan, a man with considerable backbone, to give substance to the largely powerless job of counterterrorism adviser.

A generally honest man, Eitan, like many of his generation, saw the world in black and white, never grey. He was supremely committed to Israel's survival and to stamping out terrorists with no pity whatsoever. While he despised the PLO and wanted nothing more than to exterminate them, he, along with Shamir, had opposed the Camp David agreements because he felt they left the Palestinian issue unresolved. A pragmatist, he was convinced there would be no real peace until a solution to that problem was found.

With Shamir as prime minister and Eitan running the Joint Committee, our efforts to arm Iran against Iraq did not abate. If anything, we were even more aggressive. At the same time, Eitan maintained his obsessive interest in wiping out terrorism.

One of Eitan's pet projects was an anti-terrorist scheme involving a sinister, Big Brother-like computer program named Promis. It was through Eitan that I became involved in it. This was not Joint Committee work, per se, but many of the same people who worked on our arms-to-Iran operation worked on Promis also. The most prominent of these was British media baron Robert Maxwell, who made a fortune out of it. Through some of his companies, the Israelis and the Americans were eventually able to tap into the secrets of numerous intelligence networks around the world—including Britain, Canada, Australia, and many others—and set into motion the arrest, torture, and murder of thousands of innocent people in the name of "antiterrorism."

The frightening story of the Promis program begins in the United States in the late 1960s when communications expert William Hamilton, who had spent time in Vietnam during the war setting up listening posts to monitor the communist forces, was assigned to a research and development unit of the U.S. National Security Agency. Fluent in Vietnamese, Hamilton helped create a computerized Vietnamese-English dictionary for the intelligence agency. While working there, Hamilton also started work on an extremely sophisticated database program that could interface with data banks in other computers. By the early 1970s, he was well on the way with his research and realized he had a keg of dynamite in his hands.

The program he was developing would have the ability to track the movements of vast numbers of people around the world. Dissidents or citizens who needed to be kept under watch would be hard put to move freely again without Big Brother keeping an eye on their activities.

When Hamilton saw that the program he was building had so much potential, he resigned from the National Security Agency and took over a non-profit corporation called Inslaw, established to develop a software program for legal purposes. The Inslaw program would be able to cross-check various court actions and, through cross-referencing, find a common denominator. For example, if a wanted person moved to a new state and established a new identity before being arrested, the program would search out aspects of his life and cases he had been involved in and match them up. Hamilton put his knowledge to use in Inslaw, and when his bosses at NSA found out, they were not at all happy. Their argument was that as an employee of the agency, he had no right to take knowledge gleaned there to another organization.

By 1981 Hamilton came up with an enhanced program. What he had actually done was given birth to a monster. Inslaw was turned into a profit-making organization, and Hamilton copyrighted his enhanced version.

Believing that Inslaw was invaluable for law-enforcement agencies, Hamilton sent Promis to the Justice Department in 1981, offering them leasing rights; the more they used it, the more

profit Inslaw would make. The Hamilton program was sent to the
NSA for study, but in time, through arrangements made with
Attorney General Edwin Meese III, Hamilton got his program
back. The Justice Department declined to lease the program from
Inslaw, and, it soon transpired, they were using "their own"
Promis. So was the NSA.*

The U.S. government had its own plans for Promis. Some American officials thought the Israelis might be able to sell it to intelligence agencies around the world, so in 1982, Earl Brian
approached Rafi Eitan. After studying the program, Eitan had a
brilliant idea.

He called me in to see him. "We can use this program to stamp
out terrorism by keeping track of everyone," he said. "But not
only that. We can find out what our enemies know, too."

I stared at him for a moment. Suddenly I realized what he was
talking about. *"Ben zona ata tso dek!"*—Son of a bitch, you're
right! I exclaimed. All we had to do was "bug" the program when
it was sold to our enemies.

It would work like this: A nation's spy organization would buy
Promis and have it installed in its computers at headquarters.
Using a modem, the spy network would then tap into the computers of such services as the telephone company, the water
board, other utility commissions, credit card companies, etc.
Promis would then search for specific information. For example,
if a person suddenly started using more water and more electricity and making more phone calls than usual, it might be suspected he had guests staying with him. Promis would then start
searching for the records of his friends and associates, and if it was
found that one had stopped using electricity and water, it might

---

* Hamilton and his wife Nancy sued the Justice Department, charging that
Justice stole the enhanced Promis program from Inslaw and gave it to NSA.
Justice claimed it did get a program from Inslaw but returned it unused. NSA
said it developed its own enhanced program and gave it to other intelligence
agencies, but not to the Justice Department. Since the stalling by the Justice
Department had thrown Inslaw into bankruptcy proceedings, the Hamiltons
pursued their legal remedies in Bankruptcy Court. The lower courts upheld
their claims against the Justice Department, but an appellate court ruled that
Bankruptcy Court was the incorrect venue for such claims, requiring them to
refile the suit in District Court. A congressional investigation into the matter
has also been slowly proceeding.

be assumed, based on other records stored in Promis, that the missing person was staying with the subject of the investigation. This would be enough to have him watched if, for example, he had been involved in previous conspiracies. Promis would search through its records and produce details of those conspiracies, even though the person might have been operating under a different name in the past—the program was sophisticated enough to find a detail that would reveal his true identity.

This information might also be of interest to Israel, which is where the trap door would come into play. By dialing into the central computer of any foreign intelligence agency using Promis, an Israeli agent with a modem need only type in certain secret code words to gain access. Then he could ask for information on the person and get it all on his computer screen.

According to computer experts I have spoken to in Israel, the trap door is undetectable. Nations receiving Promis might wonder if there was any trickery by Israel, but they would not be able to find anything—especially as it was experts provided by Israel who installed the program.

Rafi Eitan did not want to risk having a trap door developed in Israel. Word might leak back that the Israelis had been bugging software and then handing it out to others. He didn't even suggest that the NSA develop the trap door because he had a great sense of national pride. As far as he was concerned, it was Israel's idea and would remain so. Yet it still had to be kept secret. Eitan decided it would be best if a computer whiz could be found outside the country.

I knew just the man for the job. Yehuda Ben-Hanan ran a small computer company of his own called Software and Engineering Consultants, based in Chatsworth, California. I had grown up with him, but I didn't want him to know that I was scouting him for a possible job. I had to sound him out, to find out if he was a blabbermouth.

When I called on him, I told him I was in California on holiday and had decided to look him up. We chatted about our days as kids, and he introduced me to his wife, a Brazilian Jew. I decided he was right for the job—he was not conspiracy-minded, and it was unlikely his suspicions would be aroused. Five days after I left, he was approached by an Israeli man who hired him to build an external access to a program. Yehuda wasn't told what the program was all about. He was simply given blueprints and set about his work for a $5,000 fee.

With the trap door in place, Rafi Eitan selected Jordan as the nation on which it would be tested. Earl Brian made the sale through his company, Hadron. Brian accurately represented it as a program that would help stamp out the Palestinian dissidents who had long been a thorn in the side of King Hussein. A team of Hadron computer experts went to Amman and began setting up Promis software for Jordanian military intelligence. They also hooked it up with the various computers that had already been sold to Jordan by IBM in the late 1970s. These computers were linked to the water company, the telephone company, and every other public utility.

The Hadron team did one more thing. They hooked the Promis program to a small computer attached to a telephone line in an apartment in Amman. That apartment was occupied by a businessman who had close connections with Mossad. From his home, he was able to dial up various public services, as well as the military, and use Promis to find out everything about everybody—as well as to tap into Jordan's military secrets. Because of his business as an importer-exporter, he often had an excuse to fly to Vienna. He would take the New York-bound Aliya Royal Jordanian Airlines flight from Amman and get off in Vienna. There, he would pass computer disks loaded with information to a Mossad contact.

So what Israel and the Americans learned was that the system was workable. The two countries also found out that the Jordanians had a tracking system of their own which was being used against Palestinian movements. Israel and the U.S. were laughing. The Jordanians tracked the Palestinians, our man tapped into their information, and we knew as much about the whereabouts of one terrorist or another as the Jordanians did.

The Americans came up with the idea of selling this valuable program to governments and their intelligence networks all over the world. But first they had to produce their own version of Promis with the secret trap door. The Americans handed a copy of their program to Wackenhut, a Florida-based company that worked for the U.S. intelligence community. The company also had a computer development unit located on the Cabazon Indian Reservation in southern California. The Indian reservation was used by Wackenhut, which was contracted by the technical services division of the CIA, for developing special equipment such as special-purpose electronics, anti-terrorist devices, etc., as well as hallucinogenic drugs. It was done on an Indian reservation because there was no state jurisdiction and the federal authorities who would have jurisdiction turned a blind eye to the operation.

It was here that the trap door was built into the U.S. version of Promis, based on Israeli information.

The CIA group that was to use Promis had not handed the program back to the NSA to have the trap door fitted by them for the simple reason that they didn't want the NSA to know about it—interagency competition was fierce. Only this small CIA group, headed by Robert Gates—who was to become head of the Central Intelligence Agency in October 1991—was in on the secret. So we now had a small group in Israel and a small group in the U.S. that knew about the trap door.

The next step for both Israel and the United States was to find a neutral company through which the doctored Promis program could be sold. It was agreed that the head of the company had to be a man who could be trusted to keep intelligence secrets, who had contacts with both Western and East Bloc countries and who had a respected businessman's image. The man they came up with was Robert Maxwell.

Robert Maxwell, whose body now lies in Judaism's most revered burial ground on the Mount of Olives overlooking Jerusalem's walled city, formed his ties with Israel in the early 1960s when a meeting was arranged for him with Yitzhak Shamir, who was then in Mossad operations in Europe. Shamir's was an important role, soliciting information from all the European-based agencies employed by Mossad. The rendezvous with Maxwell was arranged through the Mapam (United Workers) Party in Israel, which was part of the labor movement and had close connections with Maxwell's leftwing colleagues in the British Labor Party.

The two men were brought together by Aviezer Ya'ari, a kibbutz member and one of the ideological leaders of Mapam. Uppermost in Ya'ari's mind was making contact with the Soviets, so it was a natural move to put Shamir in touch with Maxwell, who had intelligence links with the Soviets beginning in World War II. Shamir's past as a Stern Gang terrorist appeared to make this an unlikely pairing, but Mossad was keen to make any connections it could with the KGB, and the belief in Tel Aviv was that Maxwell, for all his pride in faithfully serving in the British Army, remained on good terms with "friends" in the East Bloc.

Maxwell, who had been elected a British Labor MP in 1964, and Shamir shared an antipathy for the Americans, and were to become friends of heart and spirit.

Rafi Eitan knew of Maxwell's long association with Shamir and with Israel, so he suggested that the British mogul would be the perfect front for selling Promis. The approach to Maxwell, on Israeli prompting, was made in 1984 by Sen. John Tower, an old friend of the publisher's, who was close to the then vice president, George Bush—in fact, many years before, Tower had helped Bush get into Congress. Always interested in military and intelligence affairs, Tower had served as chair of the Senate Armed Services Committee. According to Maxwell, when Bush was head of the CIA in 1976, Tower approached Maxwell to connect him and Bush secretly on a person-to-person basis with various Soviet intelligence people. When Maxwell delivered, Tower became his friend for life. With the relationship strengthening over the years, Tower subsequently was appointed a director of Maxwell's Macmillan publishing company in the U.S.

Tower's approach to Maxwell to use his network of companies to market Promis was made on behalf of the CIA group headed by Gates. But it was Rafi Eitan who mapped out the workings of Promis for Maxwell at a discreet meeting between the two men in Paris in 1984. I do not know whether Maxwell was made aware of the trap door and how Israel and the U.S. could use this to gain external access to the computers of whatever agencies were using the program. But Maxwell would have been made perfectly aware of the general uses of Promis and how intelligence services could keep tabs on anyone about whom they had cause to be suspicious.

Maxwell agreed he was in a perfect position to market Promis for the Americans and the Israelis. After all, his Berlitz language schools were located all around the world. All he needed to do was set up or buy computer companies through Berlitz Holdings. This would distance him personally from the massive spy project.

A perfect company for Maxwell to take over already existed. Israeli-owned, Degem was a computer business located in Israel, Guatemala, and Transkei, the Bantustan "homeland" controlled by South Africa. The Transkei connection is particularly interesting.

Menachem Begin, Israel's prime minister from 1977 to 1983, had a long-time friend, Yaacov Meridor, who was running various businesses with South Africa through Transkei. A minister without portfolio in Begin's government, he was raking in a fortune in commissions from whatever country wanted to beat the boycott on South Africa by dealing through Transkei. Everything had to go through Meridor or a company he owned. One of these companies was Degem, which was actually controlled by Israel's military intelligence and was providing computer services to the South Africans and to Guatemala.

Poor Meridor became unstuck—and opened the door for Maxwell—when he was caught up in a huge scandal. Along with a Texan, Joe Peeples, and a Romanian expatriate who claimed to be an energy professor, Meridor drew up a blueprint for using the sun as a source of energy to generate vast amounts of electricity. Although this was theoretically feasible, the Meridor blueprint went far beyond the realm of possibility. However, he and his pals succeeded in selling the idea to the wealthy Hunt brothers of Texas for $2 million. For this price, the Hunts were told they had the rights to sell the scheme in the U.S. Meanwhile, Meridor decided that he would seek a huge loan from the Israeli Treasury, but he slipped up badly. He went on TV and told the nation that he was working on a solar energy system with which Israel would never have to use oil or coal for electricity again. All he needed was a little financial backing.

Expecting the money to come pouring in, Meridor was stopped in his tracks when a scientist from the Weizman Institute went on TV three days later and declared the whole thing a fraud. Joe Peeples, who was not able to give the $2 million back to the Hunts, was jailed for fraud. The Romanian, who had not received any of the money, went free. Meridor lost his job as a cabinet minister—and his credibility. His Transkei operations were another casualty. And then along came Maxwell who, knowing exactly what he was buying it for, sank his money into Degem.

After the initial success with Promis against the Jordanians, and following Maxwell's agreement to buy into Degem, Promis was put to use in the most horrible way in a number of countries. One egregious example was Guatemala. Pesach Ben-Or, a representative for Eagle, a well-connected Israeli arms-dealing company, had been helping the military regime there set up a computer tracking system to fight the leftist insurgency. But it proved to be inadequate.

In 1984 Israeli intelligence came to an arrangement with the man who was calling himself *El Jefe de la Nación*—the Chief of the Nation—General Oscar Mejía Victores. He agreed to allow a warehouse to be used for storing weapons coming secretly out of the U.S. en route to Iran and to allow planes carrying arms from Poland to the Sandinista government in Nicaragua to fly over Guatemala and even land there on occasions. The Israelis, with a wink and a nod from the Americans, had been selling certain arms from Poland to the Sandinistas in their fight against the contras. Of course, there were other factions in the U.S. and Israel—including the Oliver North group—who supplied weapons to the contras.

The price Israel had to pay for this agreement was that the Eagle company, run by Pesach Ben-Or in Guatemala and his associate Mike Harari in Panama, and overseen by Ariel Sharon, would continue selling weapons to the Guatemalan government. On top of that, Israel would install a very sophisticated computer program that would help the military stamp out insurgents. The Mossad chief in Israel, Nachum Admoni, told Sharon not to interfere with the computer program, and in turn the intelligence community would not interrupt Eagle's unofficial sale of arms to the Guatemalan military. It was a case of everyone scratching everyone else's back.

In setting up Promis in Guatemala, Israel employed the services of Manfred Herrmann, a German expatriate in his 60s, who owned an automobile spare-parts company in Guatemala City known as Sedra. It was agreed that Herrmann would represent Israel's arms-running company, Ora, in Guatemala, while his

partner, Baldur K. Kleine, would be the representative in Maitland, Florida, from where he would coordinate all our activities
in Central America. Shortly after Maxwell took over Degem, Rafi
Eitan asked Earl Brian to meet Kleine in Maitland and give him
Promis with the trap door in place.

After Kleine passed the program over to Herrmann, I also provided Herrmann with the Israeli version. If the Americans were
going to tap into Guatemala, so were we. Because we were running
arms through the country, it was in our interests to keep a general
watch on things. However, we soon realized that Guatemala just
did not have the computer equipment or skilled operators necessary. For Promis to work, everything in the water company and the
electric company had to be computerized. Not only that, lists of
identification numbers would have to be updated and a new
census conducted. With so much information then available and
with suspicious characters going into a central computer, Israel
and the U.S. would be able to break in to the central system and
learn everything the Guatemalan government knew.

Israel turned to Honeywell, the Israeli franchise of which was
owned by Medan Computers Ltd. All the technicians working for
Medan were military intelligence reservists and experts on computers. Those at the top were made aware of the Promis program,
although they did not know about the trap door. When Medan
pointed out that their computers would not be suitable, we arranged for them to act as brokers for IBM equipment in Guatemala.

In that same year, 1984, Guatemala was swept up in a campaign
led by *El Jefe* himself to bring the nation into the computer age.
TV, radio, and newspapers lauded the move. Computers, it was
said, would give jobs to everybody. Common people would no
longer have to live in the Dark Ages. Photographs were produced,
showing lines of young women sitting behind computers. It was
compelling stuff. Every soldier in the army, many of whom could
hardly read or write, was taught to use a keyboard. Maxwell's
Degem, through Herrmann's Sedra company, moved into offices,
railway stations, and airports, and even set up terminals at the
most remote roadblocks.

The venture, from the intelligence point of view, was a major
success. Suspected dissidents couldn't move anywhere without

Big Brother watching them. Even if they traveled under a false name, various characteristics, such as height, hair color, age, were fed into roadside terminals and Promis searched through its database looking for a common denominator. It would be able to tell an army commander that a certain dissident who was in the north three days before had caught a train, then a bus, stayed at a friend's house, and was now on the road under a different name. That's how frightening the system was. By late 1985 virtually all dissidents—and an unknown number of unidentified innocents—had been rounded up. In a country whose rulers had no patience for such people, 20,000 government opponents either died or disappeared.

And how was it all funded? In 1985 Guatemala started to be used heavily as a drug transit point to the United States from South America. Mejía, the Chief of the Nation, was, in fact, a much bigger drug boss than Noriega. Massive amounts of drugs were shipped into the United States, and part of the revenue went back to Guatemala to help finance the Promis operation. This would all have been impossible without the wink and the nod that the CIA gave.

In Transkei, Degem was of immense help to the white South African regime. Promis was trap-doored because the Israelis were interested in a number of people in South Africa. Promis, in effect, was a killing machine used against black revolutionary groups, including the African National Congress. Almost 12,000 activists were affected by the beginning of 1986—picked up, disappeared, or maimed in "black-on-black" violence. "Kushi kills Kushi" became a well-known term in Israeli intelligence circles with Chief Gatsha Buthelesi's black death squads doing the dirty work.

It was a simple operation: As a result of Maxwell buying Degem, Promis was installed in the Transkei. It pulled in information on dissidents, and death lists were drawn up and handed over to Buthelesi and his group, who went out on the rampage to finish them off.

At one point a planned strike by black miners was stopped when Promis was used to find the instigators. They all disappeared as Promis tracked them down through their required identity passes. Of course the South African security network just loved it. The computer, which had become their ally, had links to the computer in the military compound in Pretoria, and although it was the Israeli version that was being used, the information went straight to the American Embassy for one very simple reason. The embassy has a common wall with the military compound, so it was nothing to string a wire between the two establishments.

The hypocrisy of it all was that Robert Maxwell was officially against any relations with racist South Africa, and his *Daily Mirror*, which he had bought in 1984 for £113 million, had championed one-man, one-vote, regardless of race. Yet under cover of his Degem company he was actually helping the South African government in a way they had never been helped before. If he had said no to Israel, no doubt some other company would have been used to get Promis going, but at least Maxwell's conscience would have been clear.

Promis was sold all over the world. With their respective intelligence connections, Earl Brian's Hadron and Maxwell's Degem engaged in friendly competition, wiring the world for intelligence purposes. The Americans, through Hadron, sold Promis to a number of countries, including Britain, Australia, South Korea, Iraq, and Canada. Many of the secrets of those nations' intelligence agencies were read through the Promis trap door by the Americans. Moreover, the CIA was making a fortune hawking Promis software. Up to 1989 they had made at least $40 million from that venture alone.

The Israelis, through Degem, sold Promis to the East Bloc and other countries, including Brazil, Chile, Colombia, and Nicaragua. An abridged version of Promis, including the trap door, was also sold by Degem to Credit Suisse in 1985. The Likud Party, which had control over Israel's intelligence network, was very interested in knowing which Israelis might have opened accounts there. After finding out who had lodged rake-off money there, the party could approach the individuals and ask for a "donation"—or threaten exposure.

Maxwell's Degem even sold Promis to the Soviet Union in the late 1980s. The path had been cleared for Degem to get into the

Soviet Union—in 1986 and 1987, a computer company, Trans-Capital Corporation, of Norwalk, Connecticut, had been allowed to export high-tech IBM computers to the Soviet Union, even though there was a general ban on selling such equipment to the East Bloc. But the CIA's Robert Gates had lifted the barriers. When the Soviets expressed a desire to have Promis, Degem technicians fitted it to the IBM computers, complete with the tell-all trap door. In early 1991, before the coup against Mikhail Gorbachev, Soviet military intelligence, GRU, was still using Promis. So whether he knew about the trap door or not, Maxwell gave the Americans a direct line into Soviet military intelligence.

I believe that one of the reasons I was arrested in 1989 on a trumped-up arms charge was that I, on behalf of the Israeli government, threatened to expose what the Americans were doing with Promis if they continued their support of chemical weapons being supplied to Saddam Hussein's Iraq.

Leigh Ratiner, the attorney who was representing Inslaw and the Hamiltons on behalf of his Washington firm, Dickstein and Shapiro, also had something strange happen to him when he began to find out about the real use of Promis. Suddenly, he was called in by his senior partners and told they wanted him to leave the case and the firm, and they started negotiating his severance agreement. Ratiner received $120,000 a year for five years, provided he agreed not to practice law during that period. Ratiner, who was always puzzled by the abrupt dismissal from a firm he had been with for ten years, assumed that the Inslaw case was the reason, but was not sure why. Some time after his dismissal, he saw a memo from his old firm's files which reported that, a week before he was called on the carpet, an assistant attorney general had been talking to one of the firm's partners and had advised that they ought to get rid of Ratiner. That was all Ratiner learned.

He did not know what I knew. A few weeks before Ratiner's dismissal I had seen a cable that came in to the Joint Committee from the United States. It requested that a $600,000 transfer from the CIA-Israeli slush fund be made to Earl Brian's firm, Hadron. The money, the cable said, was to be transferred by Brian to Leonard Garment's law firm, Dickstein and Shapiro, to be used to get one of the Inslaw lawyers, Leigh Ratiner, off the case. Ratiner, it seems, was removed for doing too good a job for Inslaw.

10

The East Bloc

WHILE THE MARKETING of Promis continued as a parallel operation through the mid-1980s, the Joint Committee's main work of selling arms to Iran was also growing. We were combing the world for arms to buy and resell to meet Iran's needs, and it wasn't always easy to find them. Once Yitzhak Shamir became Israel's prime minister in 1983, however, we were able to expand into an unexpected but cooperative new market—the East Bloc countries. And strangely enough, Robert Maxwell played an important role in this too.

To understand how this turn of events occurred, you have to know something about Yitzhak Shamir.

Unlike Menachem Begin and his Labor Party predecessors, Shamir bears a special hatred for the United States and everything it stands for. Before he became foreign minister in 1981, Shamir had visited the U.S. only once, for three days. His ardent anti-American feelings stemmed from his conviction that the U.S. was partially responsible for the massacre of the Jews by the Nazis in the Second World War. Shamir believes that if the U.S. had sacrificed British interests in the Middle East and reached some type of accord with Hitler on the region, the Jews in Europe would have been allowed to move from the concentration camps to Palestine, and Hitler could have solved the "Jewish problem" without exterminating the Jews.

Despite his reputation as a rightwinger with capitalist lean-ings, it was Shamir who first tried to open a line of communica-tion between Israel and the East Bloc. The seeds of this radical policy change were sown in the early 1980s when, as foreign minister, Shamir met his Bulgarian counterpart at the United Nations. The introduction was arranged by Shamir's old friend, Robert Maxwell. The Bulgarian quickly learned that Shamir's wife was originally from Sofia and that she longed to visit there again. A visa was arranged for her, and when she returned to Israel, she filled her husband's ear with all the wonderful things her hosts had done for her. When Shamir became prime minister in 1983, he decided he was going to open the East Bloc to Israel and try to wean his country away from its complete dependency on the U.S. The latter was to prove an impossible task.

But after Shamir assumed control, there was greater openness from the Likud Party toward the East Bloc, whereas the socialist Labor Party remained completely closed on the subject. With the door ajar, opportunities presented themselves for a whole new trade—in arms.

Viktor Chebrikov, head of the KGB, gave his personal blessing to the new venture in 1984. He simply saw the merits in the issue. The Soviets' interest was to keep the Iran-Iraq war going, to arm the Iraqis, and to make inroads into Arab money. But to maintain the conflict, Chebrikov realized it was also important to supply the Iranians. He saw that former Soviet policy was lopsided, and he believed much could be gained by starting a relationship with Israel.

Although the Soviets traditionally backed the Arabs, they had by this time started to open up to more imaginative policies. They figured that they could not be known to be selling arms to Iran, because they were already selling to the Iraqis, but, like the United States, they believed that a third country could be used. Poland was ideal. It would help Poland's financial situation, which was in a shambles; and there were merits in having a balanced Middle East policy with a tilt toward Israel because the Soviets thought there should always be a threat to the Saudi oilfields. So Viktor Chebrikov gave the okay to the Polish minis-ter of foreign trade to deal with Israel on the sale of arms to Iran.

It was about this time that I met an Austrian, Dr. Dieter Rabus, who was the son-in-law of the director of a Polish factory that made T-72 tank engines. Rabus knew Robert Maxwell, and the two men helped open doors for Israel to start business deals with the Poles. They made the necessary arrangements, Maxwell even speaking to the Polish defense minister, Gen. Wojciech Jaruzelski; and on our instructions Nick Davies flew to Warsaw, without a visa, early in 1984.

His lengthy discussion with a representative of Cenzin, an office in the Ministry of Foreign Trade that deals with the export of arms, took place at the airport. The two men met in the VIP room, where Davies spent three hours arranging for me to visit.

In mid-1984 I made my first trip to Poland, flying through Vienna. On arrival, I was met at the aircraft's steps by a major in the Polish Intelligence Service, the UB. I had no visa, and I immediately explained I wanted no Polish stamps on my passport. We certainly couldn't afford to broadcast to any official who might see my passport in another country that Israel now had links with Poland. Unlike other arrivals, I was not searched; nor did I have to slip my passport under a one-way mirror and wait. I was given an immigration card with stamps on it, and it was tucked into my passport.

These were among Poland's darkest days. The Solidarity movement had been crushed—temporarily, as it turned out—and soldiers were all over the airport. The aura of poverty overwhelmed me as the stretch diesel Mercedes swept through the capital's bleak, grey streets. The limousine drew up at the Victoria Intercontinental, by all reports the best hotel in town. As I checked in, the major hovered anxiously. It had been suggested to me that I drop the occasional "tip" to anyone who was helpful, but how much do you give a UB officer? Do you give him money at all?

I tucked a $20 bill into his hand. He almost fainted. I thought he was going to kiss the ground at my feet. He strode away, beaming.

The Polish spooks were none too subtle. In the wall of my room beside the bed was a small hole through which I could see the lens of a probing camera. I didn't worry about that so much as the lens that was aimed at the toilet seat. I covered that lens with paper.

My host for dinner that evening was a general who was head of military production in the Ministry of Defense. We went to one of the few restaurants available for foreigners. The food was supposedly French style, but I found the deep-fried fare inedible. The general didn't seem too worried—within ten minutes he was in a happy mood from the slivovitz he had downed.

The bill came to the equivalent of $4. I was about to pay when the general held up a hand of protest.

"No, no," he said. "Do you have a $1 bill?"

I peeled off a note for him, and he strode off through a side door. When he returned, he explained that the manager had been more than happy to make the bill disappear on receipt of $1—his salary was only $10 a month.

Poland's education system and medical services were good, but it remained a run-down, impoverished society in which everyone was screwing everyone else, morally and physically. Foreign men never had it so good. You asked a local woman a simple question in a foreign language, somehow making yourself understood on how to get to a certain place and she'd cling to you all the way, regarding you as a potential meal ticket. I didn't involve myself—with lenses peeping into my hotel room, I wasn't going to risk being compromised.

One day, during my discussions with various defense officials, I became desperate for some fruit. I was told that the only place I might find some was at the black market. The general took me. Even though my visit to Poland was sanctioned, I assumed we were being followed. The black market was a place where desperate Poles sold everything they owned. Anything that was new, such as mink hats or TV sets, had probably been stolen from the factory, I was told. Caviar was on sale—smuggled out of the Soviet Union by people who had worked there. Suddenly amid the chaos I found a woman who was selling oranges, a dozen of them, smuggled in from Spain by her husband. With the help of the general, she asked me if I wanted half an orange or a whole one. I said I'd take the lot and gave her $5. I'd made a friend for life.

If you knew the right people, you could make a fortune through the unofficial money exchange. The problem for most visitors was that there was a restriction in using the black market. You declared what you had in dollars when you entered the country, and you declared how much was left when you departed. If you'd officially changed only a relatively small amount of dollars, officials assumed you'd bought zlotys on the black market—and you were in trouble.

The official exchange was 200 zlotys to the dollar. The unofficial, black-market rate was about 1,100 zlotys to the dollar. The general got me a special dispensation card allowing me to pay for everything in zlotys. He also worked out a private deal with me. He would buy dollars from me for 1,000 zlotys each. He would then sell them on the unofficial market for 1,100, making himself a nice little profit. I, on the other hand, had that dispensation card, available only to the ruling élite. It meant that, unlike other foreigners, I could buy airline tickets and pay hotel bills with zlotys. And because airline tickets were subsidized by the government—no matter what the airline—I could, for example, buy an Austrian airline ticket from Warsaw to Vienna, on to New York, and back to Vienna and Warsaw for $250. And with the right to pay in zlotys, the black-market exchange rate made the airline ticket even cheaper—a round trip for less than $50!

After my introductory trip to Poland, when I established warm relations with a number of officials and expressed interest in purchasing Soviet-made Katusha shells from them, I returned to Warsaw in the bitterly cold winter of December 1984. As the snow floated down, my hosts greeted me eagerly, and I was left in no doubt that my earlier negotiations had borne fruit. The Poles said they would like to show me the factory that made Kalashnikov AK-47 assault rifles as a prelude to striking a deal. They weren't Katushas, which is what we would have liked, but there was no doubt the Iranians could use the rifles. The Iranians were happy to take anything that went bang.

The factory was in the city of Radom, some 80 kilometers from Warsaw. I thought the journey from the hotel might take an hour and a half. My friend the general, his bodyguard, and the driver of the Mercedes laughed when I mentioned this. I soon found out why. First the diesel fuel in the motor, which had frozen solid in the sub-zero temperature, had to be thawed with a small gas burner placed under the engine. Then we had to travel very slowly along a road that was thick with snow. And, of course, there were police checkpoints.

"Is there a kiosk or a restaurant on the way so I can buy some cigarettes?" I asked.

Once more they burst into laughter. "Where do you think you are—America?" the general asked.

The journey took four hours. Radom was a rail junction with smoke billowing from tall factory chimneys. Everything was grey, even the snow. At the munitions factory, we were taken to the top floor where the offices were located. I was received by an enormous fat man, who was introduced to me as the manager and who also happened to be the local Communist Party boss. He spoke no English but managed "Welcome, welcome, welcome . . ."

I presented him with the three bottles of Johnny Walker whiskey that I had brought, and he led us to a large room, which he explained through a translator was his "gift room." It was full of shelves packed with whiskey.

"These are gifts from our friends," he said. "But there is nothing here from Russia. The Russians don't bring anything worth keeping."

Onto the side of my bottles he stuck a label on which he had written "Israel." Other packages had labels in Polish reading Germany, France, Libya, and Syria. Those packages revealed a lot. You could see from the boss's gift room who was doing business with him.

He brought out four bottles of slivovitz—potent plum brandy—and led us to the dining room for lunch. The driver and the bodyguard had to wait in the outside lobby. A table had been prepared—a grand feast of meats and seafood that would have fed ten Polish families for a week. I sat next to the English-speaking production manager, facing the manager and the general.

Within 15 minutes the general and his Party companion had managed to drain two of the bottles. Meanwhile I talked to the production manager, a soft-spoken, sensible man. He told me about the factory. Many of the residents of Radom worked on the premises, which produced typewriters, sewing machines, and Kalashnikovs. He ordered a woman assistant, who was hovering to make sure our table requirements were met, to bring out a typewriter. A few minutes later a bright yellow manual contraption was placed in front of me.

"Do you make an updated model of these?" I asked, thinking he was showing me an antique.

"Nothing is fresher than this one," the production manager

proudly replied. "This has come straight off the production line. These are very popular all over Poland."

When I asked him about word processors, he said they were no good because they were too unreliable. Polish typewriters were the best. Everybody bought them. Nobody was interested in other models, it seemed, and I soon found out why. No others were available.

"Take it," he said, pushing the machine toward me through the plates of food. "This is our gift to you." I didn't have to ask whether the sewing machines were electric, and later I saw the foot-pedal versions the factory produced.

We finally got around to talking about Kalashnikovs. A sample was ordered, and we cut a deal then and there for 100,000. I knocked them down from $95 to $81.50 each. It was a bargain— spanking new weapons with a cleaning kit and two empty magazines. They were the cheapest Kalashnikovs ever bought.

The factory had to get the go-ahead from Cenzin, the arms export department. But I was assured that as long as they had a sale and there was money coming in from which officials could take their personal cuts, the price at which they were sold was irrelevant.

At about 3:00 P.M., with the deal in the bag and the fat man and the general standing up shouting "*L'chaim Israel*"—Long life to Israel—I decided it was time to go, even if I was being told over and again that Israel and Poland were now blood relatives. The Poles have a long tradition of anti-Semitism, but that seemed to have been forgotten for the time being. They couldn't do enough for me—even ordering the last of the anti-freeze at the local fire station to be delivered to the factory so it could be poured into the Mercedes to prevent any problems "for our beloved guest" on the return journey.

"What if there's a fire?" I asked.

"If there's a fire," said the production manager, "those irresponsible residents will be thrown into jail for being careless when the fire station was out of anti-freeze."

With the fluid in the car, a "Radom Industries" tie around my neck, a "Radom Industries" photo album under my arm, and the yellow typewriter on my lap, we headed off for Warsaw. I must be jinxed when traveling in other people's cars. Some 30 kilometers

along the road, we broke down. It may have been because the
Mercedes wasn't used to anti-freeze, but whatever the reason, we
found ourselves immobile on the snow-packed road. For the well-
sloshed general, there was no problem.

He drunkenly waved down the first car he saw, flashed his ID,
told the astonished driver that this was a military emergency, and
ordered him to drive us to Warsaw. We left the bodyguard and the
driver with the Mercedes . . . and the yellow typewriter.

"It's all yours," I whispered to the delighted bodyguard. There
was no doubt he would soon be down at the black market selling it.

The driver of the commandeered car was paid well—I gave him
$20, and the general gave him a note to show to the police check
points on his return journey to explain what he was doing in
Warsaw with Radom registration plates.

Anything could be bought. Even the woman in the phone room
at the hotel. There was only one international line available for
the whole premises, and I ensured I had it plugged through to my
room during the night by paying the woman $5. I told her there
would be another payment in the morning if she didn't discon-
nect me. She came to my room before breakfast, promised that I
could have the international line every night, then lay on the bed.
She knew about the camera, but didn't seem to care. I knew about
the camera and did care. I thanked her for her services, made her
another payment for the phone, and ushered her out.

The hotel security officer approached me later and said: "You
know the phones are tapped."

"Yes," I said, "I know."

"For $10 I can arrange to give you the tapes of the phone."

"Look, here's $10 for nothing. I know what I said. I don't need
the tapes."

Back in Israel, the Joint Committee decided we needed to put
up another smokescreen to cover our dealings with Poland. None
of us had any doubts that my visits to Warsaw had been monitored by various intelligence agencies. With the cooperation of
the Poles, I pulled in my unfortunate dupe, Arieh Jacobson, and
explained that Israel was hoping to buy Katusha shells from Poland to sell to the Iranians. Believing that he would make a
fortune, he traveled back and forth to Poland and Vienna, meeting

various Poles and Iranians and trying to hammer out a deal. John de Laroque also got arms dealer Richard Brenneke running around on the same kind of futile errands. And all the time, of course, the real negotiations were going on right under everyone's noses.

We continued to purchase Kalashnikovs. But Iran was now desperate for Katusha shells. Although they do not cause much physical damage, they wreak enormous psychological havoc with their terrifying whistling noise. The launchers can be used from the back of a truck, and can be reloaded every minute with 40 shells, which are all fired at once. We estimated that the Iranians had some 1,700 launchers, while the Iraqis had more than 2,000. Clearly, there was an endless need for Katusha shells.

While Israel was running low on supplies, we knew the Poles had Soviet Katusha shells to sell—but they had only 50,000. We were eventually able to strike a deal in which the Poles sold them to us for $800 each, and we sold them on to Iran for $1,100, including transport fees from Poland to Yugoslavia.

Such inventive deals led Rabus, the Austrian, to call Katusha shells "the dollar machine," a term that was picked up and used frequently in Israeli intelligence. When I first heard it, I must confess I was a bit taken aback. I had originally gone into arms dealing with a political purpose in mind—stopping Iraq—but several years later, I saw that it had indeed become a big money-making proposition, "a dollar machine," and the original goal had been obscured.

While the arms sales were running smoothly, there was chaos on the Israeli political front. The 1984 elections had ended with neither of the two major parties, Labor or Likud, able to establish a government with a majority in the Knesset. Both parties started jockeying for support from the small religious parties on the one hand and the leftist parties on the other. But the leaders, Yitzhak Shamir in Likud and Shimon Peres in Labor, soon realized that these small groups had no loyalties—they were shifting back and forth to see what they could get. So Shamir and Peres met and came up with a bizarre coalition agreement.

The basic term of the agreement was that the major portfolios would be divided up. For the next four years, Defense would go to the Labor Party and Finance and Housing would go to Likud. But the portfolios of prime minister and foreign minister would be shared by Peres and Shamir, with a swap after the first two years. Peres would be prime minister until 1986, and during those two years Shamir would be deputy prime minister and foreign minister. Then they would switch roles, with Shamir becoming prime minister and Peres stepping into the role of deputy prime minister and taking on the foreign minister's portfolio for two years.

The biggest mistake the Labor Party made was in thinking they were doing themselves a favor by allowing Finance to go to Likud. At the time, inflation was running wild and Labor was glad to be rid of the headache. But by giving up Finance and Housing, Labor was handing over the two biggest portfolios to Likud.

Calling itself the National Unity Government, the new coalition brought in other parties. These had no bargaining power, but two of them that got portfolios were orthodox parties—Shas and Mafdal—whose allegiance was more to Likud than Labor. So the balance of this coalition agreement was in favor of Likud.

There was one other vital factor to be considered. Even though the Defense Ministry was under the control of Yitzhak Rabin, a rival of Peres's within Labor, the intelligence community of Israel was controlled by Likud through various funding arrangements. The key people in the intelligence community had all been changed after Begin took over in 1977. They were now all Likud loyalists, and there was no way they were going to be removed, because the Likud was still in the coalition. So an extremely difficult situation had arisen for Peres, the Labor Party leader. While he had achieved his desperate ambition to become prime minister, even if it was to be for only the next two years, he was taking control of an intelligence community that had no allegiance to him.

The coalition was strange on another level: On the main issues of foreign policy and peace negotiations with the Arabs, the parties were deadlocked. They agreed not to agree.

The level of trust between the two parties was very low. The Joint Committee was, of course, also still controlled by Likud appointees. With the Labor Party of Shimon Peres in power, we had a genuine fear that the Americans or Peres's office were trying to find out where the slush fund bank accounts were held. With this in mind, the director of Military Intelligence at the time, Ehud Barak, instructed the committee to enlist the help of two very influential men—Robert Maxwell and Viktor Chebrikov, chairman of the KGB.

Arrangements were made for me to meet them in London in the spring of 1985. The meeting was held in Maxwell's office at the *Daily Mirror*. Maxwell had been cooperating with our arms business for more than a year by then, allowing his businesses to launder money for us and winking as his foreign editor, Nick Davies, carried out assignments for us. But Maxwell never got directly involved in the details of the arms deals. Mostly, his function was to open contact to the East Bloc for us. And that's exactly what he did in this case. For a KGB leader to slip secretly into a British newspaper publisher's office might seem a fanciful notion, but it was achieved with great success. At the time, President Gorbachev was on very friendly terms with Prime Minister Margaret Thatcher, so it was acceptable for Chebrikov to be in Britain.

The meeting was arranged for 8:30 A.M.—at least an hour before the main editorial staff started arriving. Chebrikov was driven into the ground-level garage at the Mirror building and took an elevator straight to Maxwell's floor. If Chebrikov had been spotted, Maxwell had an explanation ready. He would have instantly admitted the meeting and pointed out that he was backing the new thinking in the Soviet Union. He would say, quite rightly, that he was behind social democracy in the Soviet Union because that was the example the British Labor Party had set.

There was one other person present at that meeting—Mossad Director Nachum Admoni. Our purpose was to ask for assurances from Maxwell and Chebrikov that large amounts of the slush fund could be banked behind what was still known then as the Iron Curtain. Tucked away in the East Bloc, in the Soviet Union and Hungary, we knew it would be safe, as long as we could get hold of it when necessary. This was why we needed Maxwell, with his connections in the communist countries, and why we needed Chebrikov, with the power he wielded. I had no fear that the Soviets would snap up the funds—Chebrikov's involvement was as good as receiving a government guarantee.

Maxwell, via his Berlitz Language School, was to be the conduit for moving the money—the company was teaching languages in the East Bloc under various government institutional names. Chebrikov was happy to receive the money and become its guardian, because it meant hard currency in the bank until such time that Israel decided to pull it out. It was agreed that $450 million would be transferred from Credit Suisse to the Bank of Budapest in Hungary. A firm of accountants in London, who had control over the money on Israel's behalf, would arrange for the transfers. In addition to using Berlitz as a conduit, Israel also used a company called TransWorld, located in Canada—which sold Promis—to funnel money to the East Bloc.

It was agreed that the Bank of Budapest would disperse the $450 million to other banks in the East Bloc, and just to be safe we asked for a Soviet government guarantee. If anything went wrong, the Soviet government would make good the money in U.S. dollars, not rubles.

Maxwell was going to do well out of the arrangements. He received a flat fee of $8 million. In addition, whenever one of his companies was involved in transferring arms money, he would receive two percent of the gross. It was to bring him many millions of dollars.

The meeting in Maxwell's office lasted for about an hour. It was an important gathering because it marked a milestone in the relationship we had with the Soviet Union and its satellites. Before we parted, Chebrikov, who was also a member of the Soviet Politburo, gave Admoni a letter to be passed to the Israeli deputy prime minister at the time, Yitzhak Shamir. The contents are not known to me.

A few months later Chebrikov's relationship with Israel got closer in a most unexpected way. In late 1985 the Israelis stole almost a whole MiG-29, which had been standing dismantled in crates in the port of Gdansk in Poland. A Polish general, who had been involved in the Iran arms sales, had been paid to make sure that the plane, due to be shipped to Syria, was actually flown to Israel on a Soviet transport plane that had been used by the Poles for the Iranian arms. So Israel found itself in possession of the secrets of the most sophisticated Soviet MiG fighter to date.

One of the general's juniors found out about the missing crate, and it was reported to the Soviet Union. A furious Mikhail Gorbachev dispatched Chebrikov to Israel in February 1986.

The KGB chief met with Yitzhak Shamir, then deputy prime minister and foreign minister, and it was agreed that the aircraft parts would be flown back to the Soviet Union, that relations between Israel, Poland, and the Soviet Union would continue, and that nothing of the episode would be made public. The Polish general, meanwhile, was given political asylum in the U.S. following the intervention of the chief of Mossad, in return for the Americans receiving photos and details of the plane.

It was while Chebrikov was in Israel that the cordial relations between him and Shamir were cemented. Chebrikov paid only a courtesy call on Prime Minister Peres—he was not too keen on talking to the Labor Party because he felt they were being controlled by the U.S.

The KGB chief found common ground between Soviet interests and the Likud Party, particularly when he realized the strength of Shamir's anti-American attitude.

As a result of the Chebrikov meeting in Maxwell's office and Shamir's new friendship with the KGB man, things started moving very fast with the communist bloc—Poland, North Korea, Vietnam, and others—in terms of arms purchases and money transfers. On receipt of their weapons, the Iranians continued to hand out a fortune, which Israel quickly moved to the East, using Maxwell's companies.

It worked like this: The Iranian Bank Melli would issue a letter of credit on behalf of one of Israel's arms companies—they were all run under our mother company, Ora—and we would ask the foreign transfers department of the National Westminster Bank in London to guarantee it. We would deposit it in a Western European bank until cashing day came along, and the money would then be sent to the East Bloc. Direct cash payments moved faster, of course, going immediately through Maxwell's companies. If Israel acted on behalf of the Americans, selling their weapons to Iran, the money was paid into a CIA account at the International Bank of Luxembourg. When extra funds were needed by Shamir for Likud Party purposes, Maxwell's companies were used to bring the money out again. It would go to bank accounts in Luxembourg and Geneva, payable to Likud.

With all the new financial arrangements neatly in place, and with Israel's relationship with Warsaw cemented, we received a request from GeoMiliTech, a Washington-based CIA "cutout," or front company, run by former Gen. John Singlaub and his friend, Barbara Studley. GMT had an office on Weizman Street, Tel Aviv, run by Ron Harel, who presented himself as a former fighter pilot colonel in the Israeli air force, although in reality he was a former helicopter navigator.

By phone, the Joint Committee checked with Robert Gates if it was okay for us to deal with GMT. He told us he would be happy for that to happen. What GMT wanted was East Bloc weapons for the contras, who were fighting the Sandinistas in Nicaragua.

When the Poles heard their weapons were needed for a right-wing guerrilla group, they were very hesitant—but then came back and agreed to sell us anything we wanted as long as it was in stock. There was one condition: that they, in return, receive U.S. equipment requested by the Soviets—two General Electric engines of the type fitted in U.S. tanks. I didn't know how the U.S. was going to react to that, but put the Polish request to Ron Harel. America's response did not take long: the CIA was in agreement.

On May 15, 1985, Nick Davies drew up the list of weapons the contras wanted. It was:

5,000 AK-47 M-70 automatic rifles totaling $1,050,000; 50,000 spare magazines for the rifles totaling $450,000; 5 million rounds of 7.62mm ammunition, $550,000; 200 60mm mortars (commando type), $310,000; 5,000 60mm mortar shells, $185,000; 100 81mm mortars, $525,000; 2,000 81mm mortar shells, $104,000; 1,000 anti-personnel mines, $68,000. Total cost to GMT: $3,242,000, which included a tidy profit for us. (For example, the AK-47s we sold for $225 had each cost us only $81.50.)

The Poles, of course, did not want to be identified as the suppliers and said they would provide arms that were either unmarked or of Yugoslav origin. We found out later from our contacts that GMT actually got $5 million for the deal and that their books showed that $5 million had been paid to Ora. In fact, we had been paid "only" $3,242,000. It would be interesting to know what happened to the difference.

For the Iranians that year, 1985, we bought from the Poles a large number of RPG (rocket-propelled grenade) launchers, RPG-7 rockets, AK-47 ammunition, SAM-7 anti-aircraft missiles, 60mm mortars, 81mm mortars, and naval matériel. The Iranians continued to insist on Katusha rockets, but the Poles and the Yugoslavs couldn't supply more than 50,000. The Iranians pointed out that North Korea produced Katusha rockets and that perhaps Israel could get them from there. Israel's relations with that country were non-existent, but I worked on a simple philosophy: There was always a way.

I told my Polish contacts at a meeting in mid-1985: "You broker for us with the North Koreans, and we'll buy."

Cenzin called the North Korean military attaché to their office to meet me. He refused. He had no authority, he said, to meet with Israelis. He did finally come to the Cenzin building, but insisted on sitting in a separate office while my Polish contacts ran back and forth relaying messages from me. He continued to refuse to see me, and I decided enough was enough. I got up, acted insulted, and told the Poles I was going back to my hotel.

"But what about the North Korean?" I was asked.

"Fuck him," I replied. "And tell him what I said. Oh, please also relay to him that I'm sitting on a billion dollars, which is probably larger than the annual North Korean budget."

Two hours later the Poles came to pick me up. The attaché, they said, had telexed P'yongyang and he was now permitted to meet me face to face. I insisted I would only meet him in my hotel room.

The attaché, a slightly built, serious-faced man in his mid-40s who spoke Korean and Polish, arrived with a Polish-English translator. While mouthing niceties, he made his political points: "We have nothing against Jewish people, except for the fact they suppress Palestinian rights. Americans we don't like. The atrocities committed by Americans in my country are unbelievable. My parents were both killed by American bombs."

When he was a young boy, the attaché and many other parentless children had been evacuated to an orphanage in Poland during the Korean War. He'd spent most of his childhood in that institution. Between his reminiscing, we talked rockets—Katusha rockets. North Korea could let us have 200,000, but he conceded that the only person with the authority to close the deal was the North Korean defense minister. And no, it wasn't possible for me to talk to him by phone—everything had to be done by telex. I insisted I meet the defense minister personally.

The attaché chuckled. "He cannot come to Poland. And we cannot let an Israeli citizen visit Korea. It has never been allowed."

"OK, but if you want a deal, he and I have to meet."

"Not possible on your Israeli passport."

The Poles offered to give me a Polish passport, which would get me into North Korea. I rejected this. Traveling to North Korea would mean flying over the Soviet Union, and if anything went wrong, I wanted the protection of my own country. After more telexing, I was told the defense minister might be able to come to Poland to see me at a later date. I pointed out that was too far off, and I told the attaché, "We'll remain friends—but I don't think we can do business."

I made plans to return to Israel. There were no more deals I could strike with the Poles—we'd wiped them out of everything. But at 10:00 P.M. my Cenzin contact showed up at the hotel.

"Ari," he said, "I have good news for you. You can go to North Korea."

I was told that the North Koreans had issued a visa for me. The Soviets had already been contacted by the Poles, and the Soviet Embassy in Warsaw had issued a one-month transit visa to fly over the Soviet Union to P'yongyang. We had to leave in the morning. We would fly from Warsaw to Moscow and then fly on to Chabarovsk, in the eastern Soviet Union, in time to connect with the once-a-week flight to P'yongyang.

I hadn't been given permission by my superiors to go to North Korea, but I felt the deal was so important that I had to make an "executive decision." I phoned a Mossad contact in Vienna and asked him to tell the committee my travel plans.

My Cenzin friend and I flew with the Polish airline LOT from Warsaw to Moscow. The Aeroflot flight to Chabarovsk left two hours late, and then the plane made an unscheduled stop somewhere in the middle of the Soviet Union. When we finally touched down at the tiny airport at Chabarovsk, we were too late to make the onward connection. The plane to P'yongyang had gone. And that left us with a few big problems.

For a start, my Polish companion was terrified.

"What are we going to do?" he asked me, an Israeli who had never been to this part of the world before. "The people who live in this region are uneducated barbarians. We'll be murdered in our sleep."

"Don't worry," I said, staring around the bleak airfield at the soldiers on guard duty. "We probably won't be able to find anywhere to sleep anyway." Although we were into summer, a chilly wind swept across the runway.

A second problem was money. I had only U.S. dollars and zlotys. The Pole had only zlotys. We went into the stark terminal building. Rosy-cheeked people with Mongolian features stared at us as if we were visitors from another planet.

"Is there a telephone here?" I asked.

But of course there wasn't. However, with the help of an airport official we found a telex machine and, with some difficulty, managed to punch out a message to the Pole's office.

Within two hours we had an answer back. A Cenzin official who received the message acted promptly and contacted the North Koreans. They in turn sent a message back to Warsaw asking the Poles to inform us that a plane would be sent from P'yongyang the following day to pick us up. Things were looking brighter.

We had also found out that there was an Intourist hotel in town. For a pack of Marlboros, one of the airport officials drove us into the center, a sprawling cluster of drab concrete buildings.

The matronly woman at the hotel reception desk waved away the $100 I offered and physically turned away at the sight of the zlotys. Then I produced a Parker ballpoint pen, indicating it was for her. She fell in love with it and used it to sign us in, a single room for each of us, with food included.

Later, as we stood in my room discussing how we would spend the next few hours, there was a knock on the door. A burly man entered, a Muscovite who spoke perfect English. He shook hands and introduced himself as the chief of district security—in other words, the local KGB boss. He wanted to know how an Israeli had got this far and had managed to get a visa to North Korea.

That evening he took us out on the town, which wasn't much to see, unless you liked watching people drink vodka. I wasn't sad to say farewell to Chabarovsk the following morning as I boarded the North Korean military plane that arrived exactly on time.

The North Korean defense minister himself came to the P'yongyang airport to meet us after the two-hour flight. He was proud to welcome us to his very modern city, a relief after the drabness of Chabarovsk.

I cut a deal for 200,000 Katusha shells. Israel would deposit the money in U.S. dollars in a numbered bank account in Austria— the North Koreans were not willing to be paid through East Bloc banks. And then the shipping would start from P'yongyang direct to Iran. The charge would be $600 each, and for shipping to Bandar Abbas there would be an additional $15 a shell, insurance included. More shells could be provided, he said, but it would take some months.

In the meantime, I asked the defense minister if he could arrange for me to go to Vietnam to buy more. After three days a visa to Vietnam had been arranged. I said I would put it to use in about six weeks or so after I'd returned to Israel.

A month later, I went back to Poland, picked up a visa to travel through the Soviet Union, and flew from Moscow to Hanoi. On my shopping list were not only Katushas but a number of American C-130 Hercules cargo planes—war booty left by the South Vietnamese army after the war. I spent two weeks in Ho Chi Minh City, setting up the purchase of 400,000 Katusha shells and a number of SAM-7s, payment to be coordinated through the Vietnamese Embassy in Warsaw.

On inquiring about the C-130s, I was taken to a military airfield outside Ho Chi Minh City. The huge aircraft sat there, sad, silent relics of a war that had brought so much death and devastation. I clinched a deal to buy 85 of the planes, but I did not have the technical know-how to choose the best ones. In December, a team of experts from the Israeli Air Force and Israel Aircraft Industries was flown to Warsaw and then, with a Polish representative, traveled to Vietnam. They spent a month in Ho Chi Minh City checking over the aircraft and arranging for their shipment.

With their wings, engines, and propellers dismantled, the aircraft were shipped to various countries for repairs. As a safeguard, the crews of the Liberian vessels involved were changed in mid-ocean, so that when they arrived at their destination they were unable to tell anyone where the vessel had originated. Twelve of the aircraft ended up in the care of North West Industries in Canada; others went to Western Australia; still more were shipped to Israel. It was a massive operation, but Iran got its planes. The Vietnamese had sold them to us for $200,000 each. It cost us $2 million each to fix them up. We sold them to Iran for $12 million each.

The Americans didn't get a cent, even though originally these were their aircraft. According to the Geneva Convention, any military equipment you capture is yours, so the Vietnamese were free to sell them to whomever they wished. The Americans could not believe how Israel had had the gall to go to Vietnam, buy U.S.-made planes, repair them, and sell them for a fortune.

In times of war, sometimes you win, sometimes you lose. And sometimes after the event you go on losing.

While I was traveling through Poland and across the Soviet Union in 1985, an interesting situation was developing on another front. Israel and Nicaragua were engaged in undercover contact on the possibility of reopening diplomatic relations. These secret talks with the Sandinista government had actually begun three years earlier.

In 1982, the Nicaraguan government had reached a tentative agreement with Israel under which they would cut ties with the PLO and the Israelis would help the Sandinistas in the U.S. Congress—Israel would act as a go-between with the Sandinistas and the Democrats. But this plan did not come to fruition. Ariel Sharon, then defense minister, was involved with a group of businesspeople in Central America, who were supplying arms to the contras in their efforts to overthrow the Sandinista government.

Just before the announcement of the renewal of diplomatic ties between Israel and the Sandinistas, Sharon decided to take a private holiday on the border between Nicaragua and Honduras, close to the contra camps. A more unlikely holiday spot I could not imagine. Sharon's actions, of course, sabotaged the exchange of ambassadors between Israel and Nicaragua. The Sandinistas didn't realize that although Sharon was a government minister, he was also an independent entity as far as his relationship with the contras was concerned. The question must be asked whether he took his holiday at the suggestion of the CIA, which was supporting the narco-terrorists in their push to overthrow the Nicaraguan government.

Now, three years later, as a result of our dealings in Warsaw, the Poles, who were in contact with the Sandinistas and who had technical advisers in Managua, came up with an interesting proposal. They suggested that Israel should balance the struggle by supplying the Sandinistas as well—without U.S. involvement.

The Sandinistas needed an air force, and they had no money to set one up. Israel was very interested in the Polish idea, and so Tel Aviv proposed that, even though official diplomatic relations with Managua were cool, a number of Soviet-built MiG-23s be purchased in Angola, with the Poles acting as brokers. The Soviets couldn't sell the Nicaraguans any planes because the U.S. had threatened to invade the Central American country if they did.

But now Israel was planning to go behind America's back. The proposal was that we spend $28 million from the slush fund to buy the Sandinistas eight used MiG-23s held by the Angolans. The Poles would maintain them. There was a lot of interest in this deal, but despite the fact that they had initiated it, suddenly the Poles changed their minds, suspecting that the Israelis were trying to set the Sandinistas up. If the MiGs arrived in Nicaragua while the war fever against the Sandinistas was heating up in Washington, we would be giving the U.S. government the excuse needed to invade, the Poles believed.

"We suspect Israel is acting as a U.S. lackey," I was told by one of my Polish contacts. The deal fell through. Fortunately, it did not damage our overall relationship with Poland.

In December 1985, I was on one of my frequent trips to Poland. I had just spent some time with Freddie and Herut, but now they had gone for a visit to her family in Nicaragua. As I lay in bed trying to sleep in a freezing cold hotel room in Warsaw, the phone rang. I reached out into the darkness and grabbed the handset. The caller's chilling, final words haunt me still.

"They're dead, Ari . . . Freddie and Herut are dead."

I have experienced much in my life. I have taken the bad with the good. But I cannot clearly describe how I felt then . . . in that midnight moment something in me died too.

I sat up in the darkness. Sweat poured from my body. I knew even then that it was not an accident.

She was traveling to visit a friend, I was told, a woman doctor who was working in a number of newly established clinics in the villages of Nicaragua. The car Freddie was driving had been hit by a stolen truck in a head-on collision. The driver had escaped in another car and was never found.

There was a funeral in Nicaragua. I didn't go. I was too shattered by loss and guilt. I had never spent enough time with either of them.

It is painful for me even today to think of Freddie and Herut. At the time, I was in shock. I knew no other way to escape from it than to throw myself into my work.

Because I was the junior member of the committee, I was the gofer who had to physically search the world for aircraft and weapons that could be bought by Israel and sold to Tehran. Other committee members did their work by phone and telex. The summer before Freddie's and Herut's deaths, in August 1985, we had learned that the Ethiopian government of Mengistu Haile Mariam had a number of old F-4 and F-5 U.S. jets that were grounded because of their poor condition. Even though relations with Israel had been cut in 1978 as Mengistu leaned toward the Soviets, Israel had remained in contact with Addis Ababa.

After back-channel lobbying and help from the Poles, I was told that an audience had been arranged for me with Chairman Mengistu himself. I traveled to Addis Ababa with an Israeli Air Force expert, and we were invited to inspect the aircraft before we saw the Ethiopian leader.

We were driven to a steamy airfield outside the capital where

12 forlorn F-4s were parked, their bodies rusting, engines dead, tires rotted.

"I don't fancy going up in one of those," I told my companion.

He kicked one of the wheels. Flakes of rust fell away. "Let's see," he said. "Our people are very good."

Mengistu, who had risen up through the military, greeted us warmly. A thin, handsome man in his late 40s, he struck me as an intellectual who honestly believed in his Marxist revolution. His country was poverty-stricken, he conceded, "but when the revolution is on track, everything will be all right."

We got down to discussing the planes right away.

"You are welcome to the F-4s," he said. "The price is $250,000 each."

He added that the money should be paid in advance to a Swiss bank account.

I told him I would get back to him. As we were about to leave, he mentioned there were 19 F-5 aircraft for sale, too. My colleague and I went back to the airfield and inspected the planes. This time he shook his head.

"No hope whatsoever," he said. "But, with a lot of work, the F-4s can be fixed."

On our return to Tel Aviv I contacted the Iranians. They weren't willing to buy the jets until after Israel had refurbished them. But the Israeli government wasn't going to fix them up without an Iranian commitment to buy. We had reached a stalemate . . . until the Poles came up with a solution. They would find a financier for the planes. I traveled back to Warsaw, where I was introduced to Hans Kopp, a Swiss businessman and the husband of the Swiss minister of justice.

Over dinner, I asked him, "Isn't there going to be a problem for you? According to Swiss law, there must be no financing for arms because you're a neutral country."

He laughed. "Don't worry about it, my friend. It's a grey area. The financing will come through 'paper' companies."

While still in Warsaw, I called one of my Iranian contacts, Dr. Omshei. I extracted a commitment from him that if the Ethiopian F-4s were to be repaired to a reasonable condition, the Iranians would accept them. The Poles then arranged a three-sided meeting between Mengistu, Kopp, and myself. With the Swiss financier, I flew back to Addis Ababa. We negotiated Mengistu down to $150,000 a plane.

He continued to talk about the hopes he had for his revolution. "It doesn't look too good at the moment," I told him.

He shrugged. "There is a price to pay for every revolution," he said.

Mengistu gave me a secret bank account number in Switzerland, and I flew back to Tel Aviv. There, arrangements were made for a logistics team to travel to Ethiopia, truck the planes to the port of Asmara and then move them to Israel for refurbishing. It was a big logistics problem, but as my earlier companion had said, our people were very good.

The 12 planes were going to cost a total of $1,800,000, and we were happy to be using a middleman's money, because we were sensitive that, even though the aircraft were more than 20 years old, the Americans might still get upset. Using someone foreign was perfect.

What we decided was this: Hans Kopp would "paper out"— document a false trail—$1.8 million to a French aircraft broker, SFAIR, which had offices in Paris and at Marseille airport. The man the deal was papered through was Daniel J. Cohen, technical manager of SFAIR at Marseille. (Coincidentally, Dan Cohen was the alias Gates often used.) We asked him to put the money into a special account at Banque Worms in Geneva. In the documentation, the deal looked like it was concluded with SFAIR. In fact, the money moved secretly onward to Mengistu's account, which was handled by General Trust Company, with offices at Badener Strasse 21, in Zurich.

Before the money was deposited, Israel reached an agreement that Kopp would actually be paid $250,000 for each plane— meaning he was making $100,000 on each. But without him, the deal might not have gone through, particularly as the export to Iran was going to be run through him.

Everyone realized that it could be a year before the aircraft were in a fit state to be sent to Tehran. Apart from the financial side, there was still a lot of groundwork to be covered.

As soon as the money was deposited with GTC, Israel, in coordination with the Ethiopian Embassy in Italy, sent an Air Force logistics team to Addis Ababa. During the transit of the

F-4s to Asmara, we reached a deal with the Iranians that the refurbished versions, with new engines, would be sold to them for $4 million each.

While all this was going on, another fantastic smokescreen was started up to disguise the true negotiations. John de Laroque paid the expenses of arms dealer Richard Brenneke to fly from Portland, Oregon, to Europe, where he became involved in looking for financing for 19 F-5s from Ethiopia. Intelligence agents from other nations watched carefully, unaware that a real deal had already been struck. To add to our good fortune, Brenneke bragged to a U.S.-based correspondent for the Swiss magazine *SonntagsBlick* that he was involved in buying the planes through Hans Kopp's office.

The magazine gave the story prominence. Kopp immediately sued the publication because the reality was that he had done no deals with Brenneke and had no intention of doing so. He'd already finished his work. Kopp pursued the suit as a show because of the position his wife held.

Apart from those who were duped, everyone did well. Iran had a new supply of aircraft, Kopp made his profits, the Poles got brokering fees, Mengistu boosted his bank account, and the Israeli slush fund ballooned. The Israel-Iran Joint Committee paid $1 million per plane to Israel Aircraft Industries for the refurbishing, and that, along with other costs, including the purchase, brought the outlay on each aircraft to $1.5 million. But we sold them to the Iranians for $4 million each. Our profits were deposited in the bank accounts we set up around the world.

Once again, the Americans didn't get a penny out of it. The jets were over 20 years old, and under the strategic agreement that had been signed with Israel we had every right to buy and re-sell them.

11

The Second Channel

THE JOINT COMMITTEE'S work had thrived, but the political chaos in Israel in 1984 and the bizarre coalition forged by Labor and Likud to govern the country were to have profound consequences for us—and for the world. By 1985, with Labor's Shimon Peres as the new prime minister, the foundations for a major political scandal in the United States—the Iran-contra affair—were being laid down.

While pundits looked in vain to Peres to carry out domestic reform or initiate peace talks with the Arabs, one of his most important acts early in his tenure went virtually unnoticed. This was his appointment of a former TV newsman, Amiram Nir, as counterterrorism adviser.

A ruggedly handsome man, Nir was originally a military officer in the tank corps and had lost an eye in a training accident. He now had a glass eye, but, unlike the famous former Defense Minister Moshe Dayan, he didn't wear a patch. After his release from the army, he became a TV reporter specializing in defense matters. He met and married one of the wealthiest women in Israel, Judy Moses, the daughter of the owner of the biggest newspaper chain in Israel, *Yediot Ahronot*. It seemed, however, that Nir was in competition with his wife, and he tried to prove himself independent of her and her wealth. His public image was good, and he was so charismatic that people hung on his every word when he appeared on television.

As the 1981 elections approached, Nir fully expected Labor to defeat Likud. He resigned from his TV job and went to work for Shimon Peres as a public relations adviser. The Labor Party lost the election, so Nir found himself without a job. He certainly didn't want to work for his wife's newspaper; and if truth be told, his wife's family didn't want him there either. Feeling that he should give Nir something, Peres offered him a position as chief of staff for the chairman of the Labor Party. So Nir ended up working for Peres as a gofer. After the high public profile he'd enjoyed, it wasn't too satisfying; but it was a job.

In 1984, when Peres became prime minister for the agreed two-year period, he appointed Nir as his counterterrorism adviser. Rafi Eitan, who had used the same position to develop his U.S. spy network during the Begin years, continued his spy network from his office at LAKAM, the scientific intelligence agency he now headed. When Nir, in 1984, entered the counterterrorism office, he was faced with starting from scratch because he was going to get no help from Eitan. But Nir found documents relating to the network that Eitan had created in the U.S.—and to the Joint Committee's arms sales to Iran.

Peres and Nir found themselves in a very tough spot. The Likud-controlled intelligence community would not work with them. Moreover, the Labor Party had no real power over finances. The Finance Ministry was now Likud-run. So was LAKAM, whose huge slush fund had once financed Labor projects but was now controlled by Eitan. And support for the Labor Party among the overseas Jewish communities was virtually nonexistent. If any money was to be collected, it would be for Israel and not for the Labor Party now.

But early in 1985, Shimon Peres, who still had almost two years to run as prime minister, came up with a solution to his dilemma. He saw the profit potential that the Iran arms sales had, and he wanted a piece of the action. So he decided to take away the authority for the arms sales to Iran from the intelligence community and the Joint IDF/MI-Mossad Committee for Iran-Israel Relations and give it to people close to him.

When he found out that there was no way the intelligence community or the deputy prime minister, Yitzhak Shamir, would agree to such an arrangement, Peres came up with a completely new plan: Open a competing arms channel. This way, he believed, he could bring in a fortune for his own people and also kill off the intelligence-community channel, despite its connections with the powerful Robert Gates. The operation, he decided, would be run by Nir.

Nir was ill-prepared for such an assignment. He had no experience in intelligence or business. In way over his head, he set about finding support for the new operation. Among the people he talked to was an American-Israeli businessman, Al Schwimmer, a former Israel Aircraft Industries official who had a number of contacts in the arms world. He had been brought from the United States to Israel by Peres at the height of the Labor Party's power in the late 1960s.

Nir also talked to Yaacov Nimrodi, one of the richest men in Israel. An Iraqi Jew and a former Israeli military attaché to Iran, he had established the first official government-run arms channel between Israel and Iran in the early 1960s. In 1967, after the Middle East war, he came back to Tel Aviv and made presentations to the chief of the General Staff of the Israel Defense Forces. He wanted to be military governor of the West Bank, which had just been captured, and work as a bridge for peace between the Palestinians and Israel. Being of Middle Eastern background, he said he understood the Arabs. When the IDF general staff said they were not ready to appoint him, he told them that if he did not get the job he was going to leave the army and become a millionaire.

They all laughed about it and told him, "Go and become a millionaire."

He surprised them all. As soon as his resignation from the military went into effect, he returned to Tehran. Because of the friendship he developed with the Shah, Nimrodi reached an agreement that any arms coming to Iran from Israel would have to be brokered by him—with a built-in commission. He also developed other business interests in Iran, and today his wealth is estimated at $2 billion. However, after the Iranian revolution in 1979, he found himself with a lot of money but no interesting work. Nimrodi's allegiances were never really defined. Even though he was a sort of Labor Party man, over the years he had contributed to both parties. And he had a special liking for Ariel

Sharon, who had been his military commander when he was a young officer in the IDF.

The main players developing the competing arms channel—Amiram Nir, Al Schwimmer, and Yaacov Nimrodi—decided early in 1985 that they needed U.S. support. Nir, who had found out about Robert McFarlane's special relationship with Rafi Eitan, decided that McFarlane was the man to talk to. He was, after all, national security adviser to the president.

Nir and the others were well aware that the Israeli intelligence community's arms operations from the East Bloc, the U.S., and most of the world were going at full speed. Even the defense minister, Yitzhak Rabin, a Labor Party man, was not trying to impede us because he had no interest in helping Peres.

Still, Nir flew to Washington and met McFarlane. Over a private lunch in a restaurant in the Sheraton Hotel in downtown Washington, Nir told McFarlane to cooperate with his new channel and not the established network—or else. McFarlane read the message. He was being threatened with exposure.

Having little choice, the president's man put Nir in touch with two other people in the National Security Council. Their names were Oliver North and John Poindexter.

Marine Lt. Col. Oliver North and Deputy National Security Adviser Rear Adm. John Poindexter agreed with Robert McFarlane, their boss at the National Security Council, that running a second arms channel was a brilliant idea. And they decided that if they could get it up and running, they'd do all they could to squelch the Israeli Joint Committee operation.

In their initial discussions after meeting Nir in 1985, McFarlane and North agreed that President Reagan was not the man to approach directly about the project. They didn't think much of his ability to comprehend their plans. Instead, they went to the head of the CIA, William J. Casey.

Since his stroke in 1981, Casey had been cut out of the daily workings of the CIA by Vice President Bush and Robert Gates, who by this time was effectively running the CIA. Vice President Bush was in charge of the political oversight of the U.S. intelligence agencies as part of an agreement reached in 1980 between the presidential campaigns of Reagan and Bush to unite. In an effort to regain some of his stature, Casey was now more than willing to go along with a second channel.

So Nir, North, and Poindexter had Casey on their side, but how would Vice President Bush respond? As they anticipated, he turned a blind eye. The CIA-Israeli intelligence network had proved its efficiency and was making money for the CIA budget, and on the face of it an opposition channel might lead to complications. But as we learned later from Nir, who met three times with the vice president, Bush was looking at the wider Middle East picture. By tacitly ignoring the second operation, he was placating Israeli Prime Minister Shimon Peres, who had thought up the idea. It was very important, Bush realized, to maintain a friendship with Peres and his Labor Party if the Americans were to impose their Middle East peace plan.

The U.S. proposal was to convene a conference among Israel, Jordan, Iraq, Egypt, and the Palestinians—though not the PLO, which was not recognized by Israel—with the U.S. taking the chair. The Arabs were insisting on an "international conference," which was their way of getting the Soviet Union to join in, too. But this plan, which envisioned some type of solution for the Palestinians in the West Bank, was being thwarted by Shamir and Likud.

Shamir hated the U.S. trying to take territory away from Israel. Under no circumstances would he agree to establish an independent Palestinian state in the West Bank and Gaza Strip. He saw Jordan as the Palestinian state, and he believed King Hussein, who was a close friend of Peres and an ally of the United States, did not represent anyone in Jordan but himself and a few Bedouins, the majority of Jordan's population being Palestinian.

Also, Shamir would not trust anything Saddam Hussein said and certainly would not accept the Iraqi leader as a partner in peace negotiations. Shamir saw Saddam Hussein emerging as the leader of the Arab world and a major threat to Israel's interests.

That view of Saddam Hussein was not unjustified. Since 1981 it had been accepted wisdom in the Reagan administration that Saddam Hussein was the man to fill the vacuum in the Middle East after the ousting of the Shah. The Americans saw him as a strong leader who could protect American interests and the vast oil fields, and even though he was closely connected with the Soviets they felt he could be "pulled over."

To woo Hussein, the U.S. State Department in 1982 took Iraq off its list of "terrorist countries"—whatever that meant. One year later the weapons trade embargo against Baghdad, imposed in the 1970s because Hussein was said to have provided refuge to Palestinian terrorists, was dropped. President Reagan signed a secret presidential directive (not a finding) to enable export of arms to Iraq. A number of high-level Republicans started visiting Iraq, and in 1984 diplomatic relations between the U.S. and Iraq, which had been cut during the Middle East war of 1967, were resumed. After an exchange of ambassadors, a number of U.S. businessmen began flying to Baghdad, and they helped ensure that Saudi money continued flowing for the war effort against Iran. The Americans also felt it was not wise to end the Iraq-Iran war until they had Hussein completely in their pocket.

In order to give full force to the peace initiative, the U.S. government twisted Saddam Hussein's arm in early 1985, and he publicly announced that under the right circumstances he was willing to join the Camp David process and make peace with Israel. This, he said, would be contingent on Israel stopping its support for Iran and agreeing to the establishment of a Palestinian state.

Peres found this an acceptable framework and continued to support the idea of a peace conference. But Shamir was insistent. He said no. Effectively the leader of half of Israel's government, he was able to block the initiative.

The United States decided to force Likud's hand by turning Iraq into a major threat to Israel. The rationale for this was twofold: first, to make Iraq strong enough to repel the Iranians and keep the "moderate" Western Arab, Saddam Hussein, in power; and second, to create a viable counterweight to Israel in the Middle East, thus forcing Israel to the negotiating table. But in reality, the only way this could be done was to send Saddam Hussein missile technology and chemical weapons and perhaps give a wink and nod to his receiving some nuclear technology.

This U.S. policy started in 1985, but it had to be under cover for the simple reason that Israel had many friends in Congress, and the Jewish community in the United States would never have gone along with it.

Shimon Peres actively tried to further the new U.S. policy, remaining at odds with the other half of the Israeli government, which tried to block it. While publicly mouthing words of peace, Peres had privately agreed to participate in the American double-game of arming both the Iranians and the Iraqis. He encouraged his close friend and associate, Geneva-based Israeli businessman Bruce Rappaport, to buy military equipment from Israel, such as used M-16 rifles and 122mm shells, and divert it to Iraq.

Rappaport also participated in another very strange deal involving Iraq: The Iraqis were keen to construct an oil pipeline from their oilfields in northern Iraq to the Port of Aqaba in Jordan. They wanted to build it in that area because they were effectively blocked by the Iranians in the Persian Gulf. They might have put the pipeline along the Syrian border, but Syrian President Hafez El Assad was Saddam Hussein's blood enemy due to historical differences, and Syria was, strangely enough, an ally of Iran, which put it in bed with the Likud Party. The Turks had common borders with both Iraq and Iran and wanted to stay neutral, so they wouldn't help the Iraqis either.

That left Jordan's Port of Aqaba as the only effective outlet to the sea. There was, however, one big problem. Aqaba is only about two miles from the Israeli port of Eilat, and any pipeline coming down from Iraq to Aqaba has to be built, at least partially, along the Israeli border. It would be unacceptable to the Israelis, who didn't want Iraq to have an economic boost.

But Saddam Hussein made a smart move. He contracted the pipeline out to the Saudi Bechtel Corporation, a subsidiary of Bechtel, the U.S. conglomerate. This was no coincidence. U.S. Secretary of State George Shultz and Defense Secretary Caspar Weinberger were both former executives of Bechtel. Attorney General Edwin Meese III had been an attorney for Bechtel and was a very close friend of the Saudi ambassador to the United States, Prince Bandar. And George Bush's family, including his brother—Prescott Bush, Jr., who would later also sell arms to China during the Tienanmen Square protests—had oil interests in the Middle East.

The Saudi Bechtel Corporation approached Attorney General Meese, who was also a good friend of Bruce Rappaport, although it is not clear how they met. (Israeli intelligence speculated that Adnan Kashoggi, the broker for anything and everything, introduced them.) Saudi Bechtel Corporation's problem was twofold. It could not get war-risk insurance for the pipeline construction because it was too close to Israel. Moreover, it thought it would never have a chance to get both halves of the Israeli government to agree to such a project.

In mid-1985, Meese summoned Rappaport and offered a payment to Peres so that he would guarantee the pipeline. The Meese proposal was this: Against a "comfort letter" from Peres stating that Israel would guarantee not to bomb the pipeline, disrupt the construction activities, or disrupt the flow of oil, he would pay Peres $40 million, to be deposited in Switzerland through Rappaport's account, held by Inter-Maritime, Rappaport's umbrella company for his various businesses. The comfort letter was needed for the Overseas Private Investment Corporation, an umbrella insurance company in the U.S., which would issue war-risk insurance at a price.

Shamir, in a very stormy cabinet meeting in 1985, called Peres a traitor and threatened to leave the coalition. The pipeline deal was called off. Some time later, Rafi Eitan found out about the deal and leaked it to the Israeli press. The American press later picked up the story.

Against this background, it is not difficult to understand why George Bush agreed to look the other way as the Nir-North second-channel arms operation got under way. Any hopes of getting a peace conference off the ground lay with Peres, the second channel's sponsor.

The new operation was stepping into a busy arena. The movement of weapons in 1985 was quite fantastic. There were:

1) The original CIA-Joint Committee operations, overseen by Robert Gates and backed by the Likud Party, sending weapons to Iran;
2) The illegal Sharon-Gates sales to the contras;
3) The Soviet and French conventional weapons sales to Iraq;

4) The channeling of *unconventional* chemical and nuclear weapons systems to Iraq through West Germany, South Africa, and Chile—all with U.S. support.
5) Now, finally, came the Amiram Nir-Oliver North channel for sales to Iran and sales to the contras.

As they set up the second channel, the Nir people found an Iranian businessman who was also a CIA agent, Manuchehr Ghorbanifar, who had close ties to the prime minister of Iran, Mir Hossein Mousavi. However, the North group still did not have the necessary contacts with top Iranian officials in the Supreme Council and the Supreme Defense Council to carry out the arms sales. Realizing they were going to need all the help they could get, North and Nir also got in touch with Michael Ledeen, a Jewish part-time consultant to the U.S. National Security Council, who was known for his loyalties both to his bosses in the National Security Council and to the Peres people.

With a number of supporters behind them, North and Nir next set about trying to wreck the original channel and destroy Likud's credibility in the United States. According to Nir, they came up with the idea of leaking to the FBI details of the old spy network Rafi Eitan had set up in the United States. The North group was careful not to implicate any high-level Americans involved, but they did reveal that Jonathan Pollard, a junior civilian analyst with the U.S. Navy, was a paid spy for Tel Aviv. Also exposed with the young dupe were Pollard's wife, Anne Henderson-Pollard, who was working with him, and an Israeli Air Force officer, Col. Aviem Sella, a nuclear targeting expert.

The reason no one higher was exposed was obvious. One of the top officials working with Pollard was a man referred to in the subsequent hearings, in which Pollard pled guilty, as Mr X—actually Robert McFarlane, who was now playing such an important role in setting up North's second channel. McFarlane, in fact, had been providing computer access codes of intelligence reports to Rafi Eitan in Israel, according to Eitan. Sitting in Tel Aviv, Eitan would request computer access codes for certain items he was interested in. A LAKAM representative in Washington, a woman named Iris, would pass the request to McFarlane. He would then give her back the specified access codes. She would give the codes to Pollard, who was working for the navy. Pollard would call up the information on the computer, print it on paper, then take the papers out of the office for the night. He would photocopy them, give the copies to Iris, then return the originals to the office the next day. The purpose of all the to-ing and fro-ing was to distance McFarlane from Pollard, who, in all likelihood, had no idea himself that McFarlane was a middleman.

In this way, Israel received more than a million pieces of paper—on reconnaissance satellite data, U.S. aircraft, Soviet aircraft, spare parts listed in secret catalogs (something the Joint Committee was interested in), and just about anything else documented in the U.S. intelligence community. As part of the cooperation agreement the Joint Committee had with the Soviets to sell arms to the Iranians from the East Bloc, we provided some of the Pollard papers to the KGB, but their source was sanitized. This was authorized by Shamir himself.*

When the Likud Party and the Israeli intelligence community learned of the second channel's leaking of the Pollard story, they were furious. A decision was made to try to nip the newcomers in the bud.

When damaging information has to be spread, it is rarely done by a direct phone call to a leading official. In this case, in a casual chat between Maj. Gen. Ehud Barak, director of Military Intelligence, and his colleagues in the United States, the word was dropped that McFarlane was working for Rafi Eitan. As expected, the information reached the ears of National Security Agency boss Gen. William Odom. Determined to get to the bottom of the affair, he approached McFarlane's secretary at the National Security Council. Her name was Wilma Hall, and she happened to be the mother of Fawn Hall, Oliver North's secretary.

With Wilma's help, by taping a phone conversation between

---

* The Americans and others claimed later that I had passed to the Soviets some of the papers stolen by Pollard, but the truth of the matter was that Yitzhak Shamir himself directly authorized that some Israeli intelligence gleaned from the United States as early as 1984 and 1985 be handed to the Soviet Union on request as a way of improving the atmosphere between Israel and the East Bloc. The Americans were eventually satisfied that the spy had been found with the arrest in late 1987 of Shabtai Kalmanowitch, an Israeli businessman who had migrated to Israel from Riga as a young man. Kalmanowitch was convicted of espionage by an Israeli court.

176 PROFITS OF WAR

McFarlane and Eitan, Gen. Odom proved to his own satisfaction at the end of 1985 that McFarlane was an Israeli mole, working for Rafi Eitan. The general, according to Nir as well as Eitan, took up the issue directly with the vice president. Bush was left in no doubt that it would be extremely damaging to the administration were a spy in the White House to be exposed. McFarlane was forced to resign from the National Security Council at the end of 1985, and the issue was put under wraps.

The disgrace did not curtail McFarlane's arrangements with the Nir-Oliver North operation. He simply continued to work out of his home. But Israeli intelligence—with a little help from the Iranian defense minister—was determined that the second channel should fail. In 1985 and 1986 there were various factions in the ruling Supreme Council of Iran, and the main divisions came down almost on a personal level. Defense Minister Mohammed Jalali and Speaker of the Majlis Ali Akbar Hashemi Rafsanjani were working with the Israeli Joint Committee; on the other hand, the minister for the Revolutionary Guards Rafiqdoust was aligned with Prime Minister Mir Hossein Mousavi, who tried to open the second channel. Both factions were willing to deal with any country that was selling arms to them in their fight against, as Ayatollah Khomeini called him, "the heretic from the west," Saddam Hussein.

Late in 1985 the Joint Committee made an approach to Rafsanjani, the man ultimately responsible for the purchase of arms for the military. He told us not to worry. Iran would be loyal to the people it had learned to trust.

"Sadly, the prime minister, Mousavi, who is joining hands with the new group, is not from my faction," Rafsanjani told us. "I cannot immediately dismiss this issue. I will have to handle it my way. But I can assure you that there will be no sales to Iran through these new people."

During the first few months of 1986, the Joint Committee learned of furious negotiations to arrange a trip to Tehran by the North group. I was asked to call Rafsanjani and find out what was happening.

"Trust us," he said. "Don't worry. I'll make them look like monkeys."

* * *

By April 1986 the Nir-North operation had not made the hoped-for inroads into the arms trade. Oliver North was furious, and he began an all-out attack on his competition.

According to our informant, North dreamed up a fantastic plot intended to bring about the ruin of just about everyone involved on the Israeli side of the still-active original channel. North's motives were twofold. Not only did he want revenge, but he also wanted to gain kudos by helping to show the world how the U.S. government was quashing the activities of arms dealers by arresting them and sending them to jail. Rumors were flying around at this time suggesting that the U.S. was selling arms to Iran, and North believed that public arrests would divert attention from his country while at the same time earning respect for himself.

North's idea was that the U.S. Customs Service commissioner's strategic unit, which worked out of the World Trade Center in Manhattan, would carry out a sting against the Israelis. The men who would oversee the operation were infamous Customs agents named King and Romeo. And waiting in the wings to prosecute would be the U.S. attorney for the Southern District of New York, Rudolph Giuliani.

One other character was to be brought into play—Cyrus Hashemi, one of the three brothers who in 1980 had President Carter believing they had enough influence in Iran to bring about the release of the hostages in the U.S. Embassy. After the Reagan administration took office in 1981 and the hostages had been released, U.S. Customs started investigating the Hashemi brothers. Finally, in 1984, they were indicted under the Arms Export Control Act for the illegal sale of weapons to Iran. Cyrus and his brother Jamshid were tipped off and were able to get out of the U.S. before they were apprehended, but their younger brother, Reza, was arrested. In a way, he became a hostage. His elder brothers had to come to terms with the situation and start negotiating. They asked to be represented by Elliot Richardson, who had been Richard Nixon's attorney general until he refused to fire the independent Watergate prosecutor, Archibald Cox.

Richardson, a straightforward lawyer, dropped the Hashemi brothers when they decided to sign an agreement with Customs to become informants against the Iranian exile community in Europe and the United States. He was unwilling to involve himself in agreements that involved the U.S. Customs Service. The Hashemis then hired a lawyer who was willing to do the bidding of Customs.

With Cyrus locked into a deal with Customs, and North on his path of revenge against Israeli intelligence, King and Romeo contacted Hashemi and contrived an illegal frame-up. Cyrus was to be the bait and the trap. He allowed his phone to be tapped and himself to be wired. Next, the Customs men got the Chemical Bank in New York to falsely confirm that Cyrus Hashemi had $1 billion in the bank, in his name.

The plan was for Cyrus to "sting" on tape as many people as possible who were connected with Israeli intelligence arms sales to Iran. He was to tell them that he had a billion dollars of Iranian money to spend and was eager to purchase weapons. All he needed was for his "victim" to talk in positive terms about obtaining arms, and the U.S. authorities would be able to move in and make an arrest. I was to discover later that I was one of his main targets—along with other members of the committee.

The Israeli intelligence community, through Rafi Eitan's contacts, found out that the Hashemi sting was about to take place. Director of Military Intelligence Ehud Barak decided to throw in the "dumbest" arms-dealing ex-general we could find as bait. That was retired Brig. Gen. Avraham Bar Am. Unwitting, the general made contact with Cyrus Hashemi, who fell for the bait, believing he was delivering an Israeli general to the U.S. Customs Service.

Also working with Gen. Bar Am were two Jerusalem-based businessmen, the Eisenbergs (father and son) and a British lawyer, Samuel M. Evans, who had worked for arms dealer Adnan Kashoggi. Kashoggi, incidentally, was a friend of Prime Minister Peres and had been involved in the Nir-North operation. Evans had fallen out with Kashoggi over money before the sting, so the lawyer started representing Gen. Bar Am and the Eisenbergs for their "arms deal."

John de Laroque was also on Hashemi's hit list, but John knew about the sting, and his job was to talk to Hashemi on the phone to try to find out what was happening.

There were others on Cyrus's list, but they were not real players in the Iran arms sales; they were simply opportunists who had tried to do business with Iran. Cyrus's net had indeed been cast far and wide.

Some of the people Hashemi met and secretly recorded were also captured on videotape by Romeo. Many, uncertain about Cyrus's intentions, checked with the Chemical Bank and found there was a billion dollars in his name. With this assurance, Cyrus's targets told him they were prepared to do business. He proposed to meet them all in April 1986 in New York to sign a deal for the supply of a billion dollars' worth of arms to Iran. He also asked them to supply him with false end-user certificates.

Some of the victims came to New York and were immediately arrested, but others were not willing to sign any deals in the U.S., and Bermuda was finally agreed on as the place. Cyrus was able to lure Gen. Bar Am, the Eisenbergs, and others to Bermuda.

After Cyrus spoke to John de Laroque several times, de Laroque and his "Israeli superior" were invited to meet him and the others in Bermuda. We knew it was a sting, but we decided that I would go to Bermuda with Rafi Eitan (who was traveling under an assumed name because of the Pollard affair) to have a showdown with Hashemi. We flew to Miami, and, out of instinct, I called de Laroque at his home in southern France from the airport.

"Ari, thank God you rang," he said. "I've been calling around everywhere trying to get you. Don't go to Bermuda. You will be arrested."

Grateful for the warning, Rafi flew back to Israel, and I flew to Jamaica, stayed there for three days, and then traveled on to Peru to oversee the movement of weapons that had been removed from the U.S. and parked there.

The group that arrived in Bermuda was immediately arrested on the grounds that they were arms dealers, and had made false representations to the government regarding the purpose of their visit. They were not charged by the Bermuda authorities with any crime, and were held for deportation, not extradition. When a deportation order was brought against them, and the authorities tried to put them on a plane to New York, a lawyer was able to step in and demand they be allowed to get onto a plane of their choice.

Even though a court hearing was scheduled, they were hustled, against Bermudan law, onto a plane to New York. Upon arrival at Kennedy Airport, they were all arrested by Customs officials, charged with illegal arms sales to Iran, and thrown into the Metropolitan Correctional Center in New York. On the day of their arrest, April 22, 1986, Giuliani and Customs Chief William von Raab gave joint TV interviews telling the world how the Customs Service, together with the Southern District of New York, had been successful in arresting a huge ring of terrorists— "Merchants of Death" was how they were described—who were about to sell arms worth a billion dollars to Iran. Yet it was Giuliani, von Raab, Oliver North, and their associates who had created the crime, and now they were supposedly going to bring their captives to justice.

After completing my assignment in Peru, I flew back to Israel and became engaged in urgent discussions about the group who had been entrapped. Even though Gen. Bar Am was bait, we had to get him released and destroy the Nir-North channel.

The next month, the North group's long-sought meeting in Tehran was finally go. North, McFarlane, Nir, and others arrived in Tehran from Tel Aviv on May 25, 1986. According to Rafsanjani's account, they were disguised as Irish technicians, wearing jumpsuits and toting a Bible and a cake. They were flying with 97 U.S.-made TOW missiles and a pallet of Hawk missile spare parts on their chartered aircraft, which was registered in France. They were all detained, and, after about a day—during which no substantive discussions took place—the "Irishmen" were thrown out of Iran, but not before the military equipment was removed from the plane. As Rafsanjani, supported by Defense Minister Jalali, had promised, they had been made to look like "monkeys."*

There was more to come that would completely kill off the North-Nir group's aspirations. At first they had high hopes of getting the ball rolling because, on direct orders from Prime Minister Peres, 160 U.S.-made advanced Hawk surface-to-air mis-

---

* In later investigations, members of the U.S. delegation described varying versions of the visit. Most versions described it as lasting two or three days; some said the meetings were not at the airport, but at a hotel. They all agreed, however, that Hojjat El-Islam Rafsanjani was exceedingly uncooperative. None of these reports mentions the TOW missiles. Some of them say the plane was not French, but from St. Lucia Airways. The MI/ERD records report what I have stated.

siles were to be shipped to Tehran. As these were direct prime ministerial orders, the intelligence community and the Defense Ministry could not refuse. But there were other plans afoot.

Crates of outdated Hawk 1 missiles instead of the advanced Hawks ordered by the Iranian prime minister were assembled, and an Israeli Air Force logistics officer was given a large box containing plastic stickers. On the orders of the intelligence network, he set to work. The crates of missiles were then loaded onto the chartered ship, and it sailed away to Bandar Abbas.

In Iran there was mayhem in the Prime Minister's Office when the crates were unloaded. Not only were the missiles completely out of date, but each one carried a large sticker in the shape of the Star of David. The Iranians working with the Nir-North group refused to accept them, then found out that they had even lost their money because the letter of credit had already been released.

While this incident effectively killed off the Iran end of the second channel, North also ran into problems with his plans for supplying the contras. His attempts to get his own line into Central America got off to a bad start when Amiram Nir arranged a meeting for him with Defense Minister Rabin. Unfortunately for North, Rabin had no sympathy for Prime Minister Peres and his people, and unceremoniously and disrespectfully threw North out of his office when the contras were mentioned.

Every move North tried to make in setting up his second channel was thwarted. There was, for another example, the case of a mysterious $10 million contribution made to his group by the man reputed to be the richest person in the world—the Sultan of Brunei. The money was wired to Peres associate Bruce Rappaport, who was North's banker. Our committee had someone in Nir's camp, and when we leaked the story, North denied it, claiming it was a bank error and the money had simply gone to the wrong account. This was a lie, but of course by now a number of people knew that the Sultan was supporting Oliver North.

Battle lines had been drawn. North had interfered; he had been stopped; both sides had taken revenge. Now Likud loyalists who had been targeted by North were ready to escalate the battle.

The Joint Committee decided to make the Oliver North operation public in the United States. We did not envisage the ensuing scandal; our purpose was only to bring about the release of the captured people and to destroy North. Of course, those who had been arrested and were not connected to Israeli intelligence would also reap the benefits of anything we were about to do.

My first move was to call a Middle East correspondent of *Time* magazine, Raji Samghabadi. Of Iranian origin, he had been hired in the early 1970s by *Keyhan International*, an English-language daily newspaper in Tehran. While working there, he had also been a secret member of the pro-Soviet party, Tudeh. He was very unhappy working for *Keyhan International* because all the media in Tehran were blatantly controlled by the Shah's secret police, the SAVAK. In the late 1970s, he was hired as a stringer for *Time* by the magazine's Tehran correspondent at the time, Bruce van Voorst, who had been a CIA officer working in Addis Ababa and then Tehran.

Not long after Raji was hired, the revolution occurred in Iran, and he was arrested by the Mullahs for being a CIA spy and a Tudeh member. Given the two organizations' politics, this was something of a contradiction. Some days later, through connections he had in high places, he was released and got out of Tehran as fast as he could. He resurfaced in New York, where *Time* obtained for him political asylum status and a green card, enabling him to work in the U.S. Later he became an American citizen, and *Time*, happy with his work, hired him as a Middle East correspondent.

I had met Samghabadi in 1985, through a woman I knew from my school days and with whom he was now having an affair. He was a very attractive man with a lot of fire in him. Married with two children, he had fallen in love with Rosie Nimrodi (a distant relative of Yaacov Nimrodi), an Iraqi Jew who was working in New York for the Council on Economic Priorities, a think tank. Samghabadi eventually left his wife for Rosie, but they never got married.

In May 1986, I met Raji on more than one occasion and gave him in detail the full Oliver North-Nir story. He was astonished. It was the scoop of the year—of the decade. He agreed that the level of proof I had given him was more than enough to get the story printed in *Time*. In the meantime, Rosie introduced me to another journalist, *Newsday*'s Middle East correspondent based in Cairo, Timothy Phelps. He visited me several times at an apartment in Jerusalem, where I gave him details about the Oliver North story. Rosie Nimrodi had typed notes of the North story from me as well. And she gave them out to other journalists, including a *New York Times* reporter, Stephen Engelberg, who expressed interest. However, Military Intelligence Director Ehud Barak's office told me to avoid him, so I did. I still do not know why Barak decided not to leak the story to the *New York Times*.

I was, of course, trying to get out this information on instructions from the Joint Committee. We were hoping that after the story exploded in the U.S., Giuliani would release our people. But one day Samghabadi called me with bad news: "Sorry, Ari," he said, "*Time* is not going to print the story. It's been vetoed by the editor-in-chief, Henry Grunwald himself. The reasons must be clear to you." He laughed. "People say the media in the U.S. is not controlled."

Newsday did not print the story either.

Determined to destroy the Customs Service's case against those trapped in the Bermuda sting, we decided to target the government's chief witness, Cyrus Hashemi. Since pulling off the sting, the Iranian had been traveling back and forth between his apartments in Manhattan and London.

I flew to London and, using a number provided by John de Laroque, called Hashemi's apartment. He agreed to meet me in Lindy's, a busy café in Regent Street. I had chosen the location because it would be difficult to tape in the noisy atmosphere.

We ordered coffee. I didn't pull punches. I might be accused of interfering with witnesses, but I felt it was justified after the way the lives of the accused had been disrupted.

"Mr. Hashemi," I said, "if you testify against these people in a U.S. court, the Israeli and the world's press will come down heavily on you. You'll be seen as the rat that you are. Your name will go down in history for the dirty tricks you have pulled."

"You can't frighten me," he said. But I could see he *was* frightened.

I threw one more punch. "If you testify, you are going to wish you had never been born. And don't think your American friends are going to protect you once they've finished with you."

Having dealt out the heavy warning, I followed it up with a softener. "If, on the other hand, you don't testify, and you stay here in England, my government will look after you financially."

It was a very worried and confused Cyrus Hashemi who made his way back to his apartment. He did not realize that from that point on, he was placed under surveillance and his phones were tapped by Mossad in London.

My flight to London had not been in vain. Cyrus called the office of the U.S. attorney for the Southern District of New York and told them that he didn't care what they were going to do to him, he wasn't going to testify.

By a strange coincidence, several days later Mr. Hashemi was found dead in his London apartment. But because he had been under Israeli surveillance, we knew who had been the last person to leave Cyrus's apartment before he was found dead—Joe King, one of the Customs officers working out of the strategic unit based in the World Trade Center in Manhattan. Cyrus Hashemi's death was explained as a sudden case of virulent leukemia.

A very fast autopsy had taken place—in the presence of a U.S. Customs official. The only thing that was unusual, according to Israeli intelligence reports, was the discovery on Cyrus's elbow joint of needle punctures.

Also in the possession of Mossad's London branch were tapes of Cyrus's phone calls to the Southern District of New York, including conversations with Assistant U.S. Attorney Robert Hamel. It was clear from these recordings that Cyrus had had a falling out with his controllers. We were left with the conclusion that someone had decided it was better for Cyrus to become the victim of a mysterious death than for him to be at the center of a public scandal by announcing that he was not going to testify.

Leukemia, of course, develops over years and is not a sudden disease. And Cyrus had appeared in the best of health—only a few days before his death he had played an active game of tennis in London.

12

Coverup

THE SUMMONS TO Mossad Director Nachum Admoni's office was urgent. There had been a flurry of activity in Israel at the end of July 1986 with the visit of Vice President George Bush, and I knew that the call from the director's chief of staff had to have some connection with that.

Nachum Admoni was a very intelligent, soft-spoken man who could have passed more easily for an accountant than for the head of a vast killing machine. Politically, he did not identify with either of the two factions in the government. He was the first Mossad chief to be appointed from the bureaucracy, as opposed to the military. He got the job because the man in line to take over the post, Gen. Yekutiel Adam, was assassinated by his own people.

After being selected by Prime Minister Menachem Begin in 1981, Adam lost a number of top-secret documents when he left his briefcase behind in a Los Angeles gas station. Fortunately, it was handed over to the Los Angeles police, but there was a huge internal row about the affair. The Mossad people tried unsuccessfully to use it to stop his appointment.

On his return to Israel from the U.S., Gen. Adam went on an inspection tour of Lebanon, where he was taken to an empty building that commanded a good view of southern Lebanon. As he stood on the terrace peering through his binoculars, the building received a direct hit from Israeli artillery, instantly killing him and several Israeli officers with him. While some believed it was a mistake, according to Rafi Eitan it was an inside job. The old guard in Mossad were afraid of him because he had already told people in the Prime Minister's Office that he would make a clean sweep of the intelligence network.

With him gone, Begin appointed a professional Mossad man, a bureaucrat, who would slowly take away much of Mossad's power and move it to Military Intelligence. Begin had been inspired to do this following the intelligence failures of the October 1973 war against the Egyptians and the Syrians. Admoni turned out to be all that was expected of him. He ran a tight ship, even though his powers were less than those of my boss, the director of the Israel Defense Forces/Military Intelligence. However, on the subject of arms to Iran, the IDF/MI director and the Mossad chief had equal power.

Now, as I sat before Admoni, the seriousness in his face confirmed my hunch that this was important.

"Ari, what I'm about to tell you is of the highest secrecy," he said. "In short, Vice President George Bush wants a full briefing on the intelligence network's arms sales. He has asked to meet the people involved in these sales."

"So he wants to see me." It was a statement rather than a question.

"During his visit here," continued Admoni, "Vice President Bush has received a direct plea from Deputy Prime Minister Shamir to stop the second arms channel to Iran. You and the others who have been involved with the original channel have it running smoothly. Mr. Shamir doesn't like the idea of another group getting involved and possibly exposing the whole thing—and he's told Mr. Bush this.

"Mr. Bush has also been asked to try to stop the so-called peace initiative and has been informed of our concern about the U.S. relationship with Iraq. Robert Gates has already been told of our grave concerns about chemical sales to Iraq from Chile. Mr. Bush now wants to hear everything. As this is your field and you are able to answer any questions he might raise, I want you to brief him in detail on the arms sales to date."

"If he's going to listen to what I have to say about the original arms channel, he should also be told in detail about the Nir-North channel," I said.

Admoni nodded. "Mr. Nir will also be briefing Vice President Bush. As I said, he wants to be fully appraised of everything."

I was aware that whatever I had to present to Vice President Bush was likely to fall on deaf ears. Shamir, who was poised to take over as prime minister under the coalition government, had already told the vice president that the Likud Party would not accept a U.S. peace initiative and that it would come up with a peace plan of its own.

As I listened to Admoni's briefing, it became clear that Yitzhak Shamir himself had given instructions to the Mossad chief. We talked for three hours, at the end of which, recalling our unsuccessful efforts to expose the Nir-North channel to the media, Admoni laughed and said, "One day Bush is going to hang me by the balls because of what we are doing."

George Bush was staying at the King David Hotel in Jerusalem. Being located in the center of the old city, the King David presented enormous security problems. Even logistically it proved a nightmare getting the convoy of limousines surrounding the vice president of the United States in and out of the hotel every day. So the Hilton was chosen for his briefings because it was on the edge of the city just off Highway One from Tel Aviv.

David Kimche, now director general of the Foreign Ministry and Bush's escort, was waiting for me when I arrived at the Hilton. Kimche, the former chief of Tevel, the Mossad's counterpart of the External Relations Department of the IDF/MI, and one of the original members of the Joint Israel-Iran Committee, had been informed by Admoni about my presentation to Bush. He took me up to one of the higher floors, to a suite that had been converted into a conference room.

Greeting the Secret Service men in the corridor, we went into the room. George Bush, sitting at an oblong table, was being briefed on other subjects. At his invitation, I sat at the table with my briefcase. Kimche remained. Also present was an Israeli stenographer from Mossad, while Bush was accompanied by two aides who were also supported by a stenographer.

Bush may or may not have guessed that the Israelis had also decided to videotape the briefing secretly.

Kimche explained that I was the "man on Iran" and that I would be giving a full briefing about the joint activity of the Israeli intelligence community and the Robert Gates team.

As Vice President Bush listened in complete silence, I started briefing him in detail from 1981. I told him how we had arranged for weapons to flow to Iran from various parts of the world, including from the U.S. and Israel, and I gave him a history of the war between Iran and Iraq, giving an opinion on who was winning. I also told him about the changes that had taken place within Iran.

Much of what I told the vice president I knew he was already familiar with. He was simply hearing it again from the Israeli side. He made no comment as I talked on. But there was to be a sting in my briefing. I had been fully instructed by Admoni on what to raise. My words were along these lines: "Mr. Vice President, the United States is holding an Israeli general in one of its jails on an arms charge. We believe he and his colleagues should be released."

Bush lifted his eyes and stared at me for a moment. I assumed he was fully aware of the arrest of Gen. Bar Am in the Bermuda sting. Whatever the case, he made no comment.

"There is also the question of Iraq," I continued. "The CIA is behind a program to supply Iraq with weapons. Israel is not happy about this."

The vice president shifted uncomfortably, but again said nothing. It was obvious that he had not expected this from an official who had been sent merely to brief him, not to make veiled demands.

"Finally, Mr. Vice President," I went on, "there is the peace conference. The intelligence community is not happy about influence being given to Saddam Hussein, nor about the current proposal to have a Palestinian entity in the West Bank and Gaza Strip."

Bush was looking irritated. I knew my time was up. If I pushed further, he would actually ask me to leave, which would have meant I had exceeded my instructions. I had been told to drop in those points and then back off.

I put my papers back into my briefcase and rose when he did.

Two hours had passed. He remained extremely polite and thanked me for the briefing. But I could see he was not happy.

I went directly back to Admoni's office in Tel Aviv.

"How did it go?" he asked.

A picture flashed into my mind of the stern-faced, rigid vice president with whom I had been sitting earlier.

"If you had stuck him with a knife," I said, "he wouldn't have bled."

After the deaths of Freddie and Herut, my personal life was in shambles. Lonely and confused, I turned to Ora Ben-Shalom, a woman I'd known since we'd worked together at ERD in 1979. And of course, hers was the name I'd thought of when we decided to call our slush fund holding company the Ora Group.

Ora, a very attractive, tall brunette, had been born in the United States. Her mother, a Canadian Jew, had met Ora's father, an Austrian Jew, when he was working as a cantor in a synagogue in Ontario. Her mother later won a position in the Israeli Government Tourist Office in Chicago, where Ora was born, but her father had problems finding a job there. The family moved to Texas, where Ora's father briefly worked as a cantor, but they then decided to start life anew in Israel when Ora was 12. They changed their family name from Friedman to Ben-Shalom.

The whole family was religiously observant and also ultra-rightwing politically. Ora's older sister joined the army and married, and when Ora finished high school, she too went into the army. She was fluent in English, Spanish, and Hebrew, so she joined the External Relations Department as a first lieutenant. And that's when we met. She was 19.

We had a special friendship and even went out once or twice, but I had met Freddie by then, so nothing came of it. Ora left the ERD in 1980 to work for Mossad and was eventually appointed to a prestigious position in public relations at the Hilton International in Jerusalem. But she remained a Mossad "operative," which meant she could be called in for special jobs.

Although we'd kept in touch over the years, it wasn't until after Freddie's death that I walked into her waiting arms. In late 1986 she started traveling with me on various business trips to Europe, and soon thereafter we began living together in Jerusalem.

Even after Cyrus Hashemi's death, the Oliver North story did not surface in *Time* magazine. And the Bermuda sting prisoners, with the exception of lawyer Sam Evans, remained in New York's Metropolitan Correctional Center.

During one of my trips to Tehran to arrange more arms sales, I told Hojjat El-Islam Rafsanjani about our efforts to expose the Nir-North network. He told me, "We will do all we can to help you. But first, you try again. If you don't succeed, we'll help."

But nothing appeared in the pages of *Time*, despite further contact with Raji Samghabadi. Finally, after a direct telephone call to Rafsanjani in Iran, he told me, "We'll get it moving for you."

On November 3, 1986, a small Lebanese paper, *Al Shiraa*, published an article detailing Oliver North's secret deals with Iran. After the story appeared, Gen. Bar Am and the Israeli arms dealers were released from the Metropolitan Correctional Center on bail.

"I will not hold anybody in jail for doing what U.S. government officials are doing," declared Judge Leonard Sand, the federal judge sitting on the case. In time, the charges were dropped.

The Oliver North story fell on fertile ground in the U.S. On October 5, 1986, a plane carrying equipment to the contras had been shot down over Nicaragua, and Eugene Hasenfus had been captured alive. Documents found in the wreckage implicated the CIA. Embarrassing questions were being asked. After the Lebanese article appeared, the U.S. press could hardly avoid the issue. As a result of the publicity, the Iran-contra scandal exploded. President Reagan, who may or may not have known anything about what was going on in his own White House National Security Council, ordered a presidential commission of inquiry, to be headed by none other than former Sen. John Tower, whose then aide, Robert McFarlane, had played such an important role in the arms-for-hostages negotiations in 1980. Unknown to the American public, Tower had a great deal of inside knowledge about the weapons trade with Iran.

The commission of inquiry was to investigate only the years 1984 to 1986. The conclusions Tower reached were nothing but a coverup. He declared that some people in the National Security Council, interested in the release of hostages in Lebanon, had tried to make a deal with the Iranians, selling them 97 TOW missiles and some Hawk missiles—and that was it. Granted, the second channel had not succeeded, so there wasn't much to discover about it. But Tower knew perfectly well that there was an ongoing original arms channel. Yet the Tower Commission made no mention of it. George Bush later rewarded Tower for his loyalty by nominating him for defense secretary, but he was never confirmed by Congress.

Understandably, the Democrats were not satisfied with the Tower inquiry and pressed for hearings in Congress. And well they should have. In February 1987, while Tower was investigating a minor part of the sales to Iran, the Joint Israel-Iran Committee, together with Robert Gates, ran the biggest-ever arms supply operation to Iran. The official inquiry was better than any smokescreen we, with all our skills at such things, could have dreamed up.

Under the noses of the American people, 4,000 TOW missiles were flown out of Marana Base in Arizona to Guatemala and were shipped through Australia, where they were temporarily parked in the western part of that country. But there was a great deal more on the move. Apart from the TOWs, radar and electronic matériel, and Hawk surface-to-air missiles from the U.S., this is what was sent to Iran—while Congress and the rest of the world remained ignorant:

—From Israel: 128 U.S. tanks; 200,000 Israeli-made Katusha rockets said to have been "captured" from the PLO in Lebanon; 122mm artillery shells; 105mm artillery shells; 61mm rockets; 51mm rockets; air-to-air missiles; small arms; tens of millions of rounds of ammunition.
—Poland and Bulgaria: 8,000 SAM-7 surface-to-air missiles; 100,000 AK-47s; millions of rounds of ammunition.
—China: Silkworm sea-to-sea missiles; armored cars; amphibious personnel carriers. China helped Iran because the Iraqis weren't happy with Chinese light tanks—which

suited Beijing because Saddam Hussein had developed a
reputation as an unreliable business partner.
—North Korea and Vietnam: artillery shells; self-propelled
rockets.
—Sweden: 105mm artillery barrels.
—Belgium: Air-to-air missiles.

Israel became very good at copying weapons and alleging that
they had been captured in Lebanon, while the reality was they
had come out of Tel Aviv factories. As for the Silkworm sea-to-sea
missiles from China, they were brokered for Israel by Saul Eisenberg, who is not related to the Eisenbergs arrested in the Bermuda
sting.

One of the richest men in the world, Eisenberg at present runs
his private arms-dealing operation from an office building at 4
Weizman Street, Tel Aviv—the same block on which the CIA
"cutout" company, GeoMiliTech, was housed. Eisenberg was able
to sell Chinese weapons because he was married to a South
Korean woman who had connections with Mao Zedong and Zhou
Enlai back in the 1950s. Because of his strong links, all Israel's
business relations with China have to be conducted through him.
When a member of the Joint Committee asked him to broker
weapons for Iran, he readily agreed and even helped arrange for
"parking" temporarily in a third country—Australia. Once
again, although certain government officials in Western Australia and members of the Australian Security Intelligence Organization knew about the operation, the general public was kept in
the dark.

On July 3 and 4, 1987, I participated in two highly secret meetings with Iran's defense minister, Col. Mohammed Jalali, and
Robert Gates. The colonel had first flown to Guatemala to settle
payments to the Mejía government, because much of the matériel
that had been moved out of Arizona had been flown by cargo
plane for parking there.

Then Col. Jalali flew to Kansas City and made his way to the
Americana Hotel where Gates was staying discreetly. Ora and I
were booked into the Vista International, just across the street.

On the evening of July 3, I made my way to the lobby of my hotel and met with Gates and Jalali. Away from rooms that might be bugged, hotel lobbies were safe for private discussion, providing nobody recognized the participants.

"What I would like," said Col. Jalali, "is an assurance that despite the Iran-contra scandal, the sales to my country will continue."

"As far as Israel is concerned, they will continue," I said.

We both looked toward Gates. He smiled. "I see no problem with that."

We talked about logistics and the scandal that had put Oliver North in the hot seat. Then we agreed to meet again the following morning.

This time I visited the others in the lobby of the Americana. Once again, on this day that celebrates American independence, Col. Jalali sought and received assurances that the U.S. would continue to supply Iran with weapons.

"But I must ask you, Mr. Gates," he said, "why the United States supports the supply of chemical weapons to Iraq. We know Saddam Hussein is getting them from Chile. Why do you help us, but also help our enemy?"

Gates made no admissions or denials. Nor, as we said our goodbyes, did he make any promises.

Following my meetings with Gates and Jalali, Ora and I flew from Kansas City to Phoenix, rented a car and went on a ten-day driving holiday to California. For Ora, it wasn't much of a holiday; she had trouble ungluing me from the fascinating scenes on TV as the congressional hearings into the Iran-contra affair unfolded. Everyone was riveted to their screens. For me, it was highly entertaining to watch official after official lying through his teeth or pleading complete ignorance.

All America was gripped by a confusing spectacle that never seemed to go anywhere or result in anything substantive. Several years later, in 1991, I discussed the events of 1987 with Spencer Oliver, the chief counsel for the House Foreign Relations Committee, who had been involved in the Iran-contra hearings.

"Didn't you know they were all lying?" I asked.

"Yes," he said, "we knew it was a coverup. But at the time the Democratic congressmen and senators were very weak, and also 'for the good of the nation' we did not want to start a scandal that would bring down the president. We did not want to hear the 'I-word'—impeachment."

"To lie to the nation is for the good of the nation?"

"No. But the Democrats did not have the backbone to do what they had to do. They all knew that the witnesses were lying or telling half-truths. Everybody knew it was a cover-up, but not many knew the real truth. Casey was sick and dying. Gates and Bush were untouchable. To get them, we had to bring down the whole administration. We weren't ready for it. The Democrats didn't have any strong leadership. The only thing we did manage later, when Casey died and Robert Gates's nomination was put forward in 1987, was to force the nomination to be withdrawn."

There was a clue to the future, perhaps, in Robert McFarlane's suicide attempt during the congressional hearings. He overdosed on pills, I suspect, because he was afraid his role with the Israelis would surface. But no one was able to connect his attempt to kill himself with a national scandal that went far beyond the wildest imagination. All that happened, of course, was the decision by an independent prosecutor, Judge Lawrence Walsh, to put North, McFarlane, and Poindexter on trial. They were convicted of lying to Congress, but none of them went to jail. Later, North's conviction was thrown out. So, for the time being, the truth was buried. America was to continue living under the Big Lie.

One day in August 1987, a month after Ora and I had returned to Jerusalem from our trip to the U.S., I was replaying the messages on our answering machine. Ora was out, and I was puzzled to hear the familiar voice of the CIA station chief in Tel Aviv asking her why she hadn't "made the interview on time."

Despite our alliance, it was, of course, not unusual for Israel and the U.S. to spy on each other. And these were particularly sensitive times. What was Ora up to?

I said nothing to her, but I was determined to get to the bottom of the matter. She was put under surveillance, and it was discovered she was meeting various CIA people based in Tel Aviv.

Ora was ordered by SHABAK, Israel's internal security agency, to go to an apartment in Jerusalem for interrogation. There she admitted she was friendly with the Americans. They were talking to her about me, what I knew about Iran-contra, how I fit into the overall picture, and who had leaked the Iran-contra story to the press. Whatever her motives, she wasn't getting paid.

Later, when I confronted her, she told me the same story, emphasizing that she didn't tell the Americans much. I was stunned. I didn't know what to make of it. But I knew I could no longer trust Ora. And the Americans? What were they up to? When the Joint Committee discussed the situation, we concluded the only way the Americans could apply effective damage control was to use someone like Ora, who was close to one of the principals in the affair, to find out exactly what our role in the Iran-contra leak was and what we might do next.

When Ora's liaisons with the Americans were exposed, all her ties with Mossad were terminated. Beyond that, the SHABAK wanted to throw the book at her. It was an opportunity to prosecute and make a show out of how the U.S. was spying on Israel. And of course they had every legitimate reason to do so. She had met with another country's intelligence unit, and even though America was officially an ally of Israel, secrets were secrets.

Despite the top brass's anger, I didn't want to see Ora going down for it. I no longer trusted her, but I'd always liked her and didn't want her hurt—and, more pragmatically, she knew too much.

I came up with a scheme. I told my superiors that I would personally take charge of the situation and that she would no longer pose a threat to Israeli security. As proof of my intentions, I told them she was pregnant and that we planned to marry. As the weeks went by, we were able to show that she really was pregnant.

Ora was eager to marry me, and now that she was expecting our child, I believed it was time I committed myself. It would certainly keep Ora out of trouble with the government. We fixed a wedding date—March 13, 1988.

While Ora was out of trouble, I found myself up to my neck in it. The reverberations from the leaking of the Iran-contra story had rocked the Israeli government. Determined to cause some damage to those involved in the long-standing original arms operation to Iran, the Labor Party, which remained in the coalition, was demanding heads. In September 1987, mine rolled, along with those of three other members of the Joint IDF/MI-Mossad Committee for Iran-Israel Relations. We were told: "You no longer have a job."

But we had expected this. The signs had all been there. As I had been in the thick of the arms trade, I realized that, with the pressure on Shamir, I would be one of the first to go.

So Mossad head Nachum Admoni and I had decided before the crunch came to set some of the funds aside for our futures. We had given the government our best, shoring up the State of Israel during the terms of three prime ministers, but we believed we needed insurance against whatever might lie ahead. We weren't sure what our job prospects would be after doing work that both the Americans and the Israelis now wanted to forget ever happened. There was also a genuine risk of arrest or death—we had the examples of Gen. Bar Am, the Eisenbergs, and Cyrus Hashemi to ponder. The slush fund money had been made illegally, against all international conventions, and, as it would in time be shown in a U.S. court, neither the Israelis nor the Americans wanted to admit to owning it. So it was agreed that we would take out our insurance and let the arguments come later. We made a number of payoffs and then transferred a very large sum to South America.

What Shamir thought about our actions, I don't know. But he would have understood that, despite what had happened to me, I would not leak details about my work—at least, at that time.

Now the burden was off my shoulders. I flew to London to spend a few days enjoying myself. I had a feeling of relief—even more than that, of euphoria. I felt all-powerful. God only knew what lay ahead. I decided the best thing was to blow with the wind. It's the way I'd played it from the very beginning.

BOOK TWO

BLOOD MONEY

13

Nuclear Nation

FOLLOWING MY SUDDEN dismissal from the Joint Committee, I had plenty of money, but no job. And I get restless without a job. My plan was to go to the United States, look for work, then settle down with Ora and the soon-to-be-born baby and start life afresh.

I made a number of exploratory trips to the U.S. and Britain in late 1987. But in November, when I arrived back in Israel, out of the blue I was offered a job at the highest level—as a special intelligence consultant to the Prime Minister's Office. There were a couple of reasons for the job offer, I concluded. I had, after all, done Shamir a great favor by leaking the Iran-contra story, which helped destroy the competing arms network and hurt his old adversary, Shimon Peres. I was also still one of the guardians of the funds. And Shamir wanted access to them.

I told Shamir's spokesman and unofficial national security adviser, Avi Pazner, that I would be happy to accept the post, but I did not want to get involved in any missions that would interrupt the wedding Ora and I were looking forward to. However, they were eager for me to get started, and shortly after taking on my new position, I was called in to meet Shamir. I was to be briefed by two scientists, he told me, and should read some top-secret files as background. Then I would be asked to undertake a secret mission that was vital to Israel's nuclear program.

At the time, I knew next to nothing about Israel's nuclear

program. My only experience with it was the so-called "Vanunu affair" in 1986.

Mordecai Vanunu was a former cab driver who had been talking his head off to a church group in Sydney, Australia's red-light district, King's Cross, claiming that he had worked as a technician at a nuclear facility near Dimona, Israel.

When the Israeli intelligence community got wind of this, they immediately checked into Vanunu's background and found it was true. Born in Morocco to a rightwing Jewish family that had migrated to Israel in the early 1960s, he had grown up in Beersheba before being drafted. He was stationed in Dimona and trained as a technician. After his military service, he stayed on. While a civilian, he also started studying philosophy at the University of the Negev in Beersheba and began sympathizing with the Palestinian cause. He aligned himself with North African Jews who had migrated to Israel and told his pals how horrified he was that Israel had so much nuclear firepower. From his work he had a very good idea what Israel had.

Deciding he had had enough of life in Israel, he sold his Beersheba apartment, left his job and the university, and took off with a knapsack on his back. He headed for Thailand and Nepal, where he converted to Buddhism. He stayed free at Buddhist monasteries, although in his knapsack he had a lot of cash from the sale of his apartment. He also had something far more valuable— photographs and undeveloped film of the inside of the Israeli nuclear facility.

In their checks on Vanunu, Israeli intelligence found out that while in Nepal he had contacted the Soviet Embassy in Katmandu and, in the name of socialism, communism, and world peace, offered them the photographs. He was actually flown to Moscow from Nepal with copies, having left the originals in the monastery. He met with the KGB, handed over the photos, and was then debriefed. Although he had been given vague promises by the person who met him in Nepal, all Vanunu got out of his liaison with the Soviets was a ticket back to Katmandu.

After that trip he lost confidence in the Soviet system. Confused and feeling betrayed, he picked up his knapsack from the monastery and flew to Australia, having arranged a visa while he was in Israel. He hung around until his visa ran out and, now short of money, decided to stay on illegally. He found a place to live in King's Cross, where he joined a church prayer group.

Vanunu found many among the flock who were keen to hear him preach about the evils of nuclear power. He even brought out some of his top-secret photos and handed them around the prayer group. Encouraged by the wide-eyed response, he converted from Buddhism to Christianity and found a job as a part-time taxi driver.

Among the faithful in the prayer group was a Colombian, Oscar Guerrero. A freelance journalist, he had fallen on hard times and had taken up house painting and listening to Bible readings. When Guerrero saw the photographs, he told Vanunu that the two of them could spread "the word" by getting the photographs published—for a fee.

First, Guerrero approached the *Sydney Morning Herald*, but the photographs were rejected on the grounds that Guerrero seemed a suspicious character. However, his approach was passed on to the internal intelligence service, the Australian Security Intelligence Organization, then to the external service, the Australian Security Intelligence Service, which mentioned it to Israel. Now Tel Aviv realized it had a problem. And, there were no easy answers.

Guerrero tried *The Age* newspaper in Melbourne, not realizing it was in the same group as the *Sydney Morning Herald*. Rejected again, he decided to try the London papers. He put together all the money he had, borrowed from Vanunu's dwindling reserves, and bought himself a ticket for Heathrow Airport. In an astonishing stroke of bad luck, one of the newspaper executives he approached was none other than my associate, full-blown Israeli agent Nicholas Davies, foreign editor of the *Daily Mirror*.

Davies stalled him by telling him that the newspaper needed to bring in an expert to check out his claims. He then called me in Israel, and I sought advice from my superiors. Prime Minister Peres issued an order that Vanunu be stopped at any price and the traitor brought back to Israel. Although the intelligence community suggested that the uproar would eventually die down, Peres raged that he wanted him caught and brought back to be taught a lesson.

The same evening I flew to London. The next afternoon, posing as a journalist who was an expert on nuclear and military issues, I met with Guerrero and Nick Davies. I insisted I needed copies of the photos before the newspaper could decide whether it was going to buy the story. Guerrero handed over three samples. "Look at them," he said. "If you think they're good, I'll give you the lot."

That same evening the pictures were sent to Israel. The word came back that they were real and that I had to try to discredit Vanunu and his friend. Meanwhile Nick Davies, as ordered by his publisher Robert Maxwell, put together the framework of a disinformation story, to be used later with copies of the photographs, declaring that the *Sunday Mirror* had looked into the pictures and the men trying to sell them and that it was all a con job. To back up the story, Vanunu's wanderings were detailed.

It was at that point that we discovered that Guerrero had already struck a deal with the *Sunday Times* on an earlier trip to London. The *Times* was planning to fly Vanunu to London, interview him at length, and publish his story in detail. The arrangement was that after the story had been printed, Vanunu would get £250,000 advance on a book about Israel's nuclear capability that he would write with one of the newspaper's staff. Guerrero's cut would be 10 percent. He had approached the *Mirror* because he believed he was being cut out of the *Sunday Times* deal.

Vanunu flew to London and was put up in various hotel rooms. We realized at this stage that the story could not be stopped, although the *Sunday Times* was still a long way from printing anything. I contacted my superiors, and Prime Minister Peres himself decided to throw the full weight of Mossad at Vanunu.

The Mossad station chief in London tipped off MI-5 that Israel had a security problem—on British soil. The British intelligence agency agreed to try to help Israel track down Vanunu but warned the Israelis not to do anything that was likely to cause a political or diplomatic incident on British soil. *Sunday Times* journalists were followed, but none led their "shadows" to Vanunu's hotel.

Finally Nick Davies telephoned a journalist friend, the editor of a Sunday paper, and actually found out the name of the hotel where Vanunu was staying. Davies passed it on to me, and I relayed it to my superiors in Israel. Now, with Mossad fully aware of Vanunu's whereabouts, a plan was put into action, but without the knowledge of Mossad Director Nachum Admoni. The manner in which Vanunu was kidnapped has been well documented, except for one fascinating aspect—the true identity of the beautiful siren who lured him to his fate.

Vanunu met "Cindy Hanin Bentov" one evening while walking through Leicester Square. They started chatting, and she suggested they go to a pub for a drink. She met him two or three times in between the interviews he was giving to the *Sunday Times*, and during one of their dates she told him about an apartment she had in Rome. She invited him to come with her for a visit. The offer was too tempting to refuse.

Vanunu told the *Sunday Times* he was going away for a long weekend. When he arrived at the Rome apartment, three Mossad agents were waiting. He was grabbed, given a knockout injection and pushed into a large crate. Then the crate was taken to an Israeli ship and loaded on as diplomatic cargo, which meant the authorities could not inspect the container.

Once the ship was on its way, he was brought out of the crate, handcuffed, and taken to a guarded cabin. As soon as the vessel arrived in Ashdod in Israel, a colonel in the police presented him with a formal arrest warrant on security grounds. Even though an Israeli Air Force 707 could have flown Vanunu from Britain's Stansted Airport to Tel Aviv, Mossad had been asked by MI-5 not to kidnap him on British soil because this would have embarrassed Prime Minister Margaret Thatcher.

When Vanunu did not show up in London after his weekend away with Cindy, the *Sunday Times* decided to run with what it had, along with the photos, on October 5, 1986. The *Sunday Mirror* already had run its disinformation piece, but it did not have much effect.

The Vanunu revelations in the *Sunday Times* caused a world outcry—and there was more to follow when he was brought to court and everyone asked how he had been taken back to Israel. He was able to give the world a clue, even though he had been held in solitary confinement. On one of his trips to court in a police van, he pressed the palm of his hand against the van's window. On it, he had written the number of the flight on which he had flown to Rome.

Certain members of the intelligence community approached

Deputy Prime Minister Shamir, concerned that Peres might be using the Vanunu affair to blow open the Iran-Israel-Maxwell operations. Shamir wanted Vanunu killed, but it was too late.

Vanunu was sentenced behind closed doors to 18 years in jail for espionage and treason. The *Sunday Times* was happy because it got its story without having to pay a penny. And I heard all the fine details from "Cindy," with whom, it happened, I had worked at an earlier period.

The Vanunu affair in no way prepared me for what I was to learn from the two scientists who briefed me and the files I read in the Prime Minister's Office in preparation for my secret mission. Together, they gave me an overview of the history and scope of Israel's nuclear program. A summary of what I was able to digest follows. I do not present this without a great deal of thought. I do it because I feel it's best for the world to know all it can about secret weapons of mass destruction in every country.

The father of Israel's nuclear program in the mid-1950s was the then young Shimon Peres, who was director general of the Ministry of Defense under David Ben-Gurion, the state's first prime minister and defense minister. Peres believed that if Israel was to survive, it had to have a deterrent against the Arab countries, and the ultimate deterrent would be nuclear weapons. With this in mind, Peres flew to France in 1956 for a meeting with President Charles de Gaulle. His mission: to get a nuclear reactor for Israel.

De Gaulle, a good friend of Ben-Gurion's from their days in exile during World War II, quickly authorized the sale to Israel of a weapons-grade nuclear reactor with the technology for the development of a nuclear bomb.*

Israel's first nuclear reactor was set up on the Mediterranean coast in Nahal Sorek in the Yavne area. It was used for research with enriched uranium, which was imported from France. The idea was to see if a nuclear project could be handled with Israeli know-how—and the aid of Jewish scientists brought in from the U.S.

* Ironically, in the mid-1970s the French were to sell a reactor to Israel's enemy, Iraq.

After the initial research yielded positive results, Minister Without Portfolio Yisrael Galili, a leftwing powerbroker who directed the intelligence and security services, took upon himself with Ben-Gurion's blessing the cabinet-level supervision of the program. After tasting success in Yavne, within six to eight months he pushed through another nuclear plant in the Negev Desert near Dimona, some 40 miles northeast of Beersheba.

In a memorable speech after the groundbreaking for the super-secret Dimona nuclear plant, the usually subdued Galili stood up in a Mapai Party meeting and, with his chest proudly pushed out, declared, "The third temple is being built!"

This astonished other cabinet members, who at the time did not know what he was talking about. Galili continued by saying that the revival of Israel as a moral leader of the world was at hand and dared any of Israel's neighbors to attack.

Although the French had not given Israel the know-how, they realized Israel would create its own nuclear program and possibly achieve significant technological advances. Hence, the initial agreement that Tel Aviv would share information with Paris.

The prototype of a crude atomic device comparable to the Nagasaki bomb was developed by the early 1960s, and the first test was conducted in a joint Israeli-French operation in the Pacific off New Caledonia in 1963. With a French naval ship doing the monitoring, the relatively low-yield bomb was dropped from a French Air Force plane. The Americans and British thought it was a French test.

After the successful drop, Mapai Party leaders were so ecstatic that Finance Minister Pinchas Sapir announced at a convention that Israel's military power was equal to that of France.

The sharing of Israeli know-how, French equipment, and French money continued until the outbreak of the 1967 war, when the French accused Israel of starting the conflict. Israel didn't see it that way. It saw Egyptian President Nasser starting tensions by blocking the Tiran Straits, the waterway to the Israeli port of Eilat, for his own internal political reasons and to position himself better in the Arab world.

The Israeli government under Prime Minister Levi Eshkol had reconstituted into a wide coalition government in which even the rightwing "Begin party"—then known as the Gahal Party—

was included. Moshe Dayan, the hero of the 1956 Suez campaign, became defense minister. Basically, all of Israel's war heroes were in power, and with a depression sweeping the country in 1967, they were all itching for a war to solve the economic problems. Nasser's actions were the excuse they wanted, and they hit the Arabs hard.

The war was one of the costliest, politically, that Israel ever had—even though the result was seen as a glorious victory with the Sinai, the Golan Heights, and the West Bank falling into Israeli hands—a total land mass that was three times the size of the nation. Upset at Israel for resorting to war rather than attempting quiet diplomacy, de Gaulle slapped a military embargo on the state. He was also eyeing Arab oil. The row between the two governments meant that the nuclear cooperation came to a complete halt.

France wasn't the only nation to sever relations. All the East Bloc countries, other than Romania, cut ties as a result of the war. These countries had previously seen Israel, the home of the kibbutz, as a semi-socialist country and not as a military aggressor. Israel also tarnished its international image by refusing to sign a U.N. agreement not to test nuclear weapons, an agreement that it has not signed even today.

Israel found itself in a difficult position. France and the East Bloc had washed their hands of the nation, and military relations with the U.S. were not close. There were two very good reasons. First, in 1957 Mossad had plotted the bombing of the U.S. Embassy in Cairo to cast blame on Egyptian radicals and to force a break in relations between the U.S. and Egypt. The Israeli agents were caught, straining relations between the two countries. Then, in 1967, the *U.S.S. Liberty*, a "listening ship," was sailing off the coast of Egypt, when it was bombed by Israeli Mirage jets, killing 34 crew members, further distancing Israel from the U.S.

Out in the cold, Israel started to look for new friends with whom it could develop its nuclear capabilities. South Africa was waiting.

The door to working side by side with the South Africans had in fact already been opened by Shimon Peres as part of his early plan to give Israel a nuclear deterrent. By 1959, there had been military cooperation between the two countries, with South Africa selling uranium to Israel, mined in South-West Africa, now Namibia.

The first shipment flown up from the south in 1959 was the seed of commercial El Al flights to South Africa and South African Airways flights to Israel. The crates of uranium came through as agricultural equipment, but later the whole nuclear trade with South Africa was carried out under the guise of machinery and parts to be used for the water pipeline being built from the Sea of Galilee to the south. Under the cover of TAHAL, the government water corporation, tons of uranium were shifted, and the underground silos that were being built were also said to be for the water corporation. The reactor was the one I have mentioned in the Negev Desert, but there were also missile silos in the north built under the name of TAHAL Waterworks.

South Africa, of course, expected something in return for its cooperation. When Shimon Peres became the first Israeli official to visit South Africa in 1959, he promised the sale of arms from Israel Military Industries and a share of technology.

The first Indian Ocean nuclear testing on Israel's behalf took place in 1968 when a crude bomb with low radioactive fallout was dropped. The test was to see if the detonator mechanism worked. During that same year, South Africa and Israel signed a nuclear cooperation agreement. Israel would train South African scientists and share knowledge with them, and the South Africans would finance some of Israel's nuclear program and provide it with testing grounds in the Indian Ocean. Although Israel now had the Sinai, it was impossible to test bigger bombs there. And to test low-radiation small bombs underground was very expensive.

When South African financing started in 1968, the U.S. Congress began pressing Israel for details of its nuclear program and demanded to inspect its nuclear installations. The Israeli government, with Moshe Dayan as defense minister, caved in and agreed to show the Dimona establishment to American inspectors. Israel continued to insist its nuclear program was for peaceful purposes, like electricity. The French kept quiet. Having provided the reactor, they were not keen to incriminate themselves.

Prior to the arrival of the inspectors, the Israelis built a false control room inside the nuclear reactor building, with false panels and measuring devices. When the Americans examined it, they were fooled—or they wanted to be fooled. The team saw a low-level thermal output incapable of military-grade chemical reprocessing. They reported that Israel did not have the technology or the know-how to develop bombs and that CIA reports of cooperation with the South Africans were wrong.

Testing continued with the aid of French scientists who had been working with Israel before the embargo and had now stayed on as private citizens, enticed by big salaries.

Between 1968 and 1973, 13 bombs were built, each with a destructive power that was three times that of the weapons that wiped out Nagasaki and Hiroshima. In spite of the difficulties, some tests were carried out in underground tunnels in the Sinai; the others were in the Indian Ocean. And if anyone questioned whether Israel would ever be willing to use its nuclear capability, the answer came in 1973 during the October War with the Egyptians and the Syrians. The Syrians penetrated the Golan Heights, and there was fear they would get close to Tiberias. So Moshe Dayan ordered the arming of all 13 nuclear bombs and put 24 B-52 bombers on standby. The U.S. had sold the old planes to Israel, not realizing what Israel needed them for. (Israel had not completed its missile delivery systems at the time and needed the B-52s for bomb drops.) Following the arming of the bombs, the Soviets and the Americans were warned to keep the Arabs at bay—or else.

In response to this action, the Soviets targeted Tel Aviv, Haifa, Beersheba, and the port of Ashdod with nuclear missiles (though not Jerusalem). An alarmed President Richard Nixon announced an all-out military alert around the world and put U.S. forces on combat readiness. As it turned out, the stalemate was overcome, because a week into the war Israel reversed the Syrian advance.

Up until the 1973 war, Israel had enjoyed good relations with the black African nations. They had seen Israel as the underdog fighting the Arabs—a situation that black Africans could identify with because they had their own conflicts with the northern Moslems. But the war brought this bond to an end. The black nations claimed that in crossing the Suez Canal, considered to be the line between Asia and Africa, Israel had actually invaded Africa. Slowly but surely, most black African countries cut relations, eventually spurred on by Libya's President Muammar Qaddafi, who promised monetary rewards to African nations that agreed to wave goodbye to Israel. As it turned out, the Libyan leader never paid.

However, to counteract the move by the black nations, the South Africans, who had diplomatic relations with Israel at a consular level, quietly proposed to Israel an exchange of ambassadors. Within months, in 1974, this was implemented by the Labor government of Yitzhak Rabin.

After that, Israeli-South African relations developed rapidly. Israeli scientists helped the South Africans develop their own bomb. Curiously, some of the French scientists who were working in the late 1960s in Israel but left when the 1967 embargo was announced, met up with their former Israeli colleagues in South Africa. They started working side by side again in Capetown.

The tests proceeded so well that by 1976 Israel had a missile delivery system that was capable of hitting the Soviet Union. A year later, when Prime Minister Yitzhak Rabin was handing over office to the newly elected Menachem Begin, one of Begin's first orders was to target a number of southern Soviet cities, including Yerevan in Armenia and Baku in Azerbaijan.

Begin, conscious in his own twisted way of human rights, was unhappy about the relationship with South Africa, a country he regarded as a pariah. He found himself in a moral dilemma. While he felt that Israel had enough money and know-how to proceed alone with the nuclear program, he realized the need to maintain supplies of uranium from South Africa. Defense and military analysts also urged that the relationship continue.

Unwilling to involve himself personally, in 1978 Begin dispatched his first defense minister, Ezer Weizman, to Pretoria to meet Prime Minister P.W. Botha, who was also defense minister at the time. Even though Begin's intentions were to downgrade the relationship, Botha pushed for a wartime alliance between the two governments as the price for continuing nuclear tests. And to Begin's dismay, Weizman agreed with Botha.

After Weizman returned to Israel and reported back to Begin, the prime minister, who was never fully in control of Weizman, relented. It took two years to work out the military cooperation agreement. It was drawn up in the special assistance branch of the External Relations Department of the Israel Defense Forces/Military Intelligence. It was referred to as SIMWA, an acronym

for the SADF-IDF Mutual Wartime Agreement, drawn up between the South African Defense Force and the Israel Defense
Forces. The Israeli version was prepared by the branch head, Lt.
Col. Shimon Lavee. The provisions of the agreement were that if
either of the two countries was at war or in military operations
and there was a shortage of matériel, it could request supplies
from the other country, which would provide it from its own
stockpiles. Another provision of the agreement was that there
would be an annual meeting of the deputy chiefs of general staff,
to take place alternately in Israel and South Africa.

Between 1978 and 1979 the Israelis sold to South Africa
175mm artillery that could carry small nuclear devices. More
than money was involved. Not only did the South Africans agree
to invest in Israel's nuclear program, they also decided to give
Israel a free hand to carry out tests in the Indian Ocean without
South African supervision. In 1979 Israel carried out a number of
such tests, one of which was detected by satellite because its big
flash occurred during a break in the otherwise cloudy weather.
The South Africans rightly denied it was theirs. To this day, the
Israeli government has refused to comment on this test. It did,
however, issue a blanket denial of Seymour Hersh's book, *The
Samson Option*, which asserts that the 1979 flash was, in fact, an
Israeli atomic device. By 1979, Israel had approximately 200 very
advanced atomic bombs and nuclear artillery—175mm artillery
shells. It also had missile delivery systems that were not all that
developed but were capable of reaching the Soviet Union and
Baghdad.

The go-ahead for Israel to develop a hydrogen bomb for testing
was given in 1980 by the director general of the Defense Ministry,
Mordechai Tsippori. By 1981, Israel had the H-bomb, having
tested it in the Indian Ocean. In that year, the count was more
than 300 atomic bombs stored in silos—the structures had again
been built by TAHAL, the water company—and more than 50
hydrogen bombs. The fleet of B-52 bombers had also increased
somewhat.

A tactical atom bomb program had also started, under Defense
Minister Ariel Sharon. Israeli scientists designed a low-yield,
low-radiation atom bomb, very effective for the battlefield. But
the supplies from South Africa of the necessary metals and re-

lated chemicals were only enough for experiments. The South Africans said they would provide more, as long as Israel promised to sell them this bomb.

However, between 1985 and 1988, Israeli-South African relations deteriorated. In part, this was because of the gradual renewal of relations between Israel and the black African states. More importantly, it was because South Africa began to sell conventional equipment and missile technology to Iraq. In 1988, Israel pointed out that the Iran-Iraq war had stopped, so there was no need to help the Iraqis, but all requests fell on deaf ears in Pretoria. This rebuff brought about a complete breakdown in Israeli-South African military relations.

The immediate result was that Israel had no place to get the vital minerals and chemicals it needed to move its tactical bomb into mass production. Three critical, and rare, minerals— uranium, titanium, and molybdenum—and two even rarer chemical compounds—heavy water (deuterium oxide) and tritium—could, as it happened, be found in Peru.* So my first assignment for the Prime Minister's Office was to travel to Peru to try to arrange their purchase.

* Heavy water and tritium are usually produced in a laboratory; they can be found in nature, I was told, in areas containing certain radioactive ores. Norway is also known for this phenomenon.

14

The Revolutionary

MY WEDDING TO Ora took place on March 13, 1988, as scheduled—much to Ora's relief—and ten days after our honeymoon in the Blue Nile area, I was ready to fly on my first mission for the prime minister. It was filled with risks. The minerals could only be found in an area in Peru that was in the hands of a group known as the Shining Path, which had a formidable reputation as a Maoist terrorist group that dealt in drugs.

As I flew from New York to Peru, I wondered just what lay in store for "Professor Ari Ben-Menashe." My credentials had gone ahead of me. I was going to apply for a position to teach about the Middle East at the University of San Cristóbal de Huamanga at Ayacucho. It was an important "target." Many years earlier, Abimael Guzmán Reynoso, founder of the Shining Path, had been a professor of philosophy on its faculty. Although Guzmán had been "underground" since 1970, most of the professors at San Cristóbal University were members of Shining Path. And most of those who weren't belonged to the Communist Party of Peru.

Guzmán was legendary, considered by his followers to be the fourth sword of Marxism after Marx, Lenin, and Stalin. In 1980 he had proclaimed the armed struggle against the capitalist government in Lima, and since then the Shining Path had grown into a powerful force. As a result, the whole department (region) of

212

Ayacucho had been declared under martial law by Peruvian President Alan García.

From Lima I took a plane to Ayacucho. The aircraft was filled with women in bright Inca clothing clutching live chickens and old men with boxes tied up with string. But the passenger who sat next to me was a distinguished-looking, well-built man in his late 40s who asked me in English who I was and what I was doing flying to Ayacucho, a military zone closed to foreigners.

He continued to press me, asking if I'd been accepted at the university—in fact I had had no response to the application I'd sent—and whether I had a license from the military government. I told him I was going to talk to the officer who was head of military operations in Ayacucho, Col. Rafael Cordova, in the hope that he would help me stay in the region.

"Well, that's most interesting," said my traveling companion. "Because I am Col. Cordova."

I couldn't be sure whether he was or not, but I told him I was from Israel and would like to teach at the university and write a paper about Shining Path.

By the time the plane landed, I was convinced that the man I had hoped to meet was sitting right next to me—and that this was no coincidence. He agreed to talk to me further after our arrival. When the plane touched down at a small airfield on a mountain plateau, it was immediately surrounded by soldiers. Apart from the airport and the town of Ayacucho itself, the whole region was controlled by Shining Path. The government was taking no chances of losing a plane to the movement.

The secret police were carefully checking IDs, but Col. Cordova told them to take only my passport details and let me through. He wanted to talk to me some more. I took a taxi to the Turista Hotel—a holdover from the days when visitors were allowed in the region—and arranged for the colonel to see me later. I realized that whatever calls I made from the rather pleasant room they had given me would be recorded. So I phoned Ora and asked her to call my "doctors" and tell them I had arrived in Ayacucho.

I then made my way to the university, where I asked to see the rector. His secretary went into an inner office, then returned and asked me to wait for 20 minutes. She started chatting to me about how she represented Amnesty International, but suddenly changed tack and started talking about the visitors Ayacucho had had.

"Many of them are intelligence officers trying to find out what the Shining Path is doing," she said matter-of-factly. "They never find out much."

"Nobody tells them anything?"

"No, not that. They just get killed."

The rector welcomed me warmly, and, on presenting my academic credentials again, I explained I would like to teach and write a paper about the Shining Path. He said he saw no problem—except that I would have to obtain a permit from the military.

"I'll be honest with you," he said. "We don't like them. But they have to approve of your being here. If you stay without their permission, they'll take you away and we'll all be in trouble."

I asked why he was ready to accept me so quickly.

He shrugged. "I see your papers and you can prove yourself. If you are good at giving lectures, you can stay; if not, you can leave. If you're an intelligence officer, from the CIA, from Israel's— whatever the hell their name is—that's none of my business."

I was given a letter of appointment, and it was agreed I'd start teaching the following morning. My interviews for the day were not over, of course. Late in the afternoon, Col. Cordova arrived at the hotel. He came straight to the point. "If you're an intelligence officer trying to penetrate the Shining Path, don't bother. The Peruvian military has its own intelligence. We don't need help, whoever you may or may not represent."

I realized that what I had to say next could have resulted in my being shot. I knew he carried a gun under his suit jacket, and I was to find out later just how capable he was of using it. But I had been briefed on what to say back in Israel.

"Colonel Cordova, please excuse me, but I am going to tell you one thing. I am going to stay whether you like it or not."

His reaction was a loud belly laugh. "Oh yes?" he said. "Perhaps you'd like to explain."

"Let me remind you about the three Stingers."

His face hardened. You could feel the atmosphere change.

"We have information," I said, "that you personally got three

Stinger missiles off an Aeroflot plane in Lima and sold them to the Shining Path. A lot of people in Israel know about this. And I want to stay here."

He glared at me. "Are you trying to blackmail me?"

"No, colonel. I'm just telling you how much we know about you. And you had better make sure I am kept happy and alive. All I want to do is teach at this university, and I promise you there will be no subversive activity against the Peruvian government or military."

"You're very persistent. By the way, how did you know about the Stingers?"

I wasn't going to tell him that. In fact, we had found out as a result of a "friendly discussion" between Israel's second secretary to Lima and the Soviet Embassy's commercial attaché.

It soon became clear to me that the colonel was going to give me a permit after all. In fact, he was going to get it within the hour. He picked up the phone, asked the operator to connect him with a number, and rattled off instructions.

After he left, I went for a stroll around the town, which was dominated by the university, although it is said there are more than 40 churches there. Tourists fascinated by the Incas used to flock here up to 1980, when people started getting killed. After 1985 it was officially closed to tourism, which explained why so many of the 25,000 population stared at me, an obvious stranger.

Waiting for me under my door when I returned was my license to stay. I had hardly started reading it when I had a visitor, a police officer who told me that he knew I was a very important professor from Israel and was to be given the highest protection. In order for that to be effective, I was told I had to phone the police every day and tell them where I was. I told him he would not have to worry—I'd be at the university if they wanted me.

My first lecture, in English, at the university went well. I spoke about the economic and social structure of the Israeli kibbutz, with which the students were able to identify because they were supporters of commune-style living. I was approached after the lecture by a man called Roberto, who was head of the English department. But he was more, which he readily disclosed—he was a member of the national leadership of *El Sendero Luminoso*, the Shining Path.

"Aren't you afraid the military will pick you up?" I asked.

He shook his head. According to Peruvian law, membership in any organization was permitted unless the person was found carrying a gun or carrying out subversive activity. Members of Shining Path were followed, but at the same time there was "an understanding" between the organization and the military.

Roberto invited me to his home for lunch, where he explained that Shining Path had its own ideas about the way Peru would be after it took over. There would be a free market, but it would be based on a kibbutz-like commune, not the individual. It would also be based on the culture of the Incas, who had lived communally before the Spaniards came. If Shining Path had any ideological alignment, it was with the Albanian government, which had cut ties with the Soviet Union after Stalin died.

I asked Roberto if I could meet the movement's founder.

"You can't. The chairman is no longer alive."

But shortly afterwards, he confessed Guzmán was alive. He said there were immense difficulties in getting me to see him, among them the problem of being tailed by the military.

He agreed to do what he could in return for a favor from me.

"Look," he said, tugging at his thinning locks, "I'm losing my hair. There's a medication in England that can help. Can you get it for me?"

I said I would try. This was becoming a very personal friendship—which was perfect.

That evening I had another visit from Col. Cordova, who said he wanted to chat. While he was still there, Roberto arrived with a man who introduced himself as Marcus, an English teacher and a member of the Communist Party.

I gestured from the colonel to the new arrivals. "I assume you guys know each other?"

Roberto stared at Cordova with disgust. "Yes," he said, "this is the man who murders peasants."

Cordova rose and held out a hand, but the gesture was not returned. I spent several minutes breaking the ice, saying how nice it was that it had taken an Israeli to bring them together. I ordered coffee, but Cordova remained ill at ease. He said he had to leave and as he made his way out, Roberto called, "Don't kill any more peasants."

The colonel threw him a false smile. "We try to protect them from you guys."

Several days later, after I had given more lectures, I flew to Lima and called Nick Davies in London. He thought I was mad when I asked him to send a bottle of the hair lotion Roberto had requested, but I knew how important it was for public relations. Davies mentioned that a magazine photographer we knew was currently in Lima staying with a journalist named Barbara Durr. He told me to check on her through Israel—I might find her useful.

I found out through Tel Aviv that she was a stringer working in Peru for the *Financial Times* of London. That evening, after calling the photographer, Peter Jordan, I had dinner with him and Durr. I explained I was teaching at Ayacucho, and he mentioned to her that I had worked for Israeli intelligence until I was fired the year before. She seemed fascinated, and the three of us chatted on for hours. She was clearly a very smart woman, and I knew she might be useful to me sometime.

Back in Ayacucho, Roberto told me, "You have your wish."

The date and time was set for me to go to his home. Several days later, as instructed, I went to his home, where I was led to a van and asked to get in the back. There were no windows. I sat there, crashing around, as the vehicle hit pothole after pothole. At one stage we stopped at the back of a house where I was asked to climb into another van, also closed. It was two hours before we came to a halt.

I was led into a farmhouse, which was guarded by a number of men clutching Kalashnikovs. In the living room a balding man who looked like a college professor stepped forward. In his 50s, he was of average height, somewhat chubby, and was wearing a sports jacket with an open shirt and no tie. He did not smile as he introduced himself as Abimael Guzmán.

"For a dead man, you seem very much alive," I said.

He laughed. It was the laugh of a confident, charismatic man. In his eyes was a calm, sharp look. Guzmán was clearly very intelligent—and suspicious. "Who are you? CIA? Mossad? KGB? Whoever you are, you are lucky to have come so far and still remained alive."

I told him the truth—that I was a special consultant on intelligence with the Israeli Prime Minister's Office and that I would like to conduct business with him.

Guzmán shook his head, bemused. "You come to Ayacucho, Roberto sees you with Cordova the murderer, and now you tell me you are an intelligence officer from Israel. We were informed by our contacts in Sweden, and they are looking into your identity. And you know that if you don't check out, we're going to kill you."

Despite the Shining Path's violent reputation, I wasn't frightened. Guzmán had delivered the warning with a twinkle in his eye. I didn't take it seriously. To tell the truth, I was enjoying myself. After years of big-money Iranian arms deals, this was fun. I'd read books, of course, about heroic revolutionaries like Fidel Castro, Ché Guevara, and Ho Chi Minh. But here I was, seeing a revolution firsthand at the grassroots level. It was a rare opportunity.

Guzmán ordered coffee and talked in a friendly manner about his background. He surprised me right away by saying he had Jewish blood. He was the son of an Inca maid in a household of affluent German Jews who had emigrated to Peru from Europe in the 1920s. She was impregnated by the husband, who did not have any children by his wife. When the wife found out about the pregnancy, the maid was driven out.

Guzmán's father died before he was born, and his mother died in childbirth. His Inca grandmother then took him to his father's widow, and she agreed to raise him. She sent him to university in Sweden, but once his studies were over, he felt compelled to return to Peru. He began teaching his own philosophy, a mixture of Inca and kibbutz ideology.

I left the initial meeting impressed by Guzmán. He had a magnetic personality and was very well-educated and thoughtful. While he had a tendency to launch into passionate, self-righteous diatribes, he also had a sense of humor.

I spent the night at the farmhouse and was taken back to Ayacucho the next day. After a week of teaching, I made a short trip to Lima. On my return to Ayacucho, I was taken back to Guzmán's house, again going through the elaborate security precautions.

"You check out," Guzmán said. "What do you want with us?"

I told him about the purpose of my mission—to secure the purchase of certain minerals and compounds that we believed they had previously supplied to the French through a broker in Lima named Richtmeyer. I explained that the substances were needed for Israel's nuclear development program, to be used for a tactical battlefield weapon. Coupled with a peace treaty, it would be the best defense Israel could have.

Guzmán eyed me skeptically. "What's in it for the Shining Path?" he asked.

"Money, so you can help the Andean peasants."

"You have the right answers—but what about arms?"

I shook my head. "Not possible. Peru is a friendly country. Israel won't supply your people with arms. But with the right amount of money, you can purchase them somewhere else."

He told me they wanted $10 million for starters. After the money was deposited in a bank account in Geneva, we could get down to serious discussion. However, he still questioned whether I was trying to set him up.

From Lima, I called Shamir's adviser, Avi Pazner, to tell him that everything was going well. I gave him a bank-account number that had been passed to me, and Pazner told me that the money would be deposited. The plan was that four Cessnas would be placed on standby in Colombia to fly to an airfield in Peru that Guzmán would later designate. These planes would fly out quantities of the substances to Venezuela. Colombia had been chosen as the starting point because if the planes were detected, the Peruvians would think they were on a cocaine run; many small planes flew coca leaves from Peru to Colombia.

Next I called Barbara Durr. I asked if she'd like to interview Guzmán. She was very excited at the prospect of such a scoop being dropped into her lap, but I had an ulterior motive. I wanted her to interview Guzmán to provide public proof to my superiors that we were talking to the right man, given the rumors that he was supposed to be dead. They wouldn't be too happy about laying out $10 million for a dead man.

Shortly after my call to Durr, I realized I was being tailed—and not by the Peruvians. I talked to Nick Davies's photographer friend, Peter Jordan, and he told me that Durr had tipped off the Cubans about my contact with Shining Path. At the time, I found out, the Cubans were advising the Peruvian government in its campaign against the Shining Path. I didn't like being tailed, and I didn't like Barbara Durr going behind my back. I decided to call in the aid of the Israeli ambassador. A quick solution to the problem was found. The chief of the antiterrorism police would arrange for her to be arrested for being in touch with the Shining Path, and then we would get her out of police hands. When she was freed, she would be grateful and more than willing to help us any way she could.

At least getting her arrested might make her think twice about passing on information to the Cubans. While Durr was at police headquarters, and British and U.S. Embassy representatives along with foreign journalist association officials were demanding her release, I called on the police antiterrorism chief. He told me he didn't know what the scheme was, but he had been asked to let her go when I arrived. So she was freed, and I made sure that everyone knew who had secured her release.

That evening I called at her house, and she thanked me profusely. I then had to leave to meet Col. Cordova, who was visiting Lima. But he could spare me no time. He said he had to fly back to Ayacucho immediately because five of his officers had been killed in a Shining Path ambush.

"I'm going to teach those people a lesson," he raged. "I'm going to destroy them all."

"Are you crazy?" I asked. "You can't punish a whole village. What did they do?"

But he wouldn't listen. I raced back to Barbara Durr's house and begged her to call CBS radio, for which she also worked. I told her to get a story on the air about the ambush and that the colonel was planning to massacre a village in revenge. I reasoned that if it was broadcast, it might stop his actions. But CBS told her on the phone that if he didn't carry out the massacre, the story would be regarded as alarmist. It was never broadcast. Within days, I read in *El Diario*, the Peruvian newspaper associated with Shining Path, that dozens of innocent villagers had been slaughtered.

This incident shook me up. Because I was so close to it, ironically, it had more impact on me than the mass killing of the Iran-Iraq war, for which I bore a direct share of responsibility. I realized I needed a break, so in early April 1988 I flew back to Israel for about a week. Ora, heavy with child, was a wonderful, welcoming sight.

While I was in Israel, further preparations were made for transporting the strategic materials from Peru. We arranged for the Israeli intelligence logistics man to fly first to Colombia to hire the planes and then on to Venezuela to line up the airfields. The aircraft would be twin-engine Cessna Citations—passenger planes—with the seats taken out. Colombian drug dealers used them all the time without interference from the Peruvian government because this was one of the country's main sources of foreign currency, even if it did sometimes fall into the hands of Shining Path or the peasants.

We also planned to have an Israeli liner in port in Venezuela to pick up the substances after their arrival from Peru. Venezuela would give us no trouble—the country's intelligence network had a close relationship with Israel.

When I arrived back in Lima in mid-April, Barbara was waiting for me at the airport, as arranged by phone. I told her that the Israelis, who had saved her from going to jail, would like her to do something for them. In fact, it wasn't all that tough a job—she merely had to travel with me to Ayacucho because I needed the protection of a journalist. Things wouldn't get too hot with a newspaper representative around.

Barbara agreed to fly with me to Ayacucho. On our landing, the police greeted me, now a frequent visitor, but they stopped her. I told them that she was traveling with me, and they let her through. We took a cab to the hotel, and at exactly noon the Shining Path attacked the police station, leaving six officers dead. They announced afterwards through leaflets dropped in the square that this was their revenge for the village massacre and that there would be more vengeance killings in the future.

That evening, leaving Barbara in the hotel, I started walking to Roberto's house. He had asked me to be there at 8:00 P.M.

Suddenly gunfire broke out. Amid shouts and screams from all directions, I threw myself down flat. Then, during a lull, I ran on to Roberto's house. I was furious and asked why he had wanted me to visit him when he knew my life would be at risk.

"We can't tell you about our operations in advance," he said.

This had been some operation. The Shining Path had taken over the police station altogether and had freed every one of the prisoners held there.

Suddenly all the power went off. In the darkness Roberto told me it was time to visit Guzmán. When I pointed out that there would be a military presence everywhere, he said with a smile that it would take them two hours to get organized. His smile broadened when I handed him a package I had brought—the prescription hair restorer Nick Davies had finally managed to get hold of in London through a balding friend.

After traveling in two vans to Guzmán's place, I told the Shining Path founder the truth: that I'd like him to give an interview to a newspaper reporter, explaining there were rumors that he was dead, that I was being duped, and that I had arranged for my government to "give away" $10 million.

"I can't give an interview to a foreign capitalist newspaper," he said.

"But don't you want the rest of your money? I need some kind of proof that you are alive."

"Don't your bosses believe you?"

I told him they believed me, but the interview would help. Eventually, after a discussion about our thinning locks—these fellows really had a thing about their hair—he agreed to give an interview to *El Diario*.

Meanwhile he asked me for a few favors. He wanted the Israelis to buy a chain of five small newspapers—the Ocho Group—on the movement's behalf, and he also asked for medical equipment to be brought on the Cessnas that were coming in from Colombia. The equipment would be offloaded, and 200 kilograms of each of the substances would be put on board. It was then that he gave me the location of the airfields in Peru where the Cessnas could land. So the meeting ended on a satisfactory note.

Later I was told by phone that Guzmán had a very close friend, Cynthia McNamara, a U.S. citizen, who was in jail in Lima, accused of taking part in a Shining Path attack. Cynthia, I learned, was a former hippie in her early 40s who had visited Ecuador collecting Indian art pieces and later traveled to Peru. In Ayacucho she had fallen in love with a handsome doctor named Enrico. She had also met Guzmán and had struck up a good friendship with him. Then she had been jailed. What Guzmán wanted now was for me to do something for her, perhaps through the Israeli ambassador. I made no promises.

With the landing strips now designated, the following Friday was arranged for the pickup of the minerals. The only problem I had was getting back to Lima yet again in order to phone the logistics man in Caracas to tell him what had been arranged. I also needed a good excuse to get away from the university. I had been away quite a bit—and I had, after all, been taken on as a teacher.

Barbara provided the excuse. I told the university that my friend had sprained her ankle badly and I had to travel with her to Lima so she could get medical attention. We arrived in the capital a couple of days before the scheduled pickup and I made my call from a safe phone at the embassy. Then I phoned Roberto to confirm the arrangements.

"How are you going to manage taking the stuff off the ship in Israel?" he asked.

"That's our problem," I replied. "You just make sure it's delivered."

It was all trust. If one thing went wrong, the whole operation would collapse. I waited on tenterhooks at the Country Club Hotel in Lima, where I was staying. Finally I received word that the planes had arrived in Venezuela with the substances. It had all gone like clockwork.

The following Monday, while waiting for the flight back to Ayacucho, I saw the smiling face of Guzmán peering out from the front page of the newspaper. As with the delivery of the strategic materials, he had also kept this part of the deal.

I bought a number of copies to take to Ayacucho with me—as we were traveling on an early flight from Lima, these would be the first he would see. There was also good news for him about his friend Cynthia. Barbara had learned that only three days earlier McNamara had been released from jail.

My guilty conscience about taking so much time off from the university was relieved later that morning when we arrived back in Ayacucho. As we were traveling by cab from the airport to the hotel, gunfire burst out and the driver swerved into the curb. We threw ourselves flat against the seats. But the bullets weren't meant for us. At a roadblock ahead, soldiers had seen a machine gun in a car occupied by students, there had been an angry confrontation, shots were fired, and three students were shot dead. It was later announced that an indefinite strike had been called at the university. So I was out of a job . . . if it was ever really a job in the first place.

My other work, of course, had to continue. More of the chemicals had to be bought, which meant further negotiations with Guzmán. At his place, the discussions became tense. He tried to get a fortune from the Israeli government by asking for a house in a nice part of Lima, the newspaper chain, and $28 million. He backed up his demands by pointing out that, according to a physics professor at the university, with these substances, Israel was going to be invincible.

"It's worth paying up," Guzmán said. "Your government is nothing but an arm of American imperialism anyway. That money is American, and we want it for the Peruvian people."

Sensing that I was about to argue again about his demands, he cut in, "You're a hard-nosed Jew." Then he paused before adding, "I didn't mean to insult you. I'm part Jewish myself. But above all else we're human beings. We are all one. We are all equal," he corrected himself.

He also introduced me to more of the philosophy of the movement he had founded. He had some interesting thoughts on equality, referring to Lenin and the relationship between men and women.

"As a result of Lenin, the Soviets frowned on marriage and encouraged sexuality. When Stalin took over in the '30s, countless numbers of homeless children were roaming around Soviet cities, without any family nucleus. So Stalin announced that the family was to be a socialist institution to protect its women. This is how our Soviet friends manipulated everything. We here in the Shining Path see that the real way is eternal love between one man and one woman forever. All right, if it doesn't work, you are allowed to divorce, but it is not something to be encouraged."

Apparently, in Guzmán's idiosyncratic philosophy, communal living did not extend to sex.

"What is the big deal about sex?" he asked rhetorically. "I believe it should be one child per couple. Look at the homeless kids in Lima. It's horrible that their only hope is to be sold to foreign couples who can't have children of their own."

But how, I asked, was he really going to solve the problem? It was all right to talk about it, but what about practicalities?

He smiled softly. "We will start our calendar in Peru from the year zero. At that time everyone in Lima will leave for communes, and Lima as we know it will be erased from the surface of the earth—it's such a horrible city anyway with its slums, no good water, no drainage systems."

I found this fascinating. These were similar to the naive, idealistic thoughts I had had when I was a teenager. Bring everybody back to one level and start again.

We returned to our negotiations. It was agreed that for a further payment of $18 million—bringing the total, with the earlier $10 million, to $28 million—Israel would receive another 300 kilograms of each of the substances.

15

The Judge

HAPPY WITH MY progress, I flew to London in early June 1988. I asked Barbara to join me because I was aware that anywhere along the way things could go wrong and I might need a witness. My sudden diversion to London had been on Prime Minister Shamir's instructions. Iran's defense minister, Col. Jalali, had requested a meeting with me. The last time I'd seen him had been with Robert Gates in Kansas City when the defense minister had sought assurances that arms to Iran would continue, despite the exposure of the Iran-contra affair. Since then, however, Israel had decided to stop the flow of arms to Iran because the war with Iraq had reached an uneasy ceasefire. Now Jalali wanted to start up another channel.

Accompanied by Barbara, I caught a taxi to a large house in Belgravia. London policemen stood on duty at the gates. Iranian security men patrolled the grounds. It was, in fact, a house owned by Col. Jalali. He was waiting, his face anxious. I introduced him to Barbara as "my friend Hussein," the pseudonym he used in London.

He led us into the lounge where other guests were assembled— Jalali's wife, Mina; Jalali's aide and his wife; John de Laroque; and a German arms dealer, Werner Krüger, who was working with the Israelis. After pleasantries were exchanged, Col. Jalali and I went out to the garden and got down to business. He expressed dismay that the Iraqis were growing in strength—thanks to the Americans. The U.S. was supporting the manufacture of unconventional weapons and chemicals in Chile, which were then being flown to Baghdad.

"If Saddam Hussein doesn't attack us again," said Jalali, "he'll turn his attention to Saudi Arabia or Kuwait."

Jalali handed me an official letter from the Defense Ministry of the Islamic Republic and asked me to pass it on to the prime minister. In essence, it pointed out Tehran's concerns about Iraq's supply of chemicals. But I had a request to put to him. We needed Iran's help in securing the freedom of three Israeli soldiers being held in Lebanon.

"We'll be glad to help," said Jalali, "but we'll have to take the arrangement further. I'm going to have to show the Revolutionary Guard that we have got something out of Israel in return—even though we're already asking for your help in stopping the chemical supplies to Iraq."

"What do you have in mind?" I asked.

"We need three C-130s, and we'll pay for them, of course. I'll tell the radical mullahs that we're getting one plane for each soldier. You get us these planes, and we'll get the soldiers out."

The business end of our meeting concluded, we strolled over to the barbeque, where meats were cooking. Later, as a farewell gesture, each guest was given a gift box of pistachio nuts.

I arranged to meet Barbara in Lima and then flew by myself to Israel. In El Al's first-class lounge at Heathrow Airport I met by coincidence Gen. David Ivry, director general of Israel's Ministry of Defense. He was basically a Labor Party man, but I nevertheless mentioned to him the question of the C-130s because he would learn of the Iranian request anyway. He was not very encouraging.

"You realize, of course, that Prime Minister Shamir will not be able to arrange this on his own," he said. "He will need the support of the Labor Party in the coalition, too, because of the complete shut-down of all arms to Iran."

At Shamir's office the following day, I gave his adviser, Avi Pazner, a full briefing on the arrangements with Guzmán. I was told the extra $18 million would be paid into the Swiss bank account and money would be authorized for the purchase of the newspaper chain and a house for the Shining Path in Lima.

However, I felt I should discuss the issue of the C-130s with the prime minister himself. Pazner arranged it.

"Israel owes you a lot," Shamir told me when I entered his office, accompanied by Pazner. Directing me to the guest sofa, the prime minister sat behind his desk, his tiny body lost in a huge leather chair, his large head appearing out of proportion. The office was expensively decorated with stylish leather furniture and a coffee table at which Shamir entertained his guests. On his desk was a small Israeli flag, while on the wall were pictures of David Stern and Vladimir Jabotinski, who founded the militant Zionist Revisionist movement which had such an important role to play in the establishment of the State of Israel; and Theodor Herzl, founder of the political form of Zionism and more popularly known as the socialist father.

I told Shamir in detail about the Peruvian situation, and he was happy about how little money had been spent.

"We were expecting to spend $50 million up to this point," he said. "You have my blessing to continue to do whatever is necessary. And I appreciate the time you are giving up when your wife is expecting a baby at any moment."

I then produced the letter from the Iranians and pointed out the verbal request for C-130s. Shamir read the letter asking Israel to help with more arms and to try to stop the chemical weapons from Chile, then placed it carefully back on his desk.

"I'm not going to answer this officially," he said. "We have an agreement with the United States not to continue to supply arms to Iran at this point." I was aware of this. Earlier that year, after the Iran-Iraq war came to an uneasy halt, Robert Gates, representing the U.S., and Avi Pazner, representing Israel, had reached a secret agreement that neither country would supply the Iranians. It also said that the U.S. would try to stop the chemical weapons going to Iraq. But as I was to learn, neither country abided by the agreement. "Please tell your Iranian contact that I have received the letter and it is being considered," said Shamir.

I wondered whether this meant he was turning down the request for the C-130s. If that were the case, the soldiers would have to remain in enemy hands in Lebanon.

He appeared to read my thoughts. "Regarding those C-130s," said the prime minister, "go ahead and make the arrangements. You have my blessing in this affair."

I had to return to Peru, but I was determined to spend some time with Ora. It was June, and although it was very hot, those days together were magical. We traveled to the Dead Sea, and as she stood on the shores and looked out across the water, she looked fabulous, glowing. Then we went north to the Sea of Galilee, where we spent the night. I put my hand on her stomach and felt our baby kicking. And back in Jerusalem, after an ultrasound test, they told us we were going to have a girl. I was over the moon.

But something was on Ora's mind. I asked her what the problem was.

"Who is Barbara?" she wanted to know.

My heart leaped. There was good reason for Ora to be suspicious. What had begun as insurance for me had become a friendship and had now drifted into something more intimate. "How do you know about her?"

"Every time I've called you in Peru she's answered the phone."

"She's around because of work," I said. "An American journalist working for a prominent British newspaper. She provides protection for me—insurance." I felt like a louse as I said it. But Ora accepted my explanation—or so I thought at the time.

Five days later I took the Lufthansa flight from Tel Aviv to Frankfurt. Col. Jalali's aide, a soft-spoken man with a small goatee, was waiting for me in the lobby of the airport hotel. Over dinner, I explained that the letter requesting more arms had been passed on to the prime minister and would be considered in the cabinet. In the meantime, I said, we were ready to move on the C-130s.

"How much are you asking?" he wanted to know.

I'd been given no briefing on the price of the aircraft. I plucked a figure out of the air, based on my previous experience of Hercules sales: $12 million each.

"You want $36 million and the soldiers for three C-130s?"

"No, we want $36 million for the planes. But we also want the soldiers back." Israel would not be put into a position where it could be seen to be giving arms for hostages' release. Other governments might do that, but it was not our policy—at least not publicly.

I gave him two bank-account numbers with the request that $18 million go into each. The payment would take about ten days. He promised to do his best to get the soldiers freed.

"Are you also interested," he asked, "in getting any American hostages freed?"

"That's not Israel's business. But if you can manage to get some released, we'd be happy."

I returned to Peru in early July, and did some househunting on behalf of the Shining Path. I found a fantastic mansion with a pool and nine servants. I made no commitments to the man who showed me around, Enrique, who was selling the property for his mother. The family also owned the Ocho newspaper chain, which was perfect. I would have to speak to Guzmán, of course, and I wondered what he might make of the house and all its trappings.

Enrique suggested that I meet a friend of his, who turned out to be the Peruvian minister of finance. He wanted to know why I was investing in Peru in such an unstable political situation.

"The market is low," I said. "And one day it will go up."

"That's reasonable thinking," he said thoughtfully. "But under a *Sendero* government, it will be worthless."

I flew to Ayacucho, and, that evening I went to see Guzmán, who told me that arrangements had been made for a Peruvian businessman to receive the house and the newspaper chain once Israel had paid for them. And he had good news for me. I could call my logistics man and tell him that Friday had been set for the next airlift of the materials. That was only four days away. If I traveled back to Lima to make a safe call to Israel, they would not have much notice. I decided to chance a call from the Ayacucho hotel.

From my room, I asked the operator to connect me to Jerusalem. When Ora answered, I told her to call Avi Pazner and simply tell him it was the same plan for this coming Friday. Then I hung up. Half an hour later I received a call from the logistics man in Caracas. He just asked whether it was Friday, I confirmed it, and hung up again. I had to take as few chances as possible.

I went back to Lima and, on July 12 and 13, made all the arrangements for the purchase of the house and the newspapers—$400,000 for the house and $2 million for the newspapers. I need not have bothered. The Shining Path leadership changed its mind, deciding that to base some of its key people in Lima at this stage would be too dangerous: In the volatile political atmosphere they would be easy targets for the military.

With this shipment on its way, I planned to leave Peru. But the Israeli scientists, evidently considering that they might not get another opportunity to stockpile the necessary substances, had decided they wanted another 500 kilograms. I was instructed to get it in the works before I left. I phoned Roberto and told him I needed another shipment right away. This was arranged, again following the now familiar routine.

With this final shipment on its way to Israel, I flew back to Jerusalem—in time for the birth of my daughter Shira on July 22, 1988. I remained with Ora through the birth at Hadassah Hospital. I was overwhelmed. Right then, Lima, the Shining Path, Col. Cordova, and Barbara all seemed a long way away. I felt I had left the dangers of Peru behind me. The mission had been successful, and Israel could continue its bomb program.

Two days after Shira's birth, I was shocked to hear my next orders. There had been a miscalculation. The scientists had blundered. They decided they needed another 50 kilograms of one of the metals, and I had to return to Peru to make the arrangements.

I returned to Lima in early August. I had phoned Barbara and she met me at the airport. Roberto had also been told I was coming back, and had flown to Lima. We all met in the lobby of the Caesar Hotel and then strolled down the street. I explained why I was back.

"I'll help you," said Roberto. "I'll relay the message back to Ayacucho and let you know."

"Roberto, I don't want to hang around too long. It's getting dangerous for me here, and besides, I have a new-born daughter back in Israel. I'd like to know very quickly."

He promised to discuss the new request with "the boss" in Ayacucho first thing in the morning.

After Roberto left, Barbara told me that the U.S. consul general, Donna Hamilton, wanted to speak to me. I went to her office immediately. A very gracious woman, she told me that she needed my help. Cynthia McNamara, the American woman, had been rearrested on August 2, because a judge in Cangallo, a small village in the Andes some 40 kilometers from Ayacucho, wanted her extradited to his jurisdiction. It was a district controlled by the Shining Path, with a heavy Peruvian military presence only inside the village, and the only way she could get there safely would be with a military escort. The consulate had tried to get a court order in Lima that would effectively detain McNamara in the capital, but it was not looking good.

The charge against her was that she had been involved in smuggling medical goods to the Shining Path. When a truck containing medical supplies had been stopped for inspection, three people had been shot dead. Among the attackers, it was said, was a foreign woman fitting her description, although there was no real evidence it was McNamara.

"This judge drinks quite a bit," said Hamilton. "If someone can get to him and talk him out of this. . . ."

I knew what she was asking. Because I was able to travel in areas occupied by the Shining Path and also able to get a permit from the military to go on their base, where the judge's office was located, I was one of the few people who could do the job. I said I would see what I could do.

The following morning, over a late breakfast with Enrique, with whom I had become quite friendly, I mentioned I was planning to travel to Cangallo to see the judge. He shook his head.

"If the *Sendero* don't get you, the military will. And if they don't get you, you're still up against the village thieves, who will be after you for your shirt and your shoes. You should ask your professor friend to give you protection. It's his people who might end up attacking you."

"I don't really want to do that," I said. "I'm neutral in this war. I have nothing to do with either side."

I realized that Enrique was testing me to find out if I was a Shining Path sympathizer.

Accompanied by Barbara, I flew to Ayacucho where, after giving it much thought, I asked Roberto for safe passage to meet the judge. He assured me he would take care of things.

The following morning I asked a cab driver to take Barbara and me to Cangallo.

"You're mad," he said and drove away.

The fourth attempt to find a driver worked. I waved a $100 bill in front of him. There was no real road, he explained, and he would have to take spare tires and gas cans. Later that morning Barbara and I left for . . . well, who knew what?

It was a painstakingly slow drive along a very bad dirt road with rocky outcrops protruding from the sparse vegetation. Occasionally we were stopped by groups of Shining Path members who let us proceed after looking at me. Somehow word had gone ahead that we were on our way. I had Roberto to thank for this.

By six in the evening, we reached a bridge at the entrance to the village. On the far side of the bridge was a military post. Soldiers stared in amazement at the taxi rumbling along toward them. They raised their rifles as we approached. This time I produced a letter I had obtained in Lima from Col. Cordova, who had agreed to assist.

The judge, I had been told, could be found at the military barracks, but when we arrived there and introduced ourselves to the commander, we were told the judge would not be back until the morning.

"He's investigating a massacre," said the commander, a captain. A few more casual questions elicited the information that the judge was looking into the massacre I had tried to stop Col. Cordova from committing earlier that year.

We found a small pension in the village and treated ourselves to one room and the driver to another. We dined on rice and beans by candlelight, because there was no electricity.

In the morning we met the judge in his office. When I explained I had come on behalf of Cynthia McNamara, and he found out I was not a lawyer, he declared, "I can't talk to you." Then he thought about it a moment and added: "Actually, you can act on her behalf because, under Peruvian law, anyone can defend someone else in court."

The judge, a good-looking, informally dressed man in his

mid-30s, explained that McNamara was wanted in his court for subversive activity—aiding and abetting terrorism. He seemed very agitated, walking back and forth. He made a few phone calls, and shortly afterward a group of antiterrorist police arrived. He relaxed then and got out McNamara's file. As I glanced at the police, I wondered if he felt I had come to threaten him.

"A pretty girl," he said looking at her photo. "I would have liked to meet her, but they took her to court in Lima. I don't want to try her again; that might be double jeopardy. And I think the evidence is inconclusive. I'll rescind my order."

I was surprised at the quick decision and asked him if I could carry the papers documenting his decision. I was also interested in finding out more about the massacre, and as I started asking, I put three bottles of Johnny Walker I had brought with me on the table.

He looked taken aback, but I insisted they were for him as a friend. Then I pressed a little harder on the massacre, and he told me how he had been taken to the scene by the police—not the military—where he had been shown some 90 bodies in a mass grave. The military had blamed the *Sendero*; the peasants said it was the military.

"Sir," I said, "I'd like to give you a sworn statement about this massacre. I can tell you who was behind it."

I told him about Cordova's plans to get revenge for the death of his soldiers and how I had tried to prevent the tragedy by getting Barbara to send a radio report on his intentions. After my statement had been signed—and witnessed by two of the police—the judge said, "Rafael [Cordova] is my friend, but my friends can also make mistakes. Some peasants have also identified him, and for the past two days he has been in Lima. We have found some women who were witnesses to the killing of their husbands, and we've taken them back to Ayacucho in a helicopter. It's terrible that such a thing has happened in my jurisdiction. Whoever is responsible will be brought to justice—the *Sendero* people, Rafael, whoever. I will see to it that justice is done."

By signing the statement, of course, I was putting myself at odds with Col. Cordova. "I wonder if we're going to live long enough to make it back to Lima," said Barbara.

As a start, we made it back to Ayacucho. I had to present the judge's rescinding papers to the court there, but it was five in the evening and everyone had gone home. So I found out where the clerk of the court lived and took the documents around to his house. He refused to accept the package, saying it could only be sent by legal mail.

I told him I'd be back in half an hour and went off in search of Marcus, the Communist Party member. I gave him $300 and asked him to spread it around to the clerk of the court and the president of the tribunal. It wasn't long before Marcus returned with the message that the senior president of the court would see me at his house immediately.

There I was told by the judge that at first he had thought it was illegal to meet someone after court hours, but he had consulted his books and discovered that in an emergency situation a good citizen can carry papers. Once they had passed through his hands, however, they had to be signed by two other judges and then sent to Lima. After further discussion, he agreed to call the prosecutor and the clerk of the court together right then. An hour later we were ready to proceed with a hearing into the case against Cynthia McNamara in the judge's living room.

The prosecutor said the case against her was strong—two peasants had seen her with the group, but they didn't have any names. Acting as McNamara's lawyer, I said the judge in Cangallo had looked into the case and had found no evidence against her and that I agreed with his findings.

The tribunal president thought about things for a short time, then declared, "I accept the motion put by Miss McNamara's lawyer, good citizen Ben-Menashe. The case is dismissed."

Even so, as it happened, the Ayacucho prosecutor tried to bring additional charges against McNamara, and she was held in jail another ten days. The night of August 22, she was released, and, the next day, she left the country for Ireland.

Back in Lima a few days after my successful debut as a defense attorney, I was awaiting word from Roberto on the final shipment. There was soon shocking news: The newspapers were filled with a story about what was described as a *Sendero* attack on a military base near Cangallo, in which a judge was killed. It was the same judge I had met just a few days earlier and to whom I had described Cordova's role in the village massacre. I had no doubt who was really responsible for his murder.

Within 24 hours all hell broke loose. In the wake of more stories about the investigation into the massacre and the gradual turn of suspicion toward the military, Peruvian radio reported that two military helicopters in the Ayacucho area had been brought down by Stinger missiles. Twenty military personnel had died. It was clear to me that these were the Stingers Cordova had sold to the Shining Path. They, in turn, had used them to shoot down the colonel's helicopters. He should, of course, have foreseen that.

News of the Shining Path attack had broken shortly before Barbara and I were due to have dinner with Col. Cordova. It was an appointment I was determined to keep. We met in a fancy restaurant in Lima.

"There's a lot of news about," I told him. "And I have my thoughts on a few things." I didn't have to explain.

"Whatever you may think or hear, I am working in the interests of my nation."

"Yes, I'm sure," I said.

"Whatever I do is for the good of the people, so they will learn who is in authority. We want to build bridges and roads for these poor peasants, but if they go wild and become lawless we sometimes have to use force. Once they behave, we can start helping them. I'm sure you understand how we work. You guys kill Palestinians, don't you?"

"I don't accept your argument."

Our meal continued in this fashion. It was obvious he wanted to leave, but he was determined to have the last word. "What we do is not your business. Keep yourself out of it. In fact, I think it is time you both left the country. Guests are always welcome in Peru, of course, but I think it is becoming dangerous for you. These *Sendero* people are very angry at you."

"Oh?"

He didn't explain that, but it wasn't hard to imagine that whatever force might be used against me would be blamed on the Shining Path. Still, we had the Stinger deal on him, Barbara was with me, and anyone who killed us would have to face the wrath of the Israeli government. I was willing to take my chances.

I wanted to leave Peru, but I had to complete my work first. The next morning, Roberto called. As promised, there would be no problem in supplying the metal, but it would take three or four weeks. Although the same aircraft and airstrips would be used, it was important that our logistics man be in place in Caracas, because the phone call would come in at the last minute. I made the necessary reports.

My work in Peru was now over. I had just one more errand to perform before returning to Israel for a full briefing on my next assignment. I flew to London, where I met with Nick Davies to discuss the deal we had set up with the Iranians involving the three C-130s, an arrangement that had the full blessing of Prime Minister Shamir.

The Iranians had paid the requested $36 million into two accounts in the Cayman Islands, but it was necessary to brief Davies on the Israeli conditions. He was to tell the Iranian buyers that even though the money had been paid in advance, the planes would not leave Israel until they could assure us that our three soldiers would be released from Lebanon.

Happy that everything was in place, I returned to Israel. My experiences in Peru were to prove to be invaluable in helping me cope with the ordeals that lay ahead.

16

Never Again

PRIME MINISTER YITZHAK SHAMIR marched swiftly through the corridors of his office complex, two aides hurrying to keep up. For a small, elderly man with a seemingly frail body, he was now bursting with angry energy as he made his way to the suite in which he had called his crisis conference. It was mid-August 1988, and Israel was at its most vulnerable.

Infuriated by the chemical weapons, missiles, and nuclear technology going to Iraq from the West, Shamir decided to appoint a task force of intelligence officers to bring a halt to this supply. Shamir's chief adviser, Avi Pazner, headed the task force, which included two people from Military Intelligence research to provide background, two from Mossad operations to give operational support, and me, representing the Prime Minister's Office. Shamir wanted the matter handled directly out of his office because it involved Chile and the U.S., both friendly countries, and was therefore quite sensitive. I was to carry out whatever plan was decided upon. Shamir and Pazner were present for only parts of this August 1988 meeting. The rest of us were there the entire time.

The big worry was Iraq. The U.S. was not only refusing to listen to our concern, but was actually helping Saddam Hussein build his arsenal of unconventional weapons. Chemicals and the artillery cups to contain them were pouring in from Chile and South

Africa, and Israel felt helpless to stop the flow. But it was clear that something had to be done.

On all our minds was Cardoen Industries, an arms production company with its main offices in Santiago, Chile. The owner, with 99 percent of the shares, was Carlos Cardoen. He had relinquished the other one percent to his new (and second) wife.

As we sat around a conference table in the prime minister's suite of offices, we were briefed on Cardoen's background. He came from an upper-class Chilean family of Italian descent. In his early 20s, after attending university in the U.S.—where he received a degree as a mining engineer—he returned to Santiago immediately after General Augusto Pinochet's 1973 *coup d'état* to work for the government-owned Chilean Mining Corporation. As part of his job, he had to procure explosives for mining purposes, which turned out to be a lucrative business for him personally. Israeli intelligence officers established that various companies approached Cardoen to sell him their dynamite, and offered him commissions if he would buy it. So at a very early age, Cardoen found out what it meant to receive kickbacks.

He struck up a friendship with the mining corporation's chief engineer and turned it to his advantage. He resigned and started working as a private contractor after receiving assurances that all blasting equipment used by the Chilean Mining Corporation would be bought through him. His success as a dynamite broker set him thinking on a grander scale, and he decided to try brokering small arms. This time it wasn't such smooth sailing.

In 1979 Carlos Cardoen traveled to Israel and applied for a license to sell Israeli arms in South America. He made his approach to SIBAT, the Foreign Defense Sales Office of the Israeli Ministry of Defense. In *theory*, anyone exporting Israeli arms had to be issued a special license through this office.

SIBAT published a slick English-language brochure with color photographs on glossy paper detailing all Israel's weaponry that was for sale, whether it be a handgun or a tank. Having made a selection, a foreign country's agent would apply to SIBAT for an export license. The applicant would fill out a form and attach to it an end-user certificate from the buyer.

SIBAT's head, the deputy director general of the Ministry of Defense, in charge of foreign sales, would prepare a file on every application received, and his staff would then investigate if this material was available for sale, whether it was politically accept-able to sell, if the end-user certificate was for real, and if the broker was honest and trustworthy. This file would then be handed to the director general of the Ministry of Defense, who, in turn, would present it for final approval to a ministerial commit-tee that would sit once a week, comprising the prime minister, foreign minister, defense minister, and finance minister. If they approved the application, it would go back to SIBAT, and the export license would be issued. Sometimes conditions would be imposed. This, then, was the official, formal way of buying arms from Israel.

SIBAT was also responsible for issuing broker licenses to for-mer Israeli military personnel or others who wished to open arms-dealing companies in Israel with foreign branches. It could also issue licenses to foreign arms brokers, certifying that Israel recognized the licensee as a legitimate arms broker who could apply to Israel for weapons on someone else's behalf. It was this last type of license that Cardoen asked for when he showed up in Israel in 1979. As a reference, he presented a license issued to him by the Chilean Ministry of Defense.

In 1979, at the time of Cardoen's visit to Israel, ERD—in charge of relations between Israeli Military Intelligence and for-eign services—was asked by SIBAT to check out Cardoen with the Chilean military attaché in Israel. I had met Cardoen on that occasion. He struck me as an ambitious person who had had some education. But he didn't seem to be worried about scruples or to care particularly about the politics involved. A mercenary type, he wanted to become rich at a very young age—and he was certainly on the way with a big office in Santiago and confidence to match.

This time, though, his confidence was temporarily shattered. Israel turned down his request. He was an unknown factor who couldn't show any experience, except that he had bought dyna-mite.

At the time he did not have any established political connec-tions in Chile *to our knowledge.* If he'd had such connections, he would certainly have had a better chance. We later learned he had been walking around with one of SIBAT's catalogs in Chile,

promising people he could get them anything that was illus-
trated. But Israel dealt only with professionals, with applications
from known former generals, for example, who had connections
with politicians. There was no way this young, unknown Chilean
was going to get a license—particularly as there was a suspicion
that brokers like him had connections with Israel's enemies.

After being rejected, Cardoen flew directly from Israel to South
Africa. There he obtained a brokering license from the government weapons manufacturer, South African Arms Corporation
(ARMSCOR)—but only after he sought help from the Chilean
ambassador to South Africa, an acquaintance of his father's. He
returned to Chile with this license, and with the aid of more of
his father's connections, he obtained loans from Chilean banks.
He then started work as an arms producer and broker. But how
this part of his life generally worked was very hazy to us.

At our August 1988 meeting, Prime Minister Shamir listened
carefully. "Confidence this Cardoen certainly has," remarked the
prime minister, "but subtlety he lacks."

The rest of the briefing, which Shamir and Pazner only caught
parts of, covered how Cardoen got involved in selling arms to Iraq
and bringing us up-to-date on present developments. Sometime
in 1982, according to Israeli intelligence, Cardoen was introduced through a person in ARMSCOR to the Iraqi deputy chief of
the General Staff for Procurement in Baghdad. By early 1985
Cardoen was selling arms to Iraq.

He was doing this with the help of ARMSCOR and with the
support of certain people connected with the U.S. government.
One of them was Alan Sanders, who had links to the CIA.
Sanders's cover was ITICO—Integrated Technologies International Co. Cardoen, whose primary, and probably only, customer
was Iraq, had been receiving the technology for cluster bombs
from Sanders in the form of blueprints. In spite of a U.N. arms
embargo against Chile, Cardoen, together with Chilean Military
Industries, was producing these clusterbombs with a covert U.S.
license. Israel wanted to get its hands on those bombs.

In late 1985, I had traveled to the United States on assignment
and approached Alan Sanders. I told him I wanted to buy cluster
bombs for Israel. Although we had been receiving them from
South Africa, Israel wanted an additional arsenal of cluster

bombs, especially the Chilean ones that were made with the latest U.S. technology. But we also wanted to establish if it was even possible for us to obtain them. I was well aware that at the time the sale of cluster bombs to Israel was prohibited by the U.S.—a fact Sanders made clear to me. However, he drove me to the Virginia office of arms dealer Richard Babayan, an Armenian-Iranian CIA contract agent who had close contacts with Cardoen. Babayan, coincidentally, had also been a schoolmate of mine at the American Community School in Tehran 20 years before. Babayan explained to me that Cardoen would sell the cluster bombs to Israel, which told me everything I wanted to know.

"Cardoen," said Sanders, "will sell the bombs to anyone who pays him."

A few weeks later, an Israeli diplomatic crate was sent to New York from Santiago, and then loaded onto one of our regular military Boeing 707 flights to Tel Aviv. If we could get cluster bombs that easily, God knows what Iraq was getting from Cardoen.

During that year of enlightenment, 1985, Robert Gates, the CIA's deputy director for intelligence, was approached by Nachum Admoni, director of Mossad, regarding U.S. support for Cardoen. Admoni pointed out to Gates that the Israelis were very concerned about the support of Iraq, especially through Chile and South Africa. Cardoen by this time owned two plants for the manufacture of chemical weapons in Santiago. He operated a cluster bomb factory in cooperation with Chile's military and had a third chemical weapons plant in Paraguay. In addition, he was building a chemical weapons plant outside Baghdad.

The artillery cups, or shells, for Cardoen's Santiago-produced chemical weapons came from West Germany, procured for him by an Egyptian living in the U.S., Ihsan Barbouti. Barbouti had earlier provided equipment for chemical weapons to Libya and was known to the Israelis for arranging for former Nazi scientists to work on missile technology in Egypt in the 1950s. By the late 1950s, all these scientists had been eliminated by Mossad. But Barbouti escaped with his life by faking his death. In the early 1980s he resurfaced in the U.S. Some time after his involvement in providing chemicals to Libya, according to Israeli intelligence, he cut a deal with the CIA and started working on its behalf with Arab countries, basing himself in Texas and Florida.

During the August 1988 meeting we were reminded of how Cardoen would send the chemicals manufactured in Santiago and Paraguay, along with the German-made cups imported through Barbouti, to Baghdad by Iraqi Airways 747 cargo planes. The crates containing the chemicals and cups were openly visible on the tarmac at Santiago airport, with labels making it quite clear that they were for shipment to Iraq. Cardoen was using U.S. banks such as the Valley National Bank in Arizona to help finance his sales. He was also using a factory in Boca Raton, Florida, to get some raw materials for his chemical manufacturing. We also knew that while Alan Sanders had provided blueprints for cluster bombs to Cardoen, the Gamma Corporation in the U.S., a CIA cut-out, had sold the fuses for the cluster bombs to Cardoen.

By late 1986 Israel was expressing great concern about the arms shipments to Iraq, with Prime Minister Shamir threatening to go to Congress. So Robert Gates, now deputy director of the CIA, called a meeting in Santiago, the sole aim of which was to calm the Israelis. I described the gathering, which took place in my room at the Carrera Hotel, to the others at our August 1988 briefing at the Prime Minister's Office.

The participants at the secret meeting in Santiago were: Carlos Cardoen; Robert Gates; Sen. John Tower; Gen. Pieter Van Der Westhuizen, who had been chief of South African Military Intelligence, along with a representative of ARMSCOR; Gen. Rodolfo Stange, chief of the Chilean Carabineros (paramilitary police); and me. The representatives of Chile and South Africa produced a printed sheet identifying those weapons and other equipment that they admitted they had sold to Iraq. The list included artillery pieces, armored cars, tires, spare parts for military aircraft, and munitions, rockets, hand grenades, and firearms—but nothing unconventional.

At the gathering Gates was quite clear. The United States, he said, wanted to maintain the channel of arms to Iraq. It had to try to pull Iraq into its sphere of influence through the sale of conventional but not sophisticated weaponry. Israel was being paranoid, he said, and he gave his assurance that Israel would not be hurt. It was also understood that the Israelis would continue to supply the Iranians, and the South Africans would supply the Iraqis, to Israel's dismay.

It was quite obvious to me that this meeting had been called basically to pull the wool over Israel's eyes. As was expected, Cardoen continued to supply the wherewithal for chemical weapons and the cluster bombs to Iraq. It was a continuing source of concern for Israel, and it led to frustration with the U.S. for not putting a stop to it. During 1987 Israel repeatedly asked the Chilean government to step in and halt the sales. Our pleas to President Pinochet went unheeded, as did several to the U.S.

All this added up to a frightening situation for Israel. Our most powerful enemy, Iraq, was being systematically built up with weapons of mass destruction by our so-called friends. And we were supposed to go along simply because Robert Gates had given us his word that it would be okay.

Yitzhak Shamir was not about to sacrifice the security of Israel on anyone's word, let alone that of an American CIA official. And so, the conclusion of our August 1988 meeting was that Israel had to take the matter into its own hands. I was instructed to go to Chile, contact Carlos Cardoen directly, and offer him a carrot. If he didn't go for that, I would make it clear what came next.

I arrived in Chile in September 1988. Soaring office buildings towered over old church spires as the airport taxi took me to the apartment that Barbara, who had obtained a transfer from her newspaper, had rented.

The contrast between the haves and the have-nots was extreme. There were middle-class neighborhoods with their well-appointed homes in the northern suburbs, and then there were the slums, well hidden behind trees and walls, so that visitors traveling from the airport to the northern suburbs wouldn't notice them and would gain a completely wrong impression. A visiting journalist once described Chile as floating away from South America and taking on a European feeling—he was one of the many who have been fooled.

I remembered Chile well enough from my 1986 trip to meet

with Gates and the others to know that you could sit in an open-air restaurant in the northern suburbs and watch kids going through the trash cans of the wealthy. I also remembered that there weren't too many Native Americans. The European settlers had solved the "Indian problem" by killing them; later Chile became one of the first "democracies" in South America. That "kill-off-the-opposition-and-then-we-can-have-a-democracy" theory applies even today.

In this atmosphere of paradox, I had arrived to try to stop one of the most feared regimes in South America from continuing its deadly chemical trade with Iraq. Thousands had died mysteriously in Chile because they had stepped out of line. My only weapons were words. I knew they had to be used carefully.

My first appointment was with Gen. Rodolfo Stange, the head of President Pinochet's Carabineros.

The police headquarters was a well-protected cement office block with barred windows. I was taken to the top floor and stepped out of the elevator to face a glass door, above which a security camera peered down at me. After walking along a red-carpeted hall and being led through several offices, I was shown into an enormous wood-paneled room with Persian carpets and windows that looked out over the city. An imposing figure stepped forward to greet me. Middle-aged, balding, and dressed in a green uniform with bars that signified his various roles in the junta, Gen. Stange had not changed since I'd last met him in the Carrera Hotel two years earlier. All that had changed was the increased number of disappearances and deaths linked to his name.

"Welcome back to Chile, Mr. Ben-Menashe," he said in good English. "I hope you have a wonderful stay here. Are you booked into the Carrera Hotel?"

"No, I've rented an apartment. I'll be around for a while."

There was a moment of stunned silence. His face reflected deep concern. He tried to cover it up.

"Aha—so you will be our guest for a while. Of course, you are welcome. The weather is warming up, and I hope you enjoy Chile very much. I trust we will be able to see each other. Regard this as your second home."

He said how much he had enjoyed a visit to Israel, recalling in particular Jerusalem and Bethlehem.

"I'm sure the Israeli Embassy and your ambassador are aware of your being here?"

"General, I'm here on a confidential basis, directly empowered by the prime minister of Israel to inform you of his views about certain issues."

He frowned. "I can understand now why you are here. Do you have diplomatic accreditation to Chile?"

"No, sir, I carry my private passport as well as a diplomatic passport describing me as a roving ambassador for the Prime Minister's Office."

"It doesn't matter. Please don't regard what I asked as an impolite question. I was merely wondering about the status of your stay. I wondered whether you would be temporarily taking your current ambassador's place."

"Sir, are there any objections to my status here?"

"No, no, do not misunderstand me. You are most welcome. Everything you need will be made available to you by my office— security, protection, transportation, you only have to name it. And of course you are welcome to stay for as long as you like. This is your home. It's not Jerusalem, but I hope it will be a good substitute."

He told me he understood I was tired and ushered me into an adjoining private reception lounge. He offered me food, and when I told him I was a vegetarian, he said, "Yes, of course, I remember."

Joined by the general's chief of staff, we were attended by uniformed, black-tie waiters. I started out by telling him what he already knew, reminding him of the meeting we had had in 1986 and emphasizing the danger that the sale of unconventional weaponry to Iraq posed to Israel. I also made it clear that we were perfectly aware that the United States government was backing the Chilean effort.

As I talked, going over in detail everything that he already knew about U.S. policy and why Iraq would be a watershed from the Israeli point of view, a secretary took stenographic notes. I told him that I had brought with me a letter from Prime Minister Shamir, addressed to President Pinochet, containing a personal plea to stop the trade with Iraq. Stange politely told me that *"El Presidente"* had a lot of problems and was extremely busy. A meeting arranged for me at 10 A.M. the following day, when the letter was to be handed over, had been canceled. But it was always possible to call his chief of staff, said Stange, and then the letter would be passed on.

I stifled my disappointment. There was nothing I could do. However, there were some pertinent questions I wanted to ask about the forthcoming plebiscite in which Pinochet hoped to gain support to remain president until 1997.

"General," I asked, "what are your feelings about the plebiscite? According to the constitution, if President Pinochet loses, there'll be elections. Do you think he'll run again?"

"Of course, we'll all be pleased if he does run. But at the same time we think it's time for a fresh candidate."

"General, are you a candidate?"

He looked at me for a moment, then smiled. "If Chile needs me as a candidate, I will stand. I will do anything for the motherland. I want to prevent unwanted political forces from taking over."

Seeing him in his uniform, and hearing of his ambitions, I was reminded of the films about Nazi generals I used to see as a kid. I explained that Israeli intelligence had tracked anthrax, mustard gas, and chemical weapons being shipped from Chile to Iraq. I even pointed out that as my plane was landing at the airport just a few hours earlier, I had noticed two Iraqi 747s sitting on the tarmac.

"But of course," he said. "We do have trade with the Arab world."

"You know and I know what is happening. It has to be stopped at any price. If it means Israel going to the U.S. Congress to stop it, if it means using our intelligence services to stop it, believe me, we will."

His jaw dropped. The most feared man in the country was not used to being threatened.

"I cannot control Cardoen and the Americans," he said. "He is a private person and the Americans are . . . the Americans."

"General, you have to put a stop to this trade from your country. I'm sure you do not want to take responsibility for any Jewish children being gassed by your equipment."

He was really taken aback. He drew heavily on the fat cigar he had lit and took a drink. In the middle of our discussion, there was a phone call, picked up by his chief of staff.

"General," he said, "the president's chief secretary is here to pick up the letter."

I asked at that time if I could call my apartment to explain I would be late. Stange nodded toward the phone. I called Barbara and, making sure the general heard what I said, told her that despite his very busy schedule, Gen. Stange had been gracious enough to spare me his time.

When I hung up, he asked in a friendly tone, "You are here with a friend, or your wife?"

I told him she was the British *Financial Times* correspondent in Chile. I was with a journalist representing a very important newspaper which was not American. This of course was another veiled threat. He looked like I was sticking pins into him slowly. He took another sip of whiskey.

Pinochet's chief secretary entered the room, wearing a light brown tweed jacket with a white shirt, a dark brown tie, and dark brown trousers. With his dark brown shoes and dark brown belt thrown in, he definitely lacked color.

Looking at my options, I really had no choice but to hand over the letter. It was in a large white envelope embossed in the left-hand corner with the emblem of the State of Israel, the Menorah. Under the emblem in blue were the words: Prime Minister's Office. I opened my briefcase and handed it over. The secretary assured me it would be on the president's desk almost immediately. I told him that any response must not be made through the embassy, but through me. If I was not available, I said, the person to contact was Avi Pazner in Israel, who was aware of the situation.

As I prepared to leave, Gen. Stange invited me to his house for dinner the next day. But his chief of staff pointed out he had another appointment. "Cancel it!" he ordered.

Turning to me, he said, "I'll send a car to pick you up. And please relay my apologies to the prime minister of Israel on behalf of President Pinochet that he was too busy to see you, but I'm sure I'll be able to make it up." He added, "If there's anything you need, just say it, and it will be yours."

He offered me a lift home. I climbed into the back of a green military car with an official driver and the general's chief of staff—both in uniform—and I was taken back to the apartment on Calle Luz in the affluent suburb called Las Condes.

Barbara had bought a VCR. There was also a housekeeper who came with the apartment, with her own living quarters beyond the kitchen. I stayed up late that night watching a movie. In the middle of the night, when I had just fallen asleep, I received a phone call from Israel. It was 9:00 A.M. in Jerusalem. Avi Pazner wanted to know how things had gone.

I told him I had made progress, but the meeting with the president had been canceled. He told me to go to the embassy in the morning to talk on a secure phone. Arrangements would be made.

I overslept, and the second secretary at the embassy, who is also the Mossad representative in Santiago, called to say the safe phone system was at my disposal. I strolled to the embassy, which was close by. On reaching Pazner, I told him I had been invited to dinner at Stange's house. I pointed out I had not yet made my presence known to Cardoen.

"Be careful," said Pazner. "I don't have to remind you that you're on thin ice. But remember this is one of the most important missions you've ever had—far more important than Peru."

I told him I would wait for some of the dust to settle before I called Cardoen. We were both sure that the arms broker would already have heard I was in town.

People have the impression that the life of a spy or any kind of government undercover agent is filled with glamour. I was playing diplomat on a confidential mission, but I'd certainly seen no glamour here. In fact, I couldn't help thinking about what I was doing in Santiago at all. I'd left my wife and newborn child behind, I was living with another woman, and I had a number of difficult confrontations ahead of me. Peru had been interesting; Santiago was oppressive. I called Ora and heard her say how much she missed me. And she wanted to know if I was still with "that woman"—she wasn't sure about the relationship. And if truth be told, neither was I.

Stange sent a car for me at 5:45 that evening. On the way to the general's house, accompanied by his chief of staff, I noticed something interesting—an Israeli Uzi beside the driver. We reached a street blocked by the Carabineros, but they waved us on. At the end of the road a huge house could be seen beyond its spike-topped metal gates. The guards let us through, and there was Gen. Stange waiting at the door, dressed in blue trousers and an open white shirt with rolled-up sleeves. I felt overdressed in my blue suit and maroon tie. My host was hardly dressed for formal dinner.

He introduced me to his wife, an attractive woman with a pleasant smile. Servants scurried around as he led me into the elegant sitting room. A large painting of the general and his wife, their faces close together, dominated one wall. "By the way, Mr. Ben-Menashe," said Stange, "I have three guests I'd like you to meet."

Into the room walked a good-looking, dark-haired man in his late 30s dressed in a blue suit, white shirt, and striped tie. His wife was simply beautiful, tall and slim, with black hair and green eyes, and elegantly dressed in a light grey skirt which came to just below her knees with a slit in the side. I recognized him immediately and guessed who the woman was: Mr. and Mrs. Carlos Cardoen.

We exchanged greetings, and then the third guest stepped forward. A touch on the plump side, she was nevertheless very attractive, with short dark hair and big eyes. She was introduced to me as Mrs. Isabel Bianchi, the wife of an air force colonel who had formerly been the chief of the Chilean U.N. contingent in the Golan Heights between Israel and Syria, and she spoke Hebrew. Her husband, it was pointed out, was now commander of Chile's air force base in Antarctica. A long way away.

It seemed that an interesting night lay ahead of me.

We chatted about the coming plebiscite, and my hosts and fellow guests discussed how Pinochet wanted to stay in power for the rest of his life. But throughout the conversation I kept glancing at Cardoen. He had a smug look on his face. The unwritten message from Stange was quite clear. By inviting Cardoen to his house, the general was telling Israel: "I know this guy. He's my friend. See, he even comes to have dinner with me."

It was obvious the whole thing had been staged, but there were other aspects of the conversation over dinner that revealed their true feelings about Pinochet. They referred to him not as *El*

Presidente, but as "the old man." Stange repeated several times that Pinochet was trying to work out ways he could remain president. I had no doubt that Stange would be happy to step into his shoes.

Once in a while a woman dressed in a business suit came into the dining room and called Stange away to take a phone call. One other person was getting a lot of attention from a woman, too. It was obvious that Isabel had been brought along as a match for me, and she was putting on a good show with her eyes and her smile.

Cardoen said, "Ari, I understand you are here as our guest for a while."

"Yes—I have no immediate plans to leave."

He laughed. "Of course. Are you free tomorrow morning? Come to my office at 10:00 A.M. I'm sure you know where it is."

At 9:00 P.M., the general stood, apologized, and said he had to go to a very urgent meeting with the president over the security situation. "The president likes to have such meetings at night," he said.

Cardoen offered to drive me back, because the chief of staff had to stay with the general. It was all being played very smoothly. I sat in the back of his Mercedes 230E with Isabel. On the way back into town, Cardoen asked, "Do you know Santiago?"

"Sure, I've been here before. You remember we met in my hotel room at the Carrera."

"Yes, of course, but . . ."

Isabel interrupted, "Would you like me to show you around town?"

"Why not?" I said.

"We can do it this evening."

She asked Cardoen to take her back to her place, but I said I had a rental car and I would drive. So they drove me back to the apartment parking lot. At the car, after bidding goodnight to Cardoen and his wife, I took off my tie and jacket and rolled up my sleeves in the style of Gen. Stange and asked Isabel where we were going.

"Viña del Mar, it's only two hours' drive away."

It was now 9:30. "Sure," I said, "let's go."

We took the highway heading west, chatting about the political scene and places she had visited in Israel. As we entered a long tunnel, illuminated with orange lighting, I suddenly felt a hand on my knee.

"I like you Ari," she said. Then she added in Hebrew: "*Bo na'aseh ahava*—Come, let's make love. I've always admired Israeli men."

I drove on toward Viña del Mar, the playground of the rich. As we descended into the town the locals call the "pearl of the Pacific," I asked, "What about your husband?"

"If he catches you, he'll kill you. Then me. But don't forget, he's in Antarctica right now."

We pulled up at a hotel and went into the lobby for ice cream. Then we took a slow drive along the shore. It was a beautiful place. Little wonder President Pinochet's summer palace was located here. Shortly after midnight I suggested we return. I was playing it straight down the line. Isabel had other thoughts.

"Look," she said, "my husband isn't here, my two daughters are with my parents. Why don't we stay here for the night in a hotel?"

But I insisted. I could not afford to be sidetracked. She wasn't smiling as I turned the car around and took the Santiago road.

"Ari," she said, "I really like you. But I must say something. I don't believe you're safe. You're playing a dangerous game here. The ones who get hurt are the soldiers, not the generals. You're a soldier for 'General' Shamir. You really think you are going to stop these guys? How do you think you're going to do it?"

I knew that what I said was going to go straight back to Cardoen and Stange. I pulled no punches.

"If we have to kill every single one of them, we will. My life is not important. The State of Israel and its survival are."

"What about the Americans?" she asked. "They are supporting this business, you know."

"That's for my superiors."

It was two in the morning when we arrived at her house. I asked her how to get back to my place. She said she would drive her car and I could follow her.

"But first I want to change my clothes." We went into her home, and she brought out a tray of baklava. "There's a Palestinian here who makes it," she said with a grin. "I'm sure you don't mind who the cook is."

"No," I said, "I don't mind."

Isabel changed into jeans and a T-shirt. It was obvious she wasn't wearing a bra. Printed on the T-shirt was: "My parents went to Jerusalem, and all I got was this lousy T-shirt."

She came over to me and put her arms around me. I was physically attracted to her, but by now jet lag had caught up with me, and I was desperately tired. I extricated myself.

"You're a very attractive woman," I said, "but I have to go to bed—alone!"

I followed her Mercedes back to the apartment, where I put my head through her window and kissed her goodnight. She handed me a business card. It read: Isabel Bianchi, analyst, Cardoen Industries.

The headquarters of Cardoen Industries were in a tall building adjacent to the Sheraton San Cristóbal Hotel in a pleasant residential district on Avenida Santa María. Private security guards in the lobby checked my identity before I took the elevator up to another reception area.

A secretary led me to Cardoen's office, and the first things that struck me, more than the suave owner who greeted me, were the two large framed photos above his head—one of President Pinochet, the other of Saddam Hussein. Cardoen showed me a seat and offered me tea and cakes.

Dressed in a conservative suit and tie, he appeared nervous, unlike the confident man I had met the night before. He got down to business immediately.

"I understand you Israelis have a contract out against me."

No wonder he was nervous. "No, that's not true. At least not at the moment. On the other hand, we do have a contract for you."

Before he could say anything, I added, "You have violated prior agreements with us. May I remind you of our 1986 meeting, when I was assured that there would be nothing for Israel to worry about. Since then, right up to now, you've been playing with fire. Not only do we know that you are supplying chemical weapons to Iraq, we are also aware you are providing a financial umbrella for various people to deal with Iraq."

Cardoen was well aware that I was talking about scientists working with Ihsan Barbouti, who were providing technology for nuclear devices to Iraq, and Gerald Bull, a Canadian scientist and aeronautical engineer who was working on a "super gun" for Iraq, artillery that could shoot payloads as far as you wanted with no need for missiles.

Cardoen stared at me, flabbergasted that I was hitting him so hard. His fists were tight. I repeated: "The Israeli state will not stand by while Jewish children are gassed."

The Chilean breathed deeply, then stood up and paced the room. "First of all," he said, "your information is not accurate. Second, Saddam Hussein wants peace in the Middle East. Third, you are the guys that have nuclear weapons in the Middle East; nobody else does. And I'm certain that Israel will use them first if war comes."

"You can bet your ass Israel will use them if any of your gas hits us. Iraq will be wiped out. And, Mr. Cardoen, so will you."

He turned on me angrily. "If you're threatening me like this, I don't want to talk to you."

"If you want to cut the conversation short, fine. But you may be interested in what else I have to say."

He shrugged. "Go ahead. But let's talk sense. You must remember that I'm executing U.S. policy. You know that. In fact, you must know that I have the backing of many Western governments."

I asked him for proof. To name a few names.

He was thoughtful for a few moments. Then he said, "Look, you must understand we are working for peace in the Middle East." Suddenly he started talking as a peace-loving soul who was arming the Iraqis and serving the Iraqi people against the evil Israelis who were out to get them.

"Cut the shit," I said and tossed a handful of pages to him. "Read this."

There were no letterheads, no signatures, nothing to identify who had written it.

He sat back and took a few minutes to study it. The carrot was dangling there before his eyes. While he read the papers, I asked him, "Where's the john?" I had absolutely no respect for this man.

When I stood to go to the toilet, I made sure I left my custom-made armored briefcase open on his desk. Inside, clear for him to see, was a map of Paraguay with a large arrow pointing to a big red dot where Cardoen had his main chemical plant. When I returned, he said nothing.

I explained that the papers I had handed him described a contract under which he could open a factory in Chile and produce Uzis, Galil assault rifles, artillery shells, and 51mm mortars under license from Israel Military Industries, and he would be licensed to sell those materials exclusively all through South America. We would even help finance the operation to help him set up the factories. He would also be a broker for all Israeli military equipment in South America. We were offering him millions of dollars on a plate, just to change his style of business.

"How times change," he said. "Remember how I once came to Israel begging for a license. And now this!"

I stared hard at him. "Don't push your luck too far, Mr. Cardoen."

"You realize," he said, "that I need a permit from the Chilean government—but I also think this is a set-up because you guys are not going to abide by an agreement like this."

"Get your permit, do whatever you like. But I'm warning you that you have two weeks to think about it. You can tell your bosses in Washington, in Baghdad, and everywhere else that we're not just going to sit around and twiddle our thumbs on this business while Saddam Hussein does what he wants. You can also remind your bosses in the U.S. that we know the first thing he's going to do is turn on Saudi Arabia and the Emirates."

It wasn't the first time that this warning had been given—Col. Jalali, the Iranian defense minister, had made it clear to Gates in Kansas City in July 1987 that these were Saddam Hussein's plans.

Our conversation was over. Before I left I broke the ice by asking, "By the way, where is Isabel?"

He laughed. "I'll tell your wife. But sure, she's around. I'll give her as many days off as possible if it will make your stay in Chile happier—for her too. She's a nice girl, but she's having problems with her husband."

He called her in. She was all smiles and seemed unperturbed that I had turned down her advances the night before. "Lunch," I said, "is served at the Sheraton at 12 o'clock."

She laughed and said, "I'll come down with you now."

Cardoen showed us to the door: "You two love birds run along. I have to make a living." Despite his jocularity, I read the underlying concern on his face. You don't dismiss a clear warning from Israeli intelligence.

Over lunch of Greek salad and pasta at poolside, I held her hand and told her, "If only to teach people a lesson, if he doesn't stop his trade within two weeks and accept our proposal, we're going to kill him."

We were sitting under a sun umbrella. Tourists were lying on their recliners sipping piña coladas. They were part of another world.

Her eyes were filled with alarm. "Ari," she said, "are you guys fucking crazy?"

"No. We mean everything we say. How do you want us to play things? You want me to do nothing more than put a sticker on my briefcase saying 'Never Again'?"

"They'll kill *you*, Ari. These guys are dangerous. Very, very dangerous. If I were you, I'd leave Chile while you can. On the next flight. They're all killers even when people are nice to them. And you haven't been very nice at all."

I had not arrived in Chile with any weapons. I wasn't a Mossad hit-man. My only safeguard was the knowledge that it wasn't going to be easy for them to make me "disappear." I was there on official business. Were I to vanish, all hell would break loose. But of course "accidents" could happen.

I smiled at her and finished my lunch.

That afternoon I called Lufthansa and asked if there was a flight to Europe the next day. I told Barbara I was leaving for a while, but gave no explanations. When that plane left the next day, I wasn't on it. Instead, I got on a LAN-Chile flight to Madrid, then took an El Al plane to Israel.

I spent the weekend in Jerusalem. There was a flurry of activity. Israeli intelligence contacted a very well-connected Israeli arms dealer who lived in the same Brussels apartment building as Gerald Bull and asked him if he could help arrange a meeting between a representative of the Israeli Prime Minister's Office and Bull. The message quickly came back. Bull was excited about the proposed meeting. He obviously did not know what was in store for him. All stops were out. Israel was determined to end the trade to Iraq at all costs.

I flew to Brussels from Tel Aviv and was met at the airport by heavy Israeli security—four armed men. That was *very* heavy. But then, Europe was a killing ground. In Chile they couldn't afford to do anything to me. It was different here. There could be any number of suspects.

That evening I called Bull from the hotel and told him I was the government official who had come to meet him. I had a guest staying with me—one of the security men. The three others remained in the car outside. It was arranged that Bull should come over right away and talk with me.

Bull, I knew from my briefing, was a scientist who wanted to prove his theory that with the use of a "supergun," artillery could shoot payloads remarkable distances, depending on a number of variables. The more fuel you put in, the farther the shell went. With the correct calculations, you could fire the shell anywhere and get it to land on target.

In 1981, Bull had gone to Israel hoping to sell his project. He approached Israel Military Industries, where technicians listened to his theory and concluded that it would work. But they were interested in missile technology, not artillery.

In 1983, Mark Thatcher, the son of British Prime Minister Margaret Thatcher, introduced Bull to Gen. Pieter Van Der Westhuizen, chief of South African Military Intelligence, who in turn took him to ARMSCOR. ARMSCOR actually contracted this artillery project out with him. But on one of his trips back to where he was residing in the United States, Bull was arrested by the U.S. attorney for the Southern District of New York and the U.S. Customs Service for violating the Munitions Export Act. The charge: the export of military technology to an embargoed country—South Africa. This, at a time when the U.S. was secretly shipping arms to South Africa.

After plea bargaining, Bull spent about six months in a federal jail before he was released as a convicted felon. He left the United States a disgruntled man and set up shop in Brussels. He also intended to maintain his relationship with South Africa, but when he returned on a visit, he found the reception cooler because of his arrest. What the South Africans did for him, though, was introduce him to the Iraqi deputy chief of the General Staff for Procurement—the man who buys weapons. Bull was commissioned to develop his supergun for Iraq, but was paid through Carlos Cardoen's financial network. Which is why I was now in a Brussels hotel room facing Bull.

An informal, burly, middle-aged man with sandy hair, Bull made himself comfortable in an armchair and started talking about his supergun project. Despite his determination to trade with Iraq, I honestly liked this man. He wasn't in it for money or personal ambition or ideology. He simply wanted to prove to himself that his gun would work. "And it will work," he insisted.

"Mr. Bull," I said, "it probably will work, but what about the people who will die?"

"People have been dying for centuries for one reason or another. But this gun will be for Iraq's defense. With it, nobody would dare attack them. And that surely is a step toward peace."

"Mr. Bull, are you sure that the Iraqis only want to defend themselves? Can you tell me who is going to attack them?"

"Of course. The Americans. And you Israelis have already attacked them. You hit Baghdad in the 1967 war, and you hit Iraqi facilities in 1981."

"We blew up their nuclear plant."

"Yes, you blew up their facility, while at the time you had your own atomic bombs. You have delivery systems. If I can strike a balance of terror, there will be peace in the Middle East. And it will work."

Despite his opposing stance, I felt he wasn't really on anybody's side. "Mr. Bull, please stop," I said. "We will pay you for any breach of contract that will arise with the Iraqis."

"What do you mean?"

"We know you have reached a special deal with the Iraqis." I opened my briefcase and showed him a map. "Here is the plot of land they gave you in western Iraq to experiment."

He was aghast. "You sons of bitches have been following me."

I asked him if I could invite him to dinner in the room. He looked at the security man. "Not with this bozo around."

We dined alone. I again emphasized that if he let go, Israel would reimburse him for his financial losses.

"Will I be allowed to develop my gun somewhere else?"

"No. Absolutely not."

He drank his white wine. I asked how he had become connected with Iraq and Carlos Cardoen.

"Through my visits to South Africa. By the way, the South Africans, the Chileans, and I have a mutual friend in Mark Thatcher. I'd suggest that you guys don't muck around with me, or the British prime minister is going to get upset."

"Fine," I said. "But you still haven't told me who introduced you to Cardoen."

"I thought I had," he said. "I'm telling you it was Mark Thatcher."

We ate in silence. But I wasn't going to let up. "You know," I said, "the Israelis have a terrible reputation. They don't take too kindly to people who want to gas their population."

"Oh," he remarked, "you're pulling one of those on me. I had that in the States. You Jews are trying to guilt-trip everybody."

At that point, I said: "Mr. Bull, your time is up. Thank you for coming."

He had had his warning.

17

"Agricultural Project"

THE FOLLOWING MORNING I flew with one of the bodyguards to Frankfurt and then, leaving him in Germany, flew from there to Paraguay's capital, Asunción. An official request had been made to the president of Paraguay for a meeting on a "very urgent matter." I took a cab from the Alfredo Stroessner International Airport to the Excelsior Hotel, where a large portrait of the president peered down into the lobby.

President Stroessner had been put in power in 1954 by the CIA to protect Nazi intelligence officers and German scientists with whom the U.S. government had made deals after World War II. At the end of the war, the Office of Strategic Services did not see the Nazis as the enemy; they regarded the Soviet Union under Stalin as the real threat. So they actually recruited Nazi intelligence officers and weapons experts to glean intelligence on the Soviet Union and signed agreements allowing some of these people to live in the United States and others, with changes of identity, to go to South America. President Stroessner, with his German background and connections with the Nazi Party during the war, was an excellent candidate for the CIA to put in power. Indirectly he would be serving the United States.

The link between the Israeli government and Paraguay went back to the days when Golda Meir was foreign minister. She was instrumental in pushing for the exchange of diplomatic relations between Israel and Germany in the late 1950s when it was an extremely delicate subject in Israel. She was also instrumental in opening relations with Paraguay. President Stroessner agreed to open his embassy in Jerusalem when even the U.S. did not recognize the old biblical city as the capital of Israel and preferred instead to keep its embassy in Tel Aviv, where it remains today.

Israel's connection with Paraguay was not exactly a consistent relationship. Mossad agents continued to track Nazi groups through the 1950s and 1960s, resulting in the deaths of at least two Israelis. A truce was called, and Stroessner tried very hard to blot out his Nazi-loving reputation by promising full cooperation with the State of Israel, though he didn't end up doing much to help on the Nazi issue.

Israel, however, did take advantage of Paraguay's willingness to turn a blind eye to arms passing through its airport. Huge numbers of illegal weapons shipments to Israel from various countries were flown to Paraguay in the 1960s, and then on to Tel Aviv. Paraguay also became one of the conduits for smuggling matériel from South Africa for the nuclear reactor at Dimona—an unlikely route. The connections with Israel were so strong that even today Paraguay Airlines has a 707 flight once a month from Asunción to Tel Aviv. Each month a different aircraft is used and remains for two weeks in Israel for maintenance by Israel Aircraft Industries. When Prime Minister Begin took over in 1977, relations did not change, but neither were they nurtured. The ambassadors to Paraguay were generally Labor Party people, even under the Begin administration.

It was against this background that I received a message the evening of my arrival in Asunción in September 1988 to call a local number. It was the home of the Israeli ambassador, who told me that Avi Pazner wanted to speak to me on a secure phone at the embassy. I picked up the tightness in the ambassador's voice.

"Can you tell me who you are?" he asked.

I told him simply that I worked for the Prime Minister's Office.

"Why wasn't I informed you were coming?"

"Sir," I said, giving him the most gentle of hints, "let it go."

But he didn't. "The office of the president of Paraguay has called me asking for details about you and informing me you have a meeting with him. I insist that I be present at the meeting. Otherwise I will alert the foreign minister about it.

"We cannot harm the relations with President Stroessner that we have been working on for many years," he continued. "We cannot allow this relationship to be upset by the Likud."

And all this on the unsecure telephone.

"Sir, if you don't let go, you'll hear from the Prime Minister's Office," I said.

"What are you saying?" he demanded.

"I'm saying that you may not be holding your job for very much longer."

He hung up.

That same evening I went to the embassy to call Israel. The ambassador was not there, fortunately. I wasn't ready for another verbal war. When I got through to Israel, Pazner told me, "We've just received proof that Cardoen's chemical plant in Paraguay is their main facility."

Pazner explained we had just got hold of air photos of the Paraguay plant from "our friends," the Argentineans. It was my task to do everything in my power to persuade Stroessner to shut it down.

Before going to sleep that night, I called Ora and told her I was in Paraguay and that I was okay. It was the first I'd let her know where I was because I didn't want to risk telling anyone in advance where I was going.

The next morning my car was waiting—a black stretch Mercury, an official embassy vehicle with a flag and diplomatic plates, which I'd requested during my tense conversation with the ambassador the day before. I sat in the back seat. A bodyguard assigned to me sat in the front passenger seat.

I was driven along El Paraguayo Independiente to the Presidential Palace, which overlooks Asunción Bay. Set on spacious grounds behind a high brick wall, it was, of course, heavily guarded, but the metal gates swung open as we approached. The car followed the drive to the office wing of the building. A uniformed presidential guard opened the door, and I was escorted in by a secretary.

At the end of a high-ceilinged hall illuminated by chandeliers, an enormous portrait of the president gazed at me. The secretary led me down the long hall over a maroon carpet and then up a curved stairway and into an elegantly furnished office.

"The president will see you in his study," I was told.

Within minutes I was standing before the man who had been in power for 34 years. A man in his mid-70s, with thinning white hair which had brown stripes, President Stroessner shook my hand warmly and told me how much he had looked forward to the meeting. It was the first time, he said in good English, he had received anyone dispatched directly by Prime Minister Shamir.

"I didn't even ask about the subject," he said, "but because of the urgency implied, I assumed it was extremely important. I have canceled other appointments to meet you." He would not have bothered, perhaps, had he known what was on my mind.

"Your Excellency," I began, "I have come to see you on the most urgent of matters. Everything you hear from me, you can assume you are hearing from Prime Minister Shamir himself. We need your help."

I told him about Cardoen Industries, giving him the background of what it did and its exports to Iraq and what this could mean to Israel. "They have a plant in Paraguay."

He nodded slowly. "Yes, I know. But they don't produce gas or chemicals. If you can prove otherwise, I will call my friend Gen. Pinochet and ask him why they are producing gas in my country."

"Your Excellency, we are asking you to close down the plant altogether. It will be in the interests of your good country to do that. Quite simply, we cannot let Nazi history repeat itself and see our people gassed."

It was time to dangle the carrot. "The prime minister of Israel has authorized me to offer your country an aid package of $30 million worth of credits for military equipment." We were offering him a fortune in guns for free. Any other requests would be favorably considered, I added.

Without saying another word to me, Stroessner used an intercom to call in one of his aides. He told him, "I would like you to arrange for Mr. Ben-Menashe to go on a tour of the Cardoen Industries plant, along with a military inspection team. Arrange it for tomorrow."

I wanted more than an inspection tour. "Your Excellency," I said, "Prime Minister Shamir expects a message back from you, telling him that you are willing to do as we request—and close down the plant."

He asked if Israel would be willing to train for him a special antiterrorist unit among the Presidential Guard, and not the military. I told him I was sure it could be arranged.

Smiling, the elderly president rose. He invited me to come to his home for dinner the following evening after my inspection tour. I thanked him for his time. I had made some progress. And the following day I would find out for sure just what Cardoen was up to in Paraguay.

Back at the hotel, a message was waiting for me from the office of the head of the military school, Gen. Andrés Rodríguez, about whom the world was to hear a great deal very soon. The name was familiar to me. There had been some gossip about his daughter Marta, a woman in her early 30s, who was married to President Stroessner's second son.

The president's oldest son was an air force officer known for being gay. Because of the stigma, he couldn't succeed his father as president. As a result, Gen. Rodríguez and President Stroessner reached an agreement that in the 1991 elections Stroessner would finally give way and let Rodríguez run as the candidate of the Colorado Party—the only political party of note in town.

But there was strife between Rodríguez and Stroessner's second son, a cocaine addict, over the candidacy. Marta Stroessner had become sick and tired of her drugged-out husband, and was having an affair with the second son of Anastasio Somoza, the overthrown president of Nicaragua, who was living in Asunción at the time. He had stayed on after his exiled father had been killed by a TOW missile fired at his car, allegedly by a Sandinista agent, in 1980.

I returned the call from Gen. Rodríguez, and the man who answered identified himself as the chief of staff for the head of the military school. It was another dinner invitation. Gen. Rodríguez would be honored if I would join him that evening at his home. I accepted, wondering what line would be dropped on me this time.

A black Mercedes arrived at 7:00 P.M. Two men, immaculately

dressed, came forward and greeted me as "Señor Ambassador," and I stepped into the vehicle. I was driven to a hacienda in a wealthy part of the city. The general stood between the pillars on the veranda. A stocky man in his early 60s, dressed informally, he asked me to regard Paraguay as my second home. I had heard it all before at other dinner parties in other cities. I was beginning to think I could write the forthcoming script.

It was an ostentatious house. Plush rugs were scattered over Italian marble floors. The furniture was heavy and expensive. He introduced me to his wife and the daughter about whom I had heard so much, Marta, a very pretty woman.

"Come," he said, "let's have dinner."

It was obviously going to be a private affair. Leaving the women behind, we went into another room, where a square table had been set for two. He dismissed a servant who was standing in a corner. But he quickly called her back when he found out I was a vegetarian. Tendering his apologies for not finding out beforehand, he told me his staff would prepare the best pasta possible.

"I understand," he began, "that the president has arranged a military inspection of the Cardoen Industries plant. I don't understand why you Israelis are so interested in this."

Before I could say anything, he added, "By the way, I understand you have met Mr. Cardoen in Chile, and that you have also had dinner with my good friend Gen. Stange."

It was clear that he had good intelligence on my movements.

"The president isn't informed about everything, you know," he continued. "He's too busy a man to look at what goes on in every factory in this country. He has too many state affairs to handle. After he ordered this inspection, we took a look and found it was just a simple agricultural project."

I sat quietly, listening to him. He was obviously trying to tell me not to bother to inspect the plant. And I was left in little doubt that he had been making phone calls either to Cardoen or to Stange.

I wasn't in the mood to start arguing. Now that I had established the reasons for his inviting me to his house, I wanted to be out of there. I ate my dinner as quickly as was politely possible.

"Sir, it's a very simple thing," I said. "Your president has agreed that I can see the plant, and I have conveyed to the Israeli Prime

Minister's Office that his excellency is happy to have us shown around. So I would like to take him up on his offer."

He looked at me for a moment. "Do you have any suspicions about this plant?"

"General, I'd like to see it, if possible."

"But if you think there is something not good going on there, just tell us, and we will act on it."

I was not to be dissuaded. He reluctantly agreed to have me picked up at 7:00 A.M.

Back at the hotel, I phoned the ambassador, who was more friendly than usual. I soon established why. Avi Pazner had been on top of him, ordering him to cooperate with me. I asked what he could tell me about Gen. Rodríguez.

"After Stroessner, he's the most powerful man in town. First of all, he is thought to be a CIA agent. He has an exclusive on importing American cigarettes to Paraguay, and we don't understand how he can sell them for such a low price and still make a profit. It makes you wonder how cheap he's getting them in the first place."

"Is he known for his connections anywhere . . . Chile, for example?"

"Yes, Stroessner is a good friend of Pinochet, and Rodríguez is a good friend of Stange."

Later I spoke to Pazner. He told me what to look for at the chemical plant: large tanks containing liquid that gave off a sulphur smell, like the aroma of bad eggs. That was an indication of chemical weapon production. There might be other chemicals around, too, but that was the easiest to detect.

In the morning I was driven in a green military car to an airfield some 15 minutes away. A uniformed officer was waiting by a small two-man Bell helicopter. He introduced himself as Col. José Rodríguez—no relation to the general—and he was to be my pilot.

I looked around for the rest of the military inspection team. "There is no one else," he said. "I will be flying you to the plant, and you will be free to go wherever you wish to go." It was almost like being offered a joyride.

Landlocked Paraguay has very few highways other than the circular route surrounding the capital, Asunción. Getting out of what was once the old colonial capital of southern South America without a helicopter or a plane is difficult. The country outside Asunción is basically divided into ranches, where the Indian workers remain at the mercy of their Spanish or German masters.

With its lush vegetation and plains, Paraguay remains an ideal place to hide—or to operate a secret factory such as a chemical production plant. God only knows what happens on the infamous ranches and land tracts. The country is a black market paradise where anything goes. Marlboro cigarettes are brought in for less than their cost ex-factory. Brand new Mercedes cars, probably stolen from Brazil and driven along some secret path, can be bought for about $10,000, complete with Paraguayan license plates. Many of the goods to be found in Asunción are the spoils of blatant theft or con jobs from around the world. The biggest money launderer in India, known in financial circles only as "the Swami from Madras," had a representative in Asunción. Even military equipment being flown from the United States to South Africa would be flown via Paraguay, a perfect smokescreen.

As we took off, I looked at the compass to make sure we were going in the direction in which I knew the plant was located. I was expecting barren terrain, but instead we flew for miles over a lush forest. We traveled for some half an hour over the deep green carpet, and then suddenly I saw a clearing ahead. In the middle was the plant, four rows of flat, barracks-like buildings, with a water tower and a communications structure. A small airstrip had been carved out nearby. It was like a Hollywood set from a James Bond film.

"How many people work here?" I asked as we fluttered down.

Col. Rodríguez told me 50 or 60, most of them engineers. The director, he explained, was brought in by helicopter every day from Asunción, while the engineers were brought in by bus from nearby ranches. We landed beside a small building. From there we were driven by one of the workers to the first main building.

A man in his 50s in a tie and suit greeted me. He sported a blond goatee and spoke English with a German accent. He introduced himself as Hans Mayers. I will never forget him.

"Welcome, we were expecting you, Mr. Ben-Menashe," he said. "It is wonderful that you are interested in our agricultural project. We have a very good insecticide plant here. Would you like some coffee?"

I declined. We started the inspection tour.

He took me into the first building, where people were working with grey overalls and white masks around their faces. It was a large warehouse-style building at the far end of which were large tanks. This, I was told, was where the barrels were filled for air spraying. There was a bad smell . . . the telltale stench of rotten eggs.

"Would you like a mask?" Mayers asked.

I glared at him. "Nothing less than a gas mask will do," I said. "What do you do with this stuff—spray people?"

"Oh, people shouldn't stand in the fields when we spray," he replied glibly.

I asked where the material was flown to. He told me it was sent to Chile. His employer, Carlos Cardoen, he said, had agricultural projects in Iraq. Some of the insecticide would be sent there via Iraqi Airways 747 cargo planes from Santiago.

"We try to help the Middle East, Mr. Ben-Menashe," said Mayers, as we strolled around the storage tanks. "The Iraqis need food, and our company in Chile is helping them with their agricultural projects."

"Is Mr. Barbouti involved in this?" I asked, referring to Cardoen's Florida-based contact.

He looked at me, surprised. "Do you know him?"

"I know of him," I said.

"He has an interest in this plant, yes. It's a joint venture. We get some of our materials from Florida and Texas."

It was suggested I not go to the other buildings. The smell was worse, said my guide.

I spent only 15 minutes there. I had seen—and heard—enough.

On the way back to Asunción I asked the colonel what he thought about the building. "I have nothing to say," he replied. "I was only asked to fly you here."

I asked him if he thought the manufactured product was only insecticides.

"I know only what they tell me."

"Oh, so that's how you got to be a colonel."

He didn't like that, and the rest of the journey was completed in silence. I was back at the hotel by mid-morning.

I made a call to Pazner and told him what I had seen. He said simply, "It has to be closed down."

I asked if it was possible to arrange for a phone call between Prime Minister Shamir and President Stroessner. I believed that a call from Shamir might move the Paraguayan president to action. Meanwhile, I asked Pazner to mention to Shamir that I would be seeing Stroessner that evening. "And if you can manage to arrange for Shamir to talk to Stroessner before I get there, so much the better."

It was another private dinner, the same as before, in Stroessner's private reception suite at the palace. "We have prepared a vegetarian meal for you," he said. Then he informed me that he had spoken to Prime Minister Shamir at noon—about an hour after I had talked to Pazner.

"The prime minister and I have agreed that this plant has to be closed, even though people try to tell me it is an insecticide plant. I am well aware, of course, that such plants may be used as chemical weapons plants. I will give the appropriate orders to close it by the end of February 1989. We have agreed that Israel will train an antiterrorist unit for the Presidential Guard. And we also agreed on $30 million of credit."

I realized that Pazner had briefed Prime Minister Shamir very closely before the call had been made to Asunción.

"I will reach an agreement with Gen. Rodríguez. He will be financially compensated," said the president.

This baffled me. "Sir, what do you mean?"

"I don't know the details, but I understand he has an interest in Cardoen Industries."

"I'd like to know more details," I pressed.

He told me not to worry. It was an internal matter, and the plant would be taken care of very quickly. "If gas is being produced, the hand that is producing it will be cut off."

After our meal, I thanked Stroessner for his cooperation. I felt somewhat friendly toward this man—despite his Nazi background and the miserable conditions in his country. I had been left in no doubt from what he said that there was an internal power struggle between him and Rodríguez. And my presence had exacerbated the conflict between these two powerful men.

Back at the hotel, I called Pazner at his home, at three o'clock in the morning his time. I told him I needed a man to come to Paraguay right away and follow up on the president's promise. Meanwhile, I had to get back to Chile. There was a two-week deadline I had to deal with—the time limit I had personally delivered to Cardoen.

"But mark my words," I told Pazner, "there's a power struggle here, and it's going to explode at any moment."

Pazner told me that the chief of Mossad station in Buenos Aires, the second secretary in the Israeli Embassy there, would move in. I said I would leave only after I had briefed him. This man, the most senior Israeli intelligence officer in South America, was no stranger to me. He had been the Mossad comptroller for all the years I worked with the Joint Committee. He had overseen all our expenditures. By early 1988, after the Joint Committee disbanded, he had been sent to Argentina.

The next morning the phone woke me very early. It was he, telling me he would be in at noon. Later that afternoon, we went for a walk through the city. I briefed him on what I had seen and heard.

"You know," he said, "Rodríguez is on the CIA payroll and is a close friend of a man called Clair George, assistant deputy director of the CIA for operations. We also think Rodríguez gets a retainer from Cardoen, and is a close friend of Stange's. Rodríguez and Stange both have presidential aspirations, you know."

Yes, I knew.

He confirmed several other conclusions I'd reached: "There's a power struggle between Stroessner and Rodríguez. I'm going to try to line up a number of people we know about who are closer to the president than to Rodríguez. We can expect trouble later. But remember that the CIA is on Rodríguez's side. They don't want Stroessner's son to have any chance of becoming president because he's a coke addict and he doesn't like the United States. He's been pushing for an independent line."

We smiled at each other. We had found ourselves—and Cardoen's plant—in the middle of a bitter battle.

"By the way," he added, "Rodríguez also knows Mr. Earl Brian, the head of UPI." And a man with CIA connections, of course.

I told him I'd like to leave for Santiago the following day. But first he wanted me to make contact for him with the president's office. I spoke to President Stroessner by telephone and set up a meeting for the following day.

With everything in place in Paraguay, I flew back to Chile. It was September 18, 1988. Despite President Stroessner's promises, I could not shake off a feeling that a major crisis was developing. It hung heavily in the air.

I went straight to the apartment. Barbara was working on her computer, writing a story on Chile for the *Financial Times*. I didn't tell her I had gone to Paraguay. I'd led her to believe I'd gone to Israel, but she wanted to know why I hadn't bothered to call her. The whole journey had taken about ten days—two days in Israel, two days in Europe with Gerald Bull, and some three days in Paraguay. The rest of the time I was flying.

I didn't say anything in reply to her question, but instead asked her if she'd like to come on a trip for a weekend break to Puerto Montt, a quaint town of timber-built houses in the Lake District, some 700 kilometers to the south, for a weekend break. It was a ten-hour drive, and I suggested leaving at midnight. She pointed out we wouldn't see much scenery, so we decided to leave at three or four in the morning. All the planning turned out to be fruitless.

Around ten that night, I received a phone call from Carlos Cardoen.

"Oh, Mr. Ben-Menashe, you're back in town. Why didn't you call me? Anyway, I'm calling you with an invitation. How would you like to go for a drive to Puerto Montt?"

How curious, I thought. The man had read my thoughts. Or . . . I had a mental picture of the apartment's maid bustling around as Barbara and I were making our plans. And if it wasn't the maid, somebody else had been listening.

"That's a great idea," I said. "I'd love to come. Let's use your blood money."

"Ari, don't be like that," he said. "I'll come and pick you up at six in the morning."

I really wanted to get away from these guys for a day or two. But here they were, on my back.

I relayed the phone conversation to Barbara. "This fucking apartment," she fumed, her trip canceled. "It's like a fucking radio antenna."

Cardoen came by on time in a burgundy Mercedes 230E. He was dressed in jeans and a white shirt. We headed out of town, just the two of us. We stopped for breakfast and then changed over the driving.

The southern region of Chile is a beautiful place. Once you get out of Santiago, you are greeted by a stunning landscape, hilly and very green, with areas much prettier than Switzerland. The people reminded me of Romanian peasants, short and square. We were on the only highway, a two-lane north-south road riddled with potholes. If President Pinochet was so concerned about Chile and its infrastructure, I thought, as we got stuck behind yet another fume-belching truck, this was the first thing he should have attended to: build a six- or eight-lane highway.

Cardoen told me how great life was in Chile and what a wonderful man Pinochet was. I reminded him that only a few days earlier he was panning "the old man" in Stange's home.

"Oh, sure, there are problems, but overall it's okay." Then he asked, "How much do you make? How much is the Israeli government paying you? You spend all your life working for them, and what are you getting out of it personally?"

I stared out the window, gazing at the low-lying homes of yet another village. I found Cardoen's approach amusing.

"Have you thought about resigning from your job?" he continued. "You could work as my director of sales, or, if you like, there's an offer from the government to be national security adviser to the president. In any case, he'll be in power until at least March 1990. They'll give you a great salary. You could work for Cardoen Industries by setting up a balance of terror, making the Arab countries strong enough to threaten Israel and forcing your government to sign a peace treaty."

Yes, I thought. This was a familiar theme. I couldn't help thinking that he had been fed this line by his CIA masters.

Our drive was punctuated by Carabineros' roadblocks, where officers checked licenses and ID cards. It was impossible to drive for more than half an hour without being stopped by the green-uniformed officials.

Cardoen made it clear that if I wanted to work in Chile, Cardoen Industries would provide a house, a car, an office, and a very big salary. "And of course we could immediately provide you with a Chilean passport and Chilean citizenship."

On reaching the beautiful Lake District, we turned off the main road and parked by the shores of Lake Villarrica. Across the water, a snow-covered volcano breathed out white smoke.

"By the way," said Cardoen, "I understand you were in Paraguay recently, and that you paid a visit to my agricultural plant."

"Sure," I said, "but tell me, do you consider Jews to be insects? And I'll quote the Iraqi commander of the southern front in one of his interviews to the media after a battle with the Iranians. He said, 'We flitted them away.'"

There was a problem with this man's mentality. He thought that everything was for sale, and that everybody had a price. Yes, people may have a price, but it is not always money. I was not that hungry. Never a material-oriented person, money to me had just been a means to an end. But now I was asking for something else—a promise that the chemical trade to Iraq would stop—and perhaps the only price I would have to pay would be my life.

"Just imagine in ten years' time," I said, staring out across the mirror surface of the lake. "If you guys have your way, there'll be a nuclear reactor on this side of the water and a missile site on the other."

By seven in the evening, we had reached Puerto Montt. If it hadn't been for the company, the drive would have been rather pleasant. We checked into the best hotel in town—tourist class by international standards. This didn't deter a busload of Japanese tourists with their cameras.

Over dinner at a plain, but decent restaurant, Cardoen drank heavily. He downed a few cocktails, followed by wine. He started to get tipsy, slurring his words. But I couldn't be sure whether he was overdoing it deliberately.

"Do you like girls, Ari?" he asked. "I have some lady friends in Puerto Montt. If you like, I can call them. We could have some fun."

I thanked him for the offer, but told him I was too tired.

Before he left to go to his room, he said very precisely, "You know, Ari, nobody on earth will stop me."

He showed no signs of a hangover when he picked me up in the morning. We drove to the ferry terminal and sailed across to the large island of Chiloé, a popular holiday destination for Chileans. We strolled around the old fort town of Ancud, and ate in a small cafe. But you could never escape the knowledge that you were in Chile—the police and the military were everywhere.

"Don't worry about them," said Cardoen. "They're only looking for communist terrorists."

Early that afternoon we headed back for Santiago. En route Cardoen laid all his cards on the table. "Ari, I'll be straight with you. You either accept my offer or we'll finish you off. We're not going to do any deals with your fascist Israel Military Industries."

I didn't know whether he was making a personal threat or one against Israel—in either case, it was ugly.

"You must remember," he added, "I'm being backed by the Americans. You know that. You met Gates here with me. Gates supports us. You met John Tower here with me, too . . ."

"Tower was there on behalf of us, not the Americans."

"What do you mean?"

"Prime Minister Shamir personally intervened with his employer, the publisher Robert Maxwell, and told him that if Tower didn't go down to Chile in 1986, then he was going to have a problem."

"Are you trying to tell me Maxwell works for you guys?"

"You're a smart guy. You figure it out."

I was saying this so he understood that the rope was closing around his neck. But I had to be careful just how far I went. I had to be mindful of Israel's relationship with the United States, with Chile, and with South Africa.

Darkness had descended. The headlights of oncoming trucks lit up our faces. I saw the anger in his.

"You don't know what you're dealing with," he said. "We have a huge operation and nothing, particularly you guys, can stop us. We get all our technology directly from the CIA through Gates's office. Our equipment comes to us directly from the U.S. It's flown by Faucett from Miami to Iquitos in Peru and from Iquitos to Santiago. We have an agreement with the U.S. government. Ihsan Barbouti is the link. What the fuck else do you want to know, hey, man? If you want to fucking know it, I'll give it to you. I have investors from Australia—Alan Bond, who owns the phone company here. And investors from Britain, too. If you guys don't leave us alone, we'll finish you off. I have the backing of the Chilean government and the Americans. Just leave us alone and get the fuck out of here."

I said nothing. But Cardoen's suppressed anger was bubbling over. His driving was erratic.

"You know Richard Babayan," he went on. "He's your friend. You know Richard Secord; he shares an office with Babayan. You know Alan Sanders. You met all these guys when you bought the cluster bombs—where the fuck do you think they came from? Just leave us alone. If you have a gripe, go and see your American friends. Go and see Prime Minister Thatcher."

"Thatcher?"

"Yes, my friend. In fact, I'll save you a lot of time and trouble. I'll arrange for you to be introduced to her son this week. Perhaps that might convince you about the people who are behind me and why Israel should get its big nose out of our affairs."

He didn't allow me much time to think about this before asking, "How much did you pay Stroessner?"

It was obvious he was furious that I had obtained permission to visit his factory in Paraguay.

"You Jews never understood how the world works, Mr. Ben-Menashe." No more "Ari." "You guys think you have the monopoly on arms dealing in the world. But you're the ones who kill Palestinian children."

Suddenly he had become a big sympathizer with the Palestinian cause. His blood was boiling, he had become like a crazy man. He jammed his foot on the accelerator, and almost killed us as we tried to overtake a diesel-belching truck in the path of another smoking giant. It scared me. But he didn't even notice our narrow escape.

"I'm a private company and nobody, especially the Israelis, is going to touch my plants in Paraguay—or anywhere else. I'm going to make sure of that. My friends wouldn't allow it to happen."

He wasn't going to let up. "You dumb fucking Israelis gave nuclear technology to South Africa, and now this technology is finding its way to Iraq. Just ask my friend Gerald Bull. He talked to me the other day. He said he'd had a visit from you. You guys are throwing your weight around. But you'd better remember there are forces greater than Israel in this world."

I knew what he was going to come up with. But I let him have his say. "The Russians are also helping the Iraqis."

"Sure," I said. "But they aren't giving them chemical weapons. Or nuclear weapons."

We drove on in silence. As we entered the dimly lit outskirts of Santiago and made our way through now-quiet streets toward the apartment, I said, "Why don't you give me a call when you're ready to introduce me to your friend, Mr. Thatcher?" As I stepped out of the vehicle, I added, "I seem to remember giving you a two-week deadline. It must be almost up."

He roared away into the night.

Barbara was in an ugly mood, having been left on her own for the weekend. She complained I hadn't been there for nearly two weeks, and I'd gone off again.

"I've been spooked out here," she stormed. "I've been getting phone calls with people hanging up on me. I went out for a run, and I fell and bruised my knee. All my friends have been away. There's been no one to keep me company. I don't give a shit what you guys have to say about me. I've had enough, Ari."

"Fine," I said. "Go and find another place and live happily ever after."

"I've been staying with you out of pure conscience. I don't know what you're up to, even if you do." She turned and marched off to bed.

The following morning I went downtown and called Avi Pazner and repeated what Cardoen had told me on our trip. I gave him my thoughts about Paraguay, that Stroessner was going to go along with us. Pazner, confirming that the deadline I had set with

Cardoen was virtually up, said he would get a cabinet decision to stop all military equipment to Chile from Israel. There would be an official statement to this effect to the Chilean Embassy in Tel Aviv.

"Ari," Pazner continued, "you have to call the Iranian defense minister in connection with the C-130s deal."

I'd already received two messages from Nick Davies saying that Col. Jalali's aide urgently needed to talk to me. I'd put them off, but now, from the post office, I called Jalali's aide in Tehran. When I got through, I was asked to call the defense minister at home. Jalali had bad news. Despite all the efforts we had made, some U.S. hostages would be released, but not the three Israelis . . . yet. He was sorry.

I told him I wouldn't be able to sell this to Prime Minister Shamir.

"We can't do anything about it," he said. "We don't have ultimate control over the Hezbollah in Lebanon."

I was overcome with gloom. There I was standing in a phone booth in faraway South America and feeling my whole body going numb. One of the young soldiers in Lebanon was the son of an orthodox Yemenite Jewish immigrant family from Petach Tikva, named Al Sheik. On the weekend that I had been in Israel, I had gone to visit the family and promised them we were doing our best to bring their son home from Lebanon. I felt I was letting them down. For me, it wasn't a political issue—it was personal.

I told Jalali that if the deal didn't go through, Israel would return the $36 million the Iranians had already paid. But Jalali had not given up hope. He said, "You keep the money. We still want the planes."

I explained I'd have to consult with my superiors in Israel and assured him I'd call him back. I called Pazner again, and when I told him only U.S. hostages were going to be released, he was filled with despair. "Shit, how am I going to repeat this to Shamir? He'll blow his top. He wants our boys back. You know, Ari, I'm afraid to tell him this."

"Put me on to him, Avi."

"I'll line him up. Call back in half an hour."

I told him I couldn't talk from my apartment phone and explained how Cardoen had suggested visiting Puerto Montt shortly after I had made plans to take Barbara there. Pazner said he would send a "sweeper"—a highly trained "bug" searcher—from the Buenos Aires embassy.

Half an hour later, after I called again, I was connected to the prime minister. I explained what had happened with the Iranians. His decision was instant.

"There will be no deals," he said. "The American hostages have nothing to do with us. We need to get our boys out. Until that happens, the Iranians will not get our C-130s." Publicly, of course, Israel was on record that it would never trade arms for hostages, but in secret negotiations, the reality was quite different.

We had papered the deal through an American company, Geo-MiliTech (GMT), using one of its employees, Mike Timpani, who was to leave the company shortly thereafter. GMT was the same CIA-financed company that the Israelis, through me, had helped in its efforts to get Polish equipment for the contras in 1985. In return, the Poles had asked for U.S. equipment from GMT to hand over to Soviet intelligence. In relation to the C-130s, we had papered a deal through a company to be designated by GMT, which would get a profit of $6 million for their help. The deal had been arranged through GMT because we did not want any problems with the U.S. government accusing Israel of selling military equipment to Iran without authorization. This method of trade became a practice after the 1986 Iran-contra scandal.

Shamir said, "I don't care about any problems this may cause with the Americans. My planes aren't going to be used to get Americans out of Lebanon. I want my boys out. My planes will not be leaving without that assurance."

He slammed the phone down. The whole thing had become a real mess. The Iranians had paid their money for the planes, and I believed that if the deal still went through, they would continue their efforts to free the soldiers. But my boss, the prime minister of Israel, had changed his mind, after earlier giving his blessing. Of course, he had not foreseen that only Americans would be freed. I could understand his point of view—but he couldn't see mine.

I placed another call to Col. Jalali and explained the problem. It looked, I said, as if we would have to return their money.

"I will tell you again, Mr. Ben-Menashe," he said, "we don't want our $36 million back. We want those C-130s."

I called Nick Davies in London, explained the plane issue, and asked him to call Mike Timpani and tell him there would be no deal. I realized that the GMT people were going to be very upset because Timpani was slated to make a personal profit of $2 million, Barbara Studley and her partner in GMT, John Singlaub, would make $2 million between them, and the final $2 million would go into the company. Nick Davies said the money was already in place, but I told him that made no difference.

Frustrated, I returned to the apartment, and for the next two days did nothing. Then all hell broke loose. The Israeli ambassador was summoned by the Chilean Foreign Ministry and given a dressing-down over the fact that Israel had officially cut all supplies of military equipment to Chile. This, the ambassador was told in no uncertain terms, would have a disastrous effect on Chilean-Israeli relations. Neither the ambassador nor the Foreign Ministry had been fully briefed about the reasons for this action.

At the same time, Israel was cutting off military supplies to the South African government as well—and for the same reasons. My counterpart from the Israeli Prime Minister's Office had been present in South Africa doing the same thing I was doing in Chile—trying to stop the supply of technology to Iraq. Apparently he had a worse temper than I, and he threatened Gen. Pieter Van Der Westhuizen personally, telling him that if he didn't stop exporting missile technology to Iraq through ARMSCOR, which had in turn been given technology on a platter by Gates's people, the general would be in serious trouble. I should point out that a frequent visitor to South Africa from CIA headquarters at Langley, Virginia, was Clair George, Gates's deputy.

The cutoff by Israel against South Africa and Chile had finally come, after three years of asking, then pleading with the two countries to stop their deadly trade, carried out on behalf of the CIA. In the United States, the powerful American Israeli Public Affairs Committee had been lobbying in Congress. As for Britain, Prime Minister Thatcher had been sent a letter by Prime Minister Shamir—a very friendly letter not mentioning her son, but pointing out to her that British nationals were involved in exporting high-tech material to the Iraqi government with the authorization of the U.S. government. In fact, Israeli intelligence knew that Mark Thatcher, who was already an established arms dealer in Chile, had begun to do business with South Africa in 1983. And he was the one who had introduced his friend Gerald Bull to the South Africans.

The Americans were determined that Prime Minister Shamir was not going to have it all his way and started a campaign against him. The press was fed information from the CIA and the White House claiming that the prime minister of Israel was a warmonger who was determined to stop the peace process in the Middle East. However, the Americans had a problem. The 1988 election campaign was under way at the time, and George Bush, mindful of Jewish voters, was anxious to show how friendly he was with Israel. So there were two tunes being played by the White House—one, a newspaper campaign against Shamir; the other, telling how much Bush loved Israel and what he would do for the state if he were elected.

One thing positive emerged from all this. Toward the end of September 1988, within a week of my phone conversation with Prime Minister Shamir, a grey-haired man flew out of Washington for Santiago. Deputy CIA Director Robert Gates had arranged a secret meeting, curiously with Stange, not Pinochet.

Our information on Gates's trip was being fed to us from the U.S. by a man I didn't know, who operated under the code name Margarita.* His reports to Israeli intelligence were handled by Tsomet, Mossad's human intelligence section.

We established from Margarita that there were orders to stop the flow of arms to Iraq until after the elections in the United States. The orders came directly from the vice president's office to Gates's office, completely bypassing CIA Director William Webster. It seemed that Webster, who was appointed in 1987 after William Casey's sudden death and after Gates's nomination was withdrawn, was not aware of the arms flow from Chile and South Africa to Iraq.

When the Israelis inquired about Gates's meeting with Stange, the answer came back that its purpose was to explore the relation-

---

* Israel has repeatedly pledged that it does not spy on the United States, even after the Pollard case. But, if further proof is needed, this incident alone makes clear that this is untrue.

ship between the U.S. and a new Chile—President Pinochet was quite likely to lose the upcoming plebiscite, and the Bush administration was equally likely to take over in the U.S. Pinochet, in fact, was very worried. He didn't want his involvement in international arms deals to be exposed just before the plebiscite.

Whatever actually happened at the secret meeting, Gen. Stange told me shortly afterwards that the sales from Chile to Iraq had stopped. The Prime Minister's Office was not exactly elated. We all realized the sales to Iraq might resume after the U.S. elections. There was too much money at stake, and there were too many players for Israel to be guaranteed that everything had now stopped for good.

One of the key players was the Australian businessman, Alan Bond. At about the same time that Gates was talking to Stange, an intelligence officer from the Israeli Embassy in Canberra paid a visit to the head of Australian Security and Intelligence Services (ASIS), and briefed him about Bond's activities in Chile.

According to an Israeli intelligence informant inside Cardoen's company, Bond had been involved in joint ventures with Cardoen. Having obtained loans from various banks in Australia, Bond invested them in Cardoen's construction company in Iraq, which was to build a vast "agricultural complex" outside Baghdad. Cardoen did not really need foreign investors, but he got involved with foreigners of stature to lend more legitimacy to his activities.

It had always been a mystery to the Israelis how Alan Bond initially got involved with Pinochet, and how he convinced the president to sell the Chilean phone company to him for approximately $300 million. In fact, he made promises to Pinochet that once he bought the phone company, he would make great improvements in it. Bond was obviously not aware that phone companies need a very big initial investment plus a lot of high-tech know-how. After Bond bought the company, it went downhill, falling into worse shape than it had been in before he acquired it. Finally, he just wasn't willing to invest the money and effort necessary to improve and maintain it.

After the intelligence officer's visit to ASIS and the assurance that Bond's activities would be drawn to the attention of Prime Minister Robert Hawke, who was friendly with both Bond and

Israel, Bond almost immediately pulled out of Cardoen Industries, and later out of Chile altogether.

Had Bond remained with Cardoen, we would have known exactly what he was up to in any case. Mossad had been able to buy the services of two workers in Cardoen's company, and these employees were handing over to an agent in Santiago photocopies of documents about Cardoen's activities. They were each paid half a million dollars into two separate numbered accounts in Europe. One of these men, to this very day, works for Cardoen. The other has disappeared.

The "sweeper" who came to check the apartment for bugs was a balding man in his 50s, who greeted me in formal Hebrew. He carried a small suitcase. Before I could say anything to him, he put a finger to his lips. He took his job seriously.

The first thing he did was go to the telephone. Unscrewing the earpiece, he brought out a plastic object about the size of a little fingernail.

"This isn't Chilean," he said, after deactivating it. "This is what the Americans use—a CIA product. And it's not just a phone bug. It covers the whole room."

"Where would they be listening to this?" I asked him.

"It has a 50-meter range, so they must be in one of the adjoining apartments."

From his suitcase he brought out a kind of miniature metal detector with a rectangular head. He swept it around the apartment and found a second bug—in the base of the intercom phone on the wall.

"This must be Chilean," he said, after pulling out another plastic gadget and rendering it useless. "It's an old German model made in the 1970s. It also has a range of 50 meters. It wouldn't have been planted by the same people. There's another team out there somewhere."

Using his equipment, he checked the phone line. "This is bugged too."

He asked the maid for coffee. While she was in the kitchen, he said, "If I were you, I'd get rid of her, too."

He swept around again. "I can give you a signed guarantee that everything is okay, except the phone line, which I can't do anything about."

Later that day, after firing the maid and giving her enough money to keep her going for three months, I received a phone call inviting me to Cardoen's office the next morning. I traded in my car because I had a feeling that if they could bug the apartment, they could also bug the car. I rented another vehicle.

I turned up at Cardoen's building as arranged. A secretary led me into his office, where the head of Cardoen Industries was sitting behind his desk under the portraits of Pinochet and Saddam Hussein. There was somebody already there, a young man with his back toward me. He turned around, stood up, and stared at me.

"Mr. Ben-Menashe," Carlos Cardoen said, "I'd like you to meet a friend of mine." The young man reached out his hand. I took it. Cardoen laughed.

"I don't believe you've met Mr. Mark Thatcher," he said.

I recognized the prime minister's son from photographs I had seen. His featureless gaze changed into a smile as he shook my hand. But I wasn't going to give him the pleasure of hearing me say that his face was familiar to me.

In any case, Cardoen hadn't finished his introductions.

"Mr. Ben-Menashe works for the Israeli Prime Minister's Office, and we've been talking business together," he said. Then, looking toward me, he added: "Mr. Thatcher is an associate, and we also do business together."

"Oh yes?" I said. "What kind of business is that?"

"I'm just a private businessman," said Thatcher.

"Do you have any connection with the British government?" I inquired.

He seemed surprised by my question.

"Well, you know it's sometimes not very good to be related to a famous person," he said. I gathered he wanted to assume that I really knew who he was. "I'm a private businessman. My mother has her job, and I have my own work."

I decided to drop the pretense. "I certainly know all about you from your driving." Thatcher had gotten lost during a highly publicized car race in North Africa. "I've read about you in magazines and the newspapers. How did you get lost in the desert?"

He laughed. "That . . .! Yes, a lot of people talk about it. But I do like rally driving."

He asked me if I'd been to Britain. I told him I'd been there many times and had family members living there. We touched on the subject of royalty in Britain.

"The sovereign is a woman, the prime minister is a woman," I said. "And is it true the queen is going to abdicate in favor of her son, Prince Charles?"

His smile disappeared. It was instantly obvious he had contempt for the royal family. Yet he could not resist identifying himself with Prince Charles.

"He has his mother, the queen, and I have mine," he pointed out. "We have our similarities. But I also have to make a living, you know. Charles doesn't. Royal families remain in place, but leaders come and go."

As Cardoen sat behind his desk and Thatcher and I sat on the other side, we moved on to politics. Thatcher spoke of how much he admired Pinochet as a leader. He glanced up at the president's portrait as he spoke.

"I don't understand why the Americans knock Pinochet for human rights abuses. Why do they do that? I haven't seen or heard of any atrocities."

I asked him about the Falklands war. "Chile was a great friend to Britain during that war," he said.

I was well aware that Pinochet had allowed the British landing rights in Chile, which was crucial to the British war effort. After the war, President Pinochet and Prime Minister Thatcher had struck up quite a friendship—and Thatcher's son, not coincidentally, had sold 48 Chieftain tanks to Chile.

It was obvious Mark Thatcher did not like my line of questioning. He stood up. "I hope you'll excuse me," he said, "I have to go." Turning to Cardoen, he said, "We'll meet again this evening."

He bade me goodbye and left. Cardoen, now standing, smiled at me. He lifted his hands and let them drop.

"See?" he said.

I had seen what he wanted me to see—that Mark Thatcher and his mother were on his side. Nothing else whatsoever had taken place at this meeting.

18

Coup D'Etat

THE CHILEAN GOVERNMENT was furious with the Israelis over the ban on arms, and in early November, after the plebiscite, I spent two weeks in Israel with my family. I then headed off for a meeting in South Africa with Gen. Van Der Westhuizen.

The South Africans wanted to appear to be cooperating with us. At our meeting, the general was most gracious and told me that in that month South Africa had put an outright stop to all the technology flow to Iraq. He pointed out that CIA cutouts, such as Gamma of Massachusetts, had been providing matériel and technology that had been smuggled by the CIA through South Africa before being shipped on to Iraq.

I asked for a list of companies that Cardoen used, and the general provided it. He also gave me the names of Iraqi agents and the identity of a Texas company owned by Mark Thatcher that was moving equipment to Iraq directly from Britain. Another name that came up was John Knight, of the Dynavest company in London, which was providing parts to Iraq. Knight was familiar to us, having worked with the Tony Pearson-Nick Davies group since the late 1970s. But I was given other company names in Britain, Belgium, and Luxembourg that were new to Israel. All of them were financed by the CIA through Cardoen, and all of them were supplying Iraq with equipment to be used for nuclear and chemical warfare capability.

Gen. Van Der Westhuizen then dropped a shocker: The Scud

missiles the Iraqis had were being used in experiments with dud nuclear warheads.

"We would like Israel to know that we South Africans have nothing to do with all this," said the general.

He also confirmed that Mark Thatcher did business with South Africa, and had been doing so for a long time.

In my Pretoria hotel room I met my Israeli counterpart in South Africa. He told me that the South Africans really had made the decision to stop the flow of technology to Iraq because they were interested in going back to nuclear cooperation with Israel. Basically, he said, they were pulling the rug from under the feet of those who were helping the Iraqis. The South African government, he said, was considering dismissing Van Der Westhuizen from all official positions.

"We see an honest attempt to stop the flow to Iraq," said my Israeli colleague. "But I'm afraid it's too late. Saddam Hussein has enough technology and scientists, especially German, working in Iraq on developing nuclear warheads. The CIA has actually used South Africa's ARMSCOR to do this. The chemicals are coming from Chile, and the nuclear technology has come from South Africa. As for the personnel, that's being provided to the Iraqis through European firms."

I returned to Israel with my colleague for a top-level meeting in the Prime Minister's Office with the heads of Mossad Tsomet and Mossad Operations. It was agreed the "problem" had to be dealt with in a very personal way. We were asked to draw up lists of people involved in the whole situation—Chileans, Americans, Australians, Germans, and Britons.

In the following weeks, eight German scientists hired by Ihsan Barbouti's company in Miami who were traveling back and forth to Iraq were eliminated. Also killed were two Pakistani scientists, who happened to be in Europe. Then another German was killed in a bad car "accident" outside Munich while on a visit. His name was Hans Mayers, the man I had met at Cardoen's "insecticide" plant in Paraguay. In Britain, four Iraqi businessmen died. Three Egyptians and a Frenchman followed—a total of 19.

All were eliminated in late 1988. Four Mossad hit squads were assigned to carry out the executions. The squads were something of a novelty—they were all made up of Palestinians. Unwitting, they thought they were carrying out the killings for a Sicilian don, who was actually someone working for Mossad. Israel used unsuspecting Palestinians for one compelling reason—if any of them were killed or caught, it would be obvious they were not Israelis.

The deaths of the 19 were the start of a hit campaign by my government. Their masters had been warned.

In late November 1988, with a team of bodyguards, I traveled to see Gerald Bull again. By now the killings in Europe had already started. In fact, two of the Germans who had already been killed were working for Bull. I met him this time in his well-appointed apartment in Brussels. His face was grey. He had heard the news. I offered him $5 million to scrap his supergun project.

He said, "I'll think about it. Let's talk tomorrow."

I returned the following day. "I'm not going to accept your money," he said.

"I'm sorry to hear it," I told him. "As you know, Israel is very concerned that many of its people are going to die unless drastic action is taken. Warnings are being given. By the way, have you heard about all the terrible accidents that are happening to various people?"

"Yes," he said, "I've heard."

Then he showed me to the door.

I flew to London and visited Amiram Nir, Shimon Peres's former antiterrorist adviser, who had been involved with Oliver North in the Iran-contra affair. A man of about my age, in his late 30s or early 40s, he was due to be a major witness in North's forthcoming trial, and his testimony was expected to embarrass both former Prime Minister Peres and President Reagan. Because Nir knew a great deal about Barbouti's chemical operation in Miami, I wanted to find out more from him.

A shock was in store for me when I visited his St. John's Wood apartment, not far from my sister's. Having left his millionaire wife behind in Israel, he was now living with an attractive, dark-haired woman. I stared at her. Nir introduced her to me as a Canadian, Adriana Stanton, but I knew her from before—and though Nir didn't know it, Adriana Stanton wasn't her real name.

"Have we met somewhere?" I asked.

"I don't think so," she said and made an excuse to leave the apartment.

"Be very careful of that woman," I warned Nir. He laughed and said she posed no danger to him. He promised to come to see me in Chile. He knew Cardoen and Barbouti well and would be more than happy to help me.

Accompanied by two bodyguards, I returned to Chile late in November. Although they weren't armed during the flight, the watchdogs drew two Berettas from the Israeli Embassy in Santiago. I was well aware that the government I represented posed a big threat to the powerbrokers in this city. I also knew that word would have gotten back to Cardoen about the deaths of his scientists and that he would have little doubt who had killed them.

On November 30, four days before my 37th birthday in 1988, Amiram Nir was due to arrive in Chile to meet me as arranged. The phone rang in the apartment, and I thought it was Nir, telling me his flight arrival time. Instead, it was Ora, calling from Jerusalem.

"Ari, there's terrible news," she said. "Amiram Nir was killed yesterday in a plane crash in Mexico."

I felt my blood run cold.

Nir had reportedly been flying in a chartered Cessna T210 to inspect an avocado investment when the plane went down 110 miles west of Mexico City. There have been various inaccurate reports about the incident. According to some newspaper accounts, Nir and the pilot were killed, but three other passengers, including the woman I had met in his flat, had escaped with slight injuries.

One widely accepted report claimed he had chartered the plane under the alias Pat Weber and had died when the plane crashed.

The report said that a mysterious Argentinean who worked for Nir had identified the body and obtained custody of it.

Prime Minister Shamir ordered an investigation by Israeli intelligence, which reported back to him with a very different version of Nir's death. According to their report, it is certain Nir was shot by his woman friend. His body was never recovered by his family.

Who was behind it? Israeli intelligence has always believed it was a well-executed CIA operation. Nir's death ensured there would be no embarrassment for Peres, Reagan, or Bush at the North trial. In fact, while in London, Nir was getting bored and unhappy. He had started talking about writing a book. He even sounded out a journalist and told him some of his conversations with U.S. officials.

On December 2, just three days after Nir's death, I was leaving the post office when a window I was walking past shattered. Then something smashed into the metal custom-built briefcase I was carrying. The two bodyguards and I dived to the floor, realizing that someone was shooting at us.

The police pounced on two men. Although I was asked to go to headquarters to make a statement, I heard nothing more of the matter. I was left guessing whether it was a serious attempt on my life, or an effort to scare me—and wondering who was behind it.

Since Gen. Pinochet had lost the plebiscite, elections were to be called in Chile. In the meantime two members of the ruling junta, Gen. Stange and Gen. Fernando Matthei Aubel, chief of the air force, made it known to Israel that they were willing to come to an "arrangement" on the question of future sales to Iraq. Gen. Matthei had seen Pinochet's defeat in the plebiscite as an opportunity to further his own career, and he was already running for president.

I met Gen. Stange in his office at the Carabineros headquarters in Santiago. "We will help you put a permanent stop to this craziness and all exports, just as the South Africans did," he said. "But we need some help. We want the arms supplies from Israel to Chile to resume, and we also need to sell some of our equipment to Iran."

"Are you putting forward a proposal to stop your sales of weapons to Iraq?" I asked.

"Exactly," he said. "We have old American equipment, which we'd like you to sell to the Iranians. In exchange, we'd like to buy new equipment for Chile from Israel. As a result of the plebiscite, which was clean and fair, there are other governments that are now selling equipment to us, including the British. In addition, we promise to do all we can to stop future military exports to Iraq. We will do all in our power to stop the contraband."

I promised to relay everything back to Israel. Two days later a meeting was arranged with Gen. Stange, Gen. Matthei, and his chief of staff, Col. Mario Vila Godoy. They told me they had a number of old Northrop F-5E Tiger-2 aircraft that they wanted to sell. They didn't know where they would end up, but they had to go.

I turned to Stange. "I was under the impression that you didn't mind them going to Iran."

"Yes, yes," he said. "We've talked to Robert Gates, and he has authorized the sale to Iran. But we cannot be seen by the U.S. Congress to be making this sale. What we could do, though, is sell them to Singapore. Where they go from there is not our business. But we're aware that you could refurbish them in Israel before they are sent on to Singapore."

Details of the deal, he said, would have to be worked out with Gen. Vega, deputy commander of the Chilean Air Force, and Gen. Clark, the chief of logistics of the Chilean Air Force. Stange said he would convey to everyone involved that the American government had given the okay to the deal. (We found out later that the Chileans were lying about the U.S. government's okay. At this time the U.S. was selling to Iraq but not Iran.)

"We will assure you," said Gen. Stange, "that if we can offload these planes to Iran through Singapore, and Israel then sells us new equipment, none of the chemicals from Cardoen's plant will go to Iraq—even though the Chilean government isn't involved in this trade."

My next step was to call Joseph O'Toole, a former U.S. Air Force colonel, whose last job had been in procurement, which included much liaison with the CIA. Some years after his retirement in

1978, he became managing director of the aircraft sales division of a company called FXC International in Santa Ana, California.

FXC had produced parachutes for civilian purposes until Frank Chevrier, a French-Canadian who had arrived in California virtually penniless, came onto the scene. He started working as a laborer in this company, and the original proprietor, who had no children, liked Frank and made him director. Slowly but surely Chevrier took control of the company, and when the proprietor died, he willed the whole company to him. On taking over, Chevrier was approached by the Israeli government, as a result of which he started manufacturing, with Israeli technology, parachutes for military purposes.

The company had associates in Singapore, Australia, and other parts of the world. After Chevrier's fortunes changed and FXC became a big company, he was approached by the CIA with the idea of opening an aircraft division, through which FXC could broker secret sales of aircraft around the world on behalf of the U.S. government. Since the Israelis already had relations with FXC, it was one of the companies used to paper American equipment in what might have been perceived as illegal sales. Israeli intelligence presumed that one of the reasons the American government became involved with FXC was to keep an eye on Israel's dealings. Any sales of U.S. equipment through FXC could be closely monitored.

I explained to O'Toole that the Chilean government was interested in selling the F-5Es to Iran through Singapore and, believing the Chileans at the time, I said such a sale had authorization from the U.S. government, meaning Robert Gates himself had assured the Chileans it was all right. I told O'Toole that I wanted FXC to act as broker and buy the planes from Chile on behalf of Israel. This would put an American stamp of approval on the deal. O'Toole said it sounded good to him.

Next I called Avi Pazner and sounded him out on the sale of Israeli Kfir jet fighters to Chile as a tit-for-tat for the stopping of the sale of arms and chemicals to Iraq. The Kfir was originally developed by Israel Aircraft Industries as a copy of the Mirage jet fighter. In 1968 and 1969, blueprints of the Mirage-III were stolen from its Swiss manufacturers by Alfred Frauenknecht, a senior engineer, who received several hundred thousand dollars for his year-long efforts. The operation was exposed near its conclusion, and Frauenknecht was arrested. He spent only about two and a half years in a Swiss prison, partly because of an Israeli request for leniency. In fact, he was released in time to visit Israel for the maiden flight of the Kfir, which he had made possible.

Since Pazner had no objections to the sale of the Kfirs to Chile, I followed this call with separate meetings with Gen. Vega and Gen. Clark, the two officers designated to handle the details for Chile. Present at the meeting with Vega was Col. Guillermo Aird, who was Vega's chief of staff. They basically asked me to draw up a proposal on the deals.

Gen. Clark also agreed on the deal, but for the time being there were reports coming from our informants in Cardoen's company that the sales of chemicals to Iraq were resuming without any indication they were going to stop. It was a troubling situation, but I could only hope that once I had the F-5E deal worked out, the sales would halt.

Gen. Clark had one further request in addition to the Kfir jets from Israel—he desperately needed spare-part kits for T37s, small spotter aircraft. I felt at this point we were going forward very well and that the Israelis would be happy to negotiate this deal. After the conversations with Stange, Matthei, Vega, Clark, and their chiefs of staff, I decided not to talk to Cardoen. President Stroessner had promised the Mossad officer and me that he would close the Cardoen plant in Paraguay by the end of February 1989. It was reasonable to believe that the Americans would not interfere because President-elect Bush and others were extremely sensitive to congressional criticism.

In mid-December 1988, I decided to fly to Israel to lay out the whole scenario to Pazner. He in turn arranged for papering the sale of the F-5Es with the Singapore government through his contact, Gen. Winston Choo, who was chief of staff of the Singapore Armed Forces. I was to meet in Europe with the Iranian defense minister, and another Israeli representative would go out to Southeast Asia and sew up a deal with Singapore, which was acting as a conduit and would have to produce an end-user certifi-

cate for the Chilean government. But as for the sale of Kfir aircraft
to Chile, the subject had to be taken up with the director general
of the Ministry of Defense, Maj. Gen. David Ivry.

On being called to the Prime Minister's Office, Ivry pointed out
that the advanced Kfirs had U.S. engines, and we would risk
upsetting Congress if they were sold to the Chileans. The Israelis
decided to offer the advanced Kfir to Chile, but with engines that
had been developed by Bet Shemesh Engines, with the aid of
South African money before the row with Pretoria over Iraq.

I spent most of the rest of December in Israel with Ora and our
five-month-old daughter, Shira. But the respite was brief. Accompanied by my two bodyguards, I flew to Frankfurt on January 5,
1989, and greeted the Iranian defense minister in his suite in the
airport hotel that evening. It was a warm meeting, but the first
thing Col. Jalali pointed out was that he would not talk about the
three C-130s. It was simply expected they would come to Iran
despite Shamir's earlier refusal, and the money involved with
them was a separate issue from the planes which would be coming from Chile. Jalali asked for a price for these F-5Es.

In the late 1960s when they were manufactured, they would
have been worth $8 million each, but they would have been
"stripped down"—without any electronics, such as bomb control
and infra-red "night scope" equipment. They would just have had
standard take-off and landing radar.

Israel was going to pay the Chileans $6 million apiece, although
they were now not worth more than half a million dollars each.
The Iranians, on the other hand, would pay $14 million for each
plane. This included the price Israel had to pay, refurbishing costs
of close to $1 million each, transport, insurance, parking in
Singapore, and unseen additional costs.

The discussions with Col. Jalali continued in his suite at ten
o'clock the following morning. While it was worked out that the
total that Iran had to pay for each plane was $14 million, Tehran
had to pay $6 million each to the Chileans in advance. The rest of
the money would be cash on delivery.

Col. Jalali shrugged. "Whatever the cost, we need this stuff. We
have to defend ourselves." He was quick to point out that al-

though the war with Iraq was now over, they could not afford to take any chances.

I pushed him to agree to the payment to Chile and also asked him to send a representative to Santiago because we wanted to leak to the press that Iran was now in business with Santiago. He was happy to go along because he was very much in favor of what we were doing against the Iraqis.

I was doing all this in the hope of arranging a meeting in Chile for an Iranian representative with Israeli Maj. Gen. Ivry, Chilean Gens. Vega and Clark, and, perhaps, Matthei, as well as Joseph O'Toole, and—with any luck—Robert Gates thrown in for good measure. The more the merrier, because word would certainly get back to Iraq and cause concern to Saddam Hussein.

I flew to Santiago on January 6, 1989, and asked for a meeting with Gen. Matthei. But I was told he was on holiday in Switzerland, and Gen. Vega was standing in for him. Vega received me, and I asked him if he would meet an Iranian emissary, as well as Ivry and Gates. He agreed if Gates did.

I called Gates from Chile and asked if he would come to discuss the sale of the F-5Es. He politely said that he knew nothing about any F-5Es, and he had never okayed any sale.

Ivry came to Santiago. By this time Matthei was back in town. We met him, Vega, and Clark, and an agreement was signed between the parties that Israel would sell to Chile 12 advanced Kfirs with Israeli-made engines for the price of $14 million each. An agreement was also signed that Israel would purchase 13 F-5Es from Chile in their present condition at a price of $6 million each, to be refurbished and sent onward without specifying the final destination. Letters were provided, however, that Singapore was interested in purchasing these aircraft. Israel would buy these aircraft through the U.S. company FXC, which would act as broker. FXC would also be used to forward the aircraft after their refurbishment in Israel.

For their part, FXC was to receive $200,000 for the purchase of each aircraft and another $200,000 for each sale. It was also made clear there would be no exports of military equipment from Chile to Iraq. It was also emphasized by the Chileans that the United States government had given its approval for the sale of the F-5Es to Iran—something we knew to be untrue—and that the person who had given the okay was Robert Gates, also untrue. Gen. Stange was not at this meeting, even though he was invited. He had tendered an apology.

Ivry left Chile after these meetings, and a day later Dr. Ahmed Omshei, the Iranian arms negotiator, was sent to Santiago after the sale had been coordinated by my London contact, Nick Davies. Omshei was the aide to the Iranian Ministry of Defense who had been present at the 1980 Paris meetings to discuss the delay in the release of the U.S. hostages.

After meeting with Vega, Omshei opened a letter of credit, good for 90 days, for the Chilean government with the Bank of Luxembourg for the amount of $78 million, the total that Israel had to pay Chile for the F-5Es. The conditions for the release of this letter of credit were that the 13 F-5Es would leave Chile and be shipped to Israel by FXC. The Chilean government was to pay $1,300,000 to FXC, half its fee. The Israelis agreed to pay the other $1,300,000. The Chilean government also promised to open a letter of credit for the Israeli government in the amount of $168 million for the Kfir fighters.

The call from the Mossad chief of station in Buenos Aires was urgent. "The situation in Paraguay is grave," he said. "We have to meet immediately." He arrived in Santiago later that same day in late January 1989 and came straight to the apartment.

"We have intelligence information that Gen. Rodríguez is about to stage a *coup d'état* against Gen. Stroessner," he said. "The Americans are involved too. Earl Brian, a close associate of Gates, and Clair George, the assistant deputy for operations in the CIA, have been visiting Paraguay recently and meeting with Gen. Rodríguez."

Would the CIA go as far as overthrowing a government in order to keep Cardoen in business? President Stroessner had promised to close down the plant—and Rodríguez was power-hungry. It all seemed to fit. Nevertheless, it was incredible. I asked how reliable the information was.

"The best," he said. "Rodríguez has been spotted at the U.S. ambassador's residence several times, and there's word from colonels who are friendly with Israel that there's about to be a coup with the military taking over. The closing of the Cardoen plant is one of the issues, and it's being used as the catalyst to bring the power struggle between Rodríguez and Stroessner to a head."

I called Israel, where Pazner was very unhappy. He had already heard about the plotted coup, which was due to take place during the evening of February 2.

"Our man in Buenos Aires has told me the Americans are stabbing us in the back. There will be no Kfir deal, there will be no F-5E deal, and the chemicals to Iraq will continue. They're going as far as helping Rodríguez in planning the coup. From what we've established, there are some 10 to 15 new CIA officers in the U.S. Embassy in Paraguay."

I hung up and managed to get a call through to Stroessner himself. I guessed he already knew about the impending coup, but it wouldn't hurt to be sure.

"Yes, I know about it," he said.

I gathered from our conversation that the Presidential Guard, which, as opposed to the military, was completely loyal to Stroessner, had been put on full alert around the president. Stroessner was trying to negotiate with Rodríguez, but I couldn't see what hope he had. The Americans were clearly determined to see him overthrown.

It had been decided that I should stay where I was while the Mossad man immediately flew to Paraguay. But on February 1, he called me from Asunción. "You'd better come here, Ari. There's a possibility that Gen. Stroessner might survive because he's pulled two generals on to his side. And if he does pull through, you have to be here to massage his ego and make sure he closes the Cardoen plant right away."

I left Santiago for Asunción on February 2, arriving in the early afternoon. My colleague was waiting for me in the airport, and we drove to see Stroessner. Life was continuing in its own hectic way in the city. No one, it seemed, had got wind of the trouble, even though the guard around the palace had been strengthened.

Stroessner looked worried when he received us in his office, but he assured us he had "neutralized" Rodríguez and that there would be no move that night against him. By the morning, Rodríguez would be arrested.

"That's good news, Your Excellency," I said. "If Rodríguez had won this power struggle, it would mean big trouble for Israel. But what we'd like is your assurance that the Cardoen plant will be closed this week."

"You can take it from me it will be done," said President Stroessner. "I have already received $12 million worth of small arms since our first meeting, out of the $30 million in credits I was promised."

I seized on this to emphasize that Israel was completing its part of the bargain, and that it was now up to him to carry through his.

He smiled and raised a hand of acknowledgment. "Gentlemen," he said, "please come and see me at six o'clock tomorrow evening, when it is all over with Rodríguez." There was confidence in his voice, but I read worry in his eyes.

We were staying at the Excelsior Hotel, where guests are mainly Europeans and Americans. We each made calls to Israel and to the Israeli ambassador, who had not been fed the Mossad information. He was warned that "something was cooking" and that he should make sure his staff was in a safe place.

"If this is the case, do you need any protection?" he asked me.

"No, thank you," I said. "I have my two 'boys' with me." They weren't carrying weapons, but they knew how to take care of us—and themselves.

The four of us set out for an early dinner about six that evening, planning to eat at an Arab restaurant within walking distance of the hotel. As we walked, we saw trucks of soldiers moving into the city and taking up positions on street corners. I wondered where their loyalty lay. People stopped to stare in astonishment. A buzz of conversation was in the air, but no panic.

On our way back to the hotel after dinner, the scene had changed dramatically. The city was now full of soldiers, and the streets had emptied of civilians. Soldiers were standing in the hotel lobby, but guests were free to come and go. Rich locals mingled among the guests, ordering drinks from the lobby bar. We sat in the lobby, too, waiting for the action that now seemed inevitable. But was it Stroessner's action against Rodríguez—or vice versa? Whatever happened here tonight, we realized, also affected the security of Israel.

At about 11:00 P.M. the boom of artillery shook the hotel. We went up to my room and stared out the window at a deadly display. From the army tank base in the middle of Asunción, artillery was being fired toward the presidential palace. At least we knew whose side *they* were on.

The sight and sound of battle went on all night. It wasn't until we ventured out into the street in the silence of dawn and saw the bodies lying around that we were able to find out what had happened.

The military generals had assured Stroessner they would back him, but Rodríguez, who was commander of the military school, together with the commander of the tank unit, had decided to make the coup attempt anyway. All 2,000 soldiers in the military school had been trucked into Asunción. Command had been given to fire on the palace—the six tanks kept at a small base downtown were used to take over the city. When Stroessner had given orders for other military units to come to his aid, they refused, unwilling to come face to face with the tanks and units holding the central part of the city.

Stroessner had held out with the Presidential Guard, also totaling some 2,000. As a response, 1,000 Presidential Guard with Israeli Uzi machine guns were trucked into the city. A fierce gun battle had erupted around the tank base. Six hundred Presidential Guard were mowed down from machine-gun towers around the tank base. At 2:00 A.M., Stroessner had given up.

"Well, that's the end of that," said my friend as we walked among the mangled bodies. It was a horrifying sight. "We tried to tell him what would happen."

"And we still have our problem with Cardoen," I said. "This means, of course, that all deals are off. We're back to square one."

On returning to the hotel, we were met by military officers, who assumed we were tourists and told us not to worry. We sat in the lobby and watched them bring down Stroessner's big portrait.

The phones from the hotel were working, and I called Ora to assure her I was all right.

"What the hell are you doing there?" she demanded. "I've been watching it all on TV. I called yesterday, and they told me you were in Paraguay, and now I see there's a coup. Wherever there's trouble, you seem to be in the thick of it."

* * *

That afternoon, we decided to make contact with Gen. Rodríguez to congratulate him. We had nothing to lose. We phoned the palace. I explained I was a special emissary from Prime Minister Shamir and I would like to speak to Gen. Rodríguez.

They told me he was very busy, but they would pass on the message. Half an hour later, I had a phone call from Rodríguez's chief of staff. He was very polite, saying he did not realize we were in the city.

"We hope you were not inconvenienced by last night's events," he said, as someone might explain away a noisy party.

I asked if it was possible to see the general. "You mean the president," he said. Of course.

Half an hour later he called back again. He said the president was concerned about my personal safety and that if I was not accredited diplomatically to Paraguay, it was better for my own well-being to try to leave the country as soon as the airport was opened again that evening. Meaning, "Get your ass out of here, troublemaker."

The Mossad man and I agreed that Rodríguez wasn't going to close the plant and that it was probably wise to take the new president's advice. As the day went by and we waited for the airport to open, into the lobby of the hotel came a number of Americans. One of them I knew from before—a white-haired, distinguished-looking man, smartly dressed in a suit. His name was George Cave, the very same man who had been right in the middle of the Iran-contra affair.

I marched straight up to him. "Hello, George," I said. "How're you doing?"

He stared at me in astonishment. "What are you doing here?" he finally asked.

"I'm on government business."

"I didn't know you fellows were involved."

"I guess we're on opposing sides."

"I'm not on any side. I was here on personal business, and I got caught up in the coup."

"Sure," I said. "And what about Earl Brian? I haven't seen him, but doesn't he go everywhere with you?"

He produced a nervous laugh. "Earl *should* be here. UPI would be interested in all of this."

I didn't bother to reply. I was so sick about the whole damn business that I didn't know whether to laugh or cry.

As he moved away, my words seemed to sink in. He found some adrenaline, and turned on me. "Let me say that if anyone tries to interfere with what we're doing, we'll stop them."

At noon the next day, I flew out of Paraguay. There was nothing more I could do. I looked down over the city. At the cluster of houses, at the military vehicles I could still make out. We'd failed. The whole thing stank. I closed my eyes and wondered what I did from here.

I was met at the airport in Santiago by Joseph O'Toole, the man from FXC, who'd flown in shortly before I left for Paraguay. On February 6, two days later, we had a meeting with Gen. Clark. We hoped to press on with the aircraft deal, despite the fact that it had been made clear to us the Americans were not going to sanction it. Joe O'Toole was now acting as a private businessman, and did not care about his U.S. government masters.

Gen. Clark's message confirmed our fears. "The Chilean government has decided it will not sell its F-5Es and will not break international law at the urging of the Israeli government," he said. "We don't want Kfir aircraft—we're going to go for Mirage 2000s. We won't be opening a letter of credit for Israel, and the letter of credit opened by Dr. Omshei for the Chilean government will be left to expire."

I sensed by his firmness that a power struggle was building up among factions in the Chilean ruling junta. Pinochet was pitted against Matthei and Stange, each of whom had his own presidential aspirations. As chief of logistics in the air force, Gen. Clark should have been on the side of his commanding officer, Gen. Matthei. But Clark was a Pinochet appointee, and he was more loyal to Pinochet than to Matthei or Stange.

At an opportune moment, I asked for a meeting with Matthei, without O'Toole present. It was quickly arranged, and Matthei was able to explain the background, pointing out that he did not "agree with the politics."

It was clear to him now, he said, that the Americans weren't going to support him in his ambitions to become president of

Chile following Pinochet's defeat in the plebiscite. So he had tried to oppose the U.S.'s policies. With the backing of Adm. José Merino Castro, head of the navy, Gen. Matthei was going to try to stop the arms sales to Iraq and win over the U.S. Congress. He was attempting to hire as a consultant Edmund Muskie, a Democrat who had served as secretary of state. Muskie later turned him down, and someone in his office leaked word of Matthei's plan, but at the time, Matthei said they were still negotiating with him in the hope of setting up a Chilean lobby in the U.S. Congress.

I was encouraged by his words. He was still hoping to push the F-5E deal through and also stop the chemical trade to Iraq. It was unclear who would prevail in the Chilean political battle ahead, but if Matthei emerged the victor, perhaps our mission could still be accomplished.

My happiness was to be short-lived.

It was Robert Gates himself who telephoned Nachum Admoni, the Mossad chief,* early in February 1989, and told him the U.S. was not happy about the trouble the Israelis were stirring up in Chile. Word of Matthei's plans had apparently leaked out to the Bush administration, and Gates had been designated to take care of the potential problem. Gates asked Admoni if he was aware of what had happened in Paraguay and reminded him that the U.S. could protect its interests in whatever way it liked. Gates was also angry about my activities. He complained to Admoni that I'd arranged for accusations to be made about Cardoen in the *Financial Times*.

This was quite true. To help get world opinion on our side, I had been the source for Barbara Durr's story in the *Financial Times* exposing Cardoen's sales of chemical weapons to Iraq. Published on November 11, 1988, it was the first of such stories to make it

---

* In 1989, Admoni left Mossad. He was the first chief of the intelligence agency whose resignation was reported in the international press, which happened because of misunderstandings with the Prime Minister's Office. Despite an argument with Shamir over the disposal of the arms-sales profits and his vehement opposition to Robert Maxwell's role as a money-launderer, he remained an unofficial adviser to Shamir, while taking a management position in a public company.

into print. Subsequently, exposés of Cardoen's illegal activities were published in the *Times* and the *Independent* in London, and over the international wire services. But at the time, Barbara's was the only story published, and Gates didn't like it one bit. Even if what it said was true, he told Admoni, it had nothing to do with the Americans.

Admoni told me later that his reply to Gates was cool. The article was about Cardoen's chemical sales to Iraq, but didn't mention U.S. involvement. Admoni quoted a Hebrew saying that translates, "The hat on the thief's head is burning." He meant, more or less, that the Americans had a guilty conscience.

Gates replied that the Chileans—meaning the faction led by Gen. Matthei—were listening too much to Israel and would have to be taught a lesson.

The threatened lesson came shortly, when three grapes, out of the whole Chilean fruit harvest exported to the U.S., worth $850 million to $900 million annually, were found to be laced with cyanide. Three tiny grapes out of millions upon millions. It was an astonishing example of diligence by the U.S. Food and Drug Administration.

The FDA announced that all Chilean food imports into the United States— potentially lethal foodstuffs—would be banned. Shops and supermarkets across the nation withdrew Chilean foods. Empty shelves carried explanations that because of the danger of contamination of Chilean imports, certain articles had been removed for customers' safety.

The impact was catastrophic for Chile's economy. I was still in Chile when the effect was felt. It was tragic to watch tearful Chilean farmers trucking their grapes into Santiago and giving away carton-loads of grapes to the population. It was a demonstration of anger and frustration directed against the United States—and their own government. They were so frustrated they didn't know what to do. It was a bizarre change of scene in the streets. Instead of the Carabineros throwing gas canisters to break up demonstrations against Pinochet, it was peasants and farmers throwing grapes everywhere. Supermarkets were giving away boxes of them—in contrast to the empty shelves in the U.S. Food prices in Chile crashed, threatening to send the whole economy over the cliff. And all because of three grapes.

The American FDA tried to convince the Europeans to put a ban on Chilean exports, but it did not catch on.

Adm. Merino, one of the four members of the ruling junta, with responsibility for economics, made a nationwide telecast and calmed the Chileans down, assuring them the government would try to find the cause of the problem. He added it had not been Chile's fault—the country did not produce contaminated food, particularly fruits laced with poison.

I got an emergency call to come to Matthei's office, and he asked me what I knew about it. I gave him a full rundown of the Gates-Admoni conversation. He smiled wistfully. "I thought so," he said. Clearly, he had lost the power struggle.

Chile immediately announced to the Americans that they would not be selling their F-5Es to Iran. This meant, of course, that they would go along with the Americans and continue the trade with Iraq. The effect was almost instantaneous. Suddenly there was no problem with Chilean food in the U.S. All bans were lifted. Chilean foodstuffs appeared back on the supermarket shelves.

One for the CIA. And for Carlos Cardoen.

I called Jerusalem and said, "What do you want me to do? Go on a one-man campaign and blow up Cardoen's plants?"

"Come on home, Ari," said Pazner.

"I've failed completely," I told him.

"You've got some very useful addresses of people who are dealing with Cardoen," said Pazner. "And let's not forget that the South Africans have stopped dealing with Iraq."

I shook my head. There was something I hadn't told him over the phone. After returning to Santiago in the wake of the coup in Paraguay, I had wandered into the pool area of the Sheraton San Cristóbal Hotel and spotted two men sitting together: Gen. Van Der Westhuizen and Mark Thatcher. They were at a white metal table next to the bar with a couple of glasses in front of them. I was left in little doubt by the way they were laughing that they were the best of friends.

My suspicions were to be proved correct. While the South Africans were not dealing with Iraq, they *were* involved with

Chile, which was just as bad. Israeli intelligence reports and assessments from other intelligence agencies confirmed that Mark Thatcher was continuing to provide military equipment through Cardoen to the Iraqis. All the nuclear missile projects that were continuing in Iraq were going through the Cardoen network, which had a joint venture with Ihsan Barbouti's projects in that country. Thatcher was very well connected with Barbouti. Working with Barbouti was Sarcis Sargalian, an American arms dealer of Lebanese-Armenian extraction. Also on the project for the U.S. government was the Armenian-Iranian, Richard Babayan, my old schoolmate. Based in Washington, D.C., Babayan controlled a large network of people providing equipment for Iraq. "I'm an Iranian patriot trying to get rid of the Khomeini regime," he often used to tell me.

The Israeli government was extremely concerned about the continued trade. What could we do? Pazner said I would have to make a presentation at a meeting of present and former chiefs of intelligence organizations in Israel. They operated as a committee, with the power to deliberate and set down guidelines for execution of cabinet decisions with respect to intelligence affairs. A watchdog group of professionals, the committee also had the power of life and death. It was this secret group that decided which individuals posed a threat to the State of Israel—and decided who should live and who should die.

At these high-level meetings, who says what is not recorded. Only the final decision of the whole committee is recorded in top-secret form. In this manner, no one person can be held responsible for the decision to execute anyone. This committee included all the former and present heads of SHABAK, Mossad, Military Intelligence, and Police Intelligence. They are not all present at all times, but they need a quorum of six.

In March 1989, I made my presentation about the situation in Chile at a committee meeting at the Mossad villa near the Tel Aviv Country Club. Although we had not coordinated our reports, a Mossad analyst who was also present had drawn the same conclusions about Cardoen and Iraq.

Among the people named as enemies of the state was as prominent a figure as Robert Gates. There were also Richard Babayan, Gerald Bull, Ihsan Barbouti, Carlos Cardoen, Rodolfo Stange,

Clair George, Earl Brian, George Cave, Andrés Rodríguez, Bruce Rappaport, a number of Cardoen bankers in the United States, and a group of German scientists working with Bull in Iraq. Some of these Germans were new on the scene; others were the "survivors" from the first rampage in Europe.

I was not a party to the life-and-death decision-making. I had simply been asked to make a presentation. When the final deliberations took place, the other analysts and I were asked to leave.

Two days later I was called back to a reconvened meeting of the committee at the Mossad villa, for a more detailed presentation. It was later decided by the committee that the Egyptian-born U.S. resident, Ihsan Barbouti, and Gerald Bull, the supergun developer who was still living in Belgium, would be on the execution list, along with 12 others, mostly European scientists. It had been decided to go to the heart of the technology, as well as to some of the merchants. Carlos Cardoen was spared, however, presumably because of his closeness to the Chilean junta, and because his death would have created an uproar.

Although the committee agreed to go ahead with the executions right away, Prime Minister Shamir, fearing reprisals from the U.S., intervened. He wanted them put on hold—and he was horrified when told that Gates and Rappaport had been originally listed as enemies of the state.

In early April 1989 I made a final trip to Chile to wrap up my affairs. While I was there, Joseph O'Toole called from Santa Ana, California, to say that the three C-130s could still be sold to Tehran. An Iranian agent, explained O'Toole, had been brought into the deal by Richard St. Francis, who worked for TransCapital, a Connecticut firm licensed to sell computer hardware used for the Promis program, and by Mike Timpani, who by now was no longer working for GMT.

I said there would be no deal. Because the Iranians had not been able to secure the release of the three Israeli soldiers, Prime Minister Shamir was not going to release the aircraft, even if the Iranians had paid money up front for them.

The planes were being held by Israel, but the U.S. was claiming jurisdiction over them because they were fitted with U.S. technology. The Israeli government, of course, had discretion on resale of U.S. equipment more than 20 years old. U.S. jurisdiction was not clear in this case, because Israel had bought 85 of the planes—war booty—from Vietnam in 1985 and 1986, paying $200,000 each for them.

O'Toole also wanted to buy 12 more C-130s parked in Canada, but owned by the Israeli government. They were being refurbished by Northwest Industries in Edmonton, Alberta. At first he didn't make it clear which customer wanted them. Finally he mentioned a person called Lettner, who was apparently very keen to make the purchase on behalf of Iran. There would be no harm, said O'Toole, at least in my talking to Lettner. I told O'Toole that I doubted that Prime Minister Shamir was going to allow the sale—and we knew of no Iranian representative called Lettner.

O'Toole continued to urge me to meet this man, saying that the U.S. had given the nod for the sale of the planes. I phoned Israel, and a senior official in the Ministry of Defense told me that O'Toole had been in Israel in December 1988 talking to "the other side"—to the Labor Party people—and to the Defense Ministry. This was a surprise to me. In fact, I smelled a rat.

I called Iranian Defense Minister Jalali from Santiago to ask whether he knew anything about Lettner or about any deal with the U.S. No, Jalali had never heard of the man and knew nothing about a plan to sell C-130s to Tehran apart from those that Iran was trying to buy from Israel through me.

On the afternoon of April 20, 1989, I was scheduled to meet Robert Gates at a house in Paramus, New Jersey. This was arranged through the Prime Minister's Office to make a last-ditch plea about the Iraqi sales. On the suggestion of Pazner, who said he was intrigued to know what was going on, I also arranged with O'Toole to meet the mystery man Lettner at Kennedy Airport at 10:30 A.M., shortly after my arrival from Chile with my two bodyguards.

At the appointed time, I was approached in the main terminal by a grey-haired man in his late 40s, dressed in an elegant European-cut suit. I'd never met him before, but he introduced himself as the Connecticut businessman Richard St. Francis. He asked me to go to the upstairs coffee shop where we would soon be joined by Lettner, supposedly representing the Iranians. Sure enough, after we ordered coffee in the crowded shop, a huge man came over. He held out a hand that could have crushed an iron bar. This guy was no Sunday school teacher.

"Lettner," he said by way of introduction.

I looked him straight in the eyes. "Fine," I said. "But who are you really? And what do you want? I've called the Iranian defense minister, and he's never heard of you."

"That's crazy," he said. "I've just returned from visiting him in Tehran."

I told him that if there were to be a sale of C-130s to Iran, the U.S. and the Israeli governments each had to authorize it. Not only that, Israel didn't need any false end-user certificates. I told him that the governments would authorize the final use of the planes.

I was convinced this man was an undercover agent and that I was being taped.* It was obvious he was here to set me up. My activities in South America had clearly upset too many people, including Robert Gates. I was careful to make the comment that I was going to see Gates later that day.**

I told "Lettner" that if he was a representative of another country and he was lying, he had better watch out. If he wanted this deal to go through to Iran, he had to prove his identity, and the prime minister of Israel also had to approve the deal.

I stood up and left the coffeeshop. I took a limousine to Newark Airport and left the two bodyguards and my luggage there. It wasn't far to Paramus. I took a taxi, arriving at the house as arranged at two in the afternoon. It was a regular middle-class home with a small flower garden in front and a larger garden at the rear.

I rang the bell, and Robert Gates opened the door. It was a warm spring day, and he was dressed in a white short-sleeved shirt, open neck, blue trousers. Over his shirt he wore a light-brown vest. He ushered me into the living room. A smell of freshly made coffee wafted from the kitchen. He poured us a cup each. It didn't seem

---

* As he was later to admit in court, he was actually a U.S. Customs Service undercover agent, John Lisica.

** This comment was not in the tapes played at my trial. There was, Lettner admitted, a gap in the recording, which he said was due to his inability, at a certain point, to flip the tape over without being observed.

to be his home, but he was comfortable enough in it. I started talking about the man I had met that morning and my suspicions about him.

"Oh, don't worry about it," he said.

"But I do worry about it. It smelled of an attempt to set me up—trying to get me to agree on tape to the illegal sale of aircraft to Iran."

He brushed my comment aside with a wave of his hand, giving me the impression that it was an irrelevant incident that had already been forgotten. I decided to drop the subject. But I wasn't going to forget the purpose of this meeting and once again raised the topic of the chemical sales to Iraq.

I talked to Robert Gates for more than two hours, recounting for him what we knew about Cardoen, and the threat that Iraq held for Israel. He had heard it all before, of course. He sat patiently listening, but remained noncommittal. At 4:30 P.M. I told him I had to leave. I knew I had gotten nowhere. He called a taxi for me, and I went back to Newark Airport.

The only flight to London was on Virgin Atlantic. We had made reservations, but when we got to the counter two hours ahead of time, we were told that somebody had canceled them. It was looking as if we weren't expected to take that flight to London. I pointed out we had okayed tickets. The supervisor was called, and we were able to get our seats. I spent a few days in London and returned to Israel.

The Chile chapter in my life was over. At the time, I felt I had failed. Still, if it hadn't been for the pressure Israel applied, the Iraqi arsenal would have been much deadlier.

As it was, Iraq's Scuds used during the Gulf War of 1991 were unable to carry heavy payloads of chemicals precisely because the scientists who could have helped Saddam Hussein to that end had been eliminated before they could finish their mission. Among them was Gerald Bull, killed by the Israelis; his body had been found at his Brussels apartment in March 1990.

19

Mission to Colombo

ISRAEL'S SLUSH FUND fortune of $600 million plus interest remained safely tucked away in the East Bloc. In addition, there was also the CIA slush fund of another $600 million plus interest, which was sitting in various banks outside the U.S. A cool $1.2 billion. It was money the Americans would never be able to admit to owning, and when they started to feel vulnerable in 1987, after the failure of Robert Gates to be confirmed as CIA director, those in power in Washington decided to distance themselves from the illegal money.

A deal was cut with Prime Minister Shamir's office in which control of the CIA money was passed to Israel. It would remain U.S. money, but Israel would become its guardian. Because of the way things had been structured when I was a member of the Joint Israel-Iran Committee, I remained a signatory to the Israeli funds, and now the CIA money. The two other signatories at this time were Nachum Admoni and another member of Mossad.

I was more than happy to have this control. I was worried that the Americans were determined to "close me down" personally because of the problems I had caused them in South America. The last thing they wanted was for me to expose the deceits in the sale of Promis around the world—something I'd threatened to do as a way of stopping the chemical sales to Iraq. But while I had some control over their money, I wondered what they could do to

me. They had already tried *something*, using my newfound friend
Lettner.

A lot of money moved around in 1988. It was in that year that
Robert Maxwell approached Yitzhak Shamir and asked for a loan
guarantee to expand his publishing empire. Shamir was happy to
use the U.S. funds as a guarantee, as long as the Americans
agreed. The man who personally gave Shamir the permission,
according to Avi Pazner, was John Tower.

With a guaranteed backing of nearly $1 billion, Maxwell was
able to borrow hundreds of millions from banks. And with the
money, he went on a huge spending spree in 1988 and 1989. He
bought a communications company in Japan. He bought a con-
trolling interest in the *Ma'ariv* newspaper in Israel. He looked
forward to the launch of *The European*. He tried to buy *The Age*
newspaper in Melbourne for $750 million Australian, and he
offered $230 million for a controlling stake in the *West Austra-
lian* newspaper, moves that were thwarted only by the Australian
Labor government's foreign ownership policy.

Maxwell serviced the huge loans from the commissions he
made from numerous business arrangements he had set up with
the Israelis, including what he was getting from the sale of
Promis. For the time being, everything looked rosy for the British
businessman who claimed to have been born in Czechoslovakia.
But he was in a precarious position. The guarantees were for
renewable three-month periods; upon each renewal, we usually
moved the funds to different banks. The three of us who held
control over the accounts could close Maxwell down at any time
by refusing to renew the guarantees, signing a piece of paper, and
moving the $1 billion. But such thoughts weren't on our minds
. . . yet.

As I relaxed at home with Ora and our daughter Shira one
evening in mid-1989, I reflected on the astonishing events of the
past few years. I had an uneasy feeling that the past was catching
up with the present, and the future was going to be bleak. I knew
only too well what some of my "colleagues" were capable of
doing. Hundreds of millions of dollars were involved, a fortune
that had grown out of a small hush-hush sale of aircraft tires. No
one realized when that first under-the-counter sale was made
what it would all blow up to—least of all me.

I'd started as a naive, ambitious 29-year-old thrilled to be playing in the big leagues with the élite of Israeli intelligence. At first
the international jetting around had been exciting, the amounts
of money I was handling had been dizzying—and it was all to
serve the interests of Israel, in which I deeply believed. I felt I was
at the center, making important things happen in the world. But
by 1985 or 1986, I realized I was merely implementing other
people's policies. The initial excitement had faded, and I was tired
of the job. In the arms trade, I'd had to deal with too many
difficult, sleazy people, including Robert Maxwell, Rodolfo
Stange, and Carlos Cardoen. When I learned of Israel's involvement with South Africa, I became further disillusioned. All this
put together weighed on me. I felt like a rubber band that had
been pulled on for too long, losing elasticity, and aware that
sooner or later I would tear completely.

I wondered whether I shouldn't just throw in the job, forget
about the money over which I had a one-third control, and take up
something safe. On the other hand, I couldn't really escape. I had
been up to my neck in an international bluff, and I couldn't just
walk away from it. I knew too much.

For all his public image, Prime Minister Yitzhak Shamir was a
very private man. Having fought underground against the British
and then having spent the rest of his life in Mossad, rising to
operations chief for Europe, he had learned not to trust people. He
carried this mistrust into his position as prime minister, and
there were a number of decisions he made that he refused to share
even with his own party members. Many of his secrets were
learned only on a need-to-know basis. Some of his secrets were
known only by trusted advisers, of whom I was one. I knew, for
example, about the bank account, held by Shamir's son, Yair,
which had been started up after Admoni, I, and others had taken
some profits in 1987. I knew how often Shamir would get things
he believed were in Israel's interest done without cabinet
consent—such as sending me to Peru to collect the nuclear substances.

And I was also well aware of Shamir's closeness to the Soviets.
As early as 1984 Shamir had authorized intelligence exchanges

with the Soviets, including sanitized American intelligence reports about nuclear issues and evaluations of Soviet nuclear technology. These reports were obtained in part through Rafi Eitan's U.S. spy network. One intelligence exchange meeting took place in New Delhi between the KGB, Mossad, and Indian intelligence to discuss the Pakistani nuclear reactor and India's desire to destroy it. The three nations were all afraid of President Zia el Haq's nuclear project, which was known to the U.S. but overlooked as his prize for backing the Mujahedin in Afghanistan. Shamir saw the Libyan-financed project, known as the Islamic Bomb, as a direct threat to Israel, just like the Iraqi nuclear program. It was bizarre, but on nuclear issues our American allies and their friends such as Pakistan and Iraq were aligned against Israel, forcing Shamir to find support from the Soviet Union.

In 1986, after Chebrikov and Shamir reached an agreement on the immigration of Soviet Jews, the flow of Israeli intelligence to the Soviet Union expanded even more. Israel began regularly exchanging intelligence with the Soviets on the capabilities of the pro-American Arab countries—Saudi Arabia, Jordan, Egypt, and even Iraq, although the Soviets were also arming the Iraqis. For their part, the Soviets, as late as 1989, were handing over information to Israel from their network in Iraq about the Iraqi nuclear and chemical arsenals. They were also reporting about U.S. and other nations' relations with the Iraqis.

It was altogether a very friendly affair, particularly after the Israelis had transferred so much of the slush fund into Soviet repositories. Shamir became very chummy with Chebrikov, as did other members of the Joint Committee. As a result of these relationships with the East Bloc, I was later accused of being a Soviet sympathizer.

One of Shamir's best-kept secrets was his clandestine attempt to negotiate a solution of his own to the Palestinian situation with the PLO.

Despite Israel's generally perceived enmity with the Palestine Liberation Organization, Shamir and some of the PLO leadership shared a common belief that peace in the Middle East would come not by Israel's giving up the West Bank and the Gaza Strip, but by allowing the Palestinians to establish their own nation in what is now Jordan.

Jordan was created as the result of a feud between the sons of the Saudi King Saud bin Abdul-Aziz over who was to succeed him. The British, who controlled the area, came to a compromise and carved out a piece of Palestine and a piece of the Arabian peninsula and made a new kingdom so all the brothers would be happy. While the new Jordan had an almost 70 percent Palestinian population, the Bedouins were in control of the army, the king's power base.

Before the 1967 war between the Arabs and Israel, the ruling Labor Party never saw the Palestinians as any real threat to Israel. The PLO was considered a bunch of cutthroat terrorists who posed no political danger, so Labor never tried to deal with the broader Palestinian issue. After the war, when the Gaza Strip and the West Bank of the River Jordan fell into the hands of Israel, a million and a half Palestinians came under Israeli military rule.

One of the few people in the Labor Party who was conscious of the problems of holding these territories was the then prime minister of Israel, Levi Eshkol. He realized that some type of accommodation that included the settlement of refugees had to be reached with the Arab countries, and especially the Palestinians.

Eshkol offered to start negotiations with President Gamal Abdel Nasser of Egypt for an all-encompassing peace treatybetween Israel and the Arab countries, including settlement of the Palestinian question. He even met with Nasser secretly on two occasions to discuss the notion. But both men died within a year of each other. Nasser purportedly collapsed with a stroke while he was giving a speech; Eshkol was reported to have died of a heart attack while visiting his home kibbutz, Degania.

Nasser's successor, Anwar Sadat, believed the best way to deal with Israel was to offer peace without really settling the Palestinian question. Eshkol's successor in Israel was former Foreign Minister Golda Meir, whose perspective was very limited—she could not see beyond immediate goals. In 1948 she had struck up a friendship with King Abdullah of Jordan. They both believed the Palestinian problem would one day just go away.

But as a result of his friendship with Israel, King Abdullah was stabbed to death in 1948 in the El Aqsa Mosque in East Jerusalem, which was then under Jordanian control. After his death, his son, Talal, was made king for a few months, but he was found to be mentally disturbed and was sent off to an asylum in Switzerland where he eventually died in peace. Talal's son, Hussein, then became king of Jordan. He and his advisers began talks with the Labor Party, including Golda Meir, and once again they all believed that the Palestinian issue would go away.

King Hussein became an American favorite. As long as he ruled Jordan and there was no Palestinian state there, militant Palestinians would be no threat to America's oil supply in neighboring Saudi Arabia. Golda Meir and other Labor leaders, following America's lead, were not interested in dethroning King Hussein.

In the meantime, after the 1967 war, the PLO and other Palestinian groups moved out of the West Bank and the Gaza Strip into Jordan. Hussein thought wrongly that he would be able to contain them. The PLO with its forces became a state within a state, and the king lost complete control of large portions of his country. The PLO began hijacking civilian airliners and bringing them to Jordan. The situation reached a crisis in 1970 when the PLO landed three commercial planes in Az-Zarqa, Jordan, ordered the passengers off, and then blew the aircraft up, with the king unable to do a thing about it.

Realizing how little power he had over the Palestinians, King Hussein decided to unleash his army against them. He achieved some success until the Syrians decided, in 1970, to intervene on behalf of the Palestinians. At issue was the very existence of the king—or the establishment of a Palestinian state in Jordan. It was then that Israeli Prime Minister Golda Meir arguably made the worst political mistake in the history of Israel. She ordered the Israel Defense Forces to be mobilized against the Syrians. In doing so, she prevented the establishment of a Palestinian state in Jordan, and she kept the king in power. The threat by militant Palestinians to Saudi oilfields was prevented, which made the Americans happy, but as far as Israel's longterm strategic interest was concerned, any hopes of creating a Palestinian state in Jordan had received a major setback. Ultimately the price of this decision could still be the very existence of Israel.

As a result of Golda Meir's decision, King Hussein was able to maneuver his army within Jordan, massacre some 20,000 Palestinians, and throw all the PLO people out of Jordan. As the PLO moved into Lebanon, many Palestinian fighters came to the Jordan-Israel border and surrendered to Israeli troops rather than fall into the hands of the Bedouin army, which had a reputation for not taking prisoners.

After Likud took power in Israel in 1977, Prime Minister Menachem Begin and Egypt's President Sadat came up with a face-saving formula over the Palestinian issue and talked about autonomy in the West Bank. Begin gave the Sinai back, and Sadat let go of the West Bank and the Palestinian issue. All Sadat was interested in was getting back the Sinai. The Gaza Strip, which had been under Egyptian control before 1967, had no appeal for him because it had a large Palestinian population. For Begin, the West Bank and Gaza Strip were important for Israel to retain both for historical and strategic reasons.

After the Camp David agreements, and after the Republicans had taken over in 1981, the U.S. and the "moderate" Arab countries started pressing for a mini-Palestinian state in the Gaza Strip and the West Bank, which would not threaten U.S. oil interests, as would a Palestinian state in Jordan, which Likud wanted. Likud believed that Israel could work closely with a Palestinian state established in Jordan, but nothing was done about it. The 1984 election resulted in a hung parliament and the formation of the famous Likud-Labor coalition. Then Shimon Peres, who was prime minister from late 1984 to late 1986, agreed to consider some type of international conference to discuss the issue of a Palestinian entity in the West Bank and Gaza Strip, conforming with U.S. policy. But Likud, a major partner in the coalition, blocked the whole initiative and thus accelerated the U.S. tilt toward Iraq.

With Shamir back in power after 1986, secret attempts were made to talk to the Palestinian leadership, including the PLO—even though to this day the organization is not publicly or officially recognized by the Israeli government, especially Likud. The talks involved a plan to get rid of the king of Jordan and take over his country as a Palestinian state. The population was 70 percent Palestinian anyway. Such a plan would have outraged the

Labor Party in Israel, the U.S. Republican administration, the king of Jordan, and the Saudis, if any of them found out about it. However, various Palestinian circles, especially what was known as the radical camp, along with the Syrians and the Soviet Union, were happy to go along with it.

The Soviets believed a Palestinian state sandwiched in the West Bank between Jordan and Israel would just cause more trouble in the Middle East, reducing Israel's standing as a balancing power in the region. Even though publicly the Soviet policy was anti-Israel, privately the Soviets wanted what Shamir wanted—a Palestinian state in place of Jordan. At a secret meeting in 1986, Shamir and Chebrikov agreed that there would be no negotiations with the PLO over the West Bank as such. There would be an attempt for an overall solution in the Middle East. And the cold solution would be to "do away" with King Hussein of Jordan.

The deal between Chebrikov and Shamir was that if the Likud Party held out against a Palestinian state in the West Bank and Gaza Strip and against an American-dictated "peace treaty," the Soviets would help Israel. They would do this by helping Israel populate the West Bank with Jews; not only from their country but also with immigrants from Soviet-backed Ethiopia.

As events were to prove, the agreement was kept to the letter. By 1991 more than 250,000 Soviet Jews had emigrated to Israel with another 30,000 Ethiopian Jews airlifted from Addis Ababa.

The bond that developed between Israel and the Soviet Union was far stronger than anyone realized. Since Israel did not have diplomatic representation in the Soviet Union, the Jews were getting exit visas to Austria and Italy and then waiting. They would apply to leave the Soviet Union saying they wanted to go to their homeland, but in Vienna and Rome they would apply for immigration visas to the U.S. This was limited by opening an Israeli consular section in Moscow through which the Israeli government would grant visas to enter Israel for Soviet Jews. All paperwork was completed in Moscow, so emigrants would not go rushing off to the U.S. They had to go directly to Israel, where they were needed to populate the West Bank, thereby taking up the land and spoiling any U.S. plans to grant it to the Palestinians.

The Palestinian issue came to a head after the outbreak of the *Intifada* in the West Bank and Gaza Strip in 1987. The U.S. was talking about a peace conference with the Palestinians and had officially sanctioned a dialogue between the U.S. ambassador in Tunis and the PLO leadership. Shamir, instead of bowing to pressure and accepting the American proposals, announced he would come up with a peace plan of his own.

That peace plan, which essentially would create a Palestinian state in Jordan, was not made public. But Shamir discussed it with his advisers. In this period of time, Yasser Arafat was beating the wardrums against Jordan. It was risky, but risks had to be taken because U.S. pressure on Shamir was enormous.

It was against this background that Shamir decided that several of his advisers should meet PLO leaders around the world with a view to developing the "Jordanian option." Orders were given to one of the advisers to travel to Tunis, to PLO headquarters, and meet Yasser Arafat. It was in late June 1989; and that meeting was the first of three with the PLO leader, on behalf of Shamir.

The feasibility and theoretical scenarios of starting a war against Jordan, with Israel supporting an all-out Palestinian uprising against the king, were discussed. This was an important part of Shamir's secret plan to resolve the Palestinian situation. Surprising as it may seem, this secret was shared with Arafat.

After these discussions with Arafat, a deputy minister in the Prime Minister's Office, Ehud Ulmart, who was very close to Shamir, met the PLO leader, in a private home in Tunis City, where further discussions were held about the Jordanian option.

Based on these discussions, Prime Minister Shamir had a new secret mission for me. It was a complex plan, but if successful, it would have a twofold effect—it would free the three Israeli soldiers who were being held in Lebanon, and it would bring us closer to the PLO in our talks with them. It would require my presence in Sri Lanka.

As I flew to Colombo early in July 1989, I went over the plan, which could be likened to a political chess game in which one side moves forward but is careful to protect its interests. And at any time something could go wrong.

Despite Shamir's earlier decision that the C-130 deal was off, he decided to try again to negotiate the sale of the planes in return for Tehran's help in securing the release of the soldiers. This time we were to try to enlist the aid of the PLO, which had a representative in Sri Lanka. If Iran could find out where the soldiers were, the PLO might be able to get them freed from the clutches of the Shi'ites, who were holding them.

Sri Lanka had been chosen because it was a different "smokescreen" country to send the aircraft through, and the PLO had a man there I could talk to. Naturally, the PLO wanted a slice of the cake. The demands that Arafat had laid down during the secret meetings in Tunis were that, in exchange for their help, Israel should make a donation to the Sri Lankan Tamil guerrillas, the LTTE, who would then use the money to buy weapons from the PLO.

So we would be using the Sri Lankan government as a conduit for our aircraft to Iran—and we'd be using the LTTE as a cover for putting money into the hands of the PLO for their cooperation. It was a crazy situation. Israel had advisers helping the Sri Lankan Army in its fight against the rebels, yet here was I, acting on behalf of the Israeli government, arranging payment to the rebels so they could buy weapons to fight the army.

I checked into the Ramada hotel in downtown Colombo and, later in the evening, wandered down to the lobby, where I ordered a welcome dish of ice cream. I struck up a friendly conversation with a man who introduced himself as the Egyptian chargé d'affaires. As we chatted, neither of us could help but notice a Western man in his late 60s, with a white beard, dancing alone to the small band.

"Just look at that crazy guy," said my Egyptian companion. "He either loves dancing alone, or he can't find himself a woman."

We were soon to discover who he was. The music finished, and he flopped down in the lounge seat beside me, flapping his shirt against his chest. "That was good exercise," he said.

He reached into his shirt pocket and produced a business card. It portrayed planets circling the earth. It read:

One Universe
A Non-Profit Alliance

Leon Siff, Chief Organizer
National Food Relief—Homes for the Homeless
Counseling Without Walls—Advocates for the Homeless

Siff extended a hand, explaining he was a retired probation officer
from Los Angeles, who was now involved with charitable work.
The full name of his organization, although his card didn't say it,
was Friends of the Universe, set up, he said, to help the homeless
living in and around Venice Beach in Los Angeles.

The American explained that he was Jewish and was in Sri
Lanka to visit his son, who had become a Buddhist monk. I was to
see a lot more of Siff during my stay in the steamy city.

Later I called the PLO representative, as previously arranged,
and he was delighted to see me. We spoke in Hebrew. He had been
in an Israeli jail for 12 years after trying to plant a bomb in the
town of Afula. It had blown up prematurely and almost killed
him.

My next meeting, also arranged beforehand, was with the Sri
Lankan minister of information, at his home. As a confidant of
President Ranasinghe Premadasa, he was my stepping stone. I
explained to him over dinner that my prime minister would be
most grateful, and would ensure increased military assistance to
his army, if Sri Lanka would agree to act as the conduit for the
C-130s. The minister arranged for me to meet Premadasa at the
presidential palace the next day. The first step of my mission had
been accomplished.

The next morning I had a low-key breakfast meeting with the
PLO representative. Israel, I said, was willing to pay the Tamils $8
million if the PLO would help Iran to get the three captured
soldiers out of the hands of the Shi'ite groups in Lebanon. Officially, the money was to be used by the Tamils for "humanitarian
purposes," although we were both aware it would go to the purchase of weapons from the PLO.

Back at the hotel that evening, I spotted Leon Siff dancing on
his own again. When he saw me, he left the dance floor and made
his way over. He asked how my day had been and where I had
gone, but I dodged the topic. Then he turned the subject around to
money.

"Ari," he said, "my group needs all the support it can get. I know you can help. I'd like you to come to the U.S. some time and see what we do. How about it?"

"Sure," I said, "if I'm in Los Angeles, I'll look you up."

In the next 48 hours I met the president, the commander of the Sri Lankan Air Force, and the PLO representative, nudging them all along toward the execution of the Israeli plan to sell the C-130s in exchange for the three soldiers. I still had to meet the Tamils, even though contact had been made with their London office, to arrange their payment. Of course, this part of the deal was unknown to the Sri Lankan government.

My journey to Jaffna was not the most relaxed. I had decided to drive myself because I didn't want any witnesses to my movements or negotiations. The narrow road took me through numerous roadblocks set up by either the Sri Lankan Army or the Indian Army. The Indians were highly suspicious of a "tourist" heading north to Jaffna at a time when the rebels were active. But after a great deal of argument they allowed me to proceed, even though the area north had been designated as a military operations zone.

That night, as previously arranged through the PLO representative, I was picked up at the Subhi Hotel in Jaffna and driven to a Tamil village. My guide took me to a large house where teenage boys stood guard, each holding a Kalashnikov rifle. I was ushered inside, where a number of men were waiting in the stark light of a propane lamp. Their leader, whose codename was Tiger One, spoke reasonably good English and introduced himself and his compatriots. I was a sitting duck for their propaganda, but it had to be done.

Tiger One, a middle-aged, short, chubby, dark-complexioned man, paced the room as he informed me there were 50 million Tamils on the Indian mainland in Tamil Nadu, and they were all very unhappy with the way they had been treated by Rajiv Gandhi and his Congress Party. Gandhi had created a pro-Indian front in Sri Lanka, and he wanted to annex the Tamil areas in Sri Lanka to India.

"He has become a bully," Tiger One snapped. "He even wants the top part of Sri Lanka—our homeland. Well, let us tell you that Rajiv Gandhi will pay for his heavy-handedness. We will continue our struggle for independence to the last man. We will fight whatever and whomever they throw at us."

I explained that I was there to make a contribution to their cause. The Tamil leader was quick to point out that the Israeli government might well be offering them $8 million, but the Israelis were also assisting the Sri Lankan Army against the Tamils. They conceded, however, they needed the money. I explained it was ransom for the three soldiers, but I didn't tell them about the C-130s that were going to Iran as well.

My hosts and I struck a deal. They would accept the money from Israel, and they would contact the PLO mission in Colombo informing them of the arrangement. Hopefully, we could then expect PLO assistance in trying to secure the release of our soldiers.

The return journey to Colombo was horrendous. Inevitably, the car broke down, and I ended up being towed, sleeping in the car, and finding myself at the point of a gun as a gang of Tamil road bandits demanded money.

Back in the capital, I phoned Nick Davies and told him to go ahead. This was our prearranged signal for him to make the $8 million payment to the Tamils through their London office. Naturally, the money came out of a slush-fund account.

I flew back to Israel, right into a storm. The talks with the PLO had been leaked, I found out, by Rabbi Ovadia Yusef, leader of the Shas Party, who had himself had discussions about the Palestinian question with Arab leaders. Some coalition members were furious. Shamir was on the receiving end of their anger, and he realized he had to be seen to be backing out of his commitment. He needed scapegoats.

I guessed what was coming and decided to stay one step ahead. I consulted the other two signatories to the slush-fund accounts, and persuaded them that for the physical and financial protection of everyone who'd been on the Joint Committee, we should move the CIA money now controlled by Israel to the East Bloc.

The CIA money, by now up to $710 million, went into the East on a series of straightforward transfers, without using Maxwell's companies as a conduit. The move left Maxwell dangling. The banks that had lent him money in 1988 no longer had their guarantees. Shamir was furious that his friend had been left in such a vulnerable position, and he had to conduct a swift public relations exercise with the banks to ensure they continued to shore Maxwell up.

In early fall 1989, Shamir called me into his office. He was sitting behind his desk, his tiny body dwarfed in the large leather chair. I stood in silence, staring into his severe face. This was to be the showdown.

"You have got too close to our enemies," he said.

"If you're talking about the PLO contacts, you know I was only following orders. And we couldn't back off anyway. I have personally promised the families of those soldiers that we will do all we can to help them."

"You exceeded your authority." His face was like a stone, cold and grey. "And what about the money?" he asked. "Are you stealing it?"

An old Hebrew saying came into my head. *"Ganav mi ganav patur,"* I said. "A thief from a thief is off the hook."

He glared at me for a moment. Then with a flick of his hand he dismissed me. *"Lech!*—Go!" he ordered. I went. I knew him well enough to know that this was not the end of the affair.

Shamir's 1989 secret peace plan, from which he was now trying to extricate himself, never got anywhere. Infighting in the cabinet effectively ended any contact between the PLO and Shamir's office. King Hussein, through his own intelligence network, heard about the plan to unseat him and took precautionary steps. He aligned himself even more closely with Saddam Hussein and extracted a promise that the Iraqi leader would help the king if there were an uprising in Jordan.

The Americans, meanwhile, kept up the pressure on Shamir. They joined in full chorus with Egypt, Jordan, and Iraq, and insisted that the West Bank and Gaza Strip should be the new Palestinian state. The king of Jordan had also officially relinquished any responsibility for the Palestinians or for the West Bank and said he would no longer be interested in any negotiations over a Jordanian-Palestinian federation. This was the situation when the U.S. finally fell out with Saddam Hussein in August 1990 and decided it needed to establish its own military presence in the region.

When Saddam Hussein clashed with the U.S. in early 1991, the Palestinian populace all over the world suddenly started seeing him as their hero. Here was an Arab leader fighting single-handedly against U.S. imperialism. Arafat had no choice but to show public support for Iraq against the United States. The king of Jordan, whose loyalties were divided, did not know where to turn at first, but then decided to lean toward Saddam Hussein and show the Palestinians that he was also a protector of the Arab cause. The Syrians, however, who were anti-Saddam Hussein, suddenly changed sides and went to the Americans.

As events were to prove, when the Gulf War ended in Iraq's defeat and the loss of tens of thousands of Iraqi soldiers, Arafat lost his standing. His money sources from Saudi Arabia and other Gulf states were cut off, and what little credibility he'd built up in the West was nullified. The king of Jordan, even though he had backed Saddam Hussein in the Gulf War, quickly returned to the U.S. fold. The Syrians, for their cooperation in the Gulf War, were given control over Lebanon. Israel found itself back in one of the most difficult diplomatic situations possible, in which the Americans were saying the "moderate" Palestinians and not the PLO were to be involved in negotiations with Israel over the West Bank and Gaza Strip.

All the covert negotiations between Likud and the PLO leadership in 1988 and 1989 went down the drain. A real attempt to solve the Palestinian question, without threatening the existence of the State of Israel, was again aborted by the Americans and their friends.

20

Means of War

In October 1989, a couple of weeks after my confrontation with Shamir, Avi Pazner suggested I take a leave of absence. I welcomed the idea. It had been a hectic year, during which I could have been killed or arrested at any moment. I needed a break.

I asked Ora if she'd like to vacation for a couple of weeks in Sydney, a city I had fallen in love with on earlier visits. I promised to show her and Shira the opera house and take them out on a ferry across the harbor. Ora said she thought it was a wonderful idea.

The day before we were to leave, the phone rang. It was the travel agent through whom government employees like myself made arrangements. Our reservations on the computer had inexplicably disappeared, but the difficulty had been overcome, and the tickets would be waiting for us. Later that evening there was another call.

"Ari? It's Leon Siff. Remember me?"

How could I forget Leon Siff, the famous Sri Lankan dancer?

"Hey, this is just a contact call. You promised to look in on me some time. I'm still waiting. I'd like you to see my Friends of the Universe operation."

Leon's sense of timing was extraordinary. I suspected it was some type of operation, and my curiosity was piqued. I told him I would call him back.

I expected Ora to be pretty upset if I went to Los Angeles and let her and Shira find their own way to Sydney, but to my surprise she didn't mind at all.

"I'm not interested in what your friend has to show you, but that doesn't matter. You go see him, and Shira and I will meet up with you later."

So we left it at that. I changed the routing of my flight to Sydney, to go via Los Angeles.

I arrived in Los Angeles on Saturday, October 28, after spending two days with John de Laroque in southern France. Leon Siff was waiting. He was delighted to see me. And even though I had booked into a hotel, he would hear nothing of it—I was to be his guest at his home. The house in Hollywood had the same address as on his card for the Friends of the Universe.

"It'll be my pleasure to show you around for a few days," he said.

"That's fine, but I'm leaving on Tuesday."

Mock horror spread over his face. "You can't leave on Tuesday. I've arranged a party in your honor."

He was so insistent that I relented again and agreed to spend the whole week there. I called Ora. Again she surprised me, quickly agreeing to wait a few more days in Israel and then meet me in Sydney the following Monday.

Leon drove me around Los Angeles, taking me to Venice Beach where the homeless were sleeping. He talked about land he hoped to buy in Sri Lanka for his organization.

I was still waiting for the pitch.

On Tuesday evening Leon's friends arrived, a mixed bunch of pseudo-intellectuals and hippies of all ages who gathered in the front room. I strolled among them, the guest of honor, a little bemused by the purpose of the gathering. Suddenly a face I recognized stood out in the crowd. I was taken aback. It was my old friend Joseph O'Toole, the man who had arranged for me and Richard St. Francis to meet Lettner at Kennedy Airport several months earlier. Something was seriously wrong.

As O'Toole approached to say hello, I turned on Leon Siff. "How do you two know each other?" I asked as casually as my voice would allow.

"Oh, I heard you were in town and dropped by to say hello," said O'Toole. I had an uneasy feeling. Siff and O'Toole were obviously acquaintances. O'Toole brought the conversation around to the three C-130s.

"My company had that deal all set up," he said. "We were going to be the go-between for Israel and Iran, but you guys cut us out. You wanted to deal through Sri Lanka without involving us."

I didn't remind him that the Iranians had never heard of his associate Lettner. I didn't remind him of anything. I just didn't want to talk to the man.

Later I hit Leon Siff with one big question: "What the hell's going on?"

He shrugged and said he didn't know what I was talking about. I knew a showdown of some sort was coming. My instincts told me that if something was going to happen, it might as well happen here.

Three days later, on Friday, November 3, 1989, the day before I was due to leave, I was taking a shower in Siff's bathroom. It was noon. Allowing for time differences, I would be in Sydney on Monday. I was looking forward to it. Suddenly the bathroom door swung open. Through the steam I saw a group of people in blue uniforms—with guns, all pointing at me.

A man in a suit stepped forward.

"What's going on?" I demanded.

"Please step out of the shower and get dressed," he said. They kept their guns on me as I walked past them. There was a woman among them. I was later to learn her name was Elaine Banar, a case manager for the strategic unit of the U.S. Customs Service, and in charge of the arrest.

As I made my way to the bedroom, Leon Siff didn't protest. He didn't say a word. He just stood and watched.

They confiscated my briefcase, which contained all my papers, address book, passport, money, and credit cards. Then they let me dress, pulled my arms behind me, and clicked on handcuffs. I glared at Siff.

"Thanks, Leon," I said.

I turned to my captors. "What are you arresting me for?"

The answer shocked me. Conspiracy to sell three U.S.-built

C-130s to Iran in contravention of the U.S. Arms Export Control Act. The evidence against me, I was told, emerged from that meeting with Lettner in the Kennedy Airport coffee shop.

They led me out to a car, and I was pushed into the front seat. Elaine Banar sat in the rear. There were cars behind and cars in front, all filled with special agents. The man at the wheel of the car I was in, Special Agent Staudinger, said into the radio, "We need to start an extradition hearing to New York's Southern District for an extremely violent and dangerous criminal we've just captured."

Later, in the federal magistrate's court in Los Angeles, I acted as my own attorney and made a deal with the judge waiving my extradition to New York in return for a quick transfer there—I had heard horror stories of three-month prison bus trips from Los Angeles to New York.

The magistrate ordered that I be flown to the Southern District of New York within ten days. Then they took me, with chains around my feet and hands, to the Metropolitan Detention Center where I was to spend the next three days. International calls were not permitted and I had no address book, so all I could do was make a collect call to Leon Siff. He refused to admit having any part in my arrest and said he was looking for a lawyer for me.

He told me that Ann Magori had phoned from Israel—I'd left Leon's number as a way to contact me—and was on her way to see me. Ann was a real estate agent whom Ora and I had met while hunting for an apartment. A close relationship had developed among the three of us, and Ann was planning to join us on our vacation in Australia. She was an American-born orthodox woman. But why was she coming to Los Angeles instead of Ora?

"What about my wife?" I asked Siff.

He didn't know whether Ora had even been told about my arrest.

I was visited at the detention center by the lawyer Siff had found. He introduced himself as Harry Weiss. He was still looking into my case, he said, but he was confident of striking a deal. It was necessary, however, for me to go to New York first.

When Ann Magori arrived, she visited me in jail and told me, "There's something very wrong. I've been talking all day to Leon

Siff, and I think he and his friends are all involved with the American government. Just be careful."

At around 3:00 A.M. November 9, a Thursday, I was chained and taken out to a bus filled with other prisoners. It was a nightmare scene from the Dark Ages in which grey-faced men shuffled along to the rattle of their chains. Many of them were hardened criminals. There were to be no special privileges for a man who had done nothing more than serve his government to the best of his ability. Indeed, the opposite was true.

We were driven to an airfield, herded off the bus, and told to form a line. A circle of U.S. marshals with shotguns surrounded us, illuminated by distant lighting. And there we waited for an hour until an old 737, painted completely white, landed. It was now about four or five in the morning, but because they had taken my watch I couldn't be sure.

Struggling up the steps in our chains, we made our way onto the aircraft, a special Bureau of Prisons flight that transported prisoners around the U.S. The in-flight service was nothing to speak of. One of the prisoners asked for water and when told there was none on board complained this was unconstitutional. He demanded the name of the marshal who had refused him. The marshal told him to wait for a moment. A few seconds later he came from the rear of the plane with three others, who then began to slap the unfortunate prisoner around and call him a smartass.

The plane landed to offload some prisoners, and others were brought on, this time some women too. Then it would land at another place, and the same procedure would be played out. Men and women came out of the toilet with their clothing stained, finding it difficult to manipulate their chains in the cramped space. Our only refreshments as we hopscotched east across the U.S. were a sweet drink, a chocolate bar, and an apple.

At 10:00 P.M. we landed at Oklahoma City. My name was called along with others, and we were herded off, to be met by more shotgun-wielding marshals. I was taken to El Reno Federal Penitentiary and led down metal stairs to an underground cellblock. You could almost touch the sides of the cell with your arms spread out. On one side was a metal bunkbed. Someone had spilled sugar on it, and it was crawling with cockroaches. The concrete floor was wet. In a corner was an aluminum toilet with a sink attached. The toilet worked, but the sink didn't.

They kept me there for two days, in what I later learned were among the worst prison conditions in the U.S. It was illegal to hold anyone that long without allowing them out for exercise, but they didn't care. I had been marked as dangerous, and that was that.

My only reprieve was that they allowed me to use the phone, and I called Leon Siff collect.

"I don't want to talk to you," he said. "You're a criminal. Your friend Ann is here, she'd like to talk to you."

Her words cut me dead: "I hope you rot in jail."

I got through to Harry Weiss and asked him to connect me on a three-way line with Ora in Israel. I knew that government agents would be listening in, but at least Ora would confirm that I had been working for Israel.

When Ora came on the line, my hopes collapsed. "I don't know how I can help you, Ari," she said.

"You can help by coming here instantly and finding me a lawyer. And by telling them who I am."

"I can't do it. I've been talking to people in the government and I can't come. I can't leave. I can't do anything."

"My God, Ora. Have they gotten to you, too?"

She didn't answer. I hung up.

My world was shaken. For more than a decade I'd dealt with the slimiest, least trustworthy people on earth, who had made me cynical far beyond my years. And, of course, my marriage to Ora had been built on a foundation of distrust from the start. She had been helping the Americans. And I had certainly done my share of betraying her trust by sleeping around. Still, somewhere in my deepest soul, I wanted to believe that husband and wife were there for each other in a crisis. When her distant voice told me it wasn't so, my heart sank.

In the next hour or so, as I sat on the bed in my cell, I realized how profoundly alone I was.

On that second day I was presented with a cellmate. Although he was wearing prison khakis like the rest of us, he was tanned, clean-shaven, and, unlike any other prisoner, wearing a watch. Almost immediately he began to tell me his sob story of how he owned copper mines and the "federal government bastards" had come down heavily on him for taxes and thrown him into this jail. Suddenly he asked, "And why are you here?"

I guessed that the man was wired, so I shrugged and said nothing. I lay back on my bed and decided to wait it out.

He got nowhere with me. And I could see that the stench of that dank cell and my silence were getting to him. Suddenly he yelled to a guard, "You mother-fucking bastards, why are you keeping me here?"

The guards understood the cue. Shortly afterwards they came and took him away—I believe to freedom.

I finally arrived in New York after 12 days, not the ten that had been ordered. I knew they were trying to break me down, trying to get me to confess to a "crime" of which I knew I was innocent. It was a frightening experience, to be away from your country, your family, your friends. And I began to wonder just who were my friends. I also wondered about Ora; had they really brainwashed her about me? Had they threatened her and Shira? Or did she already know what was going to happen before I left Israel? After all, she had worked for Israeli intelligence. And she had been strangely agreeable about all my last-minute changes in travel plans. Had Ora betrayed me? I didn't want to believe that one. I forced that thought from my mind—or at least tried to.

In the prison van from the airport to the Metropolitan Correctional Center in Manhattan I sat next to a Latino man who had been flown from Miami to Oklahoma and from there to New York.

"Comrade criminal," he said, "the machine we call society has just spit you out . . . it's just spit you out."

At the correctional center I was segregated from the rest of those who had arrived with me. Everyone else was given brown jumpsuits. I was ordered to put on an orange uniform. I had been classified as dangerous. They were really determined to break me.

Two days later during a brief court hearing I asked the magistrate why I was classified as dangerous. The assistant U.S. attorney for the Southern District of New York, Baruch Weiss, immediately exclaimed: "That was a mistake, your honor."

One for me. I was declassified to the status of regular prisoner.

The lawyer Harry Weiss had found to represent me, Don Son-terelli, came up with a fascinating proposition. He and his part-ner, he said, had flown in specially from Taiwan to see me, and they wanted to hear about my North Korean adventures. I told them that was quite irrelevant to the charge I suspected they were going to throw at me—of arms dealing—and asked why they were so interested. They said they had another client who knew about C-130 aircraft in North Korea and Vietnam. I told them I wouldn't discuss it further.

"Look, it's very simple," Sonterelli persisted. "You pay our fee before you're indicted, then all you have to do is plead guilty and home you go. We'll be able to work out a deal with the prosecu-tor."

"Oh yes," I said. "And what is your fee?"

"$125,000."

"I'll make no deals," I said.

They were urging me to admit to a crime I hadn't committed. I was going to fight this all the way. They said goodbye, leaving me fully aware of the long fight that lay ahead.

That wasn't the only approach made to me behind the scenes. Leonard Joy, of the Legal Aid Society of New York, visited me one day in the holding pen after a bail hearing and offered his services "on the house" to plead me guilty and get me a deal to go back to Israel. I asked him how he knew about the case, and his mum-bling reply left me unsatisfied. I thanked him for his interest in my welfare and bade him goodbye.

Next I was sitting in a common area at MCC when I was told an attorney was there to see me. I went down to the attorney confer-ence room, and a very well-known lawyer shook my hand and introduced himself.

"You, you have come to see me?" I asked. "Are you looking after my welfare also?"

He half-smiled and said he was representing the Israeli govern-ment. He explained that I should plead guilty and go home to Israel. I politely told him no.

A second lawyer acting for the Israeli government then visited and asked me about the funds that were tucked away in the East

Bloc. He pressed so hard that I told him if he didn't back off, I'd tell the world about Robert Maxwell's involvement.

Still, he pressed. "You'll be a young, retired, well-to-do man," he said.

This really made me angry. They wanted to send me to live in "Jerusalem, Alabama," somewhere out in the boonies, and never be heard from again. Use me, betray me, spit me out. How could I trust these guys? If I did what they asked, I'd probably be dead in a couple of months, like Amiram Nir. I sent this second Israeli lawyer packing.

Then Michael Foster, a special agent of the FBI and the chief investigator for Iran-contra Special Prosecutor Lawrence Walsh, came to see me in jail. He asked about Robert McFarlane. I offered him a deal—get my case dismissed, and I'd give him McFarlane on a platter. He asked me to tell him what I knew first. I said no. He said he'd get back to me, but when he did, he wasn't willing to meet my terms.

The one deal I was willing to make was with the prosecutor, Baruch Weiss. I signed an agreement with him that I would talk to him without a lawyer present on the condition that I be granted immunity on anything we talked about. I agreed to this for one simple reason: I wanted everyone I'd ever worked with to know that I was willing to blow them all into the public eye. I assumed that Weiss, with whom I spent approximately 40 hours in presumably taped conversations, would pass the message on to those who needed to know it. And he did.

At one point I talked to Maxwell and Davies from jail, arranged by Weiss's office, and asked for their help. Both of them told me, "You're history."

My phone conversation with Nick Davies, monitored by the authorities, was most illuminating.

"Nick," I said, "why don't you tell them the truth?"

"I don't know what you're talking about," he said. "I'm only a journalist."

After that, Baruch Weiss told me that all contact with Maxwell's *Mirror* group should go through its attorney, David Zornow.

That name rang some bells. Zornow had prosecuted Oliver North as part of Lawrence Walsh's team. This time he was representing some interesting—and interested—clients: Maxwell, Davies, and John Tower. As time was to prove, he did a good job. Although he did not appear, he was able to negotiate with the prosecution to ensure that their names did not come out in open court.

I tried phoning Ora again to convince her to help me, but the call only made me angrier. She wasn't coming to America.

I was unable to hire a lawyer, because foreign currency control authorities in Israel, against Israeli law that makes exceptions for citizens in legal trouble abroad, would not allow my mother to transfer money from Israel. Yet the prosecutor objected in court to the judge's suggestion of a court-appointed attorney, because I was not indigent.

On January 18, 1990, after 75 days in jail, Baruch Weiss finally told me what would be in my indictment. The magistrate assigned me an attorney pursuant to the Criminal Justice Act. It was to be the start of a friendship. Although Thomas F.X. Dunn, a New York-born, Irish-Catholic lawyer, possessed little knowledge of the Middle East, Israel, or the international intelligence scene, he was willing to learn.

It was quite plain to me that Israel was as much to blame for my arrest as the U.S., and with Tom Dunn, who had no connections to Israel, I felt that I was in good hands.

One day Dunn broke some news to me. The U.S. attorney was going to indict Joseph O'Toole and Richard St. Francis, the man who had brought the mysterious Lettner to Kennedy Airport.

"But that's impossible," I said. "O'Toole works for the U.S. government. He was the one who set me up at the airport." I could not understand why he was being indicted.

Tom was not acquainted with the details of my case—he didn't even know what a C-130 was at first. But he asked me to fill him in. When he heard about the roles of O'Toole and St. Francis, he agreed things were looking very odd.

My hope of getting bail was disappearing. The prosecutor wanted property worth at least $130,000 as security, and it had to be located in the United States. I couldn't bring cash into the country because the Israeli government continued not to allow it.

"This is their way of keeping you in jail," said Tom.

On Thursday, February 1, 1990, I was indicted and then taken back to jail. O'Toole and St. Francis, it turned out, had been arrested before me, in April 1989, although I had not known this, and released on bail, but they were not indicted until March 1990.

The charges were not lengthy. In essence, they claimed that St. Francis, O'Toole, and I had conspired to defraud the United States, to cover up illegal dealings, and to try to sell three planes to Iran in violation of federal laws.

They claimed we were acting as intermediaries between an Israeli seller and an Iranian buyer to sell three C-130 military cargo aircraft; that we conspired to obtain a false letter of intent from a Brazilian company stating that it would be the recipient of the planes; and that we intended to conceal from the Department of State's Office of Munitions Control that the ultimate destination was Iran, not Brazil.

We could each get up to five years in jail and a fine of $250,000, depending on the determination of the degree of sophistication of the aircraft.

My trial did not begin until more than eleven months after my arrest, one of the most frustrating experiences in my life. I was locked up in jail, trying to explain a very complicated situation to a court-appointed lawyer who, though he meant well, was having a hard time understanding me.

With some reason. For one thing, the Israeli government was denying it had ever heard of me, most particularly that I had ever worked for it.

Dunn wanted witnesses, people who would show that I was working for the Israeli government and with the knowledge of the U.S. government. This turned out to be impossible. No one I had worked with would even talk to us, much less confirm anything. Dunn spent months trying to get my employment records from Israel. Originally, he was stonewalled. Four letters of recommendation from my superiors that had been sent by my mother and given to the prosecutor were described by the Israeli government as forgeries. But after Robert Parry, who was working for

Newsweek at the time, confirmed their authenticity with the signatories, the Israeli government changed its story. Now it claimed I had worked for the government, but only as a low-level Farsi translator. According to the government's scenario, I had apparently gone into business for myself, illegally selling arms.

Since the Israelis were now saying I had been a translator, there had to be some records. Of course, I knew the records would have to be forged, since I hadn't been a translator, but I hoped there might be some clue in whatever they came up with. It was only in the middle of my trial that the "records" arrived, and I discovered then that somewhere, somehow, I still had at least one, anonymous friend at my old office.

But before that pleasant surprise, Dunn finally reached the one and only person who was to be a witness for me at the trial. In the many conversations we had, trying to decide who could show that I was involved in high-level Israeli government activities, I remembered Raji Samghabadi, the *Time* magazine reporter. After all, I had told him all about the Iran-contra affair long before the information ever appeared anywhere. That ought to have some effect on the jury.

Samghabadi was not eager to be a witness for me. He was on medical leave from *Time*, suffering from a terrible case of frayed nerves, and he considered me one of the causes of his nervous condition. But, faced with the prospect of a subpoena if he did not agree, he said he would testify.

The trial began on October 17 in the United States District Courthouse in lower Manhattan, before District Judge Louis Stanton. I sat next to the straight-laced Connecticut business-man Richard St. Francis. O'Toole's case had been severed from ours, at our request, because he had cooperated with the government in setting me up. Later he was accused, falsely, of illegally trying to sell Stinger missiles from Israel to an unidentified nation. The few friends I had left in the Israeli government helped set him up, forcing the U.S. to indict him. So now O'Toole and I were even.

As I listened to the prosecutor, Baruch Weiss, outline the

charges against St. Francis and me, describing in great detail the one conversation at Kennedy Airport that included me, I wondered how much longer I would remain behind bars.

Not long, it turned out. Four days into the trial, most of which was spent describing the government's investigation and beginning a review of the transcripts of the conversations, Judge Stanton ordered me released on $30,000 bail. He had finally read the complete transcript of the supposedly damning conversations taped by Lettner (the undercover Customs agent is actually named John Lisica, but I continue to think of him as Lettner) and said he did not find it particularly incriminating. I was out of jail, after 11 months and three weeks.

The bulk of the government's case against me was the tape of the Kennedy Airport conversation. Although my own memory of it was no longer crystal clear, I knew I had tried to be truthful, and it was clear, I thought, to anyone reviewing the transcript, that I was acting officially.

Weiss, of course, having been advised by Shamir's office, insisted I was only a former military translator out to make a personal profit. "It was a business," he said.

But the tapes supported my defense that I was acting on behalf of my government. For one thing, right at the outset, Lettner tried to entice me by suggesting that, if this deal went through, there would be "a good chance of talking them into taking something else." I replied, "Forget the something else." This is not what Mr. Weiss's businessman would have said.

I also kept insisting that Lettner identify himself and his principal contact in Iran positively (neither of which he ever did), and I demanded the name of someone in Tehran who could verify that he was authorized to make this purchase for the Iranians. He never provided that either.

Also, although a part of the government's charges against us was a conspiracy to prepare and use a fraudulent end-user certificate, I remarked to Lettner, "I understand that you wanted an EUC. I don't know why." Only a government representative, not a private businessman, would be unconcerned about an end-user certificate. I also reminded Lettner the planes could be flown out by Israeli pilots.

Shortly after, the most significant part of the conversation took place. Lettner said, "Let's face it, nobody wants to have any undue publicity or anything coming back directly."

I replied, "I will be open with you about another subject, the people here said go ahead."

Lettner: "I beg your pardon?"

Me: "The people here said go ahead." I was referring to the U.S. government.

Lettner: "Uh huh."

Me: "They'll deny that they said that."

Lettner: "Of course."

Me: "But we would not do anything without some type of agreement."

Lettner: "Uh huh."

Me: "Nobody is going to check it out, no politician in Israel."

Lettner: "Of course not."

Weiss had a hell of a time explaining this to the jury. This was the clearest indication, from the government's own exhibit, that I had explained that my activities were authorized by both the U.S. and the Israeli governments.

One other item gave Weiss a bit of a problem, and let Dunn have some fun in his summation—my last passports. I did not have all my old passports, but I had three of them, and they showed some of my travels from 1985 to 1989. (My passports were usually canceled before their expiration dates and new ones issued, because I rapidly filled up the visa pages.)

The passports showed constant travels, to France, England, Guatemala, the United States, Israel, El Salvador, Peru, Jamaica, Australia, Paraguay, Argentina, Sri Lanka, Austria, and Chile, with many repeat entries and exits. There must have been 70 or 80 trips to different countries in just a few years, most of them in the Western Hemisphere. As Dunn pointed out to the jury with excruciating detail, this was a rather bizarre itinerary for a low-level Farsi translator. Weiss actually suggested they were all private vacations, which would have made me one of the highest-paid low-level translators in the world.

It was during the prosecution's case that I learned I had a friend back at my old office. After the Israelis had admitted I had been in Military Intelligence, Weiss had asked for my employment records, to introduce them in evidence to bolster the argument that I had been, at most, this low-level translator.

When they arrived in an official, sealed package from Israel, Weiss had to introduce the whole thing into evidence, including performance reports and the four letters of recommendation written when I was leaving Military Intelligence, the very letters Weiss had previously said were forgeries. (They had been written before I went over to the Prime Minister's Office, but no one was admitting that.)

The employment records had, as I assumed, been altered. They all said I was a translator, and all but two did not give any unit. But those two were the ones on which my unknown friend had left the entry in. The English translation introduced into evidence said: "Staff Officer, Means of War."

This was something Baruch Weiss could not explain. Means of war—armaments, military equipment—this is what I had said all along was my field of work. And "staff officer," that did not sound like a low-level translator.

The letters of recommendation—another present from my anonymous friend—were the icing on the cake. The first, from Col. Pesah Melowany, said, in part:

"Mr. Ari Ben-Menashe has served in the Israel Defense Forces External Relations Department in key positions. As such, Mr. Ben-Menashe was responsible for a variety of complex and sensitive assignments which demanded exceptional analytical and executive capabilities. From my acquaintance with him in the Department, I came to know Mr. Ben-Menashe and admire his proficiency and devotion. He fulfills his assignments in a very efficient and reliable manner."

Another, from Col. Arieh Shur, noted:

"During Mr. Ben-Menashe's service in the department, he was in charge of a task which demanded considerable analytical and executive skills. Mr. Ben-Menashe carried out his task with understanding, skill, and determination, managing to adapt himself to changing situations."

The other two were similar, referring to "key positions" and "great responsibility."

The prosecutor's case was finished, and the low-level translator story was dead in the water.

As we took a break before Tom Dunn was to begin my defense, my co-defendant Richard St. Francis, who'd been caught up in this whole mess unwittingly, had finally reached the boiling point and was talking to any reporter who'd listen. He insisted that he'd been set up by TransCapital, the Connecticut company he'd worked for. The reason, he explained with growing impatience, was that he'd been talking publicly about TransCapital's role in the sale of computer hardware abroad.

Finally, court reconvened, and it was our turn. Tom Dunn called our only witness, the *Time* magazine correspondent Raji Samghabadi. A heavyset, excitable Iranian, Raji was in a state, and the judge had to calm him down several times. When he was asked about his life in Iran, he started to rant about the communists and the fundamentalists, from whom he had, in fact, narrowly escaped. He had even been the subject of a mock execution.

When he was asked to describe his relations with me, he replied, "Prickly, difficult, dangerous, sometimes intolerable, almost intolerable, but I had to do a job." Once, he referred to me as "that bozo." On redirect examination, *à propos* of nothing, he said to Dunn, "You know, I don't have much respect for your client, by the way." Then, as the judge was asking him to take a moment or two to "just walk around and compose yourself," he shouted:

"Your honor, two million people crippled and killed, and we put that shrimp there in order to cover up for George Bush and Mr. Shamir? I can't tolerate that."

Some witness for the defense.

Weiss spent most of his cross-examination trying to get Raji to admit that he had only my own word for it that I was connected with Israeli intelligence, that I might well have been a low-level translator for all he knew. But when Dunn asked him if I had ever referred to myself as a translator, he blurted out, "A translator does not smoke opium with Iranian cabinet officers." The judge instructed the jury to disregard the remark, but I'm not sure they could.

The bottom line, still and all, was that Raji confirmed under oath that several months before the famous story appeared in *Al Shiraa* I had told him all about the Iran-contra weapons sales.

Thomas Francis Xavier Dunn, a tall, thin, criminal lawyer with a thick blond moustache, was now ready to address the jury in the most important case of his career. He was confident he had what he needed for his summation. A year earlier he had had nothing, he hardly understood me. Now he had developed a deep and powerful understanding of the intricate web in which he had been placed. He told the jury:

> "What we have sitting right here is another victim, an Israeli victim, a victim of a number of different parties; a victim of the U.S. Customs Service, a victim of the United States government, and, in the end, a victim of his own government, the Israelis, who have left him out high and dry. . . . The Americans are stonewalling, the Israelis are stonewalling, and now this man has been left out in the cold to swing. . . ."

He explained, "Mr. Ari Ben-Menashe had no intent to violate any American laws. He was working for the Israeli government. There was State Department approval [CIA, actually], although no one is going to admit it. And if you remember these political officials with Watergate—'We're going to stonewall, we're going to deny'; Irangate—'No, we would never do that.' Then they have to admit it eventually. It's the same story here."

Tom asked the jury to reflect on Raji's testimony. "If that man [me] had kept his mouth shut, you and I and everyone else in this country may not know about Iran-contra to this day. You don't think they're [the U.S. government] ticked off about that? You don't think they want the guy to pay?"

Tom went over the passport entries one by one. He went over the letters of recommendation and the efficiency reports word by word.

The jury retired to consider their verdict. What were they

making of it all, I wondered, as I sat in the courtroom chatting to journalists and others who had listened in on the case. I could only pray that they realized that the evidence they had heard in my defense had been the truth—because then the only verdict would have to be not guilty. After two-and-a-half hours, there was a fuss; they were returning . . . But no, they simply wanted to have the airport tape replayed to them.

It was only 30 minutes later that they returned to the court. After six weeks of evidence, the moment I had both longed for and feared—knowing I was innocent but worried that the decision would come down against me—had arrived. My heart pounded as I tried to read the decision in their faces. I had always believed I could read people well. This time I was failing. I closed my eyes. I wanted to shut out this whole courtroom and disappear into a big black hole.

"Not guilty!" The words reverberated through my mind. My eyes snapped open. They were looking at me, smiling. I sat back in my seat. St. Francis, who had also been found not guilty, was grinning all over his face. You never win federal cases, everyone had told me. You just hoped to receive a lenient sentence.

Tom reached out a hand of congratulations. It was over.

I was innocent. A free man.

It was November 28, 1991—ten years to the day since I had been appointed to the secret arms-to-Iran committee.

Afterword

A LOT HAS HAPPENED since I was acquitted. A number of journalists have investigated some of the events I've described, and at least part of the story is now emerging.

PBS's *Frontline*, in two first-rate documentaries produced by Robert Parry, delved into various aspects of the arms-for-hostages deal. Gary Sick, a former Carter administration adviser on Iran, published his important book *October Surprise*, which systematically sifts through the evidence that convinced him the Reagan camp and Khomeini did actually make a secret deal. Seymour Hersh's excellent book *The Samson Option*, caused an enormous stir with its revelations about Israel's nuclear program and about Robert Maxwell. British journalist Patrick Seale's recent book, *Abu Nidal: A Gun for Hire*, speculates about the Palestinian terrorist's ties to the Israelis. And a few enterprising newspaper and magazine reporters are now exploring Carlos Cardoen's American-backed sales of chemical weapons to Saddam Hussein during the 1980s.

The exposés in the media have had some impact. Both the U.S. House of Representatives and the U.S. Senate have begun looking into the October Surprise. The full Senate voted down a formal investigation, but the Senate Foreign Relations Committee decided to hold limited hearings on the arms-for-hostages deal, within its regular budget. The House, however, funded a full-scale October Surprise Task Force, whose chief counsel is former federal prosecutor E. Lawrence Barcella, Jr., to investigate Sick's and my allegations, among others.

In June 1992 I was interviewed at length by the Task Force staff. Unbeknownst to me, however, a deal had apparently been struck between the Democratic and Republican leaderships before the Task Force was authorized. The Task Force was required to issue

343

an interim report prior to July 1, 1992, and the deal evidently required that President Bush be completely, and quickly, exonerated. So, the interim report, issued by its chairman, Rep. Lee Hamilton, on June 30, while explaining that the Task Force had only begun its investigations, drew one, and only one, conclusion: "that Mr. Bush was in the United States continuously during the October 18–22 time period, and that he therefore did not travel to Paris, France, to participate in the alleged secret meeting."

This conclusion was drawn despite the interim report's assertions that it had interviewed only about 50 out of some 150 potential witnesses, and had obtained only a small fraction of the documents it was seeking. At his July 1 press conference, Hamilton stated that "all credible evidence" led to the conclusion that George Bush was not in Paris.

In June I also testified under oath, in closed session, before the Senate Foreign Relations Committee. I stated unequivocally that I had, indeed, seen Bush in Paris, but I am not sanguine that the Senate Committee's report will be any more forthcoming than the House Task Force's interim report. A lot of other heads may roll, but President Bush is apparently going to keep his, whether or not he is reelected.

Several official inquiries are also currently underway in Great Britain, focusing on the activities of Robert Maxwell and Nicholas Davies. And in Australia, a Western Australia Royal Commission has launched a probe that touches on some of my allegations. It is still too early to know whether these investigations will lead to further action.

A lot has happened to the main characters in my story. George Bush is still president of the United States, but his approval rating has plummeted, as the U.S. economy continues to falter and every day brings new revelations of his administration's dealings with Iraq. His reelection bid seems to be in serious trouble.

Robert Gates was nominated for a second time to be CIA director. When I and others testified in late spring 1991 before closed sessions of the House and Senate Foreign Relations Committees and the Senate Intelligence Committee, his confirmation hearings were postponed until October of that year. But then, in the shadow of Clarence Thomas's dramatic Supreme Court confirmation hearings, Gates was quietly confirmed as CIA director. He remains in that position today.

Former Sen. John Tower wrote a book about the Iran-contra affair, which said nothing new and was not widely read. He was killed in a plane crash in Georgia in early 1991.

Robert McFarlane, now a private citizen, came under FBI counterintelligence investigation in early 1991 regarding his relationship with Rafi Eitan and Israeli intelligence and his involvement in the Pollard case. The results of that investigation have never been made public. But in October 1991, an article by Craig Unger in *Esquire* magazine repeated my allegations that McFarlane had been recruited by Rafi Eitan and named him as Mr. X in the Pollard case. McFarlane sued the magazine. That litigation is still pending.

As for the Israelis, in early 1992, Shimon Peres was ousted as leader of the Labor Party by his longtime rival Yitzhak Rabin. On June 23, Labor won the national elections by a wide margin, and Rabin replaced the 76-year-old Yitzhak Shamir as prime minister. The repudiation of Shamir increased American hopes for a Bush-sponsored settlement in the Middle East, but as of August, no solution was in sight.

Rafi Eitan retired from intelligence work, and gave away all the money he got from the slush fund. According to the Israeli press, he is now, ironically, working for an international oil trader who is instrumental in selling Iraqi oil, in violation of the United Nations embargo.

Moshe Hebroni now works for the Jewish Agency; Yehoshua Sagi became a member of the Knesset. Avi Pazner, Shamir's spokesperson, was hounded by the press about the Israeli government's lies about me, among other things. He was appointed ambassador to Italy in 1991. Nachum Admoni was removed as director of Mossad in 1989, but was still advising Shamir on intelligence. He is the chair of a public utility in Israel.

My Iranian friend Sayeed Mehdi Kashani is now an adviser to Iranian President Rafsanjani. Col. Mohammed Jalali is now retired, living in Iran, with a second home in London.

Iraqi President Saddam Hussein went from darling of the

Americans to George Bush's satanic madman virtually overnight in August 1990. In January and February 1991, his country was devastated by the heaviest aerial bombing since World War II. More than 100,000 Iraqis were reported dead in the aftermath of the Gulf War. But Saddam Hussein survived and remains in power.

The turbulent Soviet Union has, meanwhile, undergone dizzying changes. In the summer of 1991, Mikhail Gorbachev survived a coup attempt but then was forced to resign. The union dissolved into separate states, and the KGB was stripped of its powers. One of its former heads, Viktor Chebrikov, who had helped us move slush fund moneys to East Bloc banks, is out of a job. He is living quietly in Russia as a private citizen.

In Peru, Abimael Guzmán died of cancer in 1990, but the Shining Path, the revolutionary movement he founded, lives on with my friend Roberto leading it. Largely to combat the Shining Path, President Alberto Fujimori suspended the Peruvian constitution in early 1992—an action that brought condemnation from around the world.

Carlos Cardoen still heads Cardoen Industries in Chile. After the appearance of a number of newspaper stories describing his involvement with Iraq, the U.S. Customs Service began an investigation, and in April 1992, charges against him were filed in Miami. His plant in Paraguay was not closed down in 1989, thanks to President Andrés Rodríguez, who continues to rule the country with the blessing of the U.S. government.

Several Australians involved in the activities I've described have run into problems. Prime Minister Bob Hawke was defeated in a special vote in the Labor Party caucus in December 1991. Forced to resign, he was replaced by Paul Keating, who had for several years been considered Hawke's natural successor until they fell out over the timing of Hawke's departure. Brian Burke, the premier of Western Australia in whose jurisdiction we were allowed to park our aircraft, was forced to resign and has been subjected to prolonged questioning in a Royal Commission. And Alan Bond, the wealthy Australian businessman who had been entangled with Carlos Cardoen in Chile and Iraq, was convicted in May 1992 of bank fraud. He was sentenced to two and a half years in prison, which he is currently serving, although an appeal is pending.

Revelations in the British press ruined both of the men I worked with most closely in London. Media mogul Robert Maxwell, of course, received more attention than anyone. The publication in October 1991 of Seymour Hersh's book, naming him as a collaborator with Israeli intelligence, was the beginning of the end. Maxwell and the Mirror Newspaper Group sued Hersh and his publishers, and the *Daily Mirror* published lengthy articles denouncing the allegations against Maxwell and Nicholas Davies. (Davies also filed a suit, but allowed it to lapse.) Almost immediately, however, some of the critical denials in the Mirror articles were shown to be false, and Hersh and his publishers filed a countersuit against Maxwell, Davies, and the Mirror Group. But, just as the claims and counterclaims were reaching fever pitch, on November 5, 1991, Maxwell's body was found floating off the Canary Islands near his yacht, causing an international uproar. A Spanish autopsy concluded the death was an accident. An Israeli autopsy called it a murder. Under British law, Maxwell's libel suit ended with his death; and in July the court threw out the Mirror Group's claim, an action it has appealed. The counterclaims are still quite alive.

After Maxwell's burial on Israel's Mount of Olives, his empire crumbled. The British press exposed him for what he was—a fraud and a crook, who stole the pension funds of his own employees to the tune of about a billion dollars. A number of stories alluded to his ties with both Israeli and Soviet intelligence. His business dealings are currently under investigation by intelligence agencies and parliamentary committees in Israel, Bulgaria, Russia, and Great Britain. In the U.S., congressional investigators are also looking into his activities. Maxwell's two sons, Kevin and Ian, who inherited the tattered remains of his empire, were arrested for fraud in London in June 1992.

Nick Davies, the *Daily Mirror* foreign editor, was accused by Seymour Hersh and several British publications of being an Israeli agent and arms dealer. Davies flatly denied the accusations, but after he was caught in some flagrant lies, he was fired from the *Mirror* in early November. In June 1992 he published a book about Princess Diana, but it was overshadowed by Andrew Morton's book on the same subject published around the same time. He is said to be currently working on a book about "the real" Robert Maxwell. Scotland Yard, MI-5, the Serious Fraud Squad, and Inland Revenue are all investigating Davies.

As for me, immediately after my acquittal in November 1990, I rented an apartment in Lexington, Kentucky. I feared for my life, and I had close friends in high office there who offered me protection. (Years earlier they had worked with the Israelis on arms deals.) I stayed in Lexington until mid-April 1991.

Then, traveling on an Israeli passport that is valid until 1994, I went to Sydney, Australia. I had a number of friends there from my arms-dealing days, among them former high government officials. They had promised that I would receive political asylum in Australia and that I would be allowed to live there, eventually receiving citizenship.

However, in the next few months I got a lot of attention in the press, I testified before congressional committees, and Seymour Hersh's book was published. Suddenly, on December 28, 1991, three days before George Bush's visit to Australia, upon my arrival from a trip to Europe and the United States, my visa was revoked at Sydney airport. The authorities allowed me into the country for only one month. This caused a furor in the Australian press, and there were accusations that the government had yielded to American pressure, since my presence in Sydney was deemed an embarrassment to the visiting president. I took the Australian minister of immigration to court. Federal Justice Graham Hill ordered the government to identify the person responsible for canceling my visa and to provide all documents used in making that decision. Rather than do that, the Australian government reinstated my visa and agreed to pay my court costs.

In the meantime, in early 1991 the CIA had contacted me through an informant, Herbert Alwyn Smith, a convicted British arms dealer whom I'd known in prison. Smith, on behalf of the CIA, offered me a deal. I would get $2 million and U.S. citizenship in exchange for my silence and my signature on a piece of paper stating that I had no legal claims or allegations against the U.S. government. I even received a letter of credit in the amount of $2 million from them, but I did not cash it or accept the deal.

Smith visited me in Australia five times over the next year, and I continued to talk to him. Through Smith as messenger, it was arranged for me to meet with two CIA officials in Ireland in August 1991 and with Robert Maxwell in the Soviet Union the same month. The purpose of both meetings was to try to get me to hand over control of part of the slush fund to the CIA. Unable to deliver a successful deal, and perhaps having learned too much, Smith died, purportedly of a heart attack, in March 1992, ten days after he left Sydney.

One thing I've learned since my acquittal in New York is the power of the printed word and how much those who seek to conceal the truth fear it. So, in June 1991, I contracted with Allen & Unwin, the Australian publishers, to write this book. The Israeli government evidently got wind of it, and shortly thereafter I had a distinguished visitor. Ehud Ulmart, then Israel's minister of health and a close crony of Shamir's, offered to see that I got Australian citizenship (just how, I never knew), and to guarantee that the Israelis would "leave me alone," if I agreed to stop writing the book. I refused.

But that was just the beginning. After Gary Sick's and Seymour Hersh's books came out in the fall of 1991, both quoting me as a prominent source, an intense, prolonged barrage of media assaults seeking to discredit me started up in earnest. *Time* magazine was first, on October 28, calling me a "veteran spinner of stunning-if-true-but yarns," and a "fabricator."

Newsweek chimed in on November 4, 1991, with a two-and-a-half-page story that described me as a "shadowy, Israeli exile," "a former translator for the Israeli government." Grudgingly conceding that I was "difficult to ignore," the article nonetheless concluded that much of what I said "does not seem to check out." The article took great pains to suggest that my involvement in the leaking of the Iran-contra story "makes no sense," but of course they never mentioned the testimony of Raji Samghabadi at my trial.

The next week, November 11, *Newsweek* was at it again, with a seven-page piece on the October Surprise, calling it "a conspiracy theory run wild." Steve Emerson then viciously attacked me in both the *New Republic* and the *Wall Street Journal*. In the former, on November 18, he called me a "low-level translator" and described the ERD as "one of the most insignificant" branches of Israeli intelligence. In the latter, on November 27, he described me as an "abject liar." Just for good measure, he asked Hersh to apologize to the Maxwell family for printing my insulting allegations against the publishing baron.

At the time, Maxwell seemed perfectly capable of taking care of himself. His newspapers in London, New York, and Tel Aviv, to no one's surprise, all took their turns slamming me.

Amidst all these smears on my credibility, there were also articles supporting my claims. Most important was a two-part piece, entitled "Who Are You, Ari Ben-Menashe?", by Pazit Ravina in the Israeli daily *Davar*, in January and February 1992. She said, "In talks with people who worked with Ben-Menashe, the claim that he had access to highly sensitive intelligence information was confirmed again and again." And, just as this book was about to go to press, on July 7, 1992, the *Village Voice* printed a long article by Craig Unger. He quoted my former colleague, Moshe Hebroni: "Ben-Menashe served directly under me. He worked for the Foreign Flow desk in External Relations. He had access to very, very sensitive material."

Aside from the media attacks, there were more subtle approaches. An old friend of mine from Mossad just happened to "bump into me" at my London hotel in December 1991 and said how nice it was to see me again after all these years. Although I made no mention of this book to him, he called a couple of days later to ask how it was going.

"Don't forget your country in all this, Ari," he said. "Whatever you did, whatever sacrifices had to be made, it was all in the cause of Israel."

"Are you saying I was sacrificed?" I asked.

"Just remember us," he replied. "That's all we ask. There are matters which should not be talked about . . ."

Other attempts to sabotage this book were less gentle. The writers who worked with me in Australia received a number of death threats. One American publisher with whom I thought I had a deal to publish the book in the U.S. was apparently intimidated and backed out. A British publisher with whom I did have a deal, refused, at the last minute, to publish the book. Fortunately, Sheridan Square Press in New York and Allen & Unwin in Sydney remained impervious to intimidation.

And what became of all that slush-fund money? There was approximately $780 million (including interest) in the Israeli slush fund, and another $780 million (including interest) in the American CIA slush fund. To a clever politician or a secret intelligence service, this would be a formidable sum, especially because it is not on any budget line and can be used without accountability.

In 1991, about $80 million of the Israeli slush fund that had been on deposit in Australian banks was transferred out of Australia to the former East Bloc. Another $100 million was taken from accounts in Eastern Europe and given to a political party in Israel (neither Labor nor Likud) that favors peace with the Palestinians. The remainder of the Israeli money—approximately $600 million—is distributed in various countries around the world, with no final resolution.

As for the American CIA money, in August 1991, we cut a deal handing control of it to Robert Maxwell, who in turn was supposed to disburse it to the Americans. But Maxwell reneged on the deal.

Today, I am a man alone. After my trial I sought a divorce from my wife Ora in the Dominican Republic, only to find out, months later, that she had already divorced me in Israel. I have not seen my daughter Shira since October 1989. I have no country. I am a citizen of the world—or a citizen of nowhere.

Looking back, I can say that the 1980s were a mean decade, perverted in their lack of humanity. It would be too easy to say simply that I regret my role—though I am deeply sorry for the human suffering of the Iranians and Iraqis. I also regret that Israel continued to develop its capacity for nuclear destruction and that we were unable to bring about peace with the Palestinians.

But I do not regret that my experience allowed me to see first-hand how secret intelligence agencies increasingly dominate the foreign policy of nations like the United States and Israel. Whereas once intelligence was supposed to inform leaders and guide them in making policy decisions, today covert intelligence operations and foreign policy are too often inseparable, one and the same. The tools of secret slush fund money, covert operations, and disinformation have been used on such a grand scale that they have changed the nature of the entire political process. A handful of people never elected by anyone are now able to manipulate politics.

And my former colleagues, the international arms merchants, with whom I had so many dealings, are not out of business, not by a long shot. If there isn't a big war going on at any given time, there are always a number of small wars. The events in Eastern Europe—in Yugoslavia and in the former Soviet republics—continue to generate profits for them. As I sit here I imagine them around their tables, waiting for the next big one, just like Iran and Iraq. Perhaps India and Pakistan. Plenty of cannon fodder to be equipped, a balanced enough conflict to last a long time, no one in the West to care who gets killed—a real goldmine.

I am a humbler man today than I was in the 1970s when I joined Israeli intelligence. I've learned the hard way that everyone makes mistakes, some of them so big that they are irrevocable. I've also changed my view of Israel and the Jewish people. When I was young, I shared with many Israelis a deep nationalistic feeling—the self-righteous and arrogant belief that we were right and everyone else was wrong, that it was more important for Jews and Israel to survive than others, that we were—as the Bible says—the chosen people.

I still believe that Jews are chosen. But no longer can I accept the premise on which the Iranian arms deals were based: "Better that their boys die than ours."

People are people. We are all chosen.

Appendices

THE FOLLOWING ARE some of the documents still in my possession, indicative of the activities discussed in this book.

The first four documents (1–4) are the letters of reference introduced at my trial, which confirmed my employment by the External Relations Department over the period 1977–1987, and refer to my "complex and sensitive assignments which demanded exceptional analytical and executive capabilities," to my "key positions," my "great responsibility," and my "considerable analytical and executive skills."

The next seven documents (5–11) relate to arms transactions conducted on behalf of the Joint Committee, including some from Nicholas Davies, who signed his name "Davis." Documents 8 and 9 are messages from me to Hojjat El-Islam Rafsanjani and his aide, Iran Nadj Rankuni; the "4,000 units" are TOW missiles. Note that all of this activity occurred during the time within which the letters of reference confirm that I was working for the ERD.

Document 12 is a letter from San Cristóbal University asking the assistance of the Israeli Cultural Attaché in Lima in my work as a lecturer in the department of language and literature.

Document 13 is a letter from Joseph O'Toole to the director general of the Israeli ministry of defense regarding the transfer of C-130 aircraft. Document 14 is a letter from me to the president of Sri Lanka also regarding C-130 sales.

Document 15 is a letter from an attorney representing me to the Office of the Independent Counsel, offering to initiate discussions concerning the transfer of the slush funds to the United States. The recipient acknowledged receipt of the letter, but no meeting ever took place.

Document 16 is the letter of credit by which I was offered two million dollars to keep quiet. I never presented it.

ISRAEL DEFENCE FORCES

4 September 1987

TO WHOM IT MAY CONCERN

Mr Ari Ben Menashe has served in the Israel Defence Forces External Relations Department in key positions. As such, Mr. Ben Menashe was responsible for a variety of complex and sensitive assignments which demanded exceptional analytical and executive capabilities. From my acquaintance with him in the Department, I came to know Mr. Ben Menashe and admire his proficiency and devotion. He fulfills his assignments in a very efficient and reliable manner.

I can vouch that Mr. Ben Menashe combines a very astute mind and fine intelligence with exceptional understanding, which I am sure will hold him in good stead in any career he wishes to pursue.

Yours Faithfully,

Pesah Melowany - Colonel
Israel Defence Forces

1. Letter of reference, dated September 4, 1987, from Col. Pesah Melowany.

ISRAEL DEFENCE FORCES

6 September 1987

TO WHOM IT MAY CONCERN

I have been acquainted with Mr. Ari Ben Menashe for approximately ten years. During this period, he served in the IDF External Relations Department in key positions. From my personal acquaintance and working relationship with him, I came to know Mr. Ben Menashe as a gifted person, who carries out his assignments with considerable capability, dedication, determination and responsibility.

During Mr. Ben Menashe's tenure of service in the IDF, the IDF and the External Relations Department underwent a very eventful and unusual period, and Mr Ben Menashe always was able to adapt himself to new and changing situations with intelligence and assiduousness.

Worthy of special mention is Mr. Ben Menashe's positive and friendly approach to those around him and his rare talent for communicating with people. These traits held him in good stead in his working relations with all those who came in contact with him.

Mr. Ben Menashe is a person known to keep to his principles, being always guided by a strong sense of duty, justice and common sense.

I believe wholeheartedly that Mr. Ben Menashe would be an asset to any academic or professional institute he chooses to join.

Faithfully Yours,

Yoav Dayagi - Colonel
Israel Defence Forces

2. Letter of reference, dated September 6, 1987, from Col. Yoav Dayagi.

ISRAEL DEFENCE FORCES
EXTERNAL RELATIONS DEPARTMENT

14 September 1987

TO WHOM IT MAY CONCERN

Mr. Ari Ben Menashe has been working in the IDF External
Relations Department for approximately ten years. During
this period, I became well acquainted with Mr. Ben Menashe
on both the personal and professional levels.

Mr. Ben Menashe fulfilled his duties in the department with
great reponsibility, expertise and dedication, down to the
finest detail.

Mr. Ben Menashe combines considerable analytical ability
with fine intelligence and common sense as well as a rare
ability to communicate with all who come in contact with
him.

I am confident that Mr. Ben Menashe's fine qualities on the
intellectual, executive and personal levels will hold him in
good stead in the future in any career he wishes to pursue.

Faithfully,

Dr. A. Granot
External Relations Department
IDF

3. Letter of reference, dated September 14, 1987, from Dr. A. Granot.

ISRAEL DEFENCE FORCES
EXTERNAL RELATIONS DEPARTMENT

14 September 1987

TO WHOM IT MAY CONCERN

I have been acquainted with Mr. Ari Ben Menashe for approximately two years, since I assumed my position in the External Relations Department.

During Mr. Ben Menashe's service in the department, he was in charge of a task which demanded considerable analytical and executive skills. Mr. Ben Menashe carried out his task with understanding, skill and determination, managing to adapt himself to changing situations.

I am convinced that Mr. Ben Menashe will excel in any future career - academic or professional - of his choice.

Faithfully Yours,

Arieh Shur - Colonel
Chief of External Relations
IDF

4. Letter of reference, dated September 14, 1987, from Col. Arieh Shur.

O R A LTD
41 BECMEAD A
STREATHAM LONDON SW16
ENGLAND
TEL.: (01) 677-2400

29 DECEMBER 1984
AZ-088-84

MR. RAN YEGNES
17 MONTEFIORY ST.
PETAH-TIKVA

RE: REQUEST FOR QUOTATION
----

1. WE WOULD APPRECIATE YOUR BEST QUOTATION AND DELIVERY TIME AND CONDITIONS FOR NEW ORIGINAL SOVIET MADE RED BAKALITE AK-47 (KLASHNIKOV) MAGAZINES.

2. SEVERAL THOUSANDS OF THE ABOVE MAGAZINES ARE REQUIRED BY OUR COMPANY FOR MARKETING IN THE UNITED STATES TO PRIVATE USERS.

3. FORM OF PAYMENT WILL BE THROUGH LETTER OF CREDIT OPENED IN A PRIME EUROPEAN BANK UPON SIGNING OF CONTRACT.

4. PROMPT ACTION AND ACCEPTABLE PRICES MAY BRING TO SUCCESSFUL COMPLETION OF THIS DEAL.

5. WE ARE LOOKING FORWARD TO DOING BUSINESS WITH YOU AND BEST WISHES.

FAITHFULLY YOURS,

NICOLAS DAVIS

5. Letter from Nicholas Davies (note that he signs the letter "Davis") to Ran Yegnes, dated December 29, 1984.

DYNAWEST INTERNATIONAL LTD.
The Bank of Nova Scotia Building,
George Town,
Grand Cayman.

'' **PLEASE REPLY TO:**
Suite 2
52 Piccadilly
London W1
Telephone 01-493 5212
Telex: 21330 DYNTEX G

Mr Ari Ben Menashe,
41, Becmead Avenue,
London SW 16.

12th January 1985.

Dear Sir,

Further to our conversation of 11th January 1985 I am pleased to confirm that we have made arrangements to re-fuel your 2 x 747 cargo aircraft in Lisbon, Portugal en route to your final client.

We will require your aircraft when filing their flight plans to ask for refueling in Lisbon.

We will want to know how many tonnes of fuel your aircraft will require 72 hours prior to their arrival in Lisbon.

I look forward to receiving your instructions.

Yours faithfully,

J. Knight.

6. Letter from John Knight to the author, dated January 12, 1985.

CONFIDENTIAL

15 MAY 1985
AN-128-85

GMT LTD.
5 WEIZMAN ST.
TEL-AVIV

RE: YOUR ENQUIRY/MILITARY EQUIPMENT
----

1. THANK YOU FOR YOUR ENQUIRY.

2. WE ARE GLAD TO INFORM YOU THAT WE ARE ABLE AND WILLING PROVIDE YOU WITH THE FOLLOWING:

ITEM	QUANTITY	PRICE PER UNIT	TOTAL PRICE
1. AK-47 M-70 AUTOMATIC RIFLE WOODEN OR FOLDING BUTT (EACH RIFLE COMES WITH 2 EMPTY MAGAZINES, 1 SLING, 1 CLEANING KIT	5000	US$210.00	US$1,050,000.00
2. SPARE MAGAZINES FOR AK-47	50,000	US$9.00	US$450,000.00
3. 7.62×39 MM REGULAR AMMUNITION	5,000,000	US$0.11	US$550,000.00
4. 60 MM MORTARS (COMMANDO TYPE)	200	US$1,550.00	US$310,000.00
5. 60 MM MORTAR SHELLS	5,000	US$37.00	US$185,000.00
6. 81 MM MORTARS	100	US$5,250.00	US$525,000.00
7. 81 MM MORTAR SHELLS	2,000	US$52.00	US$104,000.00
8. ANTI-PERSONNEL MINES (SIMILAR TO CLAYMORE TYPE)	1,000	US$68.00	US$68,000.00

1

7. Letter from Nicholas Davies (also signed "Davis") to GMT Ltd.,
dated May 15, 1985.

CONFIDENTIAL

3. ALL THE ABOVE ITEMS ARE NEW AND OF YUGOSLAV MAKE AND WILL ACCOMPANIED BY SUPPLIERS QUALITY CERTIFICATE.

4. PRICES SET ARE F.O.B. YUGOSLAV PORT AND DO NOT COVER TRANSFC CARGO COSTS OR INSURANCE.

5. DELIVERY OF GOODS IS GUARANTEED TO BE MADE WITHIN (POSSIBLY WITHIN 45 DAYS) OF OPENING OF AN IRRE DIVISABLE AND TRANSFERRABLE LETTER OF CREDIT FOR THE FULL US$3,242,000.00 IN OUR FAVOR CONFIRMED BY A PRIME EUROPE OR PAYMENT IN CASH AGAINST CONTRACT.

6. LETTER OF CREDIT SHOULD BE VALID FOR 75 DAYS AND A NEGOTIATION PERIOD AND BE RELEASABLE IN EUROPE UPON PROD OF:

    A. BILL OF LAIDING /FORWARDING AGENT'S RECEIPTS
    B. COMMERCIAL INVOICES (3 ORIGINALS)
    C. PACKING LIST

7. IF NECESSARY, ITEMS CAN BE INSPECTED BY A WEST EUROPEAN NATIONAL IN YUGOSLAVIA AFTER TRANSACTION ARRANGEMENTS HAVE BEEN COMPLETE. (TRAVEL COSTS WILL NOT BE COVERED).

8. GUARANTEES FOR THE DELIVERY OF THE ABOVE ITEMS CAN BE MADE AND WE WILL BE WILLING TO PUT UP A BOND OF 3.5% OF THE TOTAL VALUE OF YOUR PURCHASE IN YOUR FAVOR WITH A PRIME EUROPEAN BANK UP COMPLETION OF DEAL ARRANGEMENTS.

9. WE UNDERSTAND THAT A VALID AND ACCEPTABLE END USER'S CERTIFICATE WILL BE PROVIDED BY YOU.

10. THE TERMS OUTLINED ABOVE ARE VALID UNTIL 15 JUNE 1985.

11. DUE TO THE NATURE, WEIGHT AND VOLUME OF THE ABOVE GOODS WEIGHT APPROX. 200 TONS. TOTAL VOLUME APPROX. 250 CUBIC METERS WE SUGGEST THAT THE ABOVE ITEMS WILL BE TRANSPORTED BY A VESSEL WHICH WILL REACH A YUGOSLAV PORT ON A DATE MUTUALLY AGREED UPON. IF NECESSARY, TRANSPORT OF GOODS CAN BE ARRANGED B US AGAINST ADDITIONAL PAYMENT.

12. WE ARE LOOKING FORWARD TO COMPLETING THIS DEAL SUCCESSFULLY AND TO DOING FURTHER BUSINESS WITH YOU.

            FAITHFULLY,

            NICHOLAS DAVIS
            UK CONSULTANT

2

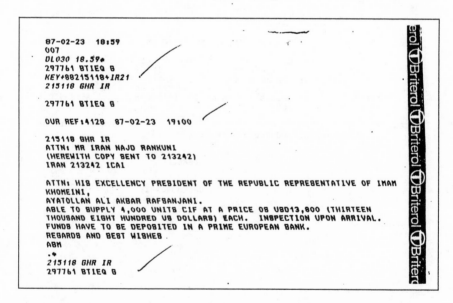

```
87-02-23   18:56
007
FJ216 18.55+
297761 BTIEQ G
KEY+88213242+IR21
213242 MOGE IR
297761 BTIEQ G

OUR REF:4127  87-02-23  18:56

IRAN 213242 ICA1

ATTN: HIS EXCELLENCY PRESIDENT OF THE REPUBLIC REPRESENTATIVE OF IMAM
KHOMEINI,
AYATOLLAN ALI AKBAR RAFSANJANI.
ABLE TO SUPPLY 4,000 UNITS CIF AT A PRICE OS USD13,800 (THIRTEEN
THOUSAND EIGHT HUNDRED US DOLLARS) EACH.  INSPECTION UPON ARRIVAL.
FUNDS HAVE TO BE DEPOSITED IN A PRIME EUROPEAN BANK. FULL DETAILS ARE
WITH MR. IRAN NAJD RANKUNI.
REGARDS AND BEST WISHES
ABM

297761 BTIEQ G+
213242 MOGE IR
```

8. Telex from the author to Hojjat El-Islam Ali Akbar Rafsanjani, dated February 23, 1987.

```
87-02-23   18:59
007
DL030 18.59+
297761 BTIEQ G
KEY+88215118+IR21
215118 GHR IR

297761 BTIEQ G

OUR REF:4128  87-02-23  19:00

215118 GHR IR
ATTN: MR IRAN NAJD RANKUNI
(HEREWITH COPY SENT TO 213242)
IRAN 213242 ICA1

ATTN: HIS EXCELLENCY PRESIDENT OF THE REPUBLIC REPRESENTATIVE OF IMAM
KHOMEINI,
AYATOLLAN ALI AKBAR RAFSANJANI.
ABLE TO SUPPLY 4,000 UNITS CIF AT A PRICE OS USD13,800 (THIRTEEN
THOUSAND EIGHT HUNDRED US DOLLARS) EACH.  INSPECTION UPON ARRIVAL.
FUNDS HAVE TO BE DEPOSITED IN A PRIME EUROPEAN BANK.
REGARDS AND BEST WISHES
ABM
.+
215118 GHR IR
297761 BTIEQ G
```

9. Telex from the author to Iran Najd Rankuni, dated February 23, 1987.

```
87-02-25   10:20
007
DG140  10.29*
24873  LONHIT G
KEY+88213744+IR21
213744 PYAM IR
24873  LONHIT G
0773  87-02-25   10:21


ATTN MR K FAKHRIAH
1. THE DETAILS OF THE REPRESENTATIVE OF ORA GROUP WHICH WILL HAVE THE
AUTHORITY TO SIGN CONTRACTS IN IRAN ARE AS FOLLOWS:
FAMILY NAME: DAVIES
FRIST NAME: NICHOLAS
MIDDLE INITIALS: AFB
CITIZENSHIP: BRITISH
PLACE OF BIRTH: BIRMINGHAM, ENGLAND
DATE OF BIRTH: 14 MARCH 1939
BRITISH PASSPORT NO: 854675 F ISSUED IN LONDON
PASSPORT ISSUED ON 18 FEB 1987
PASSPORT VALIDITY 18 FEB 1997
FATHERS NAME: BRIAN
MOTHERS NAME: ELIZABETH
HEIGHT: 1.75 M

2. WE HAVE MADE TWO ATTEMPTS TO PRESENT A USD 50.000 BANK CHECK TO
YOUR EMBASSY IN VIENNA AND IT HAS BEEN REFUSED DUE TO THEIR LACK OF
INFORMATION ABOUT THE SUBJECT. WE PROPOSE THAT SUBJECT BE DISCUSSED
WHILE MR DAVIES IS IN YOUR COUNTRY.

3. REGARDS AND BEST WISHES
ORA GROUP
ABM
*
213744 PYAM IR
24873  LONHIT G
```

10. Telex from the author to Khosro Fakhrieh, dated February 25, 1987.

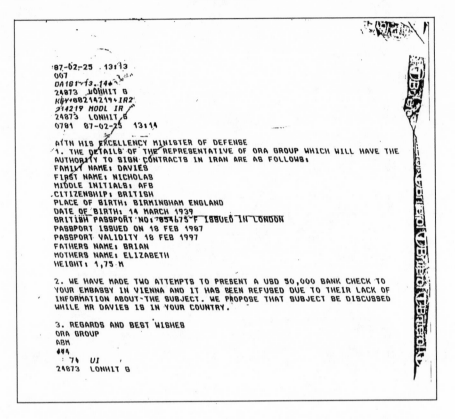

87-02-25 13:13
007
DA181-13.14
24873 LONHIT G
KEY-88214219-IR2
214219 MODL IR
24873 LONHIT G
0781 87-02-25 13:14

ATTN HIS EXCELLENCY MINISTER OF DEFENSE
1. THE DETAILS OF THE REPRESENTATIVE OF ORA GROUP WHICH WILL HAVE THE
AUTHORITY TO SIGN CONTRACTS IN IRAN ARE AS FOLLOWS:
FAMILY NAME: DAVIES
FIRST NAME: NICHOLAS
MIDDLE INITIALS: AFB
CITIZENSHIP: BRITISH
PLACE OF BIRTH: BIRMINGHAM ENGLAND
DATE OF BIRTH: 14 MARCH 1939
BRITISH PASSPORT NO: 785467S-F ISSUED IN LONDON
PASSPORT ISSUED ON 18 FEB 1987
PASSPORT VALIDITY 18 FEB 1997
FATHERS NAME: BRIAN
MOTHERS NAME: ELIZABETH
HEIGHT: 1,75 M

2. WE HAVE MADE TWO ATTEMPTS TO PRESENT A USD 50,000 BANK CHECK TO
YOUR EMBASSY IN VIENNA AND IT HAS BEEN REFUSED DUE TO THEIR LACK OF
INFORMATION ABOUT THE SUBJECT. WE PROPOSE THAT SUBJECT BE DISCUSSED
WHILE MR DAVIES IS IN YOUR COUNTRY.

3. REGARDS AND BEST WISHES
ORA GROUP
ABM
444
74 UI
24873 LONHIT G

11. Telex from the author to the minister of defense of Iran, dated
February 25, 1987.

UNIVERSIDAD NACIONAL DE
SAN CRISTOBL DE HUAMANGA
Uıidad de Cordinación en Lima
Aᵛ.Nicolás o Piérola 966-201
teléf.28261-télex 25197
   LIMA-PERU

Lima, 20 de abril de 1988

Nota No. 216-UCL-UNCH-88

Señor
ACRECADO CULTURAL
Embajada de Israel
Presente.-

De mi mayor consideración:

En nombre de la Universidad
Nacional de San Cristóbal de Huamanga y por especial
encargo del Sr.Rector de nuestra Casa de Estudios,
Ingª Alberto Morote Sánchez, es grato dirigirme a Ud.,
para hacerle llegar nuestro saludo institucional y a
la vez solicitarle el apoyo del Sr. ARI BEN-MENASHE,
quien ha sido invitado por la Universidad, a fin de
que pueda implementar el curso de inglés a nivel de
docentes universitarios del Departamento Académico -
de Lengua y Literatura de la Facultad de Educación.

Por esta razón, Sr.Agregado
Cultural, agradeceré a Ud. se sirva apoyarnos en la
invitación que formulamos al Dr. ARI BEN-MENASHE.

Válgome de la ocasión, para
ofrecerle el testimonio de nuestra mayor considera -
ción.

Atentamente,

blb.

12. Letter from the chief administrator of San Cristóbal University to
the Israeli cultural attaché in Lima, dated April 20, 1988.

FXC
international

28 NOVEMBER 1988

LOCKHEED C130H AIRCRAFT FOR KOREA/CANADA

GOVERNMENT OF ISRAEL
MINISTRY OF DEFENSE
TEL-AVIV - ISRAEL

ATTENTION: MAJOR GENERAL DAVID IVRY
               DIRECTOR GENERAL

REFERENCE: MR. ARI BEN-MENASHE DISCUSSIONS ON C130 A/C
               AND KOREAN INSPECTION - TEL-AVIV.

1. WE ARE IN RECEIPT OF THE OFFICIAL KOREAN DPA-D-8531
SOLICITATION FOR EIGHT (8) C130H AIRCRAFT TO BE PURCHASED IN
4TH QTR. 1988 OR 1ST QTR. 1989. KOREA CERTIFIES THAT
SUFFICIENT FUNDS ARE AVAILABLE (DIRECT AND BY LOAN) FOR SUCH
A PURCHASE AND, SAMSUNG INDUSTRIES HAS AGREED TO GUARANTEE
THE LOAN. MR. JAY KIM, EXECUTIVE VICE PRESIDENT, AND THE
BELOW SIGNED HAVE HAD MEETINGS RELATIVE TO SUCH A PROPOSAL
GUARANTEE OF FUNDS (LOAN) AND, FXC, NORTHWEST INDUSTRIES,
AMSUNG HAVE A MOU FOR SUBJECT SALE. FXC WAS ADVISED THAT
KOREAN SPECIALISTS INSPECTED EIGHT C130 IN SEPT/OCT 88 IN
TEL-AVIV. WE HAVE NOT BEEN ABLE TO SPECIFICALLY LOCATE THE
KOREAN TEAM LEADERS WITH THE NAMES YOU PROVIDED.

2. FXC SUBMITTED A PROPOSAL IN NOV 88 TO CANADA, DEPT OF
ARMED FORCES FOR ACQUISITION MAJOR GENERAL MORTON AND,
PROCUREMENT BRIG. GEN. WEBSTER RELATIVE TO SUPPLYING UP TO
(8) EIGHT C130H AIRCRAFT TO MEET THEIR IMMEDIATE NEED FOR
CARGO AND TANKER C130 AIRCRAFT. CANADA IS PREPARED TO
SUBMIT A LETTER OF INTENT. PROVIDE THE NECESSARY EXPORT/AND
USER DOCUMENT, HAVE AN INSPECTION TEAM VISIT TEL-AVIV (AS
EARLY AS DEC 88) AND CONCLUDE THE PURCHASE NLT 1ST QTR. 89.
THE PURCHASE MONIES WERE CERTIFIED TO BE IN THE CARGO
AIRCRAFT BUDGET.

3. NORTHWEST INDUSTRIES, MR. FLOYD MAYBEE AND THE BELOW
SIGNED ARE PREPARED TO VISIT THE AIRCRAFT PROPOSAL BY MR.
BEN-MENASHE AS DESCRIBED ABOVE.

4. NORTHWEST INDUSTRIES IS THE FOCAL POINT FOR THE CANADIAN
ARMED FORCES SINCE THEY PROVIDE ALL THE C130 DEPOT
MAINTENANCE FOR THAT COUNTRY. NORTHWEST RELATIONSHIP ON THE
KOREAN PURCHASE WOULD BE SIMILAR SINCE KOREA DOES NOT HAVE A
KOREAN FIRM TRAINED ON THE C130.

13. Letter from Joseph O'Toole to David Ivry, director general of the
    Israeli ministry of defense, dated November 28, 1988.

5. BOTH COUNTRIES APPROACHED FXC INTERNATIONAL TO BE THE CONTRACTING PARTY FOR BOTH PURCHASES. WE HAVE EXCELLENT COMPANIES (NORTHWEST, SAMSUNG) IN EACH COUNTRY.

6. MAJOR GENERAL HEALEY, DEPUTY MINISTER OF DEFENSE OF CANADA HAS BEEN BRIEFED ON THE AIRCRAFT AVAILABILITY AND WE AWAIT THE DATA SHEETS PROMISED BY MR. ARI BEN-MENASHE.

7. WE DO NOT INTEND TO HAVE DUPLICATION OF SALES BUT WE REALLY WANTED TO BE RESPONSIVE TO BOTH COUNTRIES NEEDS AND, BOTH COMPANIES ARE AWARE OF THE DUPLICATION OF OFFERINGS.

8. PLEASE PROVIDE THE DATA SHEETS TO FXC BY TELEFAX AT 714-641-5093 AT THE EARLIEST POSSIBLE TIME AS BOTH CANADA AND KOREA ARE ANXIOUSLY AWAITING FURTHER INFORMATION. WE WOULD LIKE TO HAVE COPIES OF THOSE DATA SHEETS GIVEN TO THE KOREAN INSPECTORS.

9. FXC HAS RECEIVED U.S. STATE DEPT. APPROVAL FOR THESE SALES AND MR. WHITEHEAD, UNDERSEC. OF STATE HAS COPIES OF OUR CORRESPONDENCE.

10. WE LOOK FORWARD TO AN EARLY MEETING AND CONTRACT IN TEL-AVIV; BOTH COUNTRIES ARE SERIOUS BUYERS.

BEST REGARDS
FXC INTERNATIONAL

JOSEPH W. O'TOOLE
MANAGING DIRECTOR
AIRCRAFT SALES DIVISION

ATTACHMENTS: 1. CANADA LETTER
2. KOREA SOLICITED

ora group

22 July 1989
AZ-166-89

His Excellence R. Premadasa
President
Democratic Socialist Republic Of Sri Lanka

Subject: Proposal for Sale of Five C-130 E Aircraft to the Sri
          Lankan Air Force

Your Excellency,

In two most interesting discussions I had with the Commander of
your Air Force he showed great Interest in C-130 E transport
A/C for Sri Lanka . He said he would greatly support any
reasonable proposal for such aircraft due to absolute
necessity.The following is a proposal for sale of these A/C to
the Sri Lankan Air Force directed to your Excellency in your
capacity as Defence Minister.

1. We are able and willing to provide you with up to five C-130
E Hercules transport aircraft presently in service with the
Israeli Air Force and are in excellent condition. These A/C can
be used as troop carriers and military cargo transporters as
well as civilian transporters in peace time, i.e. are very
cost effective.

2.   The price of the proposed aircraft is U.S. $ 9 million per
unit. This price will include the reconditioning of the A/C
engines to zero hours condition and a technical course for
maintaining and flying these A/C for your men. Delivery of
these A/C is immediate.

3.   If your Excellency approves of the purchase, our company
will be able and willing to arrange a credit package for this
purpose with a major western bank.

4.   There are great advantages in purchasing these A/C through
our company. If you order ex-factory A/C, as you may well know,
they will cost you U.S.$ 12 million per unit and you will have
to wait approx. two years for delivery; you will also run into
political obstacles. The package we are proposing is very
reasonable, we will handle the political problems and arrange
the easiest credit terms possible.

1586

london, 1 trafalgar avenue, tel: 01-2310115

14. Letter from the author to the president of Sri Lanka, dated July
22, 1989.

-2-

5.   Thank you for your consideration; we await your reply. Our handling agent in Sri Lanka is Globe Commercial Agencies Ltd, 40/1, Dickman's Road, Colombo, Sri Lanka, Tel, 586191, 588924, 589783, 584698. Please direct your reply to our agents in your Country.

6.   This proposal will be valid until 1 November 1989.

Yours Faithfully,

Ari Ben-Menashe
Director

c.c. Commander of Sri Lankan Air Force
     Globe Commercial Agencies Ltd.

1567

london, 1 trafalgar avenue, tel: 01-2310115

Of Counsel

John A. Jasilli
Edmund J. Bodine, Jr.
(NEW YORK)

Richard J. Amberg, Jr.
3509 Elizabeth Lake Road
Suite #100
Waterford, MI 48328
(313) 781-6255
(MICHIGAN)

MARK ANTHONY CRISTINI
Attorney at Law

235 West 48th Street - 33rd Floor
New York, New York 10036
(212) 265-0307
Fax: (212) 265-0847

Frank A. Rubino
2601 S. Bayshore Drive
Suite #1400
Coconut Grove, FL 33133
(305) 858-5300
(FLORIDA)

October 29, 1990

FEDERAL EXPRESS & FAX   **PERSONAL & CONFIDENTIAL**
Greg Mark, Esq.
Office of the Independent Counsel
555 13th Street N.W.
Suite 701 West
Washington, D.C. 20004

Dear Mr. Mark:

I am retained as counsel to **Mr. Ari Ben-Menashe**. I have attempted to contact you through Special Agent **Michael Foster** (202-383-5476) for the past several days. Today I have been in Federal Court and as a result you and I have missed each others return telephone calls. Pursuant to the instructions of my client, I am herein requesting a formal meeting with you and all relevant members of your staff on Thursday, November 29, 1990 in **Washington, D.C.**

The purpose of this meeting would be to discuss the **terms** and **conditions** as to the orderly transfer of funds that I believe to be of great interest to the **United States of America** and/or the property of the **United States of America**. According to information conveyed to the undersigned these funds are attributable to the profits of the **sale** and/or **transfer** of a massive quantity and variety of **arms, airplanes, jets, ammunition, etc.** to a hostile third-party government in the middle-east by an ally of the **United States of America** in the same region.

I am unwilling to discuss this matter with you other than in the safety and security of your office.

Nothing herein contained shall be construed as a waiver of any or all of my clients rights or remedies whether at law or in equity. All such rights are expressly reserved.

Very truly yours,

Mark Anthony Cristini
Mark Anthony Cristini

cc: Frank A. Rubino, Esq.   Richard J. Amberg, Jr. Esq.
     Robert Meloni, Esq.   Senator Alfonse D'Amato
     Adeline Ferretti, Esq.   Ari Ben Menashe

15. Letter from Mark Anthony Cristini to the Office of the Independent Counsel, dated October 29, 1990.

OMNIBANK

LETTER OF CREDIT

Susan Litwer, Esquire, Trustee,
98 Baybury Lane,
New Rochell, New York 10804

We hereby establish our irrevocable and transferable Credit in
favor of Ari Ben Manashi for the account of H.A. Smith, 2052 21st
Street, Astoria, New York 11105 available by your drawn at sight
on OMNIBANK, 3938 Wilshire Blvd., Second Floor, Los Angeles, California
90010 in the amount of $2,000,000 (two Million U.S. Dollars).

Draft may be drawn and negotiated on 12-19-90, 12:00 P.M. PST,
but not later than 12-26-90, 12:00 P.M. PST pursuant to an agreement
already in place.

This letter of credit is transferable without presentation of it to
us and the payment of any transfer fees.

The draft drawn under this credit must bear on its face the clause
"Drawn under OMNIBANK, Credit No.: 121890-1, Dated: 12-18-1990."
accompanied by a signed statement by the Beneficiary certifying that
the amount of the drawing represents indebtedness due from H.A. Smith
in connection with the loan accommodation granted to H.A. Smith.

We hereby agree with the drawers, endorsers and bonafide holders of
drafts drawn under and in compliance with the terms of this credit
that the same shall be duly honored on due presentation to us.

Philip R. Porath,
Coordinator

16. Letter of Credit in favor of the author in the amount of two million
dollars, negotiable between December 19 and December 26, 1990.

Index

THIS BOOK IS set in Trump Mediaeval and Fritz Quadrata Bold. It was produced by Ripinsky & Company, Newtown, Connecticut; typeset by Pagesetters, Inc., Brattleboro, Vermont; and manufactured by Maple-Vail, Binghamton, N.Y.

\